Endorsements for Breakfast of Champions

*N*ormally, when you read the endorsements of a book, so often they are written by famous or well-known people. We have decided to do something a little bit different. Rather than having the normal 'who's who' of endorsements, we wanted to hear from the everyday folk living everyday lives that read *Breakfast of Champions*, and let them be the ones that write the endorsements for it.

Someone once said, 'The proof of the pudding is in the eating', so here are some recommendations and comments about *Breakfast of Champions* written by everyday heroes, people who juggle family, work and other commitments daily and manage to do it successfully; people who face everyday situations and overcome them with God's help; people who live real lives in a real world and do it with God at the centre.

People just like you and me.

"I have been receiving the Breakfast of Champions *email devotional for quite some time, and have found it helpful and encouraging each day that I make time to read it. God has used it to speak to me in challenging times along the way from week to week."*

John V Stanway, *retired pastor*

"For a time I found myself avoiding daily devotionals, as they seemed to be a dime a dozen, and I didn't want to read verses out of context. While I still enjoy reading a book of the Bible start-to-finish in one sitting, I also realise we all need to start our day right and I don't always allow myself enough time. Our mornings are an opportunity to see the day's 'beginning' as a chance to start the day right with Him. After even a long, terrible night before, there's something about the morning that is fresh, open, available, exciting. As I came to know Andy Elmes in person from his visits to our home church, I was immediately drawn to his excitement, joy, and sincerity. I think we all find that a great song or sermon has that much more impact when we know it's coming from sincerity rather than simply by 'gifting' or 'duty'. Andy's Breakfast of Champions *has been the devotional for my life and I find time and again it becomes The Word for that day or week. I pray you too, as a son or daughter of the King, would carve out time and start your day right with the best breakfast for your spiritual health! Amen."*

Daniel Ray

"*I am delighted to endorse* Breakfast of Champions *because what Andy Elmes writes isn't from his own heart but from the Holy Spirit. I know this because what he writes is anointed, powerful and so relevant. His teaching about Jesus' secret place with His Father and the vital importance of every Christian spending time alone with God in order to be able to live in a world that is increasingly ungodly was 'spot on'. Many times what Andy writes in the emails is just what the Lord has been saying to me and urging me to do. We also sometimes have 'breakfasts' from Andy's wife Gina, and these are just as anointed. This couple spend a lot of time in God's presence, and it shows.*"

Ann Firth, retired nurse

"*I have enjoyed Andy's emails very much as they were very helpful when I was in the doldrums; I found them very inspirational at that time.*"

Cheryl Carter

"*I first received Andy Elmes's devotional* Breakfast of Champions *in 2012. I have since moved three times and have changed jobs three times. My social circle has changed and my life is completely different. Life is three times better to me than it used to be. One thing never changed – I continued to receive these incredible daily devotionals. No matter how much turmoil all this change brought, the content of* Breakfast of Champions *kept me moving forward and inspired me when I needed it, challenged me when I needed it and helped me help others too. Thanks, Andy.*"

Leigh Klaver

"*I have been a born-again believer for over thirty-eight years, and I believe that I need to keep my devotions and biblical input into my life fresh and varied. I picked up the contact for* Breakfast of Champions *visiting a church whilst on holiday in Paris almost two years ago. I enrolled by email and I have been reading daily for the past eighteen months. I am encouraged by this refreshing 'spiritual muesli', with all the healthy ingredients a good muesli should have: nuts – content with a bit of bite!; raisins – sweet truths to encourage my walk with God; seeds – new perspectives to 'seed' new prophetic perspective into my Christian walk; oats – something to chew, we need to meditate/chew on the depths God wants us to go. Well-balanced nourishment should give your body a variety of nourishment to 'work on in its depths/digest'.* Breakfast of Champions *addresses numerous dynamic themes with the desire to provide 'superfood' breakfast for the believer. Thank you.*"

Dr. David Willson, Cologne, Germany

"I'm a missionary/worship leader/teacher living in Brazil. I originally come from England and was a member of Andy's church. Since leaving England to work in a new culture with very different values and ways of living, Breakfast of Champions has truly been a blessing in my life. With the true wisdom it gives, and consistent encouragement to live life in abundance, it has helped me get through many situations I'm not used to and lead others to believe and know that their identity in Christ will give them hope for the future. Some children here in Brazil feel that their identity is in their drug dealer parents and aspire to follow in their footsteps. However, as Breakfast of Champions has taught us, our identity is in the true heavenly Father. On a more personal note, reading this daily devotional always reminds me of the family I have in Christ – that is, the Church – and it teaches me how the Church biblically should be, which I pass onto the church culture here in Brazil. Congratulations on the new book, Pastor Andy."

Steph Volaris, missionary

"A stroll through the religious section of a bookstore shows there's no shortage of Christian devotionals. Breakfast of Champions, though, stands apart. First, it finds the perfect balance between depth and brevity. It gives me a strong message to carry throughout the day without overwhelming me with too much to think on and remember. Second, it's more broad and pastoral than any devotional I've read. It meets me in real life situations while being true to the wide scope and variety of what the Bible teaches. Andy has sensitively and skillfully created a devotional that brings daily nourishment to the new Christian and the seasoned saint alike. I cannot help but recommend a book I have used to carry me through days when I was eager and needing to hear from God. Thank you, Pastor Andy!"

Joe Reeser

"My genuine thanks! As a sailor, a half of a degree off course is seemingly nothing if you're only traveling a mile or two, but week after week, a month, we'll never make port – we'll have drifted off course and missed our destination. These morning emails have been a blessing for me. They help with the 'magnetic interference of my environment' – a little shift in thought, a better start to the day's direction, it's a little tweak to the heading of that day. I enjoy these each day with my morning coffee without fail before I head to the docks. Course corrections are intentional and need only be subtle. I've had the pleasure to hear Andy share in person as well, in upstate New York and once down in Florida. I trust him at the helm, as well, for needed course corrections. I look for them each day. Many thanks!"

David Sior, sailor and boat builder

"I have read Breakfast of Champions *daily since it was first published. I rarely miss reading it – it is part of my daily time with God.* Breakfast of Champions *is invaluable in helping to build my personal relationship with my living, loving God. It is always good and often contains inspirational faith-building 'nuggets'.* Breakfast of Champions *is not for the faint-hearted. It provides a real challenge to live life in a way that honours God and helps build His kingdom, drawing on the strength and power of the Holy Spirit in us. Bacon and eggs, or* Breakfast of Champions? *My choice is B-of-C every day!"*

Don Payne, retiree

"In 2012 I went to bed feeling challenged by God to move on from a ministry position that I held in Nottingham. I loved the church and did not want to move but the following morning I read Breakfast for Champions where the reading was from Genesis 12. I felt God really speak to me and spoke with the leadership within a few days about what I felt God was saying. Later that year I found myself leaving Nottingham and moving to Leicester where I am now a part of the leadership of a great church here. Thanks."

Rob Gale, Managing Director

"I have loved receiving the Breakfast of Champions *emails. It's the perfect way to start my day! I love that it is sent on weekdays and that it is a manageable length. I personally have found, time and time again, that the subject matter has divine timing and speaks right into what's happening in my world where I need encouragement or direction. It gives me focus for my week, biblical references, and leadership-level teachings that spur me on in my work in ministry. Thank you for continuing to provide a 'balanced meal' in my spiritual nourishment."*

Andrea Kuhn

"I've been studying Breakfast of Champions *after registering to an online course a year to the day after I was 'saved'. This was also the same day that I started a new job. Six months down the line, Andy's devotionals have helped establish and guide me in a challenging role and has directed me to scriptures at the perfect time; from how I conduct myself at work with the spirit of Daniel, to God's promise of making a way in the desert at a time that a relationship ended. (Interestingly, my job does literally take me to the desert!) I look forward to moving on with the Bible study with a dedication to and confidence in God's word that Andy's work has helped bring into my life. Thank you."*

Andy Bullock

Breakfast of Champions

VOLUME 2

Breakfast of Champions

VOLUME 2

*260 daily devotions
by Andy & Gina Elmes*

British Library Cataloguing in Publication Data

A catalogue record for this book is available from the British Library

PRINT: ISBN 978-0-9932693-2-5
EBOOK: ISBN 978-0-9932693-3-2

Introduction

Welcome to *Breakfast of Champions Volume 2*. We are so glad that you have decided to join us for breakfast. Each midweek morning you will receive a devotional thought to encourage and challenge you to know God more and live out your Christian faith in a vibrant and impacting way. This is our second volume of 'breakfasts', and we stand truly amazed how the Lord continues to use this written devotional and its digital counterpart to minister to so many people, from all walks of life, all across the world. These days it seems wherever we visit someone is always coming up and telling us how these daily devotions have blessed and impacted their lives; whether it be the UK, US or the remotest part of the Philippines, we are amazed at how the Lord has caused this simple daily devotional to get to so many places and touch so many lives.

What started off as a simple heart-written devotional for one man has now turned into a globally-read devotional that provides a nourishing spiritual breakfast to thousands all over the world. It continues to remind us that every great oak tree starts with a small acorn. I can remember writing the very first devotional for that one recipient back in 2010! We are so blessed that now so many include it as a part of their devotional walk with the Lord.

In this devotional you will be challenged each midweek morning by a devotional written by Gina or myself, and there's even a special week written by our eldest daughter, Olivia, who seems to have a gift for writing devotionals too. Then, new for this volume, there is a 'weekend workout' – a simple challenge for the weekend to provide you with an opportunity for some life application to the things you have learned or been challenged by. The Bible teaches us that we are to 'work out our salvation' (Philippians 2:12) so these simple challenges are designed to help you do that in a number of different ways. They are simple enough for all to do but some of them will certainly cause a new stretching in your life. Also, spread throughout the book, there are random quotes written by myself or by others that I have read and have been blessed or motivated by – little extras on the breakfast table to enjoy and think about.

We are so excited about *Breakfast of Champions* and believe that it contains everything you need to start your day off in a way you won't regret. Within its pages are many lessons and revelations we have learned over the years as we have walked with the Lord. Our prayer is that these will be of great use to you as you purpose to live your life to know Him more and live out the plans He has for you. So, turn the page and let's get started, it's time for breakfast!

Andy & Gina

PLEASE NOTE

Breakfast of Champions has not been designed for you to start it according to your calendar. Week one, day one does not need to mean the first day of January. It has been laid out in a 'jump on board anywhere' style, so wherever you are in the year you can start at week one, day one, or you could start at week twenty-four, day four. We did this because we felt that not everyone is facing the same thing on the same day and this enables God to speak to different people about different things at the moment they are facing or going through them. So jump right in whatever week of the year you are in :)

Foreword

To be faithful to Jesus involves feeding on God's Word and putting it into practice. *Breakfast for Champions* is a wonderful tool that will help you to do both!

Jesus said that those who continued in His words would know the truth and the truth would set them free. Because of His great love for you Jesus wants to see you living in that freedom, and then to be a witness to others who need that same freedom in their lives. This involves using the opportunities you have to love, serve, bless and encourage others in the same way that He loves, serves, blesses and encourages you through the way the Holy Spirit speaks His words to your heart.

This the Holy Spirit will do through this book. It is written by a pastor and his wife who are experiencing a significant move of God in their lives and ministries, and in the network of churches they oversee. You will benefit greatly as they open up the truths of the scriptures to you, helping you to not only understand them more fully but also to see how relevant they are to your daily life and interaction with others.

It is important that the principles outlined here are being outlived in Andy and Gina's lives, but also in the Family Churches they lead. So this book is not full of theory but the practical realities of what it means to live as a faithful Christian. I believe you will hear the voice of God as you use this book week by week, and you will also be thankful for what you see God do in your heart and in the lives of others around you as a result.

Colin Urquhart

Apostolic leader, founder of Kingdom Faith
and well-known author of many best selling books

Dedication

We want to dedicate this book to a true General in the faith and a man who was a General in our lives. This book is dedicated to pastor, prophet and dear friend Vaughan Jarrold. He has returned to 'Headquarters' but is greatly missed here on the mission field by so many.

Thank you, Vaughan, for the legacy you have left in our lives, family and ministry.

Vaughan Jarrold
1949-2016

Breakfast is served,

with much love

Wakey, wakey, it's time to get up!

Arise, shine; for your light has come! And the glory of the Lord is risen upon you. For behold, the darkness shall cover the earth, and deep darkness the people; but the Lord will arise over you, and His glory will be seen upon you. The Gentiles shall come to your light, and kings to the brightness of your rising.

Isaiah 60:1-3

The alarm clock is going off and it's time for us all to wake up to all that we are and also to all that we are not. Let's stop living by the fickle opinions of the world, or the deceptive opinions of the devil, and even our own opinions, which are simply not good enough. Let's arise, find our identity in God's Word, and then purpose to be all that God is calling us today.

God calls you many things: He calls you forgiven, loved, mighty man or woman of valour, precious child – in fact, the list is endless and it is all good. When we make the decision to get up and live out the life He has given us it is then that we shine with His glory and have a glow that is beyond what is considered 'normal' or 'everyday'. Like the closing part of this verse reads, we will draw people to us who need God, like a lighthouse in troubled seas.

Let's face it, we are living in a time when darkness is in the world and, yes, it is deep darkness – but the light we carry is greater, Champion. Light always ruins and confounds darkness. When I look around I see things getting ever darker, and that means this is the time that our light gets brighter. As we wake up, get up, and dare to be what God has called us to be, kings are drawn to what God is doing in and through our lives. Notice it is not just normal everyday people who are drawn: the verses say that kings – people of influence and importance – will be drawn to us.

Today is a great day for us all to remember who we are and make the decision to get up and be that person and shine for Him. As we do, our lives push darkness back and give God opportunity to change people's troubled, confused lives. So today I call you to get up, see yourself through God's eyes and shine. Shine bright for the God you love, because this is our finest hour.

Never settle for short-term gratification over long-term satisfaction.

Andy Elmes

Faith is the doorway into all-sufficient grace

But He said to me, 'My grace is sufficient for you, for My power is made perfect in weakness.' Therefore I will boast all the more gladly about my weaknesses, so that Christ's power may rest on me. That is why, for Christ's sake, I delight in weaknesses, in insults, in hardships, in persecutions, in difficulties. For when I am weak, then I am strong.

2 Corinthians 12:9-10 (NIV)

It is God's grace that empowers us to be strong in times when we may naturally feel weak or even overwhelmed. We all so need His grace each and every day of our lives. It is when we operate daily in His grace that we, too, can live a life that 'delights . . . in insults, in hardships, in persecutions,' etc. knowing that we have all we need in Him.

Notice Paul says, 'When I am weak, then I am strong.' Often I have heard that preached, 'When I am weak then He (God) is strong' but it does not say that. Why? Grace (God's power) operates through us and not just outside of us, because God is in us, and we are the 'postcode' of His residence. His grace makes us strong to face any and every challenge and obstacle sent to stop us. It really is enough for us too.

There remains only one doorway into this all-sufficient grace that Paul knew, and that is faith. Religious works will not get you into it, and neither will begging. It is when you release your faith in the bigness of your God and in the validity of His promises that you will see and receive His all-sufficient grace manifested in the midst of what you are going through. To put it another way, 'God comes through.'

Champion, faith is the trigger to releasing the grace of God, so why not pull the trigger again today. You need grace today? Bask in His bigness and not the momentary threat of the situation. By faith begin to declare those hope-filled words based upon His promises, and then with expectation wait for your God to turn it all around. You do not need to know how He will do it, just that He will.

Through faith enter into grace, grace that is truly more than enough for you!

Do all the good you can. By all the means you can. In all the ways you can. In all the places you can. At all the times you can. To all the people you can. As long as ever you can.

John Wesley

Preferring others

Let love be without hypocrisy. Abhor what is evil. Cling to what is good. Be kindly affectionate to one another with brotherly love, in honour giving preference to one another.

Romans 12:9-10

This is one of those 'rubber hits the road' verses when it comes to what God desires from us as we follow Him. One of the characteristics of a follower of Jesus is that we choose to prefer others. Why? Simple – because that's the nature of God's Spirit that is in us.

So often, when people think or talk of the Spirit, they think of a vague mist or invisible force that knocks people over. Yes, God's Spirit is His power and ability but here's another way of looking at it: the Holy Spirit is the Spirit of Jesus, it's who He is, including His attitudes. Ever seen someone that prophesied and did 'all the stuff' yet they had a stinking attitude? What's the problem? They have acknowledged the gifts of the Spirit but never allowed the fruit or attitude of the Spirit to become theirs. Now that we are spirit-filled the attitudes of Jesus should be being manifested in and through us as we daily submit our lives to Him. This is, I believe, the true evidence of a life yielded – and not a person who can speak in tongues or prophesy and then live an awful life the very next moment.

God's attitudes should be our attitudes as we daily yield, and one of those attitudes is preferring others. Everything about Jesus prefers others. Generally that is so opposite to the spirit of the world that we all are exposed to on a daily basis. The spirit of this world is becoming ever more a 'me first, queue-pushing' spirit; it is concerning this that God is wanting us to wear a better attitude in life.

Imagine the impact a church would have if they decided they were going to devote themselves to preferring others, starting with each other then letting it spill out onto a self-oriented world? Now that's what would really cause a stir!

Think about that today because everything great starts with one person doing something different. How about you? Who today can you prefer above yourself? I know it hurts to do it sometimes with some, but those are the ones where you really catch God's attention. Let's live with a different spirit (attitude), let's choose again to imitate and release the character of the One whose Spirit is now in us.

Now that I've mentioned it you know you are going to have an opportunity to live it out! They've left their house and are on their way to collide with you – when it happens, prefer them!

Prayer

Heavenly Father, help me today to put others first; may I be sensitive to Your leading as You cause me to notice the needs of others over my own. Use my life to make a difference in the lives of others, I pray. Amen

Preferring others is a mark of maturity

Let love be without hypocrisy. Abhor what is evil. Cling to what is good. Be kindly affectionate to one another with brotherly love, in honour giving preference to one another.

Romans 12:9-10

*L*et's carry on with the thought we shared yesterday; in Romans 12 it shares about attitudes we should have and ways we should be living, as we live for Jesus.

We zoomed in yesterday on the attitude that simply says 'to give preference or prefer others', and noted how un-normal this can be in such a selfish, self-oriented world. Yet this is an attitude that God expects from His Kingdom people.

Giving preference shows maturity

Giving preference to others is not generally something that kids naturally do, is it? I have five and they are awesome, yet when they are relating to each other I ever long to hear things like, 'There was not enough chocolate cereal so I poured yours and I will go without', or 'Please, you need the bathroom before me, and by the way I cleaned the bath especially for you.' Rather, it is a childlike thing to think of number one all the time. But when we grow up this is one of the 'childlike things' we should put aside, and when we get God's Spirit in us we should absolutely graduate to a higher way of living, and get a kick out of putting others first.

Good exercise for the soul

If you want to hear your soul and spirit have a disagreement, as the Bible says they sometimes could, then give away something that matters to you to someone else, especially someone who you don't think deserves it. Let-in the car that has pushed alongside you as one of the two lanes of a dual carriageway merge into one because of road works. Yep, that sports car that you watched in your mirror ignoring the queue, with every intention of pushing in at the very end. Let someone else have that last chocolate cake you had your eye on as you queued-up in the coffee shop. Let someone have your place in the supermarket when there is a queue and you see they are in a hurry. The list goes on, doesn't it – so many opportunities?

So today, why not again aggravate your selfish soul by making the spiritual decision to let someone violate your driver's rights, or have that last thing you really wanted. You know, as we do that we are actually releasing the culture of another kingdom – God's kingdom – and living out the values of its King.

I pray you get some good opportunities to put this thought into practice today. (LOL!)

Ministering even when we do not feel like it

When Jesus heard what had happened, He withdrew by boat privately to a solitary place. Hearing of this, the crowds followed him on foot from the towns. When Jesus landed and saw a large crowd, He had compassion on them and healed their sick.

Matthew 14:13-14 (NIV)

*L*et's keep talking about preferring others. If we are honest it's a hard enough thing sometimes to live a life that prefers others when everything is going well and we feel good, but what about when things are not going so well and everything in us wants to curl up and concentrate on our own needs or well-being?

This is the time we minister the best because it is more about God flowing through us as we yield our lives to be used by Him without feelings.

Think about this account of Jesus:

He had just heard some terrible news about someone He personally loved – in fact, it was his cousin, John (the Baptist). Notice the effect it had on Him and what He clearly wanted to do next: He wanted to 'be alone', to go to a solitary place and work some stuff out, including the emotions He must have been feeling. So He attempts a getaway, hops in a boat and sails to another part of the sea of Galilee – great plan. But the people, being needy and so focused on their needs, followed Him along the shoreline – they were not going to give Him any time out because they had needs that they felt needed to be met now. So, when He gets out of the boat, there they are! He has not had His 'me time' and has to make a choice: do I run, or curl up in a ball and hope they go away, or do I give my life away again and prefer others and their needs? Of course He took the second option, got out of the boat and ministered to the needs of all who were present. Yep, even while He was going through something painful himself. That's ministry!

I heard someone say recently that ministry and calling is not ministering to others when you feel like it but ministering to the needs of others when you feel like it and when you don't, giving preference to others and their needs when you prefer to and when you would prefer not to. If enough of us make a fresh commitment to prefer others when we want to and when we don't then we could really cause a dynamic move of God's Spirit. Remember, preferring others is exactly that – what Jesus' Spirit (now in us) would do and the direction He would have us move in.

When God gives you a new beginning don't repeat the same mistakes.

Unknown

BLESS SOMEONE OTHERS DON'T SEE

Most men will proclaim each his own goodness, but who can find a faithful man?
Proverbs 20:6

There are many unsung heroes in this world, and they often get overlooked because they don't seek applause or limelight. I'm thinking of the people who clean the church after everyone has gone home, and the people who serve the tea and coffee at church functions. I have in mind those who serve tirelessly in the house of God because they love Jesus and want to further God's kingdom in any way there is need, such as the people who care for and teach the children on a Sunday morning so that the parents can attend the main service. Without the people who perform these services our churches wouldn't be what they are.

Find one of these faithful individuals and show them your appreciation. Maybe you could give them a card or a gift. You could always get a few friends together to give some money to buy something.

Get creative with this one! Have a lovely weekend.

Notes

_____

_____

_____

_____

_____

_____

Excellence, not perfection

Then this Daniel distinguished himself above the governors and satraps, because an excellent spirit was in him; and the king gave thought to setting him over the whole realm.

Daniel 6:3

Now that we have the Spirit of Jesus living in us, we should have a heart that wants to do things with ever greater measures of excellence than we did before. Having God's Spirit in you will never make you worse, only ever better; and this is true in every area of your life!

It is good for us to understand that there is a big difference between going for excellence and going for perfection. So often when people have a spirit of perfection they can strive to do what they are not able to, leaving them disappointed. They may try to buy what they can't yet afford and get into a whole lot of trouble and end up broke. There is a difference between excellence and perfection.

To me, excellence is simply this: to live committed to 'doing the very best you can with what you presently have in your life'. Don't live in what you have not got, but rather fully mobilise and use, to the best of its potential, what you do. Remember what God said to Moses as he stood on the edge of the Red Sea, not knowing what to do next? God's response to him was 'use what is presently in your hand'. As he dared to use the stick that was in his hand he discovered its potential was bigger than he had ever thought.

When God anoints what is in your life, incredible things can happen. What is in your hand (life) today, Champion? As you are faithful to a spirit of excellence, increase will come for your dreams and intentions to be fulfilled, both for now and in the future.

Go after excellence, not perfection. Be the best you that you can be.

Prayer

Heavenly Father, help me today to know the difference between perfection and excellence; help me to understand all of the things currently in my life and how I can use them to the best of their ability. Thank You for Your spirit of excellence that now lives in me; let that Spirit flow through everything I do and put my hand to today.

Amen

God wants the whole person and He will not rest till He gets us in entirety. No part of the man will do.

A. W. Tozer

Live content

But godliness with contentment is great gain. For we brought nothing into the world, and we can take nothing out of it.

1 Timothy 6:6-7 (NIV)

In the West we live in a society that ever pushes us to want more, get bigger things, update, upgrade, etc., etc. There is nothing wrong with prospering and upgrading in life but we should always do it from a spirit of contentment, from having a revelation of how blessed we already are.

When people say, 'I am not blessed,' it really is an issue of perspective; I was reminded of this just last week.

We were having our annual Empower Conference and finally, after three years of trying, got a dear friend from the Philippines to come over and visit for it. It was a great conference and my friend stayed around for a few days after. He started to tell me of the home he and his family were moving into and I listened and tried to imagine the layout of the home that would hold him, his wife and four kids.

We were sitting in my lounge – which is not a big one by any means, just an average-sized living room – and asked him, 'So how big is your home?' His reply shocked me: 'Oh, not as big as your living room but a very nice size for us.' He then started to show me using my living room as a template where the bunk beds were stacked, the sink and the oven were. I was amazed at how they could get so much into so little space, but he also challenged me unknowingly about my attitude – obviously having five kids we ever want or feel we need 'more room'. There is nothing wrong with wanting that but it is also important to stop and realise that what we have now is so much more than many others in the world. Come on, think about it: the roof over our head, the food we have, the clean water available at the turn of a tap – the list goes on and on, and is so much more than many have.

I suppose the message that day to me was a mixed one: be thankful for what I have, don't be afraid to believe God for more but include the well-being of others when the 'more' comes. Seeing things through a worldwide perspective will always produce a thankful heart because, let's face it, often our 'worst day' would be someone else's 'greatest day' if we were to swap lives with them. Live content; live thankful; live with others in mind.

The truth is like a lion. You don't have to defend it.
Let it loose and it will defend itself.

St Augustine

Social media: a blessing or a curse?

As they approached Jerusalem and came to Bethphage on the Mount of Olives, Jesus sent two disciples, saying to them, 'Go to the village ahead of you, and at once you will find a donkey tied there, with her colt by her. Untie them and bring them to me. If anyone says anything to you, tell him that the Lord needs them, and he will send them right away.'

Matthew 21:1-3 (NIV)

We live in an incredible time when it comes to technology and media opportunities, but we must always remember to use these things for good, to use these tools to build and establish the kingdom of God and people.

I am a modern fella, I have a website, email address, I have a Facebook account and, yes, I tweet and instagram. But I have purposed in my heart to use these incredible tools to bless and not curse, to do good and not bad, to build and not tear down. Sadly, as I scan these social media sites, I see that more Christians need this revelation.

In this account a donkey was loosed for a purpose; the donkey was made available to be a vehicle to carry something, or should I say someone, special. It was a vehicle, a tool for carrying something. Others could have used this donkey for lesser purposes – it could have been used to carry philosophy books, porn magazines, or papers filled with gossip columns. No, this day it was used to carry Jesus, the One who brings hope and life. It was not used to carry the stones with the law of Moses on but rather the Author of grace.

Simple thought this morning: let's be thankful for the awesome tools of social media that we have available to us today – tools like Facebook and Twitter – but let us purpose in our hearts to be wise and ethical concerning what we use them to carry on our behalf. Let us use them for making Jesus known and building people up. I am sure we've all been annoyed by people, who have no real influence in life, using Facebook, Twitter or a blog as a platform to preach their twisted messages of unbelief and judgement of people and ministries. They have nothing to say that brings life, hence they have no platform in life to influence – until they casually wander onto your Facebook profile and preach to your friends their philosophies of discontent. Meanwhile, the world watches and stands in amazement at how Christians, like cannibals, apparently try and eat their own!

Come on, friends, let's draw a line. These things, like the donkey, have been provided to us as great tools for cheering Christ and making Him and His love known to a dying world; for encouragement, to bless not curse. So let's not use them to carry lesser things or to smear the body of Christ and its ministers when we feel they have failed or overlooked us. Let's allow these awesome tools to carry Jesus. Remember before you write that it is a worldwide web. Use it to go into all the world and preach. Preach what? The good news of Jesus! What an awesome thought: we can use social media to fulfil the Great Commission, or we can use it for lesser things.

More than a song

And if the Spirit of Him who raised Jesus from the dead is living in you, He who raised Christ from the dead will also give life to your mortal bodies through His Spirit, who lives in you.

Romans 8:11 (NIV)

A little while ago Hillsong Church captured this awesome thought in one of their inspiring songs and, something they are always so good at, made it very catchy and easy to sing. I often find myself driving around singing it: 'The same power that conquered the grave lives in me, lives in me.'* It is a great sing-along song but it needs to be more than that in our lives. It needs to be a life-defining revelation. It needs to drop two feet from our mouths to our hearts because this really is the powerful truth that determines our true potential and capabilities.

'The same Spirit' – think about that for a moment. The same Spirit that raised Jesus from the dead lives in you. Wow! Suddenly the previously settled dimensions of what causes things to be possible and impossible for you begin to change and realign before your very eyes. That is why Paul could confidently say, 'I can do all things'. Let him finish his statement and you will see why: 'through Christ who gives me strength'. It was Paul's revelation of the indwelling Spirit of the resurrection life of Christ that brought him to this absolute. That same revelation is ours to own today.

His Spirit causes things to live!

It says if He lives in you He causes life in your mortal body. The truth is that if His life-giving Spirit is resident in your life He makes everything come alive, such as visions, dreams, health, etc. Truly everywhere the river of His presence is allowed to flow it brings life and raises things from a dead state!

Activated by acknowledgment

The daily activation of this internal potential and life force is simply the result of acknowledgement, which is a coming into agreement with what the Word says is a reality concerning you. Let me leave you with a great activation verse from Philemon:

> *That the sharing of your faith may become effective by the acknowledgment of every good thing which is in you in Christ Jesus.*
>
> **Philemon 6**

The effective outworking of your faith is the result of you acknowledging what is already in you in Christ Jesus. What is in you? The same power that conquered the grave, that's what.

I pray you have a powerful day.

---

* You Are Here (Dave George, Grant Pankratz) © 2007 HarvestOKC Music Publishing (Admin. by HMTR Ltd)/Hillsong Music Publishing (Admin. by HMTR Ltd).

Your mouth lets out what is in your heart

O God, You have taught me from my youth; and to this day I declare Your wondrous works.

Psalm 71:17

We spoke yesterday about faith-filled, God-inspired declarations. The truth is, they cannot just be in our mouth but must be flowing from our hearts to our mouths. The Bible says, 'for out of the abundance of the heart his mouth speaks' (Luke 6:45), so the reality is your sustainable (more than a moment) declaration is the outflow of the content (belief) of your heart.

It is a divinely powerful thing when the mouth and the heart are unified in the same belief. When the mouth speaks what the heart honestly believes it is then that impossible mountains move. Listen to how Jesus put it:

> *For assuredly, I say to you, whoever says to this mountain, 'Be removed and be cast into the sea,' and does not doubt in his heart, but believes that those things he says will be done, he will have whatever he says.*
>
> Mark 11:23

As we daily allow our lives to be exposed to, and impacted by, God's Word (the Bible), faith concerning His promises grows within us – faith for each and every area of the lives we live. So, then, when the gate of our mouth opens, powerful declarations flow out – not wishy-washy words of failure and impending doom. No, what projects out is declaration that has the God-given power to move stubborn things that may threaten to stand in our way.

What is it to declare? Here is a definition taken from Webster's dictionary:

> *To say or state (something) in an official or public way, to say (something) in a strong and confident way.* *

This confidence we have to declare bigger things in and over our lives does not come from mere mental assent, or base itself upon self-initiated ability; rather it comes from a confidence that God's Word, now filling our hearts with hope for better things, comes inclusive of His potential to do and to bring these things about.

Think for a moment:

- Is your declaration fear-based or faith-enhanced? Does it come from watching the news or reading His Word?

- Are your words experience-based (life so far) or defined by God-given promise (things not yet experienced)?

May I encourage you, as we enter together into this new year that has not yet been lived, to be filling your heart with His Word and promises and then letting them spill out of your mouth in confident declaration, knowing He is ABLE to do anything!

---

* Declare. 2015. In Merriam-Webster.com. Retrieved July 28, 2015, from http://www.merriam-webster.com/dictionary/declare

CHOOSE JOY

You make known to me the path of life; in your presence there is fullness of joy; at your right hand are pleasures forevermore.
Psalm 16:11 (ESV)

Joy is a fruit of God's Spirit living in you. Ultimately, true joy is cultivated in a believer as they yield to God's Spirit. When I choose joy I say to my soul, 'I will keep the soil of my life uncluttered so that the healthy fruit of the Spirit of God has no impediment in His growth in me.' Here are some good ways to keep the soil of your soul weed free and ready to produce joy. Here's your challenge:

1. Spend time in God's presence, where there is fullness of joy.

2. Be thankful and grateful for all the wonderful people and things in your life.

3. Choose not to complain, even about the little things. I live in the United Kingdom and it rains here an awful lot. There are days that I can't remember when I last saw the sun. Something as little as this can really make me feel sad, but I have to choose to remember the million and one other things God has given me on those days.

Have a lovely joy-filled weekend!

So often forgiveness means you set a prisoner free only to realise the actual prisoner was you.

Andy Elmes

Live shameless

For I am not ashamed of the gospel of Christ, for it is the power of God to salvation for everyone who believes, for the Jew first and also for the Greek.

Romans 1:16

Make the quality decision today, Champion, to live without shame concerning who God is to you and also concerning what He has done for you.

I have been ashamed at times of certain things in my life (such as behaviour, the missing of key moments, hypocrisy, etc.) but I am not ashamed of Jesus and the truth of His gospel (good news).

I have sometimes been ashamed of some of those who call themselves the church in our nation, who seem to love compromise and stupid behaviour rather than truth. They continually endeavour to try and make a holy God fit conveniently with a sinful lifestyle, and we all know that that can never be a perfect match. But I will not be ashamed of Jesus and His gospel.

When it comes to Jesus, I want to live a life that really does 'shout His fame', that knows no shame, a life that daily declares the reality of His gospel and manifests its power. How about you? Christianity is not a religion to me, rather a real relationship and a real message; a person and a message that have the potential to save absolutely anyone who dares to believe in it, independent of what culture or background they may be from.

Let us not be ashamed of the message, or a shame to it. Let us always remember it is not bad news but good, it is not a message of law and human performance but one of grace, mercy and faith. It should not leave those who believe it condemned and guilt-ridden but saved and righteous (justified). Let us stand up again today for the One who unashamedly hung on a cross for us: Jesus.

Live shameless concerning your love for Him and the truth of the good news He brings.

Prayer

Thank you, Lord Jesus, that today I will live shameless regarding You and Your kingdom. Forgive me when I have been shy concerning You with others in my life; I don't want to be like this anymore. You have done so much for me and I am so very thankful; empower me by Your Holy Spirit to be bold for You, no longer hiding behind the rocks of embarrassment, apathy or fear. Rather, let me be a person who boldly declares how good You are to all those I meet today, making the most of every opportunity You provide.

Amen

Get from every season all it has for you

Do you not say, 'There are still four months and then comes the harvest'? Behold, I say to you, lift up your eyes and look at the fields, for they are already white for harvest!

John 4:35

The journey (pilgrimage) of life is certainly a journey of different seasons. The art of living well is to make sure that you live (milk the goodness out of) each and every season by both sowing into and reaping from each and every one of them. Being alive means that we will all walk through the various seasons of life. Here is a classic verse from the wisdom of Ecclesiastes to make you think this morning.

To everything there is a season, a time for every purpose under heaven: a time to be born, and a time to die; a time to plant, and a time to pluck what is planted.

Ecclesiastes 3:1-2

If you get the chance read the rest of this classic chapter to see the different types of seasons each and every one of us faces as we journey through this thing called life. Like King David said in Psalm 37:25, we will all experience being young and being old and every season in between. I have met some older people that live in the regret of not being a teenager anymore and I have met younger people that can't wait for a later season of life (like being married), but the problem is they are missing the season they are in. Neither of these is good enough. The answer to how to get the most out of life is to love the season you're in.

You can't go back and re-live seasons gone but you can learn from them. You really don't want to fast forward to future seasons because when the ones you are in are gone, like flowers when they have flourished, they are gone for good. The key for us all today is to *carpe* (seize) the one you're in! So choose today to learn from seasons gone, love the one you're in and, with faith and expectancy, have excitement concerning the ones yet to come that are promised by your God. Every season has something for you so make sure you harvest it out!

To everything there is a season. There are seasons of age, seasons of relationship, seasons of ministry and business, seasons for everything, and in them all there is a time to plant and a time to pluck (harvest) what was planted.

Here is some food for thought for you today as you consider the seasons that you are currently in:

- What seasons are you in today? Is it time to plant (sow) or to pluck up (harvest)?

- Are you getting from this season everything that you should be or could be? Are you milking out everything that is in the season to be had?

- What else do you need to do to enjoy and seize the season you are in?

God bless you – I pray that this season of your life prospers. Don't say, 'In four months . . .' but make the decision to live large today the life God has given!

Trust, lean and acknowledge

Trust in the LORD with all your heart, and lean not on your own understanding; in all your ways acknowledge Him, and He shall direct your paths.

Proverbs 3:5-6

Here is yet another classic promise of God for our lives: God promises that He will direct our paths. Anyone else out there really desire the reality of this on a daily basis – God Almighty daily guiding you as you walk the pathways of life? Maybe you would say, 'God never directs my paths, Andy'? Let's look at that a bit closer.

I believe that, before we start accusing God of not following through, out of courtesy we need to ask ourselves if we have done (followed through) the three things that He asks us to do first?

Trust

Are you trusting in the Lord with all your heart, or are you trusting Him with some of it while trusting in other things too, in case He doesn't come through? God is looking for us to walk in faith with Him daily, to place all of our trust in Him without having the 'just in case' back up plans or safety nets that make us feel more comfortable.

Lean

Are you leaning on God concerning the things that don't make much sense? Or are you trying to work it all out according to your limited understanding and what makes perfect sense to you? Remember, we are dealing with a God that lives outside of the boundaries of what we call possible and impossible. He is able to do anything at anytime with anyone. Make sure you're leaning on Him and His promises and not your mere ability to process or reason things! Remember, He has not asked you to be reasonable (able to reason) but faithful (full of faith).

Acknowledge

Are you including Him in the different areas or sections of your life, and in each and every situation you may be facing? Or are you doing DIY (doing it yourself) and living daily outside of His council and wisdom with certain things? As I have said before, your life is like a big old pizza, and just as a pizza has different slices so do our lives: relational, financial, emotional, etc. God wants you to include wisdom and His Lordship in all the slices of your life, not just selected ones.

These are three big questions to ask yourself but I believe, when we take time to make sure that we are truly trusting, leaning and acknowledging, it is then that we will know the guiding and leading of the Lord on a daily basis, and He causes us to walk on pleasant, prosperous pathways!

Faith is a response

And Jesus, walking by the Sea of Galilee, saw two brothers, Simon called Peter, and Andrew his brother, casting a net into the sea; for they were fishermen. Then He said to them, 'Follow Me, and I will make you fishers of men.' They immediately left their nets and followed Him.

Matthew 4:18-20

*L*et us consider the power our responses have by considering the response of these young men who started the day as fishermen and ended the day as disciples of Jesus who would change the world.

What was it that changed their whole lives in a moment? Yes, it was about God making His intentions known to them, but it was equally about them responding in faith to God's Word and stepping out into the unknown. Faith is a due response and, remember, it is a response that always brings God pleasure (Hebrews 11:6).

So for them it was a day like any other. They are busy doing what they had always done when Jesus turns up and drops God's divine intention for their lives into their laps. There is no two-day seminar with PowerPoint and Q & A over an evening meal – just a single moment where a response was needed to activate a brand-new life offer. They could have turned to Him and said, 'That's great, but a bit scary – thanks, but no thanks', and Jesus would have turned and walked on. They didn't do that but instead they perceived that this was a God moment and responded to it with faith, not reason, and went with it.

Remember, this is exactly what Abraham and so many of the Bible heroes did. Abraham was also living a normal everyday life when God's intentions turned up out of nowhere and he had a choice whether or not to respond to them correctly – a whole new life started for him as he stepped out by faith into a whole new, map-less pilgrimage of faith.

God's intentions will always come to pass and if you say 'No' He will use someone else. The annoying thing about this is that you get to see it happen and have to deal with the fact that it could have been you because that was your offer. Don't miss your God moments. I believe that God prepares our hearts for these moments of challenge prior to His arrival. We do not know what is going to happen but we know something is about to. Make sure you are ready, like the disciples and Abraham, for God to arrive out of nowhere and offer you some of His great intentions. Make sure that you are not like the rich young ruler who thought he was ready for his moment but, when it came, he was not. He couldn't see beyond his present life of riches and privilege to that bigger, unseen life that Jesus was offering. When you, by faith, respond correctly to God, you always end up with more than what you imagined or came for.

Let's finish today by thinking again of the returning leper:

Then He said to him, 'Get up. On your way. Your faith has healed and saved you.'
Luke 17:19 (MSG)

Champion, look at this: he never came to get saved. He was a Samaritan and he came to get healed. He left healed and saved. When you respond correctly to God, you don't just leave with what you came for but also with what you never believed was possible! RSVP. You will be glad you did.

What's the address of your secret place?

He who dwells in the secret place of the Most High shall abide under the shadow of the Almighty. I will say of the LORD, 'He is my refuge and my fortress; my God, in Him I will trust.'

Psalm 91:1-2

Though your daily Christian life needs to have a public expression (your evangelistic lifestyle, living out what you believe on a daily basis), you cannot survive with just a public expression; it is vital that we all have a 'secret garden' or private place with the Lord. In my message *The Secret Garden*, I refer to how Jesus – in the last moments of His life, those moments before all hell would be let loose on Him – chose not a revival meeting nor public place but rather a quiet corner of a garden called Gethsemane. It was in that secret place that He found the strength and courage He needed for everything that lay ahead that night.

We must remember that we, too, find our strength and ability in the secret place we have with God and not in the public arena of our Christianity. It is in the secret place of the Most High, where there is the audience of just One, that we are, as Jesus was, made strong. Let's make sure that our Christianity is not just a public affair but that it also has a very special secret place.

Here are some questions to provoke you to thought today:

- Do you have a secret place in your relationship with God?

- Do you go there as much as you need to?

- What do you need to do to make sure that you get from the secret place everything God has for you in it?

Let's finish today by reading the next part of this Psalm to see what happens for us and to us when we choose to abide – 'make our home in' – the secret place of the Most High. As you read it ask yourself, 'Why would I NOT abide there?'

Surely He shall deliver you from the snare of the fowler and from the perilous pestilence. He shall cover you with His feathers, and under His wings you shall take refuge; His truth shall be your shield and buckler. You shall not be afraid of the terror by night, nor of the arrow that flies by day, nor of the pestilence that walks in darkness, nor of the destruction that lays waste at noonday. A thousand may fall at your side, and ten thousand at your right hand; but it shall not come near you. Only with your eyes shall you look, and see the reward of the wicked. Because you have made the LORD, who is my refuge, even the Most High, your dwelling place, no evil shall befall you, nor shall any plague come near your dwelling; for He shall give His angels charge over you, to keep you in all your ways. In their hands they shall bear you up, lest you dash your foot against a stone.

Psalm 91:3-12

Bless you and have a great day. Live out of a secret place that you have with the Most High God.

GIVE IT AWAY

Don't hoard treasure down here where it gets eaten by moths and corroded by rust or—worse!—stolen by burglars. Stockpile treasure in heaven, where it's safe from moth and rust and burglars. It's obvious, isn't it? The place where your treasure is, is the place you will most want to be, and end up being.
Matthew 6:20 (MSG)

When I was a teenager I went to a Summer Camp and met a girl who I became friendly with. For the last night of camp there was going to be a big party where we got to dress fancy and wear our best things, so I had a great outfit and some special jewellery packed. I had brought with me a necklace that I was exceptionally fond of. One night, near the end of our camping experience, as it got close to saying goodbye to all our campmates, I knew the Holy Spirit was putting on my heart to give my new friend the necklace.

I struggled with the thought for a while. It wasn't expensive, it was mostly plastic beads (don't judge me, it was the 80's!), but I liked it! I knew what God wanted me to do and, on the day before the big farewell party, I called my friend aside and gave her the necklace and a great big hug and told her how much God loved her and that He wanted her to have something that reminded her how much God loved her and desired to bless her life with good things. She broke down in tears and thanked me, telling me about the hard upbringing she had. Her mother had left her when she was only little and she struggled with the fact that God would ever do good things for her. I'm so glad I was obedient to give away this trinket.

This weekend, pray about giving something you consider precious away to someone. Ask God *WHAT*, and *TO WHOM*.

Notes

_____

_____

He doesn't need long to do something amazing

Then God saw everything that He had made, and indeed it was very good. So the evening and the morning were the sixth day.

Genesis 1:31

---

*M*orning, Champion. Maybe you are in a situation that seems impossible, and are facing things that look like they can never change; maybe you're thinking, 'I know God may be willing and able towards me but what I need for Him to do would take so long to happen.' I want to encourage you that that is not true – you see, God does not need long to do impossible things and bring incredible changes to your life!

Think about it: as Ephesians 3:20 reveals, He is the God who does exceedingly, abundantly above what we think or imagine; He thinks bigger than we could ever have the potential to dream or imagine. But Genesis also reveals Him as the unlimited God who does not need long at all, even when it comes to making apparently 'big stuff' happen.

In the first chapter of Genesis we see everything being created by God in just six days – just SIX DAYS for the whole of creation! Maybe you were taught seven days? No, on the seventh day He rested, creating one last thing: the first Sabbath. Think about what He created in each of those blocks of 'day' time: universes, oceans, vegetation, even humanity. Is what you are in need of as big a project as any of those? If God can do all that in six days what could He do in your situation in six days, or even six minutes? If God only needed 144 hours to bring all creation into existence from absolute nothingness what could He create or re-arrange for you in just one day?

Change your confession, Champion. Stop saying it's hopeless, or it will take years – unless you want it to? Stop releasing your faith for lesser things from God based on your small opinion of God's potential; instead begin to pray again and thank the God who made everything we know and see in just six days that His intentions for you and your situations can happen, and they can happen real quick!

The fact is that God could probably do what you need in a matter of seconds; He probably does not even need a full minute. Believe!

You can't start the next chapter of your life if you keep re-reading the last one.

Unknown

There are rewards for those who overcome

To him who overcomes, I will give the right to sit with Me on my throne, just as I overcame and sat down with My Father on His throne.

Revelation 3:21 (NIV)

So often life tries to convince us to just 'put up with things', to 'just roll with the punches' and just 'go with it'. Maybe with some things there is room for doing that, but with most things we actually need to make the decision that we are going to do the opposite and let God make us the overcomer He created us to be. Recently my wife Gina shared with our ladies at their Ladies' Getaway a very good message on this subject, and taught some very good points regarding not 'just going with it', whatever that 'it' may be.

It doesn't matter if the world says just put up with it or 'go with it' – if the Bible says you shouldn't or do not have to then we need to take the position of an overcomer in regard to that situation, circumstance or condition. The Bible reveals to us in Revelation that God wants us to be overcomers in life, not 'under-goers'. It also reveals that there is always a reward from Him to those who dare not to just go with things but rather overcome them. At least seven times in Revelations 2 and 3 it says, 'To him who overcomes I will give ...' So we see clearly that God gives rewards and positions to those who dare to overcome the things that others settle for.

My question today is what in your life are you putting up with when deep down inside you know you should not and don't have to? Today stand up, come into agreement with what God says and then, by the help of His Spirit, begin to kick back with a heart to overcome and make a change. Do so with the knowledge that, as well as you becoming victorious where you were not, God has a great reward on the other side for you.

One example that Gina used when teaching the ladies was the delicate and often untouchable issue of 'the time of the month' – that time when some woman can become 'a little more difficult to live with than normal' because of their menstrual cycle. The world so often teaches that it is normal and that you just have to put up with what comes with that time, because that's your lot in life and you have to just 'go with it'. Actually, it is one of those things you can choose to believe God to overcome in, if you want to. And, when you overcome, one of the rewards will be a more peaceful home (some of the men said Amen!).

That is just one example – there are many more: breaking free from addictions and habits you may have that always cause you to do what you don't want to; low self-esteem that governs your confidence in life; depressions that continually stifle you ... the list goes on and on. What I am saying is don't just 'go with it' – rise up and overcome it! Be that overcomer, and get the rewards that are there for those who overcome. Remember, it was for freedom that Christ has set you free!

Get up and kick back in Jesus' name. Those other reward references for you to check out: Revelation 2:7, 11, 17, 26 and 3:4, 21

Don't lose your first love

You have persevered and have patience, and have laboured for My name's sake and have not become weary. Nevertheless I have this against you, that you have left your first love. Remember therefore from where you have fallen; repent and do the first works, or else I will come to you quickly and remove your lampstand from its place – unless you repent.

Revelation 2:3-5

In Revelations 2 and 3 we see God have a good honest chat with a number of churches about their health and condition. Here we see Him talking to the church in Ephesus. When you read the whole conversation He has with them you see that He starts by commending them on loads of things that they have achieved. He speaks of their perseverance and hard work, and also commends them for their ability to spot false apostles and to endure hardships. These guys are getting some major pats on the back from God! Then He turns and drops this 'but' challenge on them, and addresses something that is a major problem: that, in all they're doing for Him, they had lost their first-love relationship with Him.

They were so busy doing they had stopped being! Yes, they were achieving incredible things but at a great cost – they were losing the intimate relationship with Him, that which was actually primary to God, not secondary. He tells them to remember the height from which they had fallen. Wow! When I read that I hear God saying that when we walk close with Him in a first-love relationship we sit in a place that can get no higher or be equalled by anything else. Everything else, including our labour for Him, will always be a lower position, and the further we get from our intimate walk with Him in His sight the 'further we fall'.

I think this verse can be relevant to each and every one of us at one time or another. We can all get distracted by the things we are doing and lose that which God values the most from us, an intimate relationship. The good news is it is easily rectified. Notice that God gives a very simple cure: just repent and get back to doing the things you used to do first (loving Him).

Remember, repentance is to simply change the way you think. If today you have drifted away from your first love, simply make the decision to re-prioritise things and put walking close and intimate with Him again at the very top of the list. Above all other things God desires to be our first love and for us to walk in a first-love relationship with Him; all other things and people must come second.

Let us all return to our first love again today.

Prayer

Forgive me, Lord, for when I have drifted from You being my first love. Let me be so conscious today that what I do for You is secondary to the love relationship I have with You. Help me today to get these things back into their correct order, and may the first thing in my life simply be the love that I have for You. I do not want to be lukewarm towards You in anyway, Lord; help me to be red hot of heart for You! Thank You for how You love me today with that same degree of love.

Amen

Stop praying and open the door

Peter knocked at the outer entrance, and a servant girl named Rhoda came to answer the door. When she recognised Peter's voice, she was so overjoyed she ran back without opening it and exclaimed, 'Peter is at the door!' 'You're out of your mind,' they told her. When she kept insisting that it was so, they said, 'It must be his angel.' But Peter kept on knocking, and when they opened the door and saw him, they were astonished.

Acts 12:13-16 (NIV)

This is a great account of the moment when Peter was released from prison as a result of a praying church. It is also very humorous when you read through it, as you see a church that was so busy asking (praying) that they didn't have time to receive the answer to their prayers when it stood and knocked at the door!

The church had called an emergency prayer meeting when Peter had been arrested and imprisoned for standing up for Jesus. Man, they must have lifted the roof with their heart-felt prayers because, as they were praying, God supernaturally broke Peter out of the prison. Read the chapter, it's a great read of what a limitless God can do when people dare to pray and believe.

But then you have this hilarious situation where Peter – the one they are praying for – is standing at the door trying to get in, and he can't. Rhoda, the servant girl who first opens the door, sees Peter but in her excitement leaves him on the doorstep while she goes and tells the others. When they hear, instead of rushing to the door they start over-spiritualising everything by claiming it is his ghost or angel. Meanwhile Peter stands at the door saying, 'Hello! Can I come in?'

What can we learn from this? Prayer is always good but even during it we always need to be expecting for God to answer our prayers. When we pray we must realise that God is at work at that very moment, there is no 'time difference or delay' and, most importantly, when there is a 'knock at the door', be ready to answer and welcome the manifestation of what you have been asking for. Remember He is the God of 'and suddenly' – don't wait for warnings. When God starts moving, stuff happens fast. Am I telling you not to pray? No, I am telling you to pray with expectancy, expectancy that even as you are praying your ear is open to the 'knock at the door'.

Finally, what an amazing ending – it says when they saw Peter they were amazed! Hold on, what was the theme of their prayer meeting? Wasn't it, 'Please set Peter free'? Let's keep away from token religious prayers and be a people who pray believing.

Believer, get ready for the knock at the door – what you have been asking for could be walking down the garden path towards you right now. Don't be astonished when it knocks, simply open the door and say, 'Hi, I've been expecting you!'

Be the miracle

Taking the five loaves and the two fish and looking up to heaven, He gave thanks and broke them. Then He gave them to the disciples to set before the people. They all ate and were satisfied, and the disciples picked up twelve basketfuls of broken pieces that were left over.

Luke 9:16-17 (NIV)

Everyone likes to look around for where the next miracle for the moment is going to come from; in reality, sometimes we need to stop and take a look in the mirror and realise that maybe God wants you to be the miracle this time! God forever wants to increase the output and experience of our faith to meet the needs of the world – for this to happen we need to remain committed to be ready to be the vehicle for a miracle when one is needed.

God is the one who provides the power but He always looks for everyday people to be the equipment or apparatus that He uses for the moment at hand. Will you be the equipment, positioned correctly for what God wants to do next?

- Moses was the available equipment God used to liberate a nation that was in slavery.

- David was the available equipment that God used to display His 'against all odds' power against Goliath.

- Gideon was the available equipment God used to show that His empowerment on out-numbered armies causes them to win.

God is looking for available equipment to use today. Let me put that another way: He is looking for people to partner with Him in releasing supernatural things on the earth. Do you fancy working in partnership with a living God today? All you need to do is what the people mentioned already did – make yourself available. Not some bits of yourself, but all of it. Then see what happens when an unrestricted, unlimited God partners with a submitted and yielded, available life.

That is a powerful combo, Champion!

Bless you, live extra large again today.

Those who walk with God always reach their destination.

700 Club

WORLD MISSIONS

And this gospel of the kingdom will be preached in the whole world as a testimony to all nations, and then the end will come.
Matthew 24:14 (NIV)

There are people all over this world bravely and inspiringly preaching the gospel of Jesus Christ as missionaries; people who have left their home countries to travel to other parts of the world where they feel called to minister God's Word.

1. This weekend, make a donation to a missionary you may know, or to a Missions organisation that is spreading God's Word. You don't have to give a large sum of money. Any amount would help the work these folks do. If you don't know of any, we have great partnerships with many missionaries and organisations that are making a huge impact on this earth for God. For more information regarding this contact us at **info@greatbiglife.co.uk**.

2. If finances are tight then pick a nation that needs prayer and pray that God would help the missionaries in that country.

Notes

_____

_____

_____

_____

_____

_____

Manage your busy-ness

'Martha, Martha,' the Lord answered, 'you are worried and upset about many things, but only one thing is needed. Mary has chosen what is better, and it will not be taken away from her.'

Luke 10:41-42 (NIV)

The warning here for us all is this: be careful not to let busy-ness, worries and being upset about things keep you from what is better.

Martha was busy balancing chores and all the work of having many dinner guests, and had taken her eye off the One who makes life work well. Whenever you take your eyes off Jesus and forget to take that desire-based time to sit at His feet, worry and upset about things soon re-appear and seek to dominate your attention and time, and drain you of your peace.

God does not want you living worried but rather living secure. Security is a result of faith and faith is found at the feet of the Master.

If today you are upset or worried about things, the best thing you can do is what Martha did, which is to STOP! Get yourself away somewhere quiet and sit at His feet again with empty hands and an open heart. Worship Him, listen to His words of life and you'll see that worry simply washes away.

Jesus taught a lot about the destructive force of worry and how we should live without it in Luke 12. He taught that it cannot add anything to your life, but only detract from it. Resting in the presence of Jesus, unlike worry, will always add to your life so why not hang out with Him instead. That will be time well spent.

Like Mary, know how to chill out with Jesus when you need to.

Prayer

Lord Jesus, help me today to stop unhealthy busyness in my life, and to sit at Your feet and lay all my worries down there. I trust You, Lord, in every area of my life; I know that You are working for my good. So today I choose to do what Mary did, to sit at your feet, breath and trust in You. Thank You for this new day.

Amen

A cornerstone always determines how high a structure can go, how big it will be and how much pressure it can withstand. Make Jesus your cornerstone.

Andy Elmes

Be true to the real you

But the man who looks intently into the perfect law that gives freedom, and continues to do this, not forgetting what he has heard, but doing it – he will be blessed in what he does.

James 1:25 (NIV)

*L*et us look at the account and rewards of the man who sees himself in God's mirror and does not forget!

We must look into the mirror of God's Word on a daily basis to discover our true identity and what we are truly capable of from a 'God's-eye' view. Then we must have the courage to live out what we learn, and live true to the identity we have found; it is then that our life takes on whole new divine dimensions.

It is then that the Bible promises that we will be blessed in what we do! What a great promise of reward. It does not say 'blessed in what you do in church' but rather 'blessed throughout the entirety of your life'. Why? Because the Bible speaks wisdom and truth to the entirety of your life not just the church-related bits!

If you want to experience this promised blessing throughout your life always remember to do the four things this verse tells you to:

- Look intently into perfectly fulfilled law that brings freedom.

- Continue to look, and get an appetite for it.

- Don't forget what you have read or discovered.

- DO IT – take it from information to application.

The result: YOU WILL BE BLESSED.

Prayer

Good morning, Lord. Please help me today to find my true reflection in Your Word, and then help me to live out what I have seen. Give me the courage to lay down every other, lesser reflection that this life offers and embrace Yours. As I read and apply Your Word I thank You that my life is blessed abundantly.

Amen

*P*rogress is impossible without change, and those who
cannot change their minds cannot change anything.

George Bernard Shaw

Life in the wasted places

Forget the former things; do not dwell on the past. See, I am doing a new thing! Now it springs up; do you not perceive it? I am making a way in the desert and streams in the wasteland.

Isaiah 43:18-19 (NIV)

We should not live in the past any longer but rather the now that God is doing and the future He has promised. We will be people who live with a hunger to both perceive the new thing He is doing in our lives and to 'go with it'.

When we do, it will always cause a divinely-orchestrated way to appear in the seemingly dead-end desert times of our life, and God will show you a way forward where there seemed to be none.

The promise for those who dare to live in the new thing is also that He makes streams flow in the wastelands or 'wasted places' and they become no longer wasted but refreshed, vibrant and fittingly used for His purposes. Why? Because the promised streams of His life are now running through it, and everywhere the river of His life flows things come to life.

God loves to revive, renew and re-purpose wasted things, whether they be wasted lands, buildings, people or talents. When God turns up, waste becomes potential. Walk with God with a hunger for what He wants to do today and you will witness His power of transformation, changing wasted things into flourishing successful testimonies of grace.

Are there wastelands or 'wasted areas' in your life? Commit them to the Lord today, allow Him access to them and you will be glad you did.

Have a great day, and remember God is doing a new thing so keep your eyes peeled for it!

Prayer

Thank You for this brand new day, Lord. I choose to let go of old things and embrace all that You have for me. Forgetting what lays behind I reach forward to all You have in store for me. Thank You for springtime in my life where I watch you revive, refresh and make all things new.

Amen

Always take time to bask in the bigness of God.

Andy Elmes

The potential is in the promise

Now the LORD had said to Abram: 'Get out of your country, from your family and from your father's house, to a land that I will show you. I will make you a great nation; I will bless you and make your name great; and you shall be a blessing. I will bless those who bless you, and I will curse him who curses you; and in you all the families of the earth shall be blessed.'

Genesis 12:1-3

I was driving down the road yesterday, thinking of some of the promises God has given Gina and me regarding our future – promises of things so big and so good. Promises for things I could never achieve in my own doing or by my efforts alone; that's how you identify that they're God promises, right?

Out of nowhere I felt the voice of God say to me, 'The potential is in the promise.' I thought about that for a moment and got real blessed, so I thought I would pass it on.

When God stepped into Abram's well-organised world with a promise of a better tomorrow, notice that He didn't say, 'We will . . .', but, 'I will . . .' When He gave Abram the promise regarding his future, the promise was not dependent on Abram's ability to make it happen but on God's. All Abram had to do was step out, leave Haran and trust God's promise and what it contained.

When it comes to the promises of God the most important letter in promise is I. When God gives you a promise for your life or situation, contained in that promise is the full potential to bring it into being outside of your assistance, and it is a matter of Him saying 'I will', not 'We will' or 'Can you help Me?'

All God expected Abram to do was step out into the promise and leave the rest (how it would come to pass) to Him. I believe that is what God also expects of you and me. We read later on how Abram tried to help or assist God when He promises him a miracle child. The reality is that God did not want or need Abram's help, and it only confused things in creating Ishmael. Let this simple truth penetrate your heart today: in God's promise to you is His potential to make happen what He says will happen. With child-like trust we are to simply believe.

Today, when He gives us a promise, the manifestation of that promise is not based on the potential of 'We will' but 'I will'. Contained in that promise He has given you is the full ability to make it a reality in your world, without your help! What is left for us to do, then? Only believe – all things are possible to those who believe!

God bless, don't underestimate what is contained within that promise God has given you.

Stop trying to recycle what God is trying to replace.

46

Commit what you love into His hands

It was now about noon, and darkness came over the whole land until three in the afternoon, for the sun stopped shining. And the curtain of the temple was torn in two. Jesus called out with a loud voice, 'Father, into your hands I commit my spirit.' When He had said this, He breathed His last.

Luke 23:44-46 (NIV)

*N*otice what Jesus prays in His final moments on the cross, in those moments when life as He has known it would end and He would enter into and conquer death itself: He prays, 'Into your hands I commit my spirit.' Why did He pray that? Simple: He knew His Father was able to keep that which was committed to Him or 'placed into His hands'. That which He committed to God would be safe and have a certain future. We are wise when we commit the things we care about into the secure hands of the living God regularly.

Each morning when I go for a walk and a pray – that is what I like to do, committing into His hands the people in my world that matter to me and the things in my world I have to deal with. I commit my life, my wife, my marriage and my kids, knowing He is able to do a better job of keeping them than me. As I sit watching the news, listening about riots in cities and weirdos ever on the increase, I find peace in the fact that it is God who is keeping safe what, or should I say who, I have committed to Him. When it comes to kids I have five: one boy and four girls. Sometimes I want to get t-shirts printed for my girls, making them wear them every time they go out, that read, 'This is my daughter: harm her and I will hunt you down with a chainsaw and torture you!' – but I know that's not right! I know also that a better, more effective thing to do is to daily commit them to the One who is able to keep them from all harm; He who never slumbers or sleeps.

I look at financial problems in the nation today, with international banking problems consuming the confidence that most have had for their financial futures – to tell you the truth, I don't want to be the one who handles this section of my life. I feel a whole lot safer committing the short-term and long-term provision of my life and that of my family to the hands of the One who is always one jump ahead. God is able to keep me and mine, independent of what is happening through the financial situations that the world may be facing. He caused Isaac to prosper in famine, He fed His prophets with ravens and miracles involving widows, and He is able to keep you and me when we commit all that we are into His hands.

Three days after today's verse Jesus opened His eyes in victory, never to die again. He entered the corridors of death knowing that what He would face, no matter how horrendous, could not hold Him. Why? Because His life had been positioned in the hands of God, and in God's hands things have a certain future.

Each morning commit into His hands all that you are, those you love and everything you have, then relax in perfect assurance while everyone around you stresses out.

NO SHOPPING LIST

Enter his gates with thanksgiving and his courts with praise; give thanks to him and praise his name.
Psalm 100:4

Knowing what a loving and gracious Father we have it is natural that we go to Him with our needs, desires and petitions. But sometimes I'm sure He finds it refreshing when we go to Him without the shopping list. As a parent I know how lovely it is to have my child run up to me and give me a great big hug, just 'because'.

This weekend, put all your lists aside and go to God filled with gratefulness for who He is and what He has already done. Make a conscious effort to make your time with Him all about Him.

No matter how hard you try, God is still going to give back to you. He just can't help Himself! As you selflessly delight in Him He promises to give you the desires of your heart! He already knows what you need and want, so put the list away, know He's got it all covered, and give Him thanks and praise just 'because'.

Take delight in the LORD, and he will give you the desires of your heart.
Psalm 37:4 (NIV)

Notes

_____

_____

_____

_____

_____

Created by, created for

For it is by grace you have been saved, through faith – and this not from yourselves, it is the gift of God – not by works, so that no-one can boast. For we are God's workmanship, created in Christ Jesus to do good works, which God prepared in advance for us to do.

Ephesians 2:8-10 (NIV)

These verses are fundamental and foundational to understanding real Christianity. They speak of who we are and how we came into existence as new creations, and also what we were created for, our purpose. Within these verses we see two important components; when kept together they produce effective Christian living but if divided can produce spiritual laziness and ineffective living in the life of the believer.

The first and most important thing we discover is that we are the produce of His grace (verse 9-10); we did not bring ourselves into salvation, justification and righteousness, rather it was all God outside of our help or assistance. When we were dead in our sins He saved us (made us alive) by His grace, and we enter into all He has given us and achieved for us by faith alone.

In this we can compare ourselves to Adam, the first man God created. There are many great practical and spiritual parallels to us and him, especially that his first day was God's last day. When we read the beginnings of Genesis we see God make everything and do everything that was needed for life and existence, then finally He creates man and positions him in His finished, completed work. It's the same with us in our new-creation standing: God completed everything He needed to do to save us and restore us and then through Christ brought us into being and positioned us in His finished work.

As Adam was so are we; we are God's workmanship, not finding our origins in our ability but rather in His grace, that which He did of His own potential outside of our assistance. An understanding of grace must leave you looking at God alone without any boasting of things added or achieved by you. We are indeed His workmanship, created naturally by Him (we did not come from monkeys or explosions, rather we all find our ancestry in that first man and woman, Adam and Eve), but also spiritually we have been recreated by Him in Christ.

If this is all Ephesians offered us it would be more than enough – we are left created by God and restored and re-positioned by the perfect work of His Son as a gift of His goodness and mercy. But the truth is it does not end there. The apostle Paul takes a breath and continues with the same story line as He announces in verse 10 that, 'We are God's workmanship, created in Christ Jesus to do good works, which God prepared in advance for us to do.' Wow! Created by God for a purpose – that's true destiny. This means that there is a proper response to grace and this response is not laziness or sitting on our 'blessed assurance; rather good works. Let's look into this a little further over the next few days.

Created with a purpose

For it is by grace you have been saved, through faith – and this not from yourselves, it is the gift of God – not by works, so that no-one can boast. For we are God's workmanship, created in Christ Jesus to do good works, which God prepared in advance for us to do.

Ephesians 2:8-10 (NIV)

Yesterday we paralleled our lives to the first created man, Adam, and established that, like Adam, we too are God's workmanship; we too find our existence as a result of His plans, creative ability and grace, not our doing or performance. Let's consider this further.

When God made Adam, was he made to sit in the garden and make daisy chains or was there a purpose to his existence? Obviously he was not made to sit there but rather to manage the garden (a picture of God's kingdom). He was given dominion and responsibility over what belonged to God, and found fulfilment in managing and taking care of what was God's and also his, being that he was God's workmanship and a part of His family. We must consider that He would have had spiritual as well as practical responsibilities. Imagine what it was like to tend Eden – sowing, harvesting, pruning and developing – so we can understand that there was an outflow to his God-created life. Again I believe that these verses in Ephesians teach us that there is to be an outflow to our God-created lives; we, too, have been created for good works (or should we say 'God works'). As with Adam we have been positioned to now look after what belongs to God – no longer a physical garden called Eden but rather His present-day kingdom – specifically the church and all its outworkings and projects.

Adam was not made to sit there, and neither are we. I am not talking about slave labour or obligation-based duties, but rather about having a grace-based understanding of the privilege that we have to partner with God in what He is doing and the dreams He has for our generation. The key difference is the motivation: the why we do what we do.

For me, personally, it excites me more to think that God made me for a purpose – the thought that He made me just to sit and await collection is quite boring. Again, let me underline: understanding, or having a revelation of grace, should not produce laziness but rather effective living that is rooted in the knowledge of the finished work of Christ. We are not doing to get anything; rather doing because we understand what we have already got what has been given to us freely by God in His goodness.

If it does not open it's not your door.

Unknown

Good works, not dead ones

For we are God's workmanship, created in Christ Jesus to do good works, which God prepared in advance for us to do.

Ephesians 2:10 (NIV)

We have been talking about the fact that we are His workmanship (the produce of His grace), created for a purpose – that revealed purpose being good works. At this point it is good for us to underline that we are called to good works, not dead works.

What are dead works? Simply things we may do that are pointless – pointless because what we are trying to get them to achieve or produce has been achieved already. That is what makes it a dead work. It's like spending all day trying to put a plug in the sink when there is one in there already, or shaving your head when you are already bald!

God has not called us to dead works, to try and produce what He already has. We are not Jehovah's Witnesses! One of the major differences between us and the JWs is this issue; they work hard all day evangelising and knocking doors because their chance at salvation is dependent on whether or not they knock on enough doors and fill in enough charts. If they do good they may have the slightest of chances of being included in those who go to heaven – how sad. So they are always working for or towards their possible salvation. We are different – we should be living from the assurance of perfect redemption in and through Christ. Again, we see ourselves on the other side of the perfect work of Jesus and the cross. How much more should we be knocking on the doors of the hearts of those we love, when we have such a perfect assurance based in the finished work of Jesus?

So what we do for God (good works) we do not do to get anything, but rather we do because we have revelation of what has already been done. Nothing we do can add a single thing to what is already a perfect redemption. It's not a case of Jesus only achieving 75% and the remaining 25% is down to us. It is not even that He did 99% and we have responsibility for the remaining 1%. No, He did it all; He has 100% saved us and we have no claim or involvement in achieving in His finished work. The things we now do that flow out from this understanding are the biblical good works – we do the things we were created to do because we love the One who positioned us to do them.

So repent from any dead works, stop trying to open a door that is already open, see that you have been qualified and positioned by Him, and get on with what He has created you to do – good works.

Prayer

Good morning, Lord. Today I repent and turn away from dead works in my life. Forgive me for working to achieve things that You have already established and completed for me and in me. Today I step out of dead works into good works; today I purpose to work from a position of all that You have already done. May my life bring You the glory You deserve.

Amen

Church should equip you for service

And He Himself gave some to be apostles, some prophets, some evangelists, and some pastors and teachers, for the equipping of the saints for the work of ministry, for the edifying of the body of Christ.

Ephesians 4:11-12

We have been talking about our calling to good works, that we are saved and made alive by God for a purpose. Here in Ephesians 4 we see that the primary role of church leadership is to equip and empower the saints for the 'good works' of ministry. Notice it is not pastoral care but empowerment that is primary. The role of your church leaders is to equip you to do for God the things He prepared for you to do in advance.

It's interesting when you study the Greek word used for works in Ephesians 2 and 4 – it is the same word *ergon* and it means:

> *Business, employment that with which a person is occupied with, what a person undertakes to do, an enterprise, an act or deed things done, things accomplished by the hand of a person.*

Put another way, or in context, we are all called to 'do God's business or do the business for God'.

According to today's text your church leadership is there to equip the saints – that's you! You don't become a saint when you die, or in 200 years when someone thinks you deserve it – you are one now because your life is in Christ. Your life can never be more righteous than it is now in Him.

For too many years the speed we have done and achieved things as a church has been limited sadly by the lack of people involved or equipped. We need to turn this around and increase the impact span of our church punch. How? We must all stand up in grace with a heart to do, to position ourselves where we can be equipped, and get ready to get busy with God's business. Again, let me underline that our doing does not save us or add to our righteousness, but it is, I believe, the natural result of understanding the grace of God that has been poured upon your life. Imagine how much faster our local churches could arrive at their dreams when the whole church (the saints) takes this seriously!

It says in Ephesians 2 that our good works were prepared in advance by God for us to do. Think about that – if you are not doing the things that God has prepared for you to do then someone else has to do them, right? Which means some end up carrying too much as a result of others sitting too comfortably in grace. Surely our battle cry must be one of 'All hands on deck!' not 'Can somebody please help me?!'

When the saints understand that God has prepared good works for each of them to do (in advance), and get themselves equipped and empowered by church leadership, then we can impact the world for Jesus in a way that will have lasting results and not cause the few to feel any burdens God never intended for them.

Go ask your leaders to equip you for God's business.

Our good works bring Him glory

You are the light of the world. A city that is set on a hill cannot be hidden. Nor do they light a lamp and put it under a basket, but on a lampstand, and it gives light to all who are in the house. Let your light so shine before men, that they may see your good works and glorify your Father in heaven.

Matthew 5:14-16

According to Matthew we are the light of this world, lights not to be hidden away. We are called to shine. How do we shine? By the way we choose to live in an ever-darkening world. He also says that when the world sees our good works (as we studied earlier this week, it's the same Greek word used in Ephesians chapter 2 and 4) they will give God glory. So what are the good works we should be busy with? Two categories immediately come to mind that I think are important – these are the works that God has always done and that works that matter to Him.

The works that God has always done

If we are going to be busy with good works we need to look at what God has always done, and in them see what business He would have us busy with today. Specifically we can look at Jesus and the things He did when He walked the earth two thousand years ago, and the ministry of God's spirit working in and through the first disciples (early church). In these we can see what we are called to busy ourselves with today.

Jesus' purpose for being was to destroy the works of another – that other being satan (1 John 3:8). He came to spoil and reverse everything the devil had worked hard to build: He came to heal the sick, mend the broken, save the lost. We are called to do these same works now, just as the first group of disciples was then.

The things that matter to God

As you read through the Bible you get continual glimpses of how God loves to care for the vulnerable, and defend those who are weak. When we commit to do the same we are in alignment with what God considers to be a good work; we are indeed doing His business.

> *His name is the LORD . . . A father to the fatherless, a defender of widows, is God in His holy dwelling.*
>
> **Psalm 68:4-5 (NIV)**

> *Religion that God our Father accepts as pure and faultless is this: to look after orphans and widows in their distress and to keep oneself from being polluted by the world.*
>
> **James 1:27 (NIV)**

This category has made me really think about the development of social care and people support in the life of our church. What more can we be doing to take care of those in our cities who are in need? How can we make provision for true widows, feed the hungry, strengthen those who are feeling weak? As we commit to care, support and strengthen those who are vulnerable we delight the heart of God.

These are just two categories that come to mind when I think of the subject of good works. I am sure there are many more, but in these two there is certainly enough to keep us, His church, busy – busy doing things that matter to Him, because we know what He has done for us.

SALVATION

**For God loved the world so much that he gave his only
Son so that anyone who believes in him shall not
perish but have eternal life.**
John 3:16 (Living Bible)

This weekend, think of 5 people that you want to see receive salvation through Christ
this year. Write those names down on the lines below. Spend some time praying for each
person. Believe that God desires to touch their lives and that He will send people and
opportunities their way that will cause them to want to know God.

1 _____

2 _____

3 _____

4 _____

5 _____

Notes

_____

_____

_____

Look at the tap, not the hosepipe

And my God shall supply all your need according to His riches in glory by Christ Jesus.

Philippians 4:19

Here we see Paul make a guarantee of provision to a bunch of people who had generously supported him as he pushed the gospel into places it had not been. With confidence he declares to these generous givers 'my God!'.

I love the tone of confidence that flowed from Paul, that he knew who he was representing and what He was capable of doing. He then promises that His God would provide their every need according to His divine sufficiency. But notice he does not tell them how it will happen, when it will happen, or who or what He will use to make it happen. What Paul was doing was getting them to look at the tap, not to stare at any particular hosepipe.

In my garden I have an outside tap and a hosepipe that is connected to it. The purpose of the hosepipe is to distribute or deliver that which the tap abundantly provides. It would be a crazy thing to put my confidence in that hose or any other hose and ignore or not give due attention to the tap it is joined to. Why? Because the tap is the source; the hosepipe is simply that which delivers or dispenses what the tap provides. The hose provides no sufficiency in itself.

This is an important lesson when it comes to understanding God and His provision coming into our lives. He uses different people and things at different times to get His provision to us. We must learn never to look at or put our faith in any specific hose He is using, or has previously used, but in Him. Don't get me wrong: always be grateful and thankful to the hose being used but at the same time keep your faith and expectancy in the tap (source).

I know in my ministry and life I seem to always need things from God – I suppose that is because I am a visionary leader with a heart set on ever pushing forward. I regularly need God to get His provision to me or to a project I am involved in. Over the course of my ministry I have seen Him use so many different hoses (people) to do that. When God uses a particular hose it is easy, the next time you have a need, to look at that hose again – and this is exactly what I want to tell you not to do. Yes, God may use that hose again to meet your need, but equally He may not. He may choose to use another. To only look at the hose he used last time is to put an unfair pressure on that person, a pressure that should never be. It also causes you to not live and walk by faith in regard to what God has for you next. As Paul promised these guys, so we need to remember: he didn't say who God would use, how He would do it or even when; he just said His God would.

As I said before, always be thankful for the hose God uses but don't go placing your faith or confidence in that hose. Rather, keep your eyes firmly set on the tap (God). Also remember that this is not a one-way street – it's not just about God using people to be hoses to get things to you, it's also about God being able to use your life to be a hose to get something to someone else. Be ready to be His hose sometimes, too!

God bless – whatever your need I know my God is able to provide according to riches in glory.

Your tithe empowers your church

If you start thinking to yourselves, 'I did all this. And all by myself. I'm rich. It's all mine!' – well, think again. Remember that God, your God, gave you the strength to produce all this wealth so as to confirm the covenant that he promised to your ancestors – as it is today.

Deuteronomy 8:17-18 (MSG)

When we read about the life of Abraham, a man who lived and walked with God in covenant relationship (before the law), we see the first reference to the tithe. God gave this man, who lived to honour him; victory in battle and Abraham's response was to honour God with a tenth of the spoils, which then became his lifestyle. He never read books on the tithe, or went to a conference; for him it was a natural thing to do, and it should be that way for us too. God gives us victory and the ability to prosper, and we should then honour him with the first chunk.

We also learn that God's plan for Abraham was to bless him so he could be a blessing. It was not all about him; it was about using his life to empower what God needed done on the earth. All that God is doing on the earth He does, or desires to do, through His body on the earth – which is His church. God may have great intentions for us to do things on the earth for Him, but the reality is if people do not tithe they limit what the church they say they love is actually able to do. Lack of tithers is what often ties the hands of most churches doing what they want to and getting God the postcodes/zip codes they really want Him to have.

Robert Morris, in his book *The Blessed Life* (Regal Books, ISBN 0830736735), which I highly recommend, states the sad facts. He says this: 'In 1998, the body of Christ around the world earned the equivalent of an estimated $15.2 trillion. The total amount given to all ministry-related causes, including churches, missions, etc., was $270 billion. If you do the math, you will discover that is only 1.8 percent.' Imagine that, the church does what it does in the world today running on less that 1.8 percent of the system God established for it to run by. When we look at these figures they seem so huge, but the reality is it always comes back to each of us: are we tithing correctly? Are we expecting others to and not us? Are we enjoying what other people's faithfulness has produced? Good honest questions, I think. Also, imagine with me what could happen if we dared to change those statistics in our local churches: the things we could do, the building we could get! Imagine how empowered your local church would be if we all did the right thing?

Remember, tithing is not unique to the Christian faith. Many other religions and 'faiths' do it, and sadly many do it better. Think about the Muslims: why is it they buy all the best buildings in our cities for temples? Why is it they can put their hand to so much and not live limited? Simple: tithing is non-negotiable for every member. It's something everyone accepts as the right thing to do, so they just do it and are empowered to advance in any direction they want. Think about it: should we not be leading the way? As we commit to tithe we bring the blessing of God onto our lives and also empower our church to do all that God wants it to do.

Take God and His church personally

For zeal for your house consumes me, and the insults of those who insult you fall on me.

Psalm 69:9 (NIV)

King David was a man who was extremely passionate about His God and the House of His God. In this verse you can hear very clearly that David took God and His house personally.

Zeal – 'passion' – consumed him. It 'ate him up'. How about you, Champion? Do you have a zeal and 'passion' for God that consumes you?

Are you Consumed or a Consumer?

There is a big difference between the two. One pours themself into the house and the other takes things from the house. A consumer, as we understand it commercially, is someone who goes somewhere to get what they need. Too often, sadly, church has plenty of consumers and not enough people who, like David, are consumed.

It will be a people who are consumed for God and His house who change this generation, so make the decision in your heart that you will be one of them.

I love the heart of David in this Psalm. David says that His (God's) house is my (David's) house, His (God's) insults are my (David's) insults. Wow! That is taking God personally. How do you feel when people insult your God? Do you take it personally? If you do, you could well be like David who was a nation-changer.

Again today, Champion, let love for God and His house consume your life and don't settle for being a consumer when you can be the consumed.

Prayer

Good morning, Father. Light within me a fresh fire for Your house; let me not be a consumer but rather the consumed. Help me to lay down my wants, needs and preferences so I can love and serve Your church with the passion it deserves. Holy Spirit, please light within me a fresh, all-consuming fire, not just for Jesus but for His bride, the Church. May my life add to the Church, not just take from it.
Amen

If obligation is the heartbeat of the law then desire is the heartbeat of grace.

Andy Elmes

Give God today what is reasonable

I beseech you therefore, brethren, by the mercies of God, that you present your bodies a living sacrifice, holy, acceptable to God, which is your reasonable service.

Romans 12:1

---

*L*ife is an awesome gift from God given for us to enjoy, not endure. It is also given to us so that we could have something effective to offer Him as a sacrifice. Notice He wants a living sacrifice and not a dead one. God had generations of dead sacrifices (Genesis to Malachi) and now wants some sacrifices that can walk around giving Him the glory He deserves.

Today you are a Living, Holy and Accepted sacrifice because of what Jesus has done for you (Romans 11:16). He has determined your holiness and qualified your acceptance by His completed one-time sacrifice, done on your behalf. He knew death so that you could know life.

God now wants you to offer to Him what He has given to you (life). This is not unreasonable and sounds like a very fair deal to me. Think about it, if you did not have something to offer Him as a sacrifice you would not be doing too well.

As believers, it is more than reasonable for us to daily offer our lives to God for Him to position and use us as He desires, and as we do this, it is perceived by God as an act of worship to Him. Look at how that verse sounds from another translation:

> *Therefore, I urge you, brothers, in view of God's mercy, to offer your bodies as living sacrifices, holy and pleasing to God – this is your spiritual act of worship.*
> Romans 12:1 (NIV)

In view of (take a good look at it again) His mercy, offer yourself back to Him alive and ready. This is your spiritual act of worship.

Hey, Champion, again today offer God the sacrifice of your life as a living sacrifice. As you do, you are being reasonable and worshipping Him at the same time.

*G*od is looking for people through whom he can do the impossible. What a pity we plan to do only the things that we can do by ourselves.

A. W. Tozer

No weapon formed against us

'No weapon formed against you shall prosper, and every tongue which rises against you in judgement you shall condemn. This is the heritage of the servants of the LORD, and their righteousness is from Me,' says the LORD.

Isaiah 54:17

Because you are in Christ and belong to God you can know today that God speaks this promise over your life today and over your tomorrows.

People may fashion weapons against you but they shall not prosper – those weapons may be plans or schemes, the promise of the Lord is that as you stay in your God-given righteousness and keep loving Him none of these things sent to harm you will harm you or remain.

- No arrow made for you or aimed at you will hurt you.

- It speaks not just of plans and schemes fashioned to harm you but also tongues that rise against you in judgement. Again, as you walk in your God-given righteousness (which is by faith), He will condemn lies spoken about you and defuse lies sent to harm your good name.

- The key is to daily know the righteousness you have in Him and make the daily decision to stand in it. As you do, things meant to harm you will not prosper and you will walk in God's blessing, not harm.

- According to God, this is our heritage.

Look at the life of Daniel – everything sent to harm him did not. He was set up to become lion food but the people who wrongly accused him (set him up) ended up being what the lions ate for dinner that night. Stay in truth and righteousness and God will turn things around for your good.

Also think of Mordecai, Esther's uncle – he was being set up by an evil ruler called Haman, set up for things he never did. Haman actually had gallows built to have him hanged, but at the end of the story Haman ended up hanging on the gallows he had fashioned for God's man Mordecai.

They may fashion things for your harm but when God steps in we do not get hurt by things fashioned against us, but rather witness God turning things around for our good.

NO WEAPON FASHIONED AGAINST YOU TODAY WILL PROSPER – 'GOD HAS GOT YOUR BACK'!

Just walk in truth and righteousness and, with confidence, leave everything that is going on behind the scenes to Him – that's called faith.

GET CLOSER

But as for me, the nearness of God is my good.
Psalm 73:28 (NASB)

Below is a line that represents your walk with God. This is for your eyes only, so be as honest as possible. Where on this line do you feel you could make a mark that would show how close you feel to God? Consider how much time you set aside to spend with Him. Think about how much time you give to reading the Word of God. How much and how often do you apply God's principles to your everyday life? With these things in mind, make your mark.

_____**GOD**

Now that you've made your mark, consider this thought:

Anything that is alive will grow. So a living, vibrant relationship with God should be growing and moving forward, closer to God all the time. If you were to revisit this page in six months time, and if you were to re-do the mark, ideally that mark would be moved further toward God. What three things can you implement or change in your life so that you can get that mark closer to God? List them:

1 _____

2 _____

3 _____

This weekend start taking these steps to get deeper and closer with God.

As you draw closer to Him He promises He will draw closer to you.
James 4:8

Don't worry, be happy!

Therefore I say to you, do not worry about your life, what you will eat or what you will drink; nor about your body, what you will put on. Is not life more than food and the body more than clothing. Which of you by worrying can add one cubit to his stature? Therefore do not worry, saying, 'What shall we eat?' or 'What shall we drink?' or 'What shall we wear?' For after all these things the Gentiles seek. For your heavenly Father knows that you need all these things. Therefore do not worry about tomorrow, for tomorrow will worry about its own things. Sufficient for the day is its own trouble.

Matthew 6:25, 27, 31, 32, 34

So, Champion, what do you reckon Jesus is trying to teach us in these verses? Could it be that we're not to worry?

Jesus teaches His followers not to worry about what they eat and drink and wear, and especially not to worry about their unseen yet unlived tomorrows. What was He telling them to do? Something so simple, yet they – and we – sometimes find so hard to do: it was to simply and confidently trust him. Instead of worrying about what you can't see, and have not yet experienced, trust Him. It takes the same amount of energy and conscious determination to walk by faith as it does by fear.

Faith and fear are both responses that come from our chosen beliefs or reasoning. Both of these responses – faith and fear – are produced by us when we sit, think and believe that something is going to come upon us or happen to us. Both have this in common: that the results are yet unseen. With no physical evidence – even though our emotions may be acting as if there were – their only reality at this point is the faith or fear we are fuelling them with. Choosing faith changes it from being bad stuff coming from life to good stuff coming from God.

If it takes the same amount of energy to have both, then why not choose faith over fear? Believe me, you will love what faith produces far better!

Great peace becomes yours when you make His promises the certainties of your future. God does not want His children running around worrying, getting themselves into a state, making themselves sick with worry about futures that are yet to be lived. He wants you to be calm and assured in the midst of a world that seems to be going more bonkers every day. He wants you to enjoy great sleep, to wake rested and to live with a quiet confidence that all things will turn out for good for your life. You say, 'That's what I want, how can I get that?' Simple: make the decision not to worry but rather commit your life and what you care about to Him, knowing He is able to keep, provide and sustain you far beyond what you can imagine.

Maybe yesterday it seemed like everything around you was pointing to the fact that you have had it, you have no future, and you're not going to be able to make it? Today, maybe the situations have not changed – but you know what, neither has God. He is still willing and able towards you. You release His potential when you walk by faith. How do you walk by faith? Trust Him and let go. Walk into your day knowing that He has promised over your life better things than what the world has said is going to happen, or you deserve; that it is He that has licensed you to not worry, rather be happy!

Enjoy your day, He is busy writing your tomorrow – trust Him, it's going to be good. Don't worry, be happy!

We are being watched

Therefore we also, since we are surrounded by so great a cloud of witnesses, let us lay aside every weight, and the sin which so easily ensnares us, and let us run with endurance the race that is set before us.

Hebrews 12:1

I don't know about you but sometimes the Christian walk (run) can sometimes seem a bit of a lonely, tiring thing. Some days it can feel like you're getting on a running track again to run the race that Jesus has set you to run and you're all alone, on your own. You may feel tired or that you've not got much run left in you to give. It may feel like you are standing on an empty track in a quiet, empty stadium.

But that is actually so far from the truth. We recently had a guest speaker at Family Church that reminded me of some things, and it is these things that I want to remind and encourage you with this week.

The Bible says we are actually not alone as we run our race – in fact, a great cloud of witnesses surrounds us. Notice that it does not say 'crowd'? In coliseums of old the top seats were so high up they were sometimes in the clouds, and the people would fill the stadium to the top to watch the athletes compete. Competitors would be totally surrounded on every side and as high as could be seen. In the UK we would call these seats at the theatre the 'nose-bleed seats'!

The Bible says that, as you run your race, this great cloud of witnesses surrounds you, and they are the generations of all believers and people of faith who have run before you, that completed their lap of the race. It says 'witnesses' – this means that they are all people who, in their moment or generation, bore witness with their lives and actions to the plans, truth and power of the living God. They ran their leg of the race and passed the baton of faith on to those who would run next. Now they watch and shout to you from the balconies as you purpose to run your lap. 'Run, run, you can do it!', they shout. 'You may be tired but don't drop the baton. Set your gaze on Him who is worth it. Run your best race. You're not alone. We finished our lap, now you finish yours!'

Imagine if we could see the cloud of witnesses, the believers of all previous generations that fill the seats of the coliseum of eternity: the apostles of old, the many who were martyred because they would not back down, the heroes of the last generations who stood for faith and spirit-filled living, who lived for Him and now live with Him.

Every lap is important to a relay race, but the last one is the most important. Those who ran before have handed us the baton. In the distance we see the finishing line. Maybe we will be the generation and the people of God who do not pass the baton on, but cross the finishing line and bring the race to an end? Oh, we are not alone and this was never a one-man race. Yes, you may feel weary, maybe you don't think you can run any more – then stand in the middle of the coliseum, close your eyes and see the faces of all those who ran before, many who gave their lives for this common race. Hear them shout to you even from the cloud seats.

'Run, run, run your best race.'

Imagine who is in the crowd?

Therefore we also, since we are surrounded by so great a cloud of witnesses, let us lay aside every weight, and the sin which so easily ensnares us, and let us run with endurance the race that is set before us.

Hebrews 12:1

A thought that a recent guest speaker to Family Church shared, that got the juices of my imagination going, was the thought of 'who is in the crowd?', that great cloud of witnesses that surround and cheer us on. If there is indeed a great cloud of witnesses then they are all the people who went before us, who lived by faith and died in faith, those who served the purposes of God in their generation with everything they had.

Every crowd is made up of individuals. If you took a moment to look up at the crowd, to look at the faces in the crowd, the people who are behind the shouts, imagine whom you would see?

The speaker we had began to speculate on what different people would have shouted, and as he did my imagination went berserk! This thought could turn into a really huge book but to grab just a few:

Imagine there is Abraham shouting, 'Live by faith, for God keeps His promises.'

Moses is shouting, 'Don't worry when it feels like you're standing on the edge of impossibility – He will part the ocean.'

What about the shout coming from near the top – it's Daniel and he's shouting, 'Don't fear lions, God can keep you in the lions' den.'

Maybe Daniel's friends are standing near to him – Shadrach, Meshach and Abednego – and they are shouting at you, 'Don't worry about the furnace they put you in, the Fourth Man will meet you in the flames and bring you out unharmed.'

All of these saints of old are cheering you on as you stand on the track in the coliseum of God's eternal purpose. As you look more intently you make out the weathered face of Paul and then Peter and John – imagine what would they be shouting from the balconies:

'Remember, you're saved by grace not your own works.'

Or, 'He who began a good work in you will finish it.'

Maybe, 'He that is in you is greater!'

Statement after statement of truths that cause your spirit to lift.

To the left another is standing – it's the old prophet Isaiah, and he's shouting, 'No weapon fashioned against you will prosper!'

They're all standing, cheering, shouting statements that were born out of their experiences – that's what makes them witnesses. They have run their race, finished their course, yet they know the race is not over. And it's not just the people of many years ago – the recent ones too: my mum is shouting, 'Go on, Andy boy, don't let up!' They all know there is still a generation on the track, and that their lap, this finishing one, is so important; so they stand, they scream their statements of faith.

As you listen, faith rises, spiritual adrenaline begins to pump, you set your face and run, and you run to win. RUN!

Run your best race now

Therefore we also, since we are surrounded by so great a cloud of witnesses, let us lay aside every weight, and the sin which so easily ensnares us, and let us run with endurance the race that is set before us.

Hebrews 12:1

Hope you have enjoyed the last few days as we have considered the cloud of witnesses that cheers us on. At the start of the week I said maybe you feel like you're in the coliseum, running a race with no support; then we started to consider who is in the crowd watching you. I don't know about you, but I am ready to run – not just run, but run my best race because I realise it's far more important than I first imagined.

So, if we are going to run our best race we need to make sure nothing is slowing us down, right? This is exactly what Hebrews 12 then instructs us: 'lay aside every weight and thing that hinders', because it's time to run your best race.

All of us have tolerated things that weigh us down or cause us to not gain the speed we really could – it's time to lay them aside, take them off your life and leave them on the 'bench of no return'! Insecurities, habits and secret sins – you can't carry them anymore; you've got a race to run, Champion.

Naturally speaking, if I was going to enter a race, the first thing I would do as I prepared (apart from, of course, exercising a whole lot more than I do) would be to lose some weight. Why? To look good in my running outfit? No, to make sure I am able to give my very best to the race. Those extra pounds would slow me down, so if I can get them off my life I can increase my speed and performance.

What are you carrying that you can't afford to anymore? Yes, we can pray about it but also we need to draw a line in the sand on the beach of our life and lay those things aside. Take them off, abandon them, disassociate ourselves from them. That's what it means to 'lay aside' – it does not mean to leave them somewhere safe so you can collect them later. If you don't need them for this next lap of the race then you will never need them again.

When I think about my life I know I have run some pretty good laps over the last twenty years. How about you? But I have a niggle deep inside that I have not yet run my best lap, that there is a potential inside of me that I have not yet seen and that is what is rising to the top right now – maybe because of the crowd screaming statements of faith at me? As it rises it causes a fresh desire to pump within the veins of my desire to 'lay aside what will slow me down', because I want to run my best race.

How about you?

Prayer

Thank You for this new day, Lord. Help me today to run my best race for You. Please help me, Holy Spirit, to lay aside the things in my life that slow me down and that I really do not need anymore. Let today be a day that I pick up more speed and not slow down. Let me run my race for You with passion and vision.

Amen

Jesus the Pacesetter

Looking unto Jesus, the author and finisher of our faith, who for the joy that was set before Him endured the cross, despising the shame, and has sat down at the right hand of the throne of God.

Hebrews 12:2

We have been speaking about realising that we are taking part in, even running the last lap of a race that has been run by so many throughout generations past. Now this cloud of witnesses stand in the balconies and shout 'run' at us as we take our place in the lanes of this race of eternal destiny. We have spoken how important the task is for the one who runs last, that how everybody else did with their lap can be concluded well or ruined by the man who runs the last lap, what a responsibility we now have to run our best race as those who ran before did theirs.

But the truth is everyone who takes part in a team race has an important part to play. When discussing this with a man who once ran relay races, he said that his part was to start the race; he would run at the very start when the gun went off. He explained that his role was to be the 'pacesetter'. He would, with his initial lap, set the pace for all the runners who would follow; he would raise the bar that the others needed to run by. For us our pacesetter is obviously Jesus; He is the one who we follow and run after and should set the pace we run at by.

When we see how He ran His race it inspires us that nothing we face when running ours will ever be as tough, rough of demanding as His initial one. Consider again the verse we read this morning concerning Him.

He endured the cross; imagine the physical and emotional pain in that.

He overcame and even despised the shame that came with what that initial lap required: death on a criminal cross.

Then in the next two verses we read on:

> *For consider Him who endured such hostility from sinners against Himself, lest you become weary and discouraged in your souls. You have not yet resisted to bloodshed, striving against sin.*
>
> **Hebrews 12:3-4**

Consider Him, consider what He endured, consider the blood He shed to finish well that first lap of the race for the salvation of the human race that we now have the privilege to run.

Let's look to Jesus, the Pacesetter, the Author and the Finisher of our faith.

LOVE A NEW TRANSLATION

1 Corinthians 13

When you hear a scripture read out in the same translation you have always heard it in, you can grow familiar with its great truth and wisdom. The words can lose the impact of their meaning on the mind when you recite them as if by rote, and being that the Word of God is alive and powerful this is a terrible shame. I have found that when I read familiar scriptures in a different translation of the Bible I see God's Word in a fresh way again. A good translation is one where the meaning of the words remains the same but there is a difference in the language in which it is written. There are Bibles that have many translations in one or you can go online and find a site that offers many translations.

This weekend, read 1 Corinthians 13, the very well-known 'love' chapter, in a few different translations, ones that you don't often or maybe have never read it in. Allow the different wording to impact you as if you are hearing it for the first time. After you've done this, write down something you may have learned from 1 Corinthians 13 that stood out to you in a new, fresh way.

Enjoy your weekend!

Notes

_____

_____

_____

_____

_____

_____

RSVP: the power of response

It happened that as He made His way toward Jerusalem, He crossed over the border between Samaria and Galilee. As He entered a village, ten men, all lepers, met Him. They kept their distance but raised their voices, calling out, 'Jesus, Master, have mercy on us!' Taking a good look at them, He said, 'Go, show yourselves to the priests.' They went, and while still on their way, became clean. One of them, when he realised that he was healed, turned around and came back, shouting his gratitude, glorifying God. He kneeled at Jesus' feet, so grateful. He couldn't thank Him enough – and he was a Samaritan. Jesus said, 'Were not ten healed? Where are the nine? Can none be found to come back and give glory to God except this outsider?' Then He said to him, 'Get up. On your way. Your faith has healed and saved you.'

Luke 17:11-17 (MSG)

In this account we can learn some great lessons concerning the power of response in our lives, and hopefully be challenged concerning developing our personal response-ability.

In this passage we see three responses, and all are amazing:

1. Jesus' response to the need of these ten men: Leprosy had taken away their lives and shut their world down both physically and socially. Jesus steps in and miraculously gives them their lives back. Jesus responded to their cry for help.

2. The response of the one who returned: He was a Samaritan, which meant that, out of the ten that were healed, he would have been considered the least likely one to come back to say thanks. You can hear the gratefulness and passion in his words of thanks.

3. The lack of response from the nine: They had all received miracles that day from Jesus, but only the Samaritan said thanks.

Think about the figures for a minute. Only 10% of the miracle responded in a way fitting with what had happened. Only one in ten responded appropriately for what had happened to them (basically, given their lives back).

Were they evil men? I don't think so. I think they just swiftly got back into their previously normal lives that their illness had separated them from and forgot to respond correctly by coming back to Jesus and saying thanks. They understood what it was to respond when in need (they called out to Him, 'Master, have mercy on us!') but they just forgot to respond correctly when God answered their cry. Always make sure you say thanks.

Let's make sure that we are responsive to God when we should be. Also, in our other relationships and in life, being responsive will always bring increase into your world and make things that you have more fruitful.

My observation and experience has been that God and life give 'stuff' to responsive people. Let's make sure that today we are responding correctly to the people and the situations that we should be.

Bless you and have a great (responsive) day.

The ability to respond correctly

One of them, when he realised that he was healed, turned around and came back, shouting his gratitude, glorifying God. He kneeled at Jesus' feet, so grateful. He couldn't thank Him enough – and he was a Samaritan. Jesus said, 'Were not ten healed? Where are the nine? Can none be found to come back and give glory to God except this outsider?' Then He said to him, 'Get up. On your way. Your faith has healed and saved you.'

Luke 17:15-19 (MSG)

We are looking at our responsibility, which is our 'ability to respond correctly'. Being responsive is vital for the relationships in our world to be all that they were designed to be.

God wants a responsive relationship with us. It was never meant to be a one-way road, but rather a daily interwoven relationship of us responding to Him and Him responding back – that's Christianity.

The other relationships in our world need us to remain responsive too. For example, as a pastor I deal with an element of marriage breakdown. The sad thing is many marriages break down simply because one or both of the people involved stop responding with 'due response'.

Every healthy marriage starts with a picture of volcanic response as a man and a woman stand at the front of a church like a Princess with her Prince Charming. There is no shortage of desire or response capacity. At the reception that follows the atmosphere is charged with the thought of responses yet to come (God designed it that way). The day is filled with excitement, expectation, and joyous and arduous responses by both parties. Sadly, for many, if you then press fast forward, say about ten years, you get the picture of a man behind his newspaper at the kitchen table giving automated responses to his wife, who is desperately wanting back the response and attention from the responsive stallion she once knew. Instead she hears the automated statements from behind a paper: 'that's good, dear', 'sounds nice, dear', and the vibrancy of the marriage starts to fade.

Good news! If he was to suddenly realise what had happened and remember what he once had and the promises that were made, and the dreams they started their journey with, and that morning, with fresh revelation, walked past the paper, spun her around, looked her in the eyes and sang to her their favourite love song, that marriage would come alive again, instantly – all we added was response!

When we respond correctly things come alive and stay alive. This principle covers every relationship we face on our journey of life – family and friendships, work/business relationships, teams and groups. Make sure you remain responsive and watch how things stay fresh and vibrant.

God bless, have a great day (men, go sing to your wife).

Who's your Daddy?

Therefore it is of faith that it might be according to grace, so that the promise might be sure to all the seed, not only to those who are of the law, but also to those who are of the faith of Abraham, who is the father of us all.

Romans 4:16

*I*t is interesting that Paul says that Abraham is the 'father of us all' – what does he mean? Simply that he is the father of all those who approach God and receive from God by faith, not works or performance. You may say, 'He is not my father, I am not a Jew and neither was I born in Israel.' To be considered a son of Abraham, or put another way his seed, is to consider yourself as someone who, like Abraham, has entered into the promises of God and gained a righteousness by faith, not by national birth right or achievement in keeping certain laws. You simply recognise that you, as Abraham did, stand with God by faith alone and all that you receive from God is the result of you believing in His promises outside of your ability to achieve (just like Abraham did in having his son Isaac).

God promised Abraham's natural son Isaac many times that the blessings and promises that were given to his father would be his too, simply because he was a child of Abraham. One example of this was when Isaac found himself in a time of famine and God told him to remain and sow in the famine-affected ground because the same promises and assurances of divine provision that his father had were now his.

Dwell in this land, and I will be with you and bless you; for to you and your descendants I give all these lands, and I will perform the oath which I swore to Abraham your father.

Genesis 26:3

So, we then see Isaac sow and reap and prosper in the land of famine (Genesis 26:12-14). It says of that famine in verse 1 that it was a famine on top of a famine, a little bit like the days we live in now, right? We have a recession and the media talk of a 'double dip', saying we could face another recession on top of the one we already have. We, like Isaac, have a choice: we can stop sowing (giving) because we are looking at the natural climate of how things are currently looking or we can understand that the promises given to the father (Abraham) are still relevant to his children of faith (you and me) today. And we, like Isaac, can believe in and act according to them independent of economical or environmental limitations. God will still cause us to prosper as Isaac did. Why? Because as it says in the above verse, Abraham is the father of us all, and His promises now belong to his faith-based offspring: US!

Think on that today, Champion. If you, like Abraham, have entered into your salvation and stand complete in it by faith alone, you are one of his kids, and God's intentions and promises to him are still effective towards you. Believe and begin to see them manifest in your world today.

Expect a harvest when others don't!

So also Abraham 'believed God, and it was credited to him as righteousness.'
Understand, then, that those who have faith are children of Abraham.
Galatians 3:6-7 (NIV)

Yeah, but what if?

Watch therefore, for you do not know what hour your Lord is coming. But know this, that if the master of the house had known what hour the thief would come, he would have watched and not allowed his house to be broken into. Therefore you also be ready, for the Son of Man is coming at an hour you do not expect.

Matthew 24:42-44

A few years ago the world was subjected to another end-of-the-world prophecy, where one man, apparently representing Christians all over the world, told how Jesus would return on May 21st 2012. He said that at 6 pm Pacific Time the earth would split, Jesus would return and the rapture would begin. May 21st came and went without anything that had been forecasted happening. All that sadly did occur was, once again, the media and sceptics of Christianity had more fuel to use and reasons to laugh.

But this false prophecy got me thinking, and the next day in Family Church I preached a topical message on it. After sharing on the news reports of what this man had claimed was going to happen, and of course clarifying the truth of no man knowing the exact day and the time, I posed a question: 'Yeah, but what if? What if, for some bizarre reason, he had got it right?' I then played a very loud sound clip of thunder and lightning in the hall and, as it echoed violently through our bass speakers, people stopped to think, 'Yeah, what if it was all over, what would I have changed?'

For me some things were very clear, because my life is built on His word. Would I be in heaven standing in heaven's Sonlight? Yes, I do not doubt that, or have to hope for it – rather, I have an assurance because my salvation is the result of my faith in His grace and performance, not my ability or works. But the troubling question was, if He had returned who would not be in heaven with me? Who would not be there with me because I didn't make time to tell them, or was not able to get over the pride or embarrassment that caused me not to give them their invitation? A very sobering thought and one that should cause us all to think about those we say we care for. Do we care for them enough to make sure they would be there with us?

Other questions caused me to review my life and priorities (things I thought were important). If I was now standing in heaven, how much would the things I thought I needed and had lived for now really matter? What worth would they have to me now? Was what I spent my life on worth it? Did it carry any profit in the place I now called home?

We know the Bible teaches that no man knows the hour or the day, but we also need to remember that a lot of what this fanatical man said was actually true: one day Jesus will return without warning, like a thief in the night, at a moment when people least expect, and in the twinkling of an eye it will all be over.

We know that it was not May 21st 2012, but let me leave you with this motivating thought: What if? Who do you need to reach for Christ? Do you need to take a fresh look at your priorities and what really matters? What do you need to spend the currency of your remaining days on?

I'm so glad He didn't come on May 21st 2012, as it means we still have time to invite those we need to, and live the life we always intended to. What are you waiting for, Champion? Live your best life now.

We should all be following and being followed

As Jesus walked beside the Sea of Galilee, He saw Simon and his brother Andrew casting a net into the lake, for they were fishermen. 'Come, follow Me,' Jesus said, 'and I will make you fishers of men.' At once they left their nets and followed Him.

Mark 1:16-18 (NIV)

When it comes to being followers it should be a two-fold experience.

First comes our commitment to being a follower of Christ. Like these fishermen, Jesus steps into our everyday world and says, 'Follow Me, and I will make you'. It is when we commit to being everyday followers of Jesus that we see Him change our lives into what we never imagined they could be.

But there is also the challenge that we need to always be getting people to follow us – that's what leaders do. Let me expand on that statement: we need to be ever getting people to follow us as we follow Christ. This is the greatest and most effective kind of discipleship there is. When we understand that God desires for us to live lives that lead other people to Him, a great responsibility becomes ours. We need to M.O.T. our lives every now and then to check that the lives we are living are inviting people to follow something that resembles and reflects Jesus well.

It is a very sobering thing indeed when you look back and see that people are following your life example – something that should be taken seriously.

My challenge today is two-fold and very simple: are you following Jesus? Are you going where He is going? Are you giving people something to follow in the way you are choosing to live your life? Live in such a way that people get to Jesus.

Prayer

Good morning, Lord. Help me to follow You today as I should, and to live a life that is attractive to others that need You. Let my life be a good example that others can follow and find You through. Help me today, Holy Spirit, to get rid of anything that would be a bad influence on others, or dull the shining light that my life is called to be for You. Thank You for this new day; help me as I purpose to run my best race for You.

Amen

It's the stone of your faith embedded in the forehead of your enemy that causes him to fall.

Andy Elmes

DEAR FATHER,

Your love, GOD, is my song, and I'll sing it! I'm forever telling everyone how faithful you are. I'll never quit telling the story of your love—how you built the cosmos and guaranteed everything in it. Your love has always been our lives' foundation, your fidelity has been the roof over our world.

Psalm 89:1-4 (MSG)

This is a beautiful prayer by a man named Ethan in the Bible. I cannot help but see these words as a love letter to God from his heart.

Prayerfully take some time this weekend to write your own letter to God, telling Him what He means to you. Let Him know how much you appreciate Him for all He's done for you and how glad that He is in your life.

Notes

_____

_____

_____

_____

_____

_____

A perfect family picture

Now all Judah, with their little ones, their wives, and their children, stood before the LORD.

2 Chronicles 20:13

I love the picture this verse creates: families standing before God together, loving and sold out for Him. Maybe this is the picture you are seeing each Sunday at church; when you look around the church you see your spouse and all your kids, including the little ones. Praise God if that is the case, but never let up from praying for them and encouraging them. There are so many distractions sent to draw our kids away, remain a praying parent.

But what if that's not the picture today and your heart aches for those who are not with you as you stand before Him? Take hope, knowing that God wants the picture to look like that more than you do, and will not stop working with those who are not with you at present to bring them back. What you must never do is quit praying, believing and prophesying their return. Whether the missing part of the picture is a spouse, parent or child, never become weary or stop believing them back into the picture, so it can be perfect again.

I think of the father in the parable of the wayward child (Luke 15:11-24): it says that his youngest son set off for a distant land (v13). His son had become deceived, and indeed had totally 'lost the plot', but while he was 'afar off' his dad never stopped believing for his return. Guess what: the end of the story is that he returned and the family stood again a complete picture. Thank goodness the father never stopped believing for a return.

I did the journey of the wayward child for eight years, and was adamant I would never come back to church or God. I am so grateful that both God and my parents never gave up on me, even when I made the chance of my return look impossible. I am grateful that, when my mum and dad's perfect picture was spoiled, they closed their eyes and saw me back in it; they refused to believe that the Elmes family that stood before God had changed to Mum, Dad and just one son. They got a promise from God and stood on it, claiming me back into the picture. Guess what: one day Mum and Dad looked around in church and the picture was complete again: Dad had his wife and both kids again, 'standing before the Lord'.

Here is the promise they claimed for me; maybe it's one that you can use if a child is currently missing from the picture:

All your children will be taught by the LORD, and great will be their peace.

Isaiah 54:13 (NIV)

When it comes to believing a family member back into the picture remember the words of Winston Churchill: 'Never, never, never give up!'

Faith works

What does it profit, my brethren, if someone says he has faith but does not have works? Can faith save him?

James 2:14

*I*f we want to function in faith correctly we need to add Hebrews 11 to the thoughts of the apostle James, above.

This actually makes a lot more sense when we read it from the NIV translation.

> *What good is it, my brothers, if a man claims to have faith but has no deeds? Can such faith save him? Suppose a brother or sister is without clothes and daily food. If one of you says to him, 'Go, I wish you well; keep warm and well fed,' but does nothing about his physical needs, what good is it? In the same way, faith by itself, if it is not accompanied by action, is dead. But someone will say, 'You have faith; I have deeds.' Show me your faith without deeds, and I will show you my faith by what I do. You believe that there is one God. Good! Even the demons believe that – and shudder. You foolish man, do you want evidence that faith without deeds is useless.*
>
> James 2:14-20 (NIV)

Faith is all about trusting God to create what is needed but, as the NIV says so well, faith should be accompanied by actions. We should always be found acting in accordance to what we say we believe. We need to be living it out, walking the walk and not just talking the talk. If a man says he believes he will fall off a cliff if he gets too close does he then jump around on the edge of it expecting nothing to happen? No, he would be a hypocrite, one who says he believes one thing then has unaccompanied actions.

When God gives us a promise for us to place our faith in, there is normally always instruction that accompanies it. When we walk in what God says to do we release what He promises will happen.

God said to Noah to build an ark and He would save his family. Noah then built the ark according to God's instructions. Would his household have been saved if he had sat upon the promise without accompanying actions (building the boat)?

Abraham was promised that the world would be blessed through his life when he left what he knew. Would anything have happened if he had waited in Haran for the promise to be delivered? No, it was his walking in what God had said that released what God had promised.

So, Champion, get the promise for your situation and then act or live in accordance to what you say you believe. Add that accompanying action. A great closing example would be to look at one of the classic promises of divine provision which is, 'Give and it will be given to you – pressed down, shaken together.'

1. You can wait for the 'given back to you, pressed down' bit and have a long wait.

2. You can live out the accompanying action – which is to give – and then you will release the potential of the promise – which is God giving back to you, pressed down, shaken together.

Add James 2 to Hebrews 11 and you will have a very exciting life!

Acknowledge what has already been given!

That the sharing of your faith may become effective by the acknowledgment of every good thing which is in you in Christ Jesus.

Philemon 6

This powerful little verse, found in the book of Philemon, reveals to us that the sharing (living out) of our faith is dramatically affected by the acknowledgment of every good thing that is now present in you in Christ Jesus. As we daily consider and discover His divine potential and power already resident within the temple of our lives, the realisation of this is what will make you think differently about the life you live and take you to a whole new level.

In fact, it is the acknowledging of 'every good thing' that God has put in you through Jesus that causes true effectiveness in every single part of who you are. What did we get placed in us through Christ? That's a very good question and it would take a very long list to answer! Here are a few of the many things that we need to be so grateful for:

- Abundance of grace, come to us through Jesus;
- The gift of righteousness, ours because of Jesus;
- Forgiveness, healing and divine health;
- Faith and hope;
- New life, and freedom from condemnation;
- Restored innocence;
- Love, power and a sound mind.

The list really could go on and on!

Oh, that you may fully understand all that you have already received in and through Christ Jesus your Lord! Start today to release, and see manifested, more of what He has already deposited in you. How? You guessed it – by faith! By acknowledging (coming into agreement with) what He has given as revealed in His word, and by thanking Him for these things by faith. Faith is the divine phone call that activates whatever God gives and has already given.

Let's stop begging Him for more and take a moment to realise and acknowledge what we already have.

Are you expecting abundance from God, or just enough?

Do you know today, Champion, that your God is a God of abundance? And all of His plans and intentions towards you are always plans and intentions of abundance, not 'just enough'. Here are some verses to think on today; they all reveal to us God's abundant intentions towards us for different areas of our lives.

1. The measurement of His saving grace (unmerited favour).

> *For if by the one man's offence death reigned through the one, much more those who receive abundance of grace and of the gift of righteousness will reign in life through the One, Jesus Christ.*
>
> **Romans 5:17**

Notice that it is abundance, not 'just enough'. It's when you understand this truth, and also that you have been made perfectly righteous through the perfect sacrifice of Jesus, that you will reign in life as promised!

2. His provision in our lives – again, notice it does not say 'just enough'!

> *And God is able to make all grace abound toward you, that you, always having all sufficiency in all things, may have an abundance for every good work.*
>
> **2 Corinthians 9:8**

All grace, not some. All sufficiency, not some. All things, not some.

3. The quality of new life He has for us in Christ.

> *The thief does not come except to steal, and to kill, and to destroy. I have come that they may have life, and that they may have it more abundantly [in abundance].*
>
> **John 10:10**

4. The giving of His Spirit, to transform us into all we are called to be.

> *Not by works of righteousness which we have done, but according to His mercy He saved us, through the washing of regeneration and renewing of the Holy Spirit, whom He poured out on us abundantly through Jesus Christ our Saviour.*
>
> **Titus 3:5-6**

His ability matches His intentions. God does not just want to do abundantly for us in these areas of life and so many more – He is able to! He is the God who is able to and wants to do abundantly in your life, so start expecting abundance. Sadly, some of those damaging doctrines of religion made by men have left us all for too long expecting nothing or very little from God. It's time to bring our thinking into alignment with His word and truth – God wants to do abundantly for you so make room in your life for it!

> *Now to Him who is able to do exceedingly abundantly above all that we ask or think, according to the power that works in us.*
>
> **Ephesians 3:20**

Stop expecting a bit, Champion, and start thanking Him for abundance!

Don't take your life into your own hands, but place it in His

And it shall come to pass that whoever calls on the name of the LORD shall be saved.

Acts 2:21

When you called on the name of the Lord, as promised, you were saved. Saved from what? You were saved from your sins, yes, but you were also saved from the consequences and fallout of everything that Adam and Eve did wrong in their moment of deception and fall.

Your faith in Jesus reinstates and restores you as a citizen of God's kingdom. Now you need to make the decision to no longer live independently, but rather dependently. Before we believed in Jesus we did not have a choice. Our lives were independent, separated by sin from the governing and covering of God and His kingdom, but not now!

We used to have to hold our own lives in our own hands but now there is a better way. We can place our lives lock, stock and barrel into the loving, strong hands of a mighty God. As you yield your life into His hands, pledging your trust in Him, it is then that you experience all the blessings, protection and grace that Adam knew before his moment of foolishness.

So here is the choice, Champion: you can keep your life in your hands and do the best you can to make things happen, maintaining your independence; or you can humbly place it in the hands of your ever-redeeming God and watch Him lift you, protect you, and provide for you far beyond what you could have ever imagined.

Therefore humble yourselves under the mighty hand of God, that He may exalt you in due time.

1 Peter 5:6

Put your life (all of it) back into His hands because it's a better place for it to be. Faith is simply 'dependence on God'!

You have enemies? Good. That means you've stood up for something, sometime in your life.

Winston Churchill

TAKE ONE A DAY

Blessed is the one who finds wisdom, and the one who gets understanding, for the gain from her is better than gain from silver and her profit better than gold. She is more precious than jewels, and nothing you desire can compare with her. Long life is in her right hand; in her left hand are riches and honour. Her ways are ways of pleasantness, and all her paths are peace.
Proverbs 3:13-18 (ESV)

Proverbs is a book of incredible wisdom. There are 31 chapters in the book of Proverbs, which is just about one a day for a whole month. You may have to double up on one day if there are only 30 days in the month you begin.

This weekend start a *Proverbs Month of Wisdom*.

Notes

_____

_____

_____

_____

_____

_____

_____

Give honour where honour is due

Give unto the LORD the glory due to His name; worship the LORD in the beauty of holiness.

Psalm 29:2

Put another way:

> *Bravo, GOD, bravo! Gods and all angels shout, 'Encore!' In awe before the glory, in awe before God's visible power. Stand at attention! Dress your best to honour him!*
> **(MSG)**

Let us remember that all glory and honour belong to Him because He is the one worthy and most deserving of it. It is He that has saved us so wonderfully and keeps us so faithfully. I like what this Psalm reminds each of us to do today, which is to give Him that which is rightfully His.

The great Baptist preacher Charles Spurgeon put it this way: 'The moment we glory in ourselves, we set ourselves up as rivals to the Most High. Shall the insect of an hour glorify itself against the sun that warmed it into life? Shall the pot exalt itself above the man who fashioned it upon the potter's wheel? Shall the dust of the desert strive with the whirlwind? Or the drops of the ocean struggle with the tempest? Give unto the Lord, all ye righteous, give unto the Lord glory and strength; give unto Him the honour that is due His name.'

Well put, Charles! Let us take a moment in our busy, successful lives to remind ourselves that all the glory and the honour belongs to Him. Without Him how successful, prosperous or significant would we really be? As we daily live to bow our knees humbly and give all glory and honour to Him, He daily honours us with continual goodness and mercy.

> *You are worthy, our Lord and God, to receive glory and honour and power, for you created all things, and by your will they were created and have their being.*
> **Revelation 4:11 (NIV)**

Today is another opportunity to give Him what He is due; so don't hold back, give it to Him, Champion!

Prayer

Heavenly Father, today I want to take a moment to honour You. You are worthy of honour and today I lift You high above all others. Thank You for all You have done for me; thank You for Your constant faithfulness towards me. I extol Your wonderful name today, Lord, because You are so worthy of praise. Help me to live a life that honours You.

Amen

When things do not go according to plan

Many are the plans in a person's heart, but it is the LORD's purpose that prevails.

Proverbs 19:21 (NIV)

*H*ow true this proverb is!

How often is it that we have our heads filled with so many plans: plans based on what we think or want or judge should happen; plans based also on what we think will work best according to what we know or have experienced? Most often these plans are not evil or wrong, they are just often not as big or as good as God's plans, and certainly never as inclusive as His purposes. His purposes always include and artfully interweave together so many seemingly independent components of a person's life.

I have forgotten the number of times I have pushed forward with plans, then at the end of them discover His purposes. More often than not my plans fitted with His purposes because my desire is always to do His will, but at the end of the day His purposes were always so much bigger than what I had planned for.

His purposes are always, like Ephesians 3:20 says, 'exceedingly, abundantly above all that we ask or think'. We will normally plan in accordance with what we can imagine as possible, but will many times find ourselves arriving at a place that is so much larger, called God's actual purpose for what was happening.

When we grasp this truth it causes even the things we do not understand to be more manageable, because we can trust that God's purposes for our life involve what is happening in one way or another even if it seems to go against what we planned. That is where faith can replace anxiety and fear. We can know that as we live for His long-term purpose, not just our current plans, we can experience all things working together for good. One day we will look back and it will all make sense and fit together.

> *And we know that all things work together for good to those who love God, to those who are the called according to His purpose.*
>
> Romans 8:28

> *We humans keep brainstorming options and plans, but GOD's purpose prevails.*
> Proverbs 19:21 (MSG)

Put your confidence in His purposes, not your current plans.

Prayer

Good morning, Lord. Today I purpose to trust You, in the things I understand and the things I don't. Lord, I trust You and believe that You will cause all things to work together for my good. My life could be in no safer place than Your hands, Father, and into Your hands I again commit my life. Help me to walk through this day simply trusting You with childlike faith.

Amen

Why not sharpen the axe head?

If the axe is dull and its edge unsharpened, more strength is needed but skill will bring success.

Ecclesiastes 10:10 (NIV)

O r put another way:

> *Using a dull axe requires great strength, so sharpen the blade. That's the value of wisdom; it helps you succeed.*
>
> (NLT)

Sometimes, when we enter a new season or take on a new situation or challenge, we can be tempted to simply expend more energy even when we know we may not have more energy to give. Let's talk about this – imagine that the new situation or challenge you face is a log that needs to be chopped in two: you would have two choices. Firstly, it's a bigger log than you've chopped before, but you use your axe and just expend more energy, hitting it harder, giving more than you have given before. Or the second option, which is wiser, is to stop and take a moment to sharpen your axe head. This will enable you to achieve more with each strike and to spend less energy; you can then invest the energy you saved on advancing faster and finishing sooner if you choose.

How about you and the new challenges or opportunities you have been handed or face, what are you going to do? Are you going to try and find more energy from somewhere? Are you going to try and give what you know you can't sustain for a momentary advance? Why not take the advice found in this passage and stop, think and sharpen.

God's wisdom will always cause things to sharpen in your life. If you want a sharper edge to what you are doing get rubbing on His wisdom; it will always result in you achieving more and spending less effort and energy. Don't hit harder, hit wiser.

> *Remember: The duller the axe the harder the work; use your head: The more brains, the less muscle.*
>
> (MSG)

The devil whispers, 'You cannot withstand the storm.'
The warrior replies, 'I am the storm.'

Unknown

Bread to eat and seed to sow

Now He who supplies seed to the sower and bread for food will also supply and increase your store of seed and will enlarge the harvest of your righteousness. You will be made rich in every way so that you can be generous on every occasion, and through us your generosity will result in thanksgiving to God.

2 Corinthians 9:10-11 (NIV)

Here we see a two-fold promise for those whose hearts are set on sowing in life. God will provide bread to eat and seed to sow!

God does not want to just provide for you what you need for your daily life (bread) but He wants to entrust you with seed so that you can:

1. Sow for your future: like a wise farmer you do not need to be subject to others determining what your harvest in life will look like, but rather you can plan what your harvest will look like yourself by using your God-given seed with wisdom and faith.

2. Sow into the purposes of His kingdom and the lives of others to create a harvest for kingdom purposes, not just your own benefit.

Believe God today not just for bread (daily provision) but also for seed to sow (future harvest).

He gives seed to the sower

God is not fooled. He can see when the heart of a person is set on sowing, and He promises that He will provide seed for that person to sow. Make sure today that your heart is set on sowing, not just getting daily bread. Then you can, with faith and confidence, wait for a delivery of seed from the Divine Supplier.

It is very important to remember when God gives you seed that its purpose is different in your life than bread. Make sure you do not eat it or treat it as daily provision, but rather you view it as seed and get it into fertile ground as quickly as you can so that you can get that future harvest started straight away. Never eat your seed! If a farmer was to eat his seed you would call him a fool because he would be sentencing himself to a future of lack.

He gives bread to eat and seed to sow

Today, with a grateful heart, thank God for both the bread He provides for your provision today, and the seed He provides for you to sow, which is all about your future.

And remember, God promises that He will increase the store of the sower so that he can be positioned to sow on every occasion. What occasion do you want to sow into? Thank the One who gives seed to the sower today and wait for that delivery.

Sing!

'Sing, barren woman, you who never bore a child; burst into song, shout for joy, you who were never in labour; because more are the children of the desolate woman than of her who has a husband,' says the LORD.

Isaiah 54:1 (NIV)

Sing, O Daughter of Zion; shout, O Israel! Rejoice, be in high spirits and glory with all your heart, O Daughter of Jerusalem. The Lord has taken away the judgements against you; He has cast out your enemy. The King of Israel, even the Lord [Himself], is in the midst of you; you shall not experience or fear evil any more.

Zephaniah 3:14-15 (AMP)

Why does God give the same advice to the barren woman and the nation needing victory and restoration? Simple – it's great advice!

It's advice that causes a desperate person to launch themselves towards guaranteed fruitfulness and victory. It does not say, 'Sing after it all happens' – anyone can do that. No, it says, 'Sing when it still feels like barrenness and failure, sing a song of faith declaring what the Lord says about the situation.'

Why does God want you to sing songs of faith while in the midst of the situation or circumstance? I believe the answer to this is found in verse 17: when you sing you are not performing a solo, but rather creating a harmony with your God who is singing songs of freedom and victory over you! Read it for yourself:

The Lord your God is in the midst of you, a Mighty One, a Saviour [Who saves]! He will rejoice over you with joy; He will rest [in silent satisfaction] and in His love He will be silent and make no mention [of past sins, or even recall them]; He will exult over you with singing.
Zephaniah 3:17 (AMP)

My friend, you are not singing some lonely solo of faith – you are coming into agreement with the words that God is singing over you, and when heaven and earth sing the same song you better believe an explosion is going to happen. Don't believe me yet? Then remember Paul and Silas in the prison as they created a faith harmony with God: the prison walls shook and the doors undid themselves.

Stop whining and SING! Your freedom and breakthrough are contained within that divine duet you have with your Maker.

SING!

GET TO KNOW THEM BETTER

For whatsoever things were written aforetime were written for our learning.
Romans 15:4 (KJV)

We all have our favourite characters from the Bible, like King David or Queen Esther, and then there are the ones we don't know very well at all.

This weekend get to know one of the men or women mentioned in God's Word that you don't know that much about. There are so many interesting people and colourful characters in God's Word. For example, did you know Josiah was one of the greatest kings to ever rule Israel but he began his rule at the tender age of 8 years old?

You can check them out on Google or another search engine and learn two things you never knew about them.

Character: _____

Two Facts:

1 _____

_____

_____

2 _____

_____

_____

Have you got a problem with God's breath?

All Scripture is God-breathed and is useful for teaching, rebuking, correcting and training in righteousness, so that the servant of God may be thoroughly equipped for every good work.

2 Timothy 3:16-17 (NIV)

Our verse today teaches us that all Scripture is useful to us – not some, not just the bits we like but all. It also says that it is 'God-breathed': this means it finds its origins in Him. Not just those bits that are good for teaching and training also the bits that bring rebuke and correction.

I believe one of the signs of maturity in the life of the believer is that we develop an ever-growing appetite for God's Word, independent of what it may be coming to do. When you are a babe in Christ you just want the nice bits that make you feel warm, loved and fluffy. When you begin to mature you gain an understanding that all of His word is good for you and that when His word comes into your world to bring correction or rebuke these words really are good for you and are as equally inspired by the love He has for you as the nice fluffy ones.

Never forget that, as Hebrews 12:6 reveals, God also chastens (brings discipline to) the child that He loves – not abuses or ill treats, but brings correction to.

So, is God's breath offending you today? Is what He currently wants to address annoying or aggravating you? Or are you responding to His daily bread in a mature way, knowing that it is indeed all good, and when allowed has the potential to equip you for every good work that God has for you?

My advice: give God open access to speak to you about what He needs to speak to you about. If He is bringing teaching or training – great; if He is trying to correct or rebuke don't get offended or bent out of shape by His breath, rather celebrate what He is doing and watch the way your life goes again from good to great.

Prayer

Thank you, Father, that today I will not be offended by the words You have spoken. Rather, I purpose to apply them to my life, and as I do I know my life will be blessed. Thank You for helping me to do this again today, Holy Spirit.

Amen

A farmer does not reap a harvest by just looking at an empty field in despair, he sows a seed. Whatever you lack in life, sow.

Andy Elmes

Don't shoot the Postman

All Scripture is God-breathed and is useful for teaching, rebuking, correcting and training in righteousness, so that the servant of God may be thoroughly equipped for every good work.

2 Timothy 3:16-17 (NIV)

Being a pastor can sometimes be the strangest of things to do; as well as daily caring for God's lambs and leading His sheep, we have the privilege of delivering God's message to His people week in and week out. Sometimes it's a bit like being a postman – our role is, as a postman's, to simply deliver the message He wants delivered to whom He wants it delivered to.

This is great when the messages are nice, friendly and 'right where people feel they are at', but what about when God wants to pass on a message that steps right into the 'no go' area of a person's life? Maybe He wants to address how they don't honour Him with their finances, how they want to reap but never sow; or He wants to speak to them concerning how to treat their wife and kids in a way that pleases Him that is different to what they currently do? There are so many examples we could use but these are good ones to make the point.

So the pastor gets to represent God's breath (His words and truth) and one day, instead of maybe teaching or training, he speaks words that maybe correct or rebuke a person. It amazes me when this happens how people do not turn on God or His breath but on the pastor. They forget that all Scripture is God-breathed, and that the pastor is just the postman – but let's face it, they are a much easier target to shoot at than God, right?

Think about how fickle the attention a postman is given can be – one day he walks up the path holding good news or something you want to hear, so you celebrate him, give him big smiles and morning greetings. What about when he walks up the driveway holding a bill you were expecting or apparent bad news? Suddenly the unsuspecting postman gets an altogether different reception.

Sometimes being a pastor can be like that: a pastor's commitment should be to bring to you what God is saying. The truth is, sometimes they are unaware of what you are going through, just being faithful to deliver heaven's mail, so, hey, give them a break. If what is in the message cuts close to home do your pastor a favour – remember who breathed the message and who is the one simply delivering it, and stop trying to shoot the postman!

Crowning benefits

Bless the LORD, O my soul; and all that is within me, bless His holy name! Bless the LORD, O my soul, and forget not all His benefits: who forgives all your iniquities, who heals all your diseases, who redeems your life from destruction, who crowns you with loving kindness and tender mercies.

Psalm 103:1-4

*L*et's remind ourselves of some great benefits – the King of kings crowns you with two incredible things:

1. Loving kindness – not judgement, wrath and disappointment; these were all poured upon His Son at the cross as He hung there on our behalf. Remember, we are now qualified by Christ to live continually in the benefits of the divine exchange of the cross. He took what was rightfully ours and gave us what was rightfully His.

> *God made him who had no sin to be sin for us, so that in Him we might become the righteousness of God.*
>
> **2 Corinthians 5:21 (NIV)**

2. Tender mercies – continual undeserved goodness and grace towards us from the hand of a gentle and loving Father. The perfect work of the cross put the Father's crown of delight upon our heads, as well as upon the head of His beloved Son. His heart is again turned towards you to do you good.

Different Bible translations put it the following ways:

> *He crowns you with love and mercy – a paradise crown.*
>
> **(MSG)**

> *Who beautifies, dignifies, and crowns you with loving-kindness and tender mercy.*
>
> **(AMP)**

- He has made all things beautiful (Ecclesiastes 3:11).
- He has restored our dignity.
- He has crowned us with love, kindness, and mercy.

Take time to think about that today and go into the rest of the week praising Him, because He did not have to do this but rather He chose to!

Prayer

Good morning, Lord. Thank You for the many benefits that You have given me; help me to never forget any of them. Morning by morning Your goodness, mercy and provision I see. Let me walk conscious of Your benefits today.

Amen

Satisfied with good things

Who satisfies your desires with good things so that your youth is renewed like the eagle's.

Psalm 103:5

---

*L*et's continue to consider the benefits that are ours in Christ. To remind ourselves of our benefits list so far:

1. Forgives all your sins.

2. Heals all your diseases.

Then there's also:

3. Redeems your life from destruction!

4. Crowns you with loving kindness and tender mercies.

Benefit 5: He satisfies your desires with good things.

Notice that it says, 'He satisfies'! When you purpose to seek God and His kingdom first He satisfies your desires with good things. Why? When you are seeking Him and His kingdom first, most, if not all, of your desires will be in alignment with His will: 'two hearts beating as one'.

> *Delight yourself in the LORD and He will give you the desires of your heart.*
> **Psalm 37:4 (NIV)**

- He is a satisfier, not a disappointer!

- He is interested in your desires and, if truth be told, is the author of most of them.

- He knows your deepest and shallowest desires, and has interest in every one.

As with any loving father, the desires of God's kids mean a lot to Him – not just the big ones but also those seemingly little desires too.

Romans 1:24 (NIV) says concerning wicked people with evil desires that He 'gave them over in the sinful desires of their hearts', but when it comes to a righteous person with good desires He does not give them over to them but rather gets involved and makes those desires manifest realities, dreams come true.

Bless you, love God first and watch Him turn even the smallest desires into manifest blessings.

Forget none of His benefits

Who satisfies your desires with good things so that your youth is renewed like the eagle's. The LORD works righteousness and justice for all the oppressed. He made known His ways to Moses, His deeds to the people of Israel: the Lord is compassionate and gracious, slow to anger, abounding in love. He will not always accuse, nor will He harbour His anger for ever; He does not treat us as our sins deserve or repay us according to our iniquities. For as high as the heavens are above the earth, so great is His love for those who fear Him.

Psalm 103:5-11 (NIV)

Through satisfying your desires He renews your youth like the eagles. Through grace we experience our youth renewed.

God stands in front of us and works righteously and justly for us when oppression comes into our world to harm us.

As with Moses and the children of Israel He makes His ways and deeds known to us by revelation so that we can know what is happening when others don't.

God is abundant towards us with compassion and grace, and doesn't harbour anger or repay us what we deserve for iniquities committed. Instead of punishing us He sees all iniquity paid for by the sacrifice of His beloved Son.

Finally, what a great measurement He uses to reveal the quantity of His love towards us: as high as the heavens are above the earth. That is a long way, my friend, and that love is yours again today because of Jesus.

Bask in that love today and forget none of His benefits!

Prayer

Father, again today I thank You for the many benefits You have given to me and pour upon my life. Thank You that today my life is renewed like the eagle's, and I can fly high with You. Thank You that today You are my Provider, Protector and the source of all I need. I declare that in You I live, I move, and I have my being.

Amen

Selfish faith will change your life, but selfless faith can change the world.

Andy Elmes

LISTEN

My sheep listen to my voice; I know them, and they follow me.
John 10:27 (NIV)

In a world that is so very noisy it is not easy to get quiet and listen, but God is continually speaking and it is very often in a still, small voice (1 Kings 19:12, KJV). If you are a child of God then you have the ability to hear Him.

This weekend, find some time to get quiet and to listen for what God is saying to you. How will I know it's Him? You'll know it's God because He will never say anything that contradicts what is in the Bible. Write down what He says to you so you can reflect on His words.

_____

_____

_____

_____

_____

_____

_____

Return to the blueprint

Consequently, you are no longer foreigners and strangers, but fellow-citizens with God's people and members of God's household, built on the foundation of the apostles and prophets, with Christ Jesus Himself as the chief cornerstone. In Him the whole building is joined together and rises to become a holy temple in the Lord.

Ephesians 2:19-21 (NIV)

Is it time for the 21st-century church to return to a 1st-century vision? Two thousand years ago Jesus, the Architect of the Church, rolled out a blueprint for the church He wanted built and declared, 'I will build my church and the gates of hell with not prevail against it.' As with any architect He was not confused concerning what He wanted it to look like or the effect He wanted it to have on the earth. For most of us when we look at an architect's blueprint we just see lines and numbers, but when an architect or builder looks at one he sees the finished, desired building, complete in every way.

Jesus was not confused concerning the church He wanted built – a church that was to be originally opened in the nation of Israel but would be effective and relevant to all generations and nations. My pursuit of late has been to make sure that I am building the church He wants, not one that I think could work better. I believe that when it comes to 'building the church' we can all sometimes be guilty of concentrating on 'conservatories and extensions', things that in themselves are not wrong or evil but sometimes do distract us from building that which He is so very passionate about.

The world we now live in desperately needs to see His church shining again in all its power and glory, relevant and very much alive; a church that is over two thousand years old but still shaking and impacting people and nations.

When it comes to building the church, are we looking at His blueprint? Or have we overlaid it with a blueprint we feel is more effective or iconic? Is it time to blow away the dust that we have allowed to gather on that original one He was so passionate about and purpose in our hearts that, once again, we will build according to the pattern (blueprint) He handed to us through His apostles?

When I say that we are to be a 21st-century church with a 1st-century vision I am not saying we need to revert to doing things in an Israeli or Jewish style because that was the nation the church was originally established in; rather we need to consider: are we still as passionate about and putting value on things like the Great Commission, discipleship and the manifest power of God in the church, or have we settled for putting on nice meetings and getting people seated comfortably when God never wanted them to be?

'GO'

And Jesus came and spoke to them, saying, 'All authority has been given to Me in heaven and on earth. Go therefore and make disciples of all the nations, baptising them in the name of the Father and of the Son and of the Holy Spirit, teaching them to observe all things that I have commanded you; and lo, I am with you always, even to the end of the age.' Amen.

Matthew 28:18-20

We spoke yesterday concerning the need for us to 'return to God's Blueprint' when it comes to the church and the building of it. As you study that original blueprint you instantly see the importance Jesus placed on what we term the Great Commission. The church that Jesus wanted built was to be a place that would mobilise, equip and send out its people to make a difference in their world, and indeed the world. It would be a place where the people, to their very hearts, would be a bunch of 'goers' not 'stay-and-watchers'!

How much does this simple yet life-changing word 'GO' affect us today? Are we passionate about this Great Commission, as Jesus was passionate about it, or have we reduced it to being a Great Suggestion – or worse, a Great Omission? These are the question I believe the 21st-century church is to ask itself, and keep asking until we get the answers and results that we should get.

Have we reduced the Great Commission to 'go to church' instead of something that changes the worlds of others? Are we as individuals and as churches making plans and doing what we need to do to let Jesus be known and experienced in our 'Jerusalem, Judea, Samaria and ends of the earth' – put another way: locally, nationally and globally.

Before a person looks at their Jerusalem or the ends of the earth they need to make the decision to live beyond the boundaries of their own existence, to live beyond what they prefer and find more comfortable and convenient, for the benefit of others. Until they do this they are not a goer or a missionary anywhere; but when they do they are a missionary wherever they find themselves.

'Go' is such a small word but can do so much in the life of a person and a church. 'Go' is important to Jesus so it needs to be important to us. If you feel your Christianity is lacking adventure you need to realise that the adventures of God are always connected and linked with 'Go'. Read the Bible, you'll see that it was when the early church 'went' that they experienced incredible adventures and got loads of great stories to tell. When we purpose to be a people who 'Go' we will again get stories, and our boredom will turn to adventures that will bless many. 'Go' puts the zing back into lifeless Christianity.

It's great that church these days is so 'attractional' – by that I mean that it is nice looking and makes it easy for people to access and feel welcome. But attractional church needs to always contain a strong missional agenda. Attractional draws a person, missional gets them saved, equipped and sent out to do what God has for them. It is a missional-minded church that will turn our generation upside down, just as that 1st-century missional church turned their world upside down.

As a friend of mine once said, when it comes to the Great Commission, what part of GO do we not get – the G or the O?

Go and what?

Then Jesus came to them and said, 'All authority in heaven and on earth has been given to me. Therefore go and make disciples of all nations, baptising them in the name of the Father and of the Son and of the Holy Spirit.'

Matthew 28:18-20 (NIV)

The last two days we have spoken about 'returning to the Blueprint' when it comes to building church. Yesterday we looked at the calling we all have to the Great Commission or, as we simply put it yesterday, to God wanting us to be a people who 'GO'.

It is equally vital that the 21st-century church re-embraces the passion of the 1st-century church for equipping the saints – God's people – to be goers, not people who sit and watch.

So when we go what are we to do? We could answer this in a number of ways. One way would be according to Ephesians 2: 'to go to do good works'. But here in the text we have been studying together we see that the next natural progression of the Great Commission is that we are called to go and make disciples.

As we dare to re-embrace this Great Commission that means so much to God we must also be ready to fully complete what He desires for us to do: that we be a people who 'make disciples'. Again, this can cause a whole number of good questions to arise in our minds. Are we making disciples? What is discipleship? What does discipleship look like in the 21st century? Is discipleship about more meetings or is it worked out in a more personal context too?

Discipleship can be both. It can be done in a group setting but also by walking with people on a daily basis, helping them to discover God for themselves each day, and to understand His wisdom and how to apply it to their everyday lives and situations. As we help people to replace the subtle, wrong wisdom they have been believing for God's wisdom, it is then that their internal belief system changes and, as a result, their lives start heading in a new and better direction.

According to our text today disciples are made! They are the result of people giving time to other people, the result of imparting what you have learnt as you have journeyed with God to those who have not been walking with Him so long.

Two questions:

1. Who is discipling you? Have you positioned your life where you need to grow?

2. Who are you discipling? To whom are you passing on what you have learnt?

Prayer

*Good morning, Lord. Help me today to be the disciple You have called me to be, and be busy helping others to be Your disciples. Let Your 'Go' ever be in my heart and equip me to make more disciples for You. Today I acknowledge that the Great Commission is **my** commission, and You have empowered me to be busy with it.*

Amen

Created for a reason

For we are God's handiwork, created in Christ Jesus to do good works, which God prepared in advance for us to do.

Ephesians 2:10 (NIV)

Ephesians 2:9-10 reveals to us that we are the produce of God's grace; that we have been created by Him, for Him; that we find our origins in Him both in our first birth and also our second one. It reveals to us that we are His handwork and as 'new creations' we are indeed the produce of His intentions and His ability to save and make righteous, not our own effort or performance to exist.

What I really love is that it also reveals that we were created for things – those things being 'good works'. Notice that it does not say 'dead works' – dead works are pointless things that only ever try to achieve what has already been achieved, like a person spending all day trying to put a plug in the sink when there is already one in it. Rather we are called to 'good works' – the Greek word basically means 'to do business', more specifically to do God's business!

Just as the donkey in Matthew 21 was loosed for a purpose, so our lives have been loosed because: 1) He loves us and wants us free, but also 2) because He has things for us to do, things that were 'prepared in advance for us'.

A person's Christianity finds its fulfilment in knowing that you were created by God and created to do for God, not out of a works-based mentality but rather out of a heart that understands all that He did to save us – a heart of gratitude and adoration that has a desire to be involved with what He is doing.

The natural Adam in Genesis was God's very first piece of human workmanship. Notice as you read on in Genesis that he was not made to sit and make daisy chains; he would never feel fulfilled in doing that because he was made in the image of a productive God. In the same way we, as new creations, need to understand that we too, by grace, are His workmanship and we too find our fulfilment in discovering what He has called us to do and in doing it.

Today, remember that you are His handiwork; you are saved by grace alone, which removes any boasting of self-achievement, but as His handiwork you were created to 'do His business'. What has He got for you to do? Ask Him, or maybe start by asking the pastor He has given to equip you.

Created by, created for, living from desire not obligation – that is an effective, fulfilled life!

A wholehearted Church will influence, change and even redefine the culture it exists in.

Andy Elmes

Will you move with the cloud?

Sometimes the cloud stayed only from evening till morning, and when it lifted in the morning, they set out. Whether by day or by night, whenever the cloud lifted, they set out. Whether the cloud stayed over the tabernacle for two days or a month or a year, the Israelites would remain in camp and not set out; but when it lifted, they would set out. At the LORD's command they encamped, and at the LORD's command they set out.

Numbers 9:21-23 (NIV)

Change has always been present in the life of those who purposed to follow God; think about what it was like being one of the children of Israel, for instance. The Bible reveals that for a time they were led by day by a pillar of smoke and by night by a pillar of fire. This represented God's presence and they were commanded by God to follow it whenever and wherever it moved. This makes a very interesting read; especially for those who hate change and love things to just stay the same. Every now and then without any warning the cloud would up and move and everything would change for everyone. The Bible reveals that sometimes it would stay days, other times weeks and months, then without warning off it went. When it moved it meant that change was here again; also a choice concerning how the children of Israel would respond to change.

Imagine you had been there – maybe you had moved 20-30 times already, set up home in 20-30 different places; sometimes you were by the river, other times not; sometimes under trees where you and your family could enjoy some nice shade, but next time no tree around. The last time you got a great deal, maybe you were by a well or under the cover of a palm tree; it's only been a few weeks, you're growing some nice vegetables, all is good – then all of a sudden you hear it: the voice of a messenger running through the camp shouting, 'The cloud is moving again!' which basically meant, 'It all changes again!'

Surely sometimes some of the people must have thought, 'OK, that's enough now, I think I will stay here. I have had enough change for one life.' The reality is if they stayed they may have had a degree of comfort but they would never see what God was doing or where He was going next. They would never experience the long-term plan of God, just the moment they were in.

Change is normally inconvenient, involving uprooting and rearrangement, but if it happens because God is moving then you need to be ready to pack up your security, put up with a bit of inconvenience and move again. Today we may not follow a physical cloud of smoke and fire but God is still moving and looking for people who will live beyond the inconvenience of momentary change to experience what He is doing next and has planned for them later. Remember in Jeremiah 29, it says He has plans to prosper you, give you future and hope? Sometimes He has to move you or something you're doing to position you for what He has for you; this is where you, like the children of Israel, have to trust Him.

How about you, Champion, will you move with the cloud?

UNPLUG

Don't become so well-adjusted to your culture that you fit into it without even thinking. Instead fix your attention on God.
Romans 12:2 (MSG)

Take some time this weekend to unplug from every form of technology and social media. When you do this you may realise how much it has become a part of your life! Use this time instead to spend with the Lord, your family and friends.

Enjoy your screen-free time! Happy weekend!

Notes

_____

_____

_____

_____

_____

_____

_____

_____

_____

Thoughts on Friendship

True friends can hear your life yelling 'help' when your lips are not moving and no words have been spoken.

Many may refer to you as their 'good friend' but there's nothing like a time of trouble to allow you to truly see who your good friends really are. Though often painful, these times will truthfully filter for you who's who in your friendship circles. Resolve to love all who call you friend passionately, but with wisdom's eyes watch and learn from these very valuable times.

Proverbs 18:24 teaches us that 'a man who has friends must himself be friendly'. This is a simple yet honest truth to building healthy friendships. It's basically the golden rule of 'what a man sows, that he will reap' in a relational context. It reminds us that if we lack friends or want more friends then we need to be proactive by being friendly ourselves. If you want good friends, be a good friend!

Andy Elmes

Characteristics of a blueprint church
PART 1

Those who accepted his message were baptised, and about three thousand were added to their number that day. They devoted themselves to the apostles' teaching and to fellowship, to the breaking of bread and to prayer. Everyone was filled with awe at the many wonders and signs performed by the apostles.

Acts 2:41-43 (NIV)

These verses show us a really good day in the life of the early church. What a result: three thousand people added in one day by one message! How would you like a response to your personal evangelism like that?

The other great thing that these verses give us is a glimpse into the culture or DNA of that early 'blueprint' church. In these verses we see a number of values that they chose to give great emphasis to. I personally think that when we hold these verses against the ones in Matthew 28:18-20 (the Great Commission) and Acts 1:8 (the promise of empowerment to a GOing people) we find the co-ordinates for the destination we are to still take as 21st-century relevant churches, and indeed the 'blueprint' for building what God wants built. We need to still find our DNA for building effective Christian lives and churches in that which Jesus was passionate about and commissioned us to do and that which the first church spent their time, energy and money doing. What He desired and what they dedicated their lives to transcends style or natural culture and still gives us a great and effective building plan for our lives and churches today.

They devoted themselves

Here we find the first ingredient to their effectiveness. There was within the church, not just the leadership, a spirit of self-devotion. People daily 'devoted themselves'. They had great preachers but they were not spoon-fed; they were self-feeders taking responsibility to get the spiritual nourishment they needed. They had great meetings and fellowship but did not need to be constantly phoned or dragged there or reminded with constant bulletins like they had memory problems; they got themselves were they needed to be, when they needed to be there.

So much of modern church is sadly about motivating people to do what they should naturally want to do, encouraging people to do things that really should be their spiritual lifestyle. Imagine if we could get even more self devotion into the DNA of the modern Western church – how much more effective would our local churches be if each member took personal responsibility for even the little things, like getting to church on time so church services could start as strong as they could do, serving on the teams that needed them and turning up when it was their turn without a text, being faithful in honouring God with their finances and time without subtle reminders and encouragements from the stage?

I am always amazed at how people can downgrade the 'God bit' of their life and sentence it to a lesser devotion than the other bits; one great example again being time-keeping. In every other area of life they are on time: meetings with the dentist, bank manager, work – but why not church? What is that switch that needs to be fixed? Surely the greatest of our devotion belongs to God, right? Surely the place we manifest the greatest personal self-devotion should be in His House? Imagine what we could achieve if just this one thing was to change – suddenly no challenge would be too great. Hey we might even see 3000 people get saved on our Sunday morning; 3000 people moved by His message but also moved by a group of people so sold out and devoted to what and who they believed in.

Let's be a devoted people.

Prayer for my Church

Heavenly Father, today I pray for your Church, both your Church globally and my home church. Let there be a fresh desire in Your people for devotion. Lord, I pray today that people would begin to have a greater desire to move away from a spoon-fed church experience to personally being devoted to a pursuit of You. Let a fresh fire be lit and burn within the hearts of those who belong to You to make their pursuit of You something that is their personal responsibility. As the people of the early church had a powerful personal devotion for You that affected the church they were in, let it be the same for us. Break chains this week that hold people back from being personally devoted, and let Your people break free and fly higher with You then they ever have before. This is my prayer, Lord; let it start with me.

Amen

Each stage of our pilgrimage causes our lives to be enhanced and empowered for the road and journey that still lies ahead.

Andy Elmes

Characteristics of a blueprint church
PART 2

And they continued steadfastly in the apostles' doctrine and fellowship, in the breaking of bread, and in prayers. Then fear came upon every soul, and many wonders and signs were done through the apostles.

Acts 2:42-43

*Y*esterday we looked at the subject of 'they devoted themselves'. We looked at the need for self-devotion in some of the modern church. 'What did they devote themselves to?' is my next question. There was probably a whole lot that they could have devoted themselves to but in the book of Acts the writer selects a specific handful of things; not that they were not devoted and passionate about other things but obviously God wanted these ones highlighted.

Apostles' Doctrine

It says that they were devoted to the apostles' doctrine. So what is a doctrine? Other translations often use a more understandable word 'teaching'.

The Dictionary says that *Doctrine* is, 'Teaching, instruction, the body of principles in a branch of knowledge or system of belief.' Basically, the apostles' doctrine was the teaching of the first church leaders (apostles). The foundational teaching for the New Testament church was based on their teaching, especially Paul's. Their teaching formed the 'branch of belief' for what we still believe, live by and hold to as true today in regard to everything including God, His church and how we are to live.

I suppose the challenge today is, do we teach and personally live by the truths found in the apostles' doctrine (teaching)? Does it still form the margins of what we believe today to be truth or do we attempt to mix it with other doctrines (teachings)? Notice that it does not say they devoted themselves to the doctrine of Moses or the doctrine of religion; no, it clearly says they devoted themselves to the doctrine of the apostles (leaders of the early church).

The doctrine of Moses was not wrong for its time or dispensation, but as Paul stood up to preach daily everything had indeed changed. Christ had now died for the sins of the world, the old covenant was no longer effective or relevant because a new covenant had been established and had replaced it – a covenant (agreement) cut with the very blood of God's only Son, not of bulls and goats that could only provide a mere covering for sin that would last a moment. Full punishment for sin had now been placed on Christ as He hung on the cross as our substitute; full forgiveness had now been given and God's wrath towards us settled because of His one-time redemptive work. So much had now changed. It wasn't that Paul could not or did not refer to Moses, the law or the previous covenant, but now what he taught, and the doctrine he was establishing, was based on the grace of God and the perfect finished work of the cross, and nothing else. The doctrine he now preached and established would leave a person redeemed and free outside of their own performance or merit; it would give the offer of a new beginning to all who would believe based on faith not works; it would reveal God's eternal plan to get His life inside the life of the believer, to empower a person to overcome and live the new life they had been freely given.

This is a big subject, so let's carry on tomorrow, but let me leave you with this challenge: are you living and building by the apostles' teaching or are you trying to add a bit of Moses, or maybe a bit of law, maybe a dash of your reasoning? My friend, build upon the platform handed to you by Paul and the other apostles, devote yourself like the people in that early church to 'the apostles' doctrine'; believe me, the Spirit of God was guiding their understanding and it really does include everything you need to know.

Prayer for my Church

Heavenly Father, today I want to pray for the Church and specifically my home church. Let it be a place where your Word is loved by Your people. Let Your Word take centre place in all that we do. Help us to embrace as we should the teachings of your Son, Jesus, and apostles He empowered to lead the Church. Let the teachings of these Holy Spirit-inspired men be the words we teach today and that the people purpose to live by. I pray today for a fresh hunger in Your people for the truth of Your Word. I pray today for my pastors and leaders as they prepare to teach Your Word; may they know the empowering and leading of Your Holy Spirit the Great Teacher. May they know a fresh anointing and excitement as they prepare to feed Your people. Father, let Your Church get hungrier for Your truth, and let it start with me.

Amen

Walking in the power of the Spirit comes from walking around knowing that the power is always 'turned on', despite how you feel.

Andy Elmes

Characteristics of a blueprint church
PART 3

And they continued steadfastly in the apostles' doctrine and fellowship, in the breaking of bread, and in prayers. Then fear came upon every soul, and many wonders and signs were done through the apostles.
Acts 2:42-43

This week we have been looking at what the early church devoted themselves to. We looked yesterday at how they devoted themselves to the 'apostles' teaching'. We laid the platform that this teaching the people in the first church dedicated themselves to was that which came from Paul and the other apostles. It never excluded or denied the law or old covenant but what the apostles taught put them in their rightful place in the sequence of God's eternal master plan. Their teaching always left the focus and pre-eminence on Jesus and the perfect and finished work of the cross.

When I started to think about 'the apostles' doctrine' I was intrigued to find out exactly what it was, to make sure I was not guilty of mixing covenants in a wrong way, or of believing partial or diluted truth. I studied a bit deeper than normal and found out what the epicentre of the apostles' doctrine was. I was not surprised but certainly encouraged as I discovered the apostles' doctrine orbited and found its strength in a couple of basic truths or realities. Firstly the finished redemptive work of Christ and secondly the reality of the new creation.

Think about that: everything that Paul taught and established was based and rooted in the simple yet profound truth that when anyone believes in Jesus as Saviour they become a 'new creation' – they are born again and it is as if they had never lived before or ever sinned in the sight of God.

One of Paul's foundational truths for all he taught in regard to this reality was of course this one found in 2 Corinthians 5:17 (NKJV): 'Therefore, if anyone is in Christ, he is a new creation; old things have passed away; behold, all things have become new.' The NIV translation puts it like this: 'the new creation has come: The old has gone, the new is here'. Paul had a deep-set revelation that the new creation was God's master plan – not a patch-up job of the old man, behaviour modification or a rust maintenance programme, rather a brand-new beginning for a person based on God's unfailing grace.

The truth is when a person believes in Christ they identify with His death, burial and resurrection and come by faith to a brand-new existence based on Christ alone (Romans 6:3-6). As God's Word says in Romans 6, the old man is crucified with Christ and, as Paul said so well, our only boast is in the cross where we were separated from the world and who God has called us to be (Galatians 6:14). As you read on in that verse you actually see Paul defy or replace the doctrine of Moses with this new creation reality.

Neither circumcision nor uncircumcision means anything; what counts is the new creation.
Galatians 6:15 (NIV)

Circumcision was a major part of the previous covenant based on law. What was Paul saying? Simple: it's a new day, it's no longer about circumcision, festivals and such; it's about faith in Jesus Christ. When a person places their faith in Him, they die and are raised again to newness of life (Romans 6:4), they become a new creation without a past, they awaken to a new beginning, and all of this is a gift from God. From the position of being a new creation they begin to build and live out God's ways and plans for their life.

Maybe that's why the gospel means 'good news'. Champion, today count your old life dead and enjoy your new one!

Prayer for my Church

Good morning, Lord. Today I come before You to pray for my church. I pray for health and prosperity in our church leadership. I pray that You would guide them with Your wisdom in the decisions they need to make. I pray today, Father, that the revelation of the new creation would explode afresh in the hearts of our leaders and the people in my church. Thank You that we will not be busy trying to maintain the 'old man' but rather helping people to discover the 'new man' they have become through Christ. Father, I lift my hands and bless the church You have put me in. I thank You for my leaders and I pray that they would know Your voice today in their leading and preparation. Let the new creation revelations of the Apostle Paul be the guiding truths in the church I call home. Thank You that today I can declare, as Paul did, that the 'old has gone, the new has come'. Born again, born again, my life is born a new!

Amen

Forgiving people is a manifestation of God's love now living in and flowing through you.

Andy Elmes

Characteristics of a blueprint church
PART 4

They devoted themselves to the apostles' teaching and to fellowship, to the breaking of bread and to prayer. Everyone was filled with awe at the many wonders and signs performed by the apostles. All the believers were together and had everything in common.

Acts 2:42-44 (NIV)

A re you attending meetings or doing life with the church?

We have been looking at what the first church devoted themselves to. We saw that the Apostles' teaching was a very high priority and that each person who called that first church home had a personal devotion to it. Next on the list comes the word 'fellowship'; this was another high priority to them and needs to be to us. So what does it mean by fellowship? I love the way The Message translation puts this verse:

'They committed themselves to the teaching of the apostles, the life together, the common meal, and the prayers.'

I love that statement and the image it creates: they devoted themselves to 'the life together'. The early church put great emphasis on simply 'doing life together', they never defined their church experience as two hours on Sunday but rather committed to live more community-minded in their relationship with the church.

To get the best out of any church I believe this is the bottom line: if you just pop into church for a couple of hours a week the reality is you are so robbing yourself of what you could have, of what God provided for you to have. Family Church is a biggish church now – even our church plants are getting bigger and developing their own crowds on Sunday – but a reality I always share with people is this: if you really want the best of what we are you have to commit time to big church and little church. What do I mean by that? Simply that it's great that you are a part of the crowd on Sunday morning, but you also need to experience the weekly community aspect of church. Get locked into a small group, maybe a life group or outreach team, something where there is a smaller group of people committed to doing daily life together, to building and developing real friendships.

It's in the smaller part of church you can support others, ask the question you can't ask on Sunday morning, be there for people and let them be there for you. One of the reasons I believe Family Church is a strong church is not that we have big Sunday services but rather we constantly push for people to get into the 'apart-from-Sunday-event' life of who we are. Every time someone does, like a flower his or her life begins to blossom and flourish, just as God planned.

How about you, are you still settling for being a Sunday Spectator? Why not step beyond that and experience the family life of your local church. Position yourself where the community side of church is happening and let His family become your home.

The modern church has still got a fair way to go before we truly know what the early church actually had. How can I say that? Simple, look at the end of the verse: 'All the believers were together and had everything in common'. People were flogging homes and land to make sure everyone had what they needed, people cared more about people's needs than personal stuff. We may not be at that point of community living, and I am certainly not saying we should by a farm and live together, but I am saying maybe we can all move forwards in our understanding of making church a place that we do life with others, not just sit next to people on Sunday?

How about you – is there room for application? Is it time to get into a life group? Speak to your Pastor about all that is happening midweek, find a team that you can link in with, maybe the worship team or outreach team; find out if discipleship programs have a place for you? Go on, you will be glad you did.

It's time for the 21st century church to return to a 1st century vision

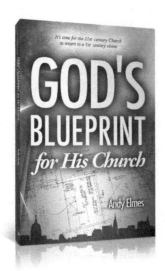

God's Blueprint for His Church

by Andy Elmes, available from **greatbiglife.co.uk** and **greatbiglifepublishing.com** for £9.99

ISBN 978-0-9928027-2-1, Great Big Life Publishing

Characteristics of a blueprint church
PART 5

And they steadfastly persevered, devoting themselves constantly to the instruction and fellowship of
the apostles, to the breaking of bread [including the Lord's Supper] and prayers.

Acts 2:42-44 (AMP Classic Edition)

We have looked at how the original blueprint church devoted itself to doctrine (teaching) and fellowship (doing life together); next on the list comes the breaking of bread. Did this mean that they spent all day doing communion? I don't think it did. I like the way that the Amplified version puts it: 'to the breaking of bread [including the Lord's Supper]'. Personally I think this fits well with the culture of Israel at that time and links well with previous value and priority of doing life together. Remember, when Jesus instituted the original communion, or breaking of bread as we know it today, where was He? In a synagogue? No, He was at a meal with His friends, hanging out with them, eating and breaking bread with them; He then takes the bread and wine and talks His friends through what has become a significant ordinance still in His church today.

Is God saying in this verse that we are to devote ourselves to the act or ordinance of communion? That we are to do it all day and every day? Or, like the Amplified version says, that we are to be taking time to eat and fellowship together and, in the midst of that ongoing fellowship, we are to make time to take bread and wine to specifically remember what He has done like He instructed us to do)? This feels more natural and 'lifestyle' to me than just making the bread and wine something we do in certain meetings we hold together.

Again, I don't think it is an issue of 'either or', rather 'both'. I think we should still have significant bread-and-wine times (communion) together when we meet corporately, but also as we build the community side of the church. As we meet together not just to pray but to fellowship and eat, in the midst of us doing that we take time to give thanks and remember what He did for us when He gave His body (represented by the bread) and shed His blood (represented by the wine or grape juice).

Once again, maybe the book of Acts speaks to us of a lifestyle of Christianity, rather than just events and ceremonies, of fellowship and including Jesus and what He has done for us in our everyday lives? What a great picture this gives us – friends who love Jesus spending good time together, then in the midst of their time together taking a moment to remember what Jesus accomplished. No need to ring a priest – all you need is bread, juice and some friends who love Jesus!

Finally, wherever you break bread, whether in church or at your friend's house, always believe for Jesus to save, heal and restore, always apply faith to what you're doing and watch what happens. Why? He is alive, so communion is not a sad memorial of someone who is no more, but rather a proclamation that He lives and is mighty to save.

SERVE

Even as the Son of Man came not to be served but to serve, and to give his life as a ransom for many.
Matthew 20:28 (ESV)

This weekend, if you don't already, make a plan to serve in your church. Maybe you can help set up chairs, serve on the welcome team, pass out refreshments or help tidy up. Ask someone in charge of an area what would help the team to run smoother and then offer your services. Whatever you do, serve with your whole heart, like Jesus did when He came to serve humanity.

Enjoy your weekend!

Notes

_____

_____

_____

_____

_____

_____

_____

Is anybody out there?

But, speaking the truth in love, may grow up in all things into Him who is the head – Christ – from whom the whole body, joined and knit together by what every joint supplies, according to the effective working by which every part does its share, causes growth of the body for the edifying of itself in love.

Ephesians 4:15-16

When we look at the task ahead, this Great Commission to change nations given us by Jesus, starting with our own personal 'Jerusalem', it is indeed a mammoth task, but then we remember that God did not give the challenge to one man but rather to His Body, the church. In His Body, with all its individual members, is everything needed to get the job done, and indeed done well. The trouble is that some of the members or ligaments of the body do not function or give themselves to be used, and the strain always falls on the remaining ligaments that will. This can often, just as in the natural body, cause un-needed strain or injury to the ever-willing ligaments, and this should never happen in a church.

The church is God's Body, and as a part of this glorious Body each of us has a responsibility to be active with the gifts, talents and time we have to spare. As we dare to give what we are and have, we mobilise the local church to be all it was destined by God to be.

So why are so many departments within our churches short of workers? Why do we need to invade what we do on Sundays with pleading requests of, 'Please come and help kid's church or another needy team'? I don't think it is that people really won't, often it's because people think that someone else will; trouble comes when a whole bunch of people step away from helping because they think someone else will – the problem is never solved, nor the need fulfilled.

It's time to be the 'Anybody' when appeals for help are made and we have the time, energy or gifting to help. When the 'will anybody help us?' appeal is made, we need to say, 'I will be that anybody'. If we could get this in the culture of our churches in a greater way imagine the advancing we could achieve together.

I want to finish this morning's breakfast with what I think is a modern-day proverb or pearl of wisdom – within it lies both the problem and the answer for most churches seeking more people to 'come on team'. Give it a read and take it personally.

> *Everybody, Somebody, Anybody and Nobody*
> *This is a little story about four people named Everybody, Somebody, Anybody, and Nobody. There was an important job to be done and Everybody was sure that Somebody would do it. Anybody could have done it, but Nobody did it.*
> *Somebody got angry about that because it was Everybody's job. Everybody thought that Anybody could do it, but Nobody realised that Everybody wouldn't do it. It ended up that Everybody blamed Somebody when Nobody did what Anybody could have done.**

Will you be an Anybody?

* Author unknown

Stewards or owners

As each one has received a gift, minister it to one another, as good stewards of the manifold grace of God.
1 Peter 4:10

The Bible instructs us here that we are stewards of the manifold grace of God – what a privilege we have been given. The reality is that we are actually stewards of a whole lot more: how much? Everything we have! We all need sometimes to have a fresh realisation that in regard to 'all things' we are not 'owners of' but 'stewards of' – whether that be finances, resources or even our children. All these things belong to God and come from God into our worlds for us to use, enjoy and care for.

Everything we have has been given to us by God to enjoy but also to be a trustworthy steward of. Having this way of thinking enables you to hold things with a much lighter grip without losing any diligence or needed responsibility – simply, any unhealthy possessive attitude we may have.

Especially concerning wealth, we must always remember, as it says in Deuteronomy 8:18, 'It is He who gives you power to get wealth, that He may . . . ' It was not just our strength, education or natural abilities that enabled us to prosper, it was God who gave all those things and more. Don't forget also that last bit: that He may . . . ' God has a purpose for what He has blessed you with – just as His agenda with Abraham was to bless many through him, so it is God's agenda for you and me. Will you let Him, or does the chain reaction of blessing stop when it hits your life?

When we get wealth it is good to remember who enabled and empowered us. As we do we no longer see ourselves as the wealth's owners but its stewards for God. I heard it put this way once: 'God does not just want to get stuff to you, He wants to get stuff through you.' What a greater privilege that is, being someone God can trust and use to pass things on not just someone who has testimonies of what God gave or managed to get to them.

When we understand that we are stewards we then purpose to live beyond ourselves; we enjoy what God allows us to have but we are not scared to use those things for what He needs or wants, to let things flow through us and not just to us.

We come into the world with nothing, we leave with nothing, except the lives we influenced and affected with the things He let us use while we were here.

Be His faithful steward again today and watch what else He starts to trust you with.

What does He mean by 'all'?

Bring all the tithes (the whole tenth of your income) into the storehouse, that there may be food in My house, and prove Me now by it, says the Lord of hosts, if I will not open the windows of heaven for you and pour you out a blessing, that there shall not be room enough to receive it.

Malachi 3:10 (AMP Classic Edition)

What do you mean when you say 'all'? Do you mean some, a measure of or maybe what is left over? Or when you say 'all' do you mean everything that is due? Guess what: so does God. When it comes to us honouring God with the tithe we need to remember a couple of basic things: firstly, God sees everything, so don't try and make out that all is all when it is really some. Secondly, remember that you are not paying anything, you are returning something. We don't pay our tithes, we return the tithe (tenth part) to God and as we do this He, as promised, causes great blessing on the remaining 90 per cent. When you have a revelation of this it's no longer a matter of 'have to' but rather 'why wouldn't I'.

When you study the tithe (honouring God with the tenth part), both in the old and the new testaments, you see that it must be a joyful, heart thing – not an obligation. You also soon notice that God loves the first tenth or first part. Why? Because it demonstrates a number of things:

1. Your priorities. When you give God the first part or tenth you are saying, 'You come first, all others who are lining up for my money come after what I first return to You, Lord.'

2. Your faith. It says, 'I chose to trust you.' Let's face it, most of us have a whole bunch of other stuff we could spend the tithe on – I know I do. When you honour God with it you say, 'I trust You, I place faith in You for what I need, want and even desire.'

3. Your obedience. God told you to do it. The tithe is not a law but a kingdom principle, which means it is effective both sides of the cross, in both covenants. If God asks you to do something and does not ask you to stop you demonstrate obedience in remaining faithful to it.

It's amazing when you start to talk about God and people's money how you suddenly get different responses from people: everything from passion to anger, depending on their revelation of it. We must remember, as we have learnt before, to not get angry with the postman (minister/church) who is delivering the message but check out the facts with the One who actually sent the message.

When it comes to the tithe, in my opinion there is a difference between those who can't and those who won't. When I meet people who want to and can't I always apply faith and grace and challenge them to start were they can, en route to getting to the tenth. God will see the activity of the heart and work with them to make them able to do what they desire to. But when someone can and won't, I don't apply the same reasoning. I actually don't know what to say except read the Bible, ask God to reveal His truth in your heart so you get a revelation of its significance in your life.

Remember, He is not trying to rob you – He is trying to bless you.

The Test

'Bring the whole tithe into the storehouse, that there may be food in my house. Test me in this,' says the LORD Almighty, 'and see if I will not throw open the floodgates of heaven and pour out so much blessing that there will not be room enough to store it.'

Malachi 3:10 (NIV)

---

pparently this is the only time in the Bible where God invites you to test Him! What is this invitation to test Him in reference to? Yep, you got it, you and your money. For some I know that is annoying, but read the context of the verse. God is asking you to trust Him with this area of your life, just as you trust Him with other areas that are non-wallet related. What an incredible invitation! Think about it, God Almighty is inviting you to test Him. The God, whose arm is not too short to save, whose ear is not to deaf to hear, the God who spoke and everything came into existence, says to you and me, 'Test me, see if I am faithful to My word in regard to your provision'.

The reality is that God does not need our money. I believe He actually uses money to test our hearts, to see how free we are and how much trust we actually have in Him. This verse is all about us being invited to test Him, but in reality all of us, as we daily handle our finances, are also passing or failing tests He is giving us. Why would He test us? Why does a parent do little tests with their kids? Is it not because there is an agenda within the parent to entrust the child with more responsibility? When I let my younger kids walk down the street without me those first couple of times, in my heart I am looking to the day I can entrust them to go to the local shop on their own.

This principle is in the Word: it says, 'What a man does with little, he will do with much.' This is fact. Just as I do little tests on my kids with a heart to give them more, so God uses money, among other things, to test our hearts and motives. A man might say, 'When I have loads of money I will honour God and be generous,' but the reality is they most probably won't, because if they can't be faithful with little why would they be faithful with much? Listen, we can't kid God. He looks beyond the greatest projections we give to the realities of the activity of the heart, He knows what we will do and what we won't.

When it comes to tithing and giving, God is watching. When it comes to what we do with our wealth, our level of generosity, God is watching. Why? Because He is mean and untrusting? No, the opposite: because He longs to entrust us with more and watches to see if we are good stewards who are able to handle more. Will we, like Abraham, let our lives be vessels He can flow stuff through or will our knuckles grip white anytime anything comes our way?

So, Champion, God is inviting you to test Him with your finances. Go ahead and do what He is asking and see if He will not follow through with what He promised. But also know that He uses finances and blessings to test us, to see where we are at. Will you pass the test and see what He has for you next?

Have a great day, live to give.

Imagine what God opening heavens floodgates looks like

'Bring the whole tithe into the storehouse, that there may be food in my house. Test me in this,' says the LORD Almighty, 'and see if I will not throw open the floodgates of heaven and pour out so much blessing that there will not be room enough to store it.'

Malachi 3:10 (NIV)

We have spoken a lot this week about the act of tithing, honouring God with the first tenth of your increase. Let's finish off by talking about the result.

Personally I do not give my tithes to get – that is not my primary purpose in giving. I give my tithes to honour God but I'm not unaware that God promises, when I do, it will result in great blessing. It is always good to have a motive for giving that is beyond you getting, but also if God promised it know it will happen.

Listen to the terminology He uses when describing His response. In different translations you see different words used: 'heaven's windows', 'floodgates'. I also like what it says in *The Message* translation: 'Test me in this and see if I don't open up heaven itself to you and pour out blessings beyond your wildest dreams.' Beyond your wildest dreams! What would that look like? Have you ever dared to imagine what that could look like? If you don't tithe you don't have to but if you do it's worth taking a moment to think about. Remember, we do not serve a God who uses words in an idle way. When He uses 'floodgates' and 'open windows', and 'not enough room to receive it', you'd better believe that is exactly what the God who according to Ephesians 3:20 does exceedingly abundantly far above means.

My personal belief is that it is not just about money – though money is good, right? It meets needs in your life and the lives of others. When I say I am wealthy I am certainly not referring just to finance – I am referring to everything in my life: great wife, healthy kids, healthy body, opportunities, friendships – the list could go on and on. When we honour God by returning the tenth to Him, He opens heaven's windows and more than money falls out. He blesses you with what you need or what you need for someone else. Yes, I believe in the principle of seed producing after its own kind – 'plant carrots, get carrots' – but I think God is far more generous than that. He causes carrots (money) to come when we honour Him with or sow carrots (money), but then He looks around heaven's cupboards and says, 'What else have I got in here I can throw at them?'

When I was on holiday in France this year, each morning I had the joy of walking by a canal. As I walked, every now and then I would come across a floodgate or lock. On one side the level of the water was low, waiting for the canal boat to arrive, but on the other side of the floodgate the water was high, pushing hard, wanting to flood the void, it just needed an excuse or hand to open it. My friends, according to Malachi, God is just looking for a reason to put His hand to the floodgate and let what's behind it pour out. Maybe if we believe the Bible that reason or hand-moving thing could be your tithe? What can I say: test Him.

KEEP A CLEAN SLATE

For if you forgive men when they sin against you, your heavenly Father will also forgive you. But if you do not forgive men their sins, your Father will not forgive your sins.
Matthew 6:14-15 (NIV)

At times there will be people who you don't see eye to eye with and you will have plenty of opportunity in life to get offended with some of them. Your heart was not designed to hold unforgiveness, and the consequences of holding onto it are terrible.

Forgive, if you want to receive forgiveness from God; harbour unforgiveness and you will not be forgiven.

Today, keep the slate of your life clean and forgive anyone you have any unforgiveness toward.

Notes

_____

_____

_____

_____

_____

_____

Your will be done, in my life as it is in heaven

'For I know the plans I have for you,' declares the LORD, 'plans to prosper you and not to harm you, plans to give you hope and a future. Then you will call on Me and come and pray to Me, and I will listen to you. You will seek Me and find Me when you seek Me with all your heart. I will be found by you,' declares the LORD, 'and will bring you back from captivity.'

Jeremiah 29:11-14 (NIV)

God knows the state of the world and knows what is needed to help people and change situations. He has everything that is needed in heaven but needs to get them present and active on the earth. God has always chosen to use everyday, normal people to release and fulfil His incredible plans and blessings.

He looks for a faithful person who will say, 'Yes!' That's it. The only qualifications He needs are faithfulness and agreement. Think back to how He got the greatest gift and plan of all time (Jesus) to the earth – it was through an agreeing young virgin called Mary. God knew that all the world needed was Jesus, His Son, that He would save and change humanity by perfect redemption and grace. But Jesus did not just appear – He came through the womb and life of a young girl whom God had chosen to use for His plans; indeed, those plans brought prosperity, hope and future not just to Mary but to the human race.

In Luke 1 we read how an angel of the Lord comes to Mary, as with Jeremiah, out of the blue and announces the Father's plans for Jesus to come to the earth, born through her. God makes His plans known, but nothing happens yet; she does not become pregnant till she says these famous words of humility and submission:

Let it be to me according to your word.

Luke 1:38b

Mary was not violated! It was after she said, 'Yes, Lord, use me' that she supernaturally conceived and the miracle began. Nine months later she gave birth to a God master plan: Jesus!

What is God saying to you that He wants to do or bring to the earth through you?

Will you say, as Mary did, 'Let it be according to Your plans', or stick with your own?

The world needs you to be a carrier and point of release for heaven's intentions. That may be a ministry or a business, or both. God will use what He has made you good at. You have been prepared for His purposes and at the right time ignition is made with the simplest 'Yes!'.

Mother Teresa was another lady who said yes, and thousands of forgotten, overlooked children were cared for, who would have died unloved and hungry. Saying 'Yes!' to God can cause incredible things to happen in our world!

Your will be done, Lord, in me as it is in heaven.

Have another great, God-filled day.

Wise up and 'Team Up'

For this reason a man shall leave his father and mother and be joined to his wife, and the two shall become one flesh. So then, they are no longer two but one flesh. Therefore what God has joined together, let not man separate.

Matthew 19:5-7

This one goes out to the husbands and wives!

God made marriage and it is a powerful union between two people; a union that is very spiritual as well as physical, a union like none other where, in the sight of God, two individuals become one new person, one new life force. Do not underestimate the power of your unity as a team and what happens when you take time to pray together as a team. You sit down to pray as two people but in God's opinion you actually sit down as one, representing one voice and one desire! When you take time to come together in agreement in prayer with one heart, one desire and one purpose you cause big mountains to move and devils to run.

Being in unity with each other is so important. The devil knows it, and that's why he works full on always trying to cause disunity between Mr and Mrs, normally with petty things that really don't matter. He knows that if he can disrupt your unity together, when you pray there will be a degree of confusion. Remember, when God looks at us He sees two that have become one – if we are not in agreement with each other in our prayers it's like a man sitting down to pray who does not agree with himself, all that he will produce is confusion.

I was reminded of these things when today I took some time to join hands with my beautiful wife Gina and pray change into some situations we are facing, also to commit some other very important things to Him. It's amazing how, when you do this, His presence instantly embraces you both; also a confidence that His hands are loosed to work on your behalf floods your hearts.

Hey, Man and Wife, this is so important if you want an effective prayer life – and by that I mean that you see stuff happen! It says at the end of today's verse, 'let not man separate'. Think about that: what is it that tries to separate you and your spouse that comes to weaken the true potential of your prayers? Don't let life, embarrassment, busyness or any other things keep you from taking time when you need to, to pray in unity together. When a husband and wife come together, with one heart and one prayer, mountains really move! Think about it: your family, your finances and all the things you are going through need you to wise up and 'team up'!

1 Peter 3:7 speaks a lot about marriage and how we should honour each other for the parts we play in the marriage. It says this to encourage us to walk at peace with each other. Why? Simple, this is what it says at the end: 'So that nothing will hinder your prayers' (NIV). I don't know about you but I can't afford hindered prayers, and I will do what I need to to get them unhindered.

Make sometime today to come together with the other part of you to talk to God.

How do you handle change?

God, who is enthroned from of old, who does not change, He will hear them and humble them, because they have no fear of God.

Psalm 55:19 (NIV)

The Bible says of God that He changes not; this gives us, His followers, great assurance and stability in our relationship with Him. We can build strong, stable lives and ministries knowing He does not change His mind every five minutes. He may not change but He causes a whole lot of ongoing change in the life of someone who follows Him, that's for sure. Also, life causes change constantly with its sudden turns and surprises. Like somebody once said, the only thing that is certain is change, yet in the midst of change we have a God who changes not.

Living a real life means that you will experience moments of change – sometimes these may be desired, other times they may take you by surprise and even be totally unwanted. Most change is actually good for you and it does a number of things in us. Change keeps you moving and keeps you fresh; change tests where your securities really are; change stops life becoming boring; change causes you to find new ways of doing things; change forces you to think differently, often to discover your former thinking was far too limited. I suppose the question really is, how do you handle change?

When you read about all the key figures in the Bible you see they lived lives where change was certainly the norm. When you look in the Old Testament at people like Moses, David or even Joseph, you see people who were constantly experiencing change. If you look in the New Testament at the disciples and apostles, it seems that almost every new page you read sees change coming into the world of these early pilgrims of faith, almost on a daily basis.

Whether in the Old or in the New you see people that constantly looked out at the horizon of their life and saw changes on it. You also see people that, when they knew God was in the change, chose not to run and hide but rather run to embrace the change, even when it did not make sense to their current moment. You see, they knew that if God had authored it then God was in it, working behind the scenes for their good.

It takes faith (that stuff that pleases God) to live a life where you choose to embrace change. How about you, Champion – are you experiencing change or sensing it on the horizon? Do you believe God is causing it? Then run to it, not from it. He changes not but He brings change into our worlds to keep us moving into all He has for us. You do not have to fear it if you know that God is the author of it.

Prayer

Dear Father, help me to be brave as change comes to my life. Give me Your strength and perspective as challenges come. I will lean heavily upon You today, my Father, my unchanging God. Amen

---

Called to be agents of change

So Joshua ordered the officers of the people: 'Go through the camp and tell the people, "Get your provisions ready. Three days from now you will cross the Jordan here to go in and take possession of the land the LORD your God is giving you for your own."'

Joshua 1:10-12 (NIV)

Here we see Joshua's first moments of stepping into the leadership role he had received from God, a leadership role that once belonged to Moses; a role that involved taking God's people where they could not go before. This was a role that meant he had to bring change; he had to courageously lead God's people from where they had settled into what God had for them. Straight away we see him arise in his role and make preparations to lead them forwards into God's intentions. He sends messengers throughout the people instructing them to pack up and get ready to move again – yep, you guessed it, he was unapologetically out to cause more change. Why? Because Joshua could see the promised future.

When you read the Bible you soon notice that all of God's best leaders have always been 'agents of change', people who don't fear stepping into stagnant situations to bring new direction and life. God's leaders today still do it, they also are called to stir up the settled, and re-arrange the stable. They, too, are driven by a desire to keep what God is doing fresh and moving. Like we learned yesterday if they are following God they are predictably going to lead things into change at any given moment or, put another way, whenever 'the cloud moves'.

Are you sitting waiting for change? I believe that we should be people who don't just wait for change but actually get up and cause it to happen, when we sense it's time for it. We are to be God's agents of change that look to the future and don't just do things because they have always been done a certain way; a people who embrace change, not resist it; a people who actually enjoy change because they have seen the fruit and new life it can produce.

What situation are you in at the moment that needs you to stop waiting for change and get up and create some? What is that thing that you know God has been highlighting and trying to get you to look at through new eyes? What is that old thing or season it's time to leave, and that new opportunity you need to courageously run towards?

Sometimes we have to sit and wait for certain things and people to change, but other times we don't and God is actually waiting for us to get some gumption, get to our feet and cause the change, to be an agent of change for Him.

Go for it, Champion! If you don't like what is happening in your life, get God's wisdom and make some changes.

Change in your mind

Do not conform to the pattern of this world, but be transformed by the renewing of your mind. Then you will be able to test and approve what God's will is — His good, pleasing and perfect will.

Romans 12:2 (NIV)

We have been speaking a lot about change, looking at how we handle change when it comes into our lives and what we do when we actually need to create change.

I believe the most effective change that can take place and cause true transformation in a person's life is when change is made in your thinking – that moment when you dare to get 'out of the box' of thinking in a certain way, especially if that box is a non-truth-based one. You see, when genuine change occurs in a person's heart and in a person's mind it then causes that person's life to go in new directions they never dreamed possible in a sustainable way.

Change taking place in the way a person's 'thought life' is, I believe, the truest definition of New Testament repentance. There are two different words that are commonly used for repentance: one is found mostly in the Old Testament and that is *nacham* and normally relates to being 'mournfully sorrowful' or filled with remorse. This is a very emotionally driven type repentance that does not produce much more than sorrow. The other type of repentance that is the one mostly used in the New Testament is *metanoia*. This word means to 'change your mind or to change the way you think'.

Effective New Testament repentance is when your thought life is presented with a better kingdom-based option and you dare to go with it; not that you don't feel bad for things you may have done but rather you more importantly see a new way forward and dare to make the needed changes to embrace it. In doing so you set your life on a new flight plan for that area of your life.

When we allow God to bring change into our thinking, serious redirection to better and bigger things can begin. When we allow His wisdom to challenge the wrong philosophies we may have believed a freedom can break out that is second to none and lasting. A lot of the changes that come into our world are external and we have to make choices either to go with them or not, but there are also many changes that happen within that place nobody else sees – in your mind. It's these changes that can be the most productive, like when a person finally gets sick and tired about feeling sick and tired about something, maybe like living in debt or an on-going addiction, and finally makes some radical choices to change behaviour patterns that keep creating the same undesired effects. It's then that things that are no longer wanted, like a debt-ridden lifestyle or addictive behaviour patterns, are finally walked away from and a new storyline can begin.

What thinking is God trying to get you to change or update? What wisdom from God is challenging a wrong belief within your present thinking, maybe in one you inherited? Champion, go with God; apply God's Word; change the way you think and watch the way your life changes direction for good.

THE WORD

**As your words came to me I drank them in, and they
filled my heart with joy and happiness because I
belong to you.**
Jeremiah 15:16 (NET)

God's Word is so very powerful. Even one verse can change your life beyond recognition, if
you allow that small seed into your heart and mind.

Today, choose one scripture from God's Word. Maybe there's an area of your life you would
like to see some positive change. Find a scripture regarding your situation. Write this
verse down below, or on a piece of paper. You 'artsy' types can really go to town and
make it all fancy! Non-artsy types, fear not – the Word of God is just as powerful without
little flowers and butterflies drawn around it!

Stick this scripture to your wall or wherever you will see it all weekend. Read it often. Say
it out loud. Close your eyes and think carefully about the words you have read.
Remember, these are God's words; His very thoughts and intentions for you. Allow the
Word to wash over you and to bring about His life in your heart and mind.

Scripture

_____

_____

_____

_____

_____

_____

One more night with the pigs?

But when he came to himself, he said, 'How many of my father's hired servants have bread enough and to spare, and I perish with hunger! I will arise and go to my father, and will say to him, "Father, I have sinned against heaven and before you, and I am no longer worthy to be called your son. Make me like one of your hired servants."' And he arose and came to his father.

Luke 15:17-20

Here we see the journey of the wayward child in the parable Jesus told called The Lost Son. We join him at a very important point of his journey. Briefly to recap, he had left his home, against his father's advice, lost and squandered everything he owned, and ended up living with the pigs at a farm he worked at and was so hungry he wanted to eat the pigs' food. Oh, how the story had not turned out like he had planned. Bottom line was, he now realised he was wrong and that he had made a series of dumb choices that created some terrible changes and consequences in his life.

It's great that he finally came to his right mind – which means he finally lost his wrong one – and that he had this moment of realisation, but nothing was actually any different for him. He was still with the pigs, away from his father, so hungry that he wanted to eat pig food. A couple of things would have to now happen to cause the changes he needed in the life he now lived. One was that he would have to do something about his realisation – it alone was not enough, he had to put some actions to it. Good intentions are nice but they don't achieve much.

Watch what he does: he makes a choice to embrace the change. He changes his thinking and says, 'I will arise.' Enough thinking about it, let's do it. He then makes a plan of what he will say to his father. After that he does something that really starts the ball rolling: 'He arose and went to his father.' He put legs on his desire for change, became an agent of change, stepped out of the pigsty and walked towards the future he actually really wanted.

Think about it: if he had not allowed change to start in his mind and then not had the courage to act on it, he would have stayed another night with the pigs, then another night, and ... you guessed it, another one too. He probably would have died with the pigs and with his un-acted-upon realisation. No, this young man acted on it and, as you read on, his whole life from that point experienced grace and got better and better, beyond what he ever could have imagined.

The lesson today is, if you are in a place you do not want to be, and know what you need to do to change it, get up, get out and start moving towards where you know you should be. It's never too late to make a change; every new journey starts with one step.

Prayer

Father, I pray that You will give me the wisdom and courage to make the changes in my life that will help me to live the life You have planned for me. Forgive me for the things I have done to hinder my own journey, and by Your grace give me the next step to take in fulfilling my God-given destiny.

Amen

Your God will fight your fights

He said: 'Listen, King Jehoshaphat and all who live in Judah and Jerusalem! This is what the LORD says to you: "Do not be afraid or discouraged because of this vast army. For the battle is not yours, but God's. Tomorrow march down against them. They will be climbing up by the Pass of Ziz, and you will find them at the end of the gorge in the Desert of Jeruel. You will not have to fight this battle. Take up your positions; stand firm and see the deliverance the LORD will give you, O Judah and Jerusalem. Do not be afraid; do not be discouraged. Go out to face them tomorrow, and the Lord will be with you."'

2 Chronicles 20:15-17 (NIV)

Hey, Champion, if you are facing a big problem or a situation that makes you feel somewhat 'out-numbered' draw your hope from these verses today. The promises of God to King Jehoshaphat are the same promises to you today in Christ.

Here is some real good advice if you are facing something that needs a win:

1. Don't be afraid or discouraged because of the vastness of the situation; just remember, your God is bigger!

2. Remember you're a covenant kid. The battle is not yours, it is God's; so, by faith, tag Him and let Him in the wrestling ring of this situation or fight.

3. Remember, you will not have to do the fighting but you do need to turn up and position yourself for a win. Why turn up? You need to position yourself so you can see the deliverance of your God. You won't be able to see how incredible God's deliverance is if you're hiding behind a rock of fear.

4. Finally, we are reminded again not to let fear be the atmosphere of our lives or this present situation, but faith (child-like trust in God). Turn up for the fight knowing what your problem does not know – God Almighty is on your side and has made your fight His fight!

Take these keys today and apply them to your situation, and as you do you will see that the God who was for King Jehoshaphat is the God who is for you, too.

Go fight that battle and win it, without fighting!

Good deeds are not done by walking into a church. They are done when you walk out of the church and help others.

Unknown

Deal with the hand, not the puppet

Then Peter took Him aside and began to rebuke Him, saying, 'Far be it from You, Lord; this shall not happen to You!' But He turned and said to Peter, 'Get behind Me, satan! You are an offence to Me, for you are not mindful of the things of God, but the things of men.'

Matthew 16:22-23

This can seem a very strange thing for Jesus to do, if you don't fully understand what was happening; especially as this very fierce rebuke came just seconds after Jesus had commended the same guy for having a revelation that He was the Christ. To fully understand what was happening, you need to see who Jesus was actually rebuking or dealing with. Many have interpreted this portion in different ways – I look at it this way: Peter was just the puppet; he was unknowingly being used to say something that was contrary to the heaven-sent plans that were directing the life of Jesus. He was not possessed by satan but was unknowingly allowing some suggestions or very subtle thoughts of satan to be voiced through his mouth, making him the puppet not the actual originator of the problem-induced words.

Notice Jesus does not say, 'Get lost, Peter.' He says, 'Get behind me, satan' – He was speaking to the voice of His enemy that was subtlety using one of His team to direct Him off course. Read on – directly after this encounter it is as if nothing had happened and He continues to teach His team more stuff, including Peter who must have still been in shock.

The lesson here is to always know and be spiritually discerning when it comes to the guiding voice of God in your life, and also to know when it is not the voice of God speaking words of direction to you. In the same way that Jesus experienced, it is amazing how people who are close to us can sometimes be the ones who, through lack of understanding or revelation, say something that could potential take you off course or cause you to doubt something you should not.

What do we do when this happens? The same as Jesus: look beyond the (puppet) person and consider what spirit is actually in operation with an alternative agenda to that of God's. Remember, the Bible says we wrestle not with flesh and blood but with principalities and powers (Ephesians 6:12), which means if we punch the person who is speaking we have so missed the point. We need to deal with what is going on beyond the person involved.

The devil is like a snake, he will always try and slip into the ear of people whose hearts are set on doing something for God. When it comes to whom he will try and use he is no respecter of persons and will use those close to you to say the most destiny-disturbing things. The shock comes when they are really close, like Peter was to Jesus. When that happens you must remember not to fall out of love with the person but realise they do not know the weight of the statements and thoughts they are sharing. Equally I would hold back from staring at them and telling them to 'Get behind me, satan' – that's never good for keeping friends! It worked for Jesus but it may not work so well for you. I would deal with it spiritually, away from the person, around the corner. I would say, 'satan, you filthy liar, get out of here, you are not knocking me off track.' I can't say that I would never say it to the person, but would be very careful who it was if I did. I heard once of a man who used to say that to his wife – listen, that will never produce a happy home, be wise!

So the lesson today: be a sheep that knows the shepherd's voice. When you hear another voice don't always accept it because you recognise the puppet speaking. Take all things back to God's Word and wise council, and you will always walk in the right and God-designed direction.

Prayer

Heavenly Father, I pray that You will give me discerning ears today. Help me to know when it is You speaking and encouraging me and when the voice of the enemy is speaking discouragement or distraction into my life. I want to be wise in choosing people whom I trust will speak God's Word to me in season, and I want to be strong enough to dismiss the voice of the enemy when I recognise it.

Amen

A revelation of our inability leads us to a revelation of His ability now within us, in which we find everything we need.

Andy Elmes

Join in the 'tug of war' for your kids

Train up a child in the way he should go, and when he is old he will not depart from it.

Proverbs 22:6

This one goes out to the parents.

Question: who is training your kids? I want to encourage you today to continue to put good time and effort into raising your kids up to love God and understand His ways. Church programmes should only compliment, never replace, the godly input and standards you provide in the home life of your kids. You need to see yourself working together with the children's church programmes in your church, working with them hand-in-hand during the week to balance off the wrong things that your kids are being exposed to each and every day of their lives.

Oh, how innocently we can wave our kids goodbye when they go to school each morning, not fully realising how things have changed since we went and how the pull of wickedness is greater than what we knew, while the discipline is ever less. If only we could see for ourselves what and whom we are releasing our kids into to be trained, it would certainly make you think twice.

I once used this following example as a visual message to our church. Imagine a tug-of-war rope: on one side is the ungodly influences that your child is exposed to in any given week – think what that looks like: teachers teaching good stuff but also a lot of error about God and life with subjects that promote evolution over creation and alternative lifestyle as the norm; the music they listen to; the stuff they watch on TV; their mobile gadgets – these gadgets also providing them with a mostly unmonitored, open access to the world wide web; then there is the peer pressure that comes as they do life with kids that come from often ungodly, confused and messed up homes, again defining for them what is really good, fun and normal; what about the magazines and shows that bombard them with images of what is cool; the movies with their ever-decreasing moral standards that come to train your kids for you concerning what is normal and acceptable when it comes to morality, bad language and violence.

But what about the other side of the rope, the end which represents God's influence on their life on a weekly basis? Oh, it's OK, isn't it? You take them to church for two hours a week and let them go to Kids' Church and Youth. Think about it: two hours out of 168 every week. Visualise that for a moment – that's like a rugby team on one side with two children's church workers on the other. Parent, it's simply not enough if you really want your children to go God's way. We have to be active Christian parents who lead our kids to Jesus and His ways in our homes throughout those 168 hours of each and every week. They simply won't be trained up effectively in God's ways without you being the godly parent you need to be!

Make the decision, if you haven't already, that you will not leave the God bit to the church workers, but rather you will be proactively working with them during the week, teaching your kids about God's ways, praying with them, talking to them about the stuff they see at school and modelling the God life for them.

Don't wait until it's too late!

Live to give God the best

But the king replied to Araunah, 'No, I insist on paying you for it. I will not sacrifice to the LORD my God burnt offerings that cost me nothing.'

2 Samuel 24:24 (NIV)

King David was looking for a threshing floor to build an altar to God for worship so that he could break the plague that was on his people (read chapter 24 if this needs more explanation). He approaches Araunah to ask if he can buy what he needs and Araunah offers him everything he needs for absolutely nothing (read verses 21-23). Many of us would have thought, 'What a great bargain, I got that cheap!' But not David; he actually refuses to not pay. Why? Because of his revelation of worship: he knew that worship was all about giving your best, not what you have left or got cheaply.

Whenever David gave (worshipped) the Lord anything he always gave Him the very best – whether it was time, energy, song or finance. His worship was always based on God's worth to him. That is why he never held back. God meant everything to him.

How about us? Would we take the bargain offer? When it comes to us worshipping the Lord with who we are and what we have, will we give the bare minimum or what is considered normal, or will we be extroverts of worship, like David?

I suppose the only thing we need to really consider, to determine the measure of our worship response, is what God gave to us in Jesus. Did He hold back or give second best? No, Jesus was the very best and He gave Him for us, which again leaves us with a due response. Purpose in your heart that, like David, you won't give God songs, offerings, service or anything that costs you nothing. As you do, you set yourself up for a very blessed life.

Have a great day and don't hold back. Give the King the worship He deserves and not what you got cheap or had left over. When giving to God always remember: if you feel a seed leave your life you will always feel the harvest when it comes back.

We love to fill buildings, He loves to fill people and then send them into the world to turn it upside down.

Andy Elmes

FEED OTHERS

Jesus answered, "It is written: 'Man shall not live on bread alone, but on every word that comes from the mouth of God.'"

Matthew 4:4 (NIV)

This weekend, pray for someone you know, maybe a friend or a family member. Ask God to give you a verse from His Word that will encourage, inspire, or bring peace to them or whatever else they may need. Write this verse of scripture down in a card or on a piece of paper, along with a note telling them that you were praying for them and that you feel God gave you this verse for them. Maybe a card is not your style and you would rather send a text or an email. Go right on ahead and do that.

Allow yourself to be used by God to bring the sustenance of His Word to others. Have a beautiful weekend!

Notes

_____

_____

_____

_____

_____

_____

Look up

Then He came to Bethsaida; and they brought a blind man to Him, and begged Him to touch him. So He took the blind man by the hand and led him out of the town. And when He had spit on his eyes and put His hands on him, He asked him if he saw anything. And he looked up and said, 'I see men like trees, walking.' Then He put His hands on his eyes again and made him look up. And he was restored and saw everyone clearly.

Mark 8:22-25

This was always one of my favourite stories when I was a kid; I think it was the 'spit in the eye' bit that caught my attention and always made me smile. Once again we see Jesus being 'out of the box' and very unconventional when it came to how He chose to help this man, and I know for sure the blind man never saw that coming! He never imagined in his wildest dreams the miracle he needed would involve someone who claimed to be God's Son spitting in his face!

But notice before the spitting took place, the first thing Jesus did was lead him out from where he was presently at. If you are believing God for a miracle or breakthrough in your life the first thing you may have to change is your location. I am not necessarily talking about a physical location but other places our lives can be presently located at. Among other things this could mean coming out from where you are at in your thinking, your expectations and beliefs. For example, if you do not believe God heals today you may need to leave that place of unbelief and let Him position you somewhere new, so He can do what He wants to do for you.

I believe that Jesus could not do what He wanted to do where the man was currently at. Maybe the thing that is holding up what God wants to do in your life is where you presently are – maybe it's not your faith or thinking but something else, like unforgiveness, or jealousy, a bad attitude or even small thinking. Just as Jesus had a breakthrough in mind for this blind man that day, He has one in store for you. Let His Spirit lead you out of where you do not need to be anymore; let Him position you where you need to be so He can do what He wants to do. Remember also, it says He led him out – at this point the man was still blind and could not see where he needed to go, so he placed his hands in the hand of Jesus and allowed Him to lead him into a correct position. Today, God's Spirit is that same hand extended to each of us, offering the same assistance. Pray today, 'Lord, lead me to where You need me to be so that You can do what You have planned to do for me.' I know He will. Let's carry this thought on tomorrow.

Look up
CONTINUED

Then He came to Bethsaida; and they brought a blind man to Him, and begged Him to touch him. So He took the blind man by the hand and led him out of the town. And when He had spit on his eyes and put His hands on him, He asked him if he saw anything. And he looked up and said, 'I see men like trees, walking.' Then He put His hands on his eyes again and made him look up. And he was restored and saw everyone clearly.

Mark 8:22-25

So Jesus leads this man out and then prays for him to receive the miracle of sight that he desperately needed. Notice that He actually does this in two stages: it does not happen fully straight away but in two individual moments. Firstly, it says that the man looked up and, as he did, he saw, 'men like trees, walking'. This means he saw a bit clearer but not yet with perfect clarity; things seemed clearer than they did before but not perfect. I am so glad Jesus didn't say, 'Well, there you go; it's better than what you had before, right?' No, He took the man by the head and 'made him look up', and as he did the man's clarity of sight became perfect; he no longer saw shadows moving but clear and precise images with fully restored vision.

What I learn from this is that when you look up things become clearer; when you keep looking up they get perfectly clear!

Making the choice, like this man did, to look up and see Jesus in your situation is a choice we all need to make daily. Though we may not be physically blind, sometimes it can feel like we have lost our vision for life and cannot see the way forward, in the way we used to. In these times the best thing we can do is 'look up', and then keep looking up! As with this blind man, when you first look up to Jesus things begin to get a bit clearer – but God does not want you to settle for that, He wants you to keep looking up till you see all things perfectly clear.

Hey, Champion, will you let Jesus take you by the hand today and cause you to look up again? Don't settle for 'slightly better' vision for your life or the situation you may be going through – keep looking up to Jesus until things are as clear as can be and you can see the way forward for yourself. Jesus led this man when he could not see the way forward for himself, but then He restored him so that he could. When he came to Jesus he could not see a thing; after spending some time with Jesus things looked clearer; but after gazing on Him he had 20-20 vision and could now walk on his own.

He is still the lifter of our heads.

Prayer

Good morning, Lord. Help me today to look up and see You in the things that I face. Help me not to look at the things around me but at you, as I set my gaze on you Lord cause the things that don't seem clear to become clearer.

Amen

Keep looking up

My voice You shall hear in the morning, O Lord; in the morning I will direct it to You, and I will look up.

Psalm 5:3

---

*L*et's continue with our thoughts on 'Look up'. If you want to walk in breakthrough in your life you need to make the decision that daily you will intentionally look up! In today's text we hear David talking about his personal lifestyle for doing this: he basically says in this Psalm, 'Every morning, God, I will talk to You and I will make the decision to look up and see You.' This choice set him up to live an overcoming life, and this daily choice will set you up for one too. You have three choices as to where you look each day: you can look down, look around or look up.

When you look down all the time you can trip over your own feet and you can become despondent because you do not see anything ahead, just the moment you're in. This is not healthy.

When you look around it is better, but still not good enough, because when you look around you just see what is currently happening and the people around. The problem is that people can't help you like God can – people do not understand what you are going through like God does. Also, when you look around you see what others have and what you don't, and what others have and you need, and this can – among other things – cause frustration and jealousy.

No, your best choice is to look up and see Jesus and see what He says about your life and future. This is where hope is born and faith rises.

I recently had to get new glasses and moved from reading glasses to what they call varifocals. These are glasses that enable you to see three different things with only one pair, to stop you having to change your glasses all the time. These new glasses took some getting used to but really exemplify what I am saying today. When I looked down I could see what I was reading or concentrating on very clearly. When I looked straight ahead they enabled me to see the larger moment I was in clearer. But when I looked up my long distance vision was empowered and I could see what was coming very clearly. I soon noticed it was actually dangerous to walk around looking down because things were too magnified! I could easily trip over because they looked too close or too big. Looking forward is very clear, helping me to function with day-to-day stuff, seeing things clearer. But when I look up through the top of the glasses, everything I am walking towards is now so very clear.

It's the same for us all – when it comes to walking through life it is when you choose to look up that the things in your life and future will become clear again. Do what David did and make the choice every morning to talk to God and to look up!

Look higher

I will lift up my eyes to the hills – from whence comes my help? My help comes from the LORD, Who made heaven and earth. He will not allow your foot to be moved; He who keeps you will not slumber.

Psalm 121:1-3

Often you just need to make the decision to tilt your head a little higher to enable you to see what you need to see.

Notice in today's text where the question mark is positioned. The writer of this psalm first asks a question and then makes a statement of his belief. He starts by asking the question, 'Where does my help come from, the hills?' Looking to the hills is certainly looking up but the problem is, it's not looking high enough! He then says, 'No, I choose to look higher than the hills – I look to God because He made everything.'

Maybe you are in a time of need – what could 'the hills' represent to you? They could represent a number of things: things that are not bad or evil, just not as good as God. Things that maybe offer you a measurement of help or future for the situation you are in; maybe the hills are the promises of people. We've all seen this at one time or another – people promise you things and you then set your hope in their promise, but then maybe they forget or are unable to follow through with what they said they would do, and you are left feeling abandoned or ripped off.

Maybe your 'hill' is your job or employer; then one day the job is taken away and you are replaced. There are many things that we can naturally lift our eyes to, trying to find the help and security we need, but none of them can guarantee what God can: that He is the only one who can offer a permanent successful future. Most other permanence that is promised by people, even those close to us, actually is just mere illusion – they have no guarantees, people die, people don't follow through, relationships and jobs change. No, the only true permanence you can know and build on in your life is God and His promises for your life.

So today, Champion, don't settle for just looking to the hills (people, employment and other momentary things) – rather look higher, tilt your head even more and look to the Timeless One who keeps His promises and covenants from generation to generation; the One who made heaven and earth; the One who will not allow your foot to be moved, who keeps you and will not slumber.

Keep looking up, even when you think you can't

For innumerable evils have surrounded me; my iniquities have overtaken me, so that I am not able to look up; they are more than the hairs of my head; therefore my heart fails me.

Psalm 40:12

This whole week we have been speaking about making the choice to look up; to always make sure we are always looking high enough, looking to the One who offers true permanence, security and future: Jesus.

We are to make looking up our lifestyle – something we do in every season. Not just when things are going well and it's easy to do, but when things are not going so well and it takes effort to do so; when the storms are beating against the boat of your life and everything in you wants to stare at the ocean of problems that is besetting you. No, Champion, these are the times when, more than any other time or season, we need to look up and see Him because as we do He restores our current and long-distance vision to see beyond the storm to better days.

The writer of the psalm in our text today obviously had these very real moments too, moments where he felt overtaken by problems. Moments where problems were too many to even count, where it felt like his heart would fail him because of what he had to face. We have all been there – the worst thing you can do in these moments or seasons is to look down. If you look down you will stay down. The best thing to do is, by faith, look up. Stare again into the face of Him who calms every storm.

Like we said earlier this week, looking down won't help you it will only magnify the horror of the present moment you are in. Looking around won't help you – people may be able to help for a mere moment but what you really need comes from Him who is seated higher than the hills of natural assistance. No, you have to look up, even in the midst of storms. It can feel so unnatural to do this, which is why it needs to be a spiritual decision, not an emotional one.

Jesus will always help you to lift your head when He sees you have the heart to do so. Let Him help you to lift your head so that your eyes can see beyond the moment you are in to better things and peaceful shores. Don't quit – look up! Even concerning the end of the world and the return of Christ to collect His people, we are instructed to not look around but look up. Let's live our lives with eyes set on the Author and Finisher of our faith, in every situation we may face.

Now when these things begin to happen, look up and lift up your heads, because your redemption draws near.

Luke 21:28

YOUR STORY FOR HIS GLORY

They triumphed over him by the blood of the Lamb and
by the word of their testimony; they did not love their
lives so much as to shrink from death.
Revelation 12:11

Your testimony is very important; the story of how you came to be a follower of Christ. It is
a story of redemption and how God came into your life and rewrote your story for His glory.

Take time this weekend to recall how you came to know the Lord and write below the
highlights of your redemption story from the time you met Him to where you are today.

We have a site called iamredemption.org where we publish people's redemption stories to
encourage others that God is still in the business of changing lives. Feel free to send
your 350-word testimony to **info@iamredemption.org**. We cannot make any promises, but
we may publish the ones that we feel would be of particular encouragement to others.

Enjoy your weekend!

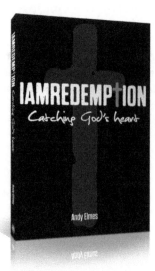

Visit
iamredemption.org
for testimonies and stories, resources and training,
and merchandise.
iamredemption, by Andy Elmes, available from
iamredemption.org and
greatbiglifepublishing.com for £6.99
ISBN 978-0-9928027-4-5, Great Big Life Publishing

We are still a Commissioned People

And Jesus came and spoke to them, saying, 'All authority has been given to Me in heaven and on earth. Go therefore and make disciples of all the nations, baptising them in the name of the Father and of the Son and of the Holy Spirit, teaching them to observe all things that I have commanded you; and lo, I am with you always, even to the end of the age.' Amen.

Matthew 28:18-20

*L*et us never forget that we are still a commissioned people.

Two thousand years ago, when Jesus said to that first-century primitive church, 'Go,' He was speaking to us too. It was not a momentary commission given to an individual church in a specific generation, but rather the marching orders for His church through all generations. It was and is a commission intended to remain as a central heartbeat to who we are until His return.

This Great Commission should still be one of the fundamental priorities and concerns of the twenty-first-century church – not just its leaders or the eccentric few but the whole body. We must realise that the Great Commission mattered to Jesus so it needs to matter to us.

Indeed, we are living in times when the church in the West desperately needs to be mobilised again. So much of our modern entertainment-based Christianity, instead of mobilising the saints, has left them comfortably seated without any intention of reaching out to others with the love of God's message, the gospel. A spiritual alarm clock is ringing – it's time for us to stop being seated so comfortably, arise from finding such fulfilment sitting on our 'blessed assurance' and get busy again about the Father's business. The Father's business always involves people being reached and souls being saved.

A Canadian missionary called Oswald J. Smith put it very well when he said, 'Any church that is not seriously involved in helping fulfil the Great Commission has forfeited its Biblical right to exist.'

Let me underline again that the Great Commission was never the Great Suggestion! It was something that Jesus was very serious and passionate about. He wanted His church to be a people that go, that live beyond themselves to the reaching and saving of others. Notice that He did not give this commission to angels; He gave it to His Body. I have seen Christians get pretty wacky when it comes to teaching on angels, and we always need to keep a good biblical balance in how we teach such things. But I have also seen many Christians living like the Commission was given to angels and not to them, living in omission rather than commission to this divine mandate and calling. No, the responsibility for reaching this world with the saving gospel of Jesus was never given to a gathering of angels but to us, His church, and it remains the responsibility of you and me.

So let us arise with a new passion when it comes to this two-thousand-year-old commission, given by the One who saved our souls. Let us lay aside every fear and excuse and join the ranks of the Army of the Lord, busy again carrying Him wherever He desires to go. Whether it is in the workplace or school, to the down-and-outs or the rich and famous, whatever world God has placed you in, remember that He has given you the mandate and commission to reach the people in that world for Him: 'GO.'

Commissioned and empowered

But you shall receive power when the Holy Spirit has come upon you; and you shall be witnesses to Me in Jerusalem, and in all Judea and Samaria, and to the end of the earth.

Acts 1:8

When Jesus commissioned His church to 'Go', He also empowered His church to 'Go'. Jesus never had any intention of sending us into the world merely in our own strength and ability – rather He always had a plan to empower us with His divine ability so that we would be fully equipped and have everything we needed to do what He had called us to do, and to be the witnesses He desired us to be.

He said, 'You shall receive power when the Holy Spirit has come upon you.' Let us just ask another fundamental question: why was this power given?

Was it so that we could experience goose bumps in our meetings? Was it so we could play power games in our services and experience tingles in our worship? It's not that any of these things are wrong – I also love to feel God's Spirit moving in meetings – but we must remember the primary purpose for the giving of the Spirit's power: that we would be empowered to be His witnesses in our Jerusalems, Judeas and End-of-the-Earths!

Notice the very next thing Jesus mentions after telling of the empowering of the Spirit – that we will be witnesses for Him. Let us never forget this primary reason for the giving of the Spirit's power. The good news is that when you decide you are going to stand up in your world for the one who saved your soul you can have an inner confidence that He will back you up and give you everything you need to do it effectively.

What an incredible thought! He is not expecting us to represent Him in our own strength or ability, but rather He has provided an empowerment to accompany the commission He has given us. The reality is you won't feel it until you purpose to be a witness. Many Christians want to feel everything before they do anything; in my experience that is not how God works. Everything He does is triggered by, or involves, faith. The reality is it's when we dare to step out, believing in what He has promised, that we see His promise come into manifestation and effect.

It's when you daily purpose to live a missionary life for Him in your local world, as well as further afield, and leave your home to be a witness for Him – ready to seize every opportunity and divine appointment He gives you – that you can have a righteous expectancy of His accompanying power. In those moments when you don't know what to say, He will give you the perfect words. In those moments when you need to see His power move in a person's life, you will see His power move. In those times when you need divine courage to make your stand, from deep within it will suddenly be there in abundance.

He has called us to go – but also given us everything we need to go. So Go!

His blessings come without sorrow

The blessing of the LORD makes one rich, and He adds no sorrow with it.

Proverbs 10:22

*L*et's face it – everyone wants to be blessed, right?

But when pursuing blessing, make sure you go after the blessing that comes from God and not just that which you arrange yourself. Why? Because His blessing has no sorrow attached to it.

When it comes to blessing it is so easy to go off in a couple of directions. You can walk the path of reason and try to make it happen yourself, or you walk the path of faith and simply trust in the promises God gives regarding His blessing, and with faithful diligence and patience see Him bring them to pass in your life.

When God gives you a promise of blessing, He intends to make it happen in His strength and timing. Believe me, if He needed your help, He would ask! What He actually wants us to do is wait and watch Him bring it to pass. My experience has been that, whenever I became too involved in making a blessing happen in my life, it normally brought with it an element of sorrow or trouble. But when God blesses no sorrow accompanies it.

Think of Abraham, the one who is called the father of faith. He gives us a perfect example of the reality of this truth. God steps into his world and, among other blessings, promises him what his heart truly desires: a child. What did God want him to do? Simple: faithfully wait for it. What did he do? Exactly what many of us have done: he decided to help God out to make the blessing come or exist. So, after making a plan with his wife he sleeps with Hagar, the maidservant of his wife, and he produces a child. The child was called Ishmael and certainly looked and sounded like the blessing God had promised, but the reality was it was not. It was man-made, the produce of reason not faith.

So baby Ishmael is born – there is probably a big party, everyone is happy, and Abraham thinks he has received what God promised. But then another child is born miraculously – Isaac – and he soon realises that God had always had another plan. When you read on, from that moment you see that the blessing he had produced (Ishmael) actually became a great sorrow, not just to him but to generations and nations that were yet to come.

It did not have to be like that. If Abraham had just patiently waited for the blessing that God had promised he would have had a blessing that had no sorrow accompanying it.

How about you? Have you, like Abraham, received promises from God concerning blessing in your life? Do they also seem like they are taking their time? What are you going to do? Will you help God out and have a blessing that has an element of sorrow and management attached to it, or wait patiently with confidence for God to bring into existence the blessing He intends for your life, blessing that will make you rich and will add no sorrow to you?

Things we should not forget

Then I saw a great white throne and Him who sat on it, from whose face the earth and the heaven fled away. And there was found no place for them. And I saw the dead, small and great, standing before God, and books were opened. And another book was opened, which is the Book of Life. And the dead were judged according to their works, by the things which were written in the books. The sea gave up the dead who were in it, and Death and Hades delivered up the dead who were in them. And they were judged, each one according to his works. Then Death and Hades were cast into the lake of fire. This is the second death. And anyone not found written in the Book of Life was cast into the lake of fire.

Revelation 20:11-15

Recently God in His goodness reminded me of some things that I had forgotten, or lost a correct perspective and understanding of. Maybe it was because of the busyness of modern church life or maybe just the often self-centred busyness of life itself. For whatever reason, I had become distracted – and God felt it was time to remind me of a couple of things that would jump start my passion for seeing souls saved in a more profound way than ever I had known. What were these things He wanted to remind me of? Simple: a white throne, a book of life and a lake of fire.

The truth was, something about this all-singing, all-dancing Christianity of the 21st century had caused me to lose a realistic viewpoint of some things beyond this life that carry eternal consequence for both the people I know and love and those I am yet to meet. I am not wanting to preach 'hellfire and brimstone' to you this morning, just bring you back, as God did me, to the reality of what is taught in the book of Revelation concerning what awaits a person beyond the life they now live on earth. It's indeed a very sobering thought to take a fresh look at these facts. I believe sobering enough to even awaken our hearts to a fresh passion for reaching the lost friends and family in our worlds for Christ before it is too late.

This text in Revelation teaches us that when a person's life is spent, or Christ returns, Christians will stand before God to give an account for how they spent their lives and the things and talents entrusted to them. This judgement is a reward-based one that carries no punishment of hell because faith placed in Christ's divine exchange removed every penalty of hell and death; but we will be accountable and rewarded for how we lived for God and what our lives produced – or indeed, didn't – for His kingdom while we lived.

But then we read of a white throne judgement that determines where a person will spend their eternity, namely heaven or hell. What will purpose the eternal destination of a person's life will be whether their name is in the Lamb's Book of Life or not. Their destination will not be based on what they have done, owned or achieved in life, but simply on whether they acknowledged and received Jesus as Saviour in their life. For those who did, an eternity with God awaits where there is no more pain and every tear is wiped away. But for those whose names are not in this Book, a lake of fire and a second death of never-ending torment will become an eternal and inescapable reality. When the trumpet blast has sounded and the Book is opened there will be no place for turning things around or changing minds or opinions. What is, will be for all eternity.

I don't know about you but when I read this passage I find new resolutions springing up within me.

1. I want to live for heaven's rewards, not earth's momentary comforts of applause.

2. I want to get everyone I know named in that Book of Life

3. I want to stop as many people going into that lake as possible so, one day, when this prophetic vision becomes a reality, I am not left saying, 'If only, if only, if only.'

Today, live in the light of eternity, my friend. Live with praise in your heart that your name is in the Lamb's Book of Life and that lake of fire has no claim on you; but also let a passion for souls rise within you. Speak to people about our Saviour Jesus, while you still can.

Prayer

Heavenly Father, help me to remain conscious of these important things today; let me keep them as a priority in my life and for the lives of others. Give me the boldness I need to speak when I should. Let me live in the light of eternity and may my life cause many other entries in the Lamb's Book of Life. Amen

Pentecost was never meant to be a moment or a meeting but a new lifestyle, a whole new way of life.

Andy Elmes

He wants none to perish

The Lord is not slow in keeping his promise, as some understand slowness. Instead he is patient with you, not wanting anyone to perish, but everyone to come to repentance.

2 Peter 3:9-10 (NIV)

*Y*esterday we spoke about the sobering truths revealed in the book of Revelation regarding what happens when a person's life is finally spent. We spoke about the white throne and how, if a person's name is not found in the Lamb's Book of Life, they will be thrown into a lake of fire. These things are a reality that should inspire us to see the soul of man saved.

But we need to understand in all of this that God's heart is that none would perish. He does not want to throw anyone into a lake of fire; rather He is longing that people's names would be in the Book of Life.

You have to understand God's redemptive heart when reading any part or book of the Bible – that God wants no one to go to hell, and sends no one but satan . If a person goes to hell after death it is because they chose to reject Jesus as God's Son and their Saviour. I believe the Father heart of God for the creation He loves and sent His Son to redeem will do everything to give each person more than enough opportunity to hear of Him and receive Him as Lord.

On that day when judgement is carried out, heaven won't be laughing, and the Father will not be in delight. Rather He will watch on as people that should have been in eternity with Him get cast into something so terribly different, when it did not need to happen – if only they would have placed their faith in His Son. It is not God's will that any should perish but all would come to the knowledge of His saving grace, and through repentance enter into a better inheritance.

Recently, when the Lord began to underline these things afresh to me, I wondered how I would communicate them to my wife Gina in a way she would understand. I was actually in hospital at the time, and the next day when she visited I began to tell her how God was speaking to me about souls going to hell and how we needed to live to see more people saved. Gina interrupted me and told me of a dream she had had the night before. Bear in mind that Gina rarely dreams, so that in itself was a God thing! In this dream God gave her a very clear picture of what the judgement moment would be like for God the Father.

In this dream she saw a big white room with a fire burning hot. She was conscious of the presence of a father and a child. She then heard the child say, 'Dad, this is going to burn, isn't it? Dad, please, I don't want to go into the fire.' She then heard the father respond with tears, 'Son, it will burn but there is nothing I can do,' She heard in his voice sadness and sorrow and the sense that he had no ability to intervene even though he loved the child dearly. The father kept saying, 'I can't do anything to change the choices you made while you were able.' She became aware that the child was going into the fire because of its own choices, outside of the father's ability to help or change anything. But the father did not want the child to perish; there was sadness in his heart, not delight.

We need to understand that God has done everything He can through the giving of His own Son to stop anyone of His creation going into the fire, but He can't choose for them or violate their will. Every person must choose or reject the salvation that comes through the Son for themselves. What does God want? That none would perish.

What can we do? Carry daily a message of reconciliation and invitation, letting people know that God has made a way, through His Son, for everyone to escape hell and be entitled to heaven; that God is no longer angry with man and desires all to be saved. This commission that God has given us is one that brings eternal life and eternal redemption. Let's realise the power in the message we carry and not keep it a secret!

We need never shout across the spaces to an absent God. He is nearer than our own soul, closer than our most secret thoughts.

A. W. Tozer

Churches do not just need good leadership they need good 'followship' too.

Andy Elmes

DO SOMETHING YOU'VE NEVER DONE

I can do all things through Christ who strengthens me.
Philippians 4:13

This weekend why not try something that you have never done before?

Don't put limits on yourself, try something that you have always wanted to but for one reason or another you never did. There's a great big world outside your front door and you can go and discover something new in it. Maybe you've never tried an exercise class before or painted pottery. Write a poem, play tennis . . . the list is endless. What do you want to try? Invite a friend or a family member to join in.

Go for it!

Notes

_____

_____

_____

_____

_____

_____

_____

Do you feel at home with God?

Jesus answered and said to him, 'If anyone loves Me, he will keep My word; and My Father will love him, and We will come to him and make Our home with him.'

John 14:23

Do you want an intimate daily relationship with God or a vague acquaintance? Once again God leaves the choice with us. What will we settle for? What will we desire? God's desire is for you to know the intimacy and companionship of His presence daily, not just have a theological understanding of Him being 'ever present'. The Bible indeed teaches us the reality of His presence ever being with us when it says things like we are 'the temple of the Holy Spirit' (1 Corinthians 6:19), and 'I will never leave you nor forsake you' (Hebrews 13:5). But I suppose my question is: does God enjoy being in you and watching the life you choose to live? Is your life somewhere He owns (because He purchased you with His blood) or somewhere He likes to 'make home' in?

Notice what Jesus says that is needed concerning our lives being a place that He likes to make home in and not just have ownership of. Love Him, keep His word. In truth these things should be established in the life of every believer, but sadly sometimes they are not. Sometimes the distractions of life, and even modern-day Christianity, can leave you believing in Jesus but not intimately loving Him like maybe you first did. It's time to get that first love back, to make sure it remains the protected centrepiece of your life.

Again, when it comes to keeping His word, many people just keep the bits that are convenient or that fit well with the life they want to live. Jesus never said keep some of it or the bits you like; He wants you to keep all of it. He wants you to bring your life in alignment with His Word and not try and make the Word fit into the life you are choosing to live!

If you want to know the incredible, indescribable feeling of God making home with you it's simple: purpose to love Him more than any other and to make His word the final authority and guide for your life, in all things. Believe me, when you experience the intimacy of His companionship you will never want anything less. Mere ownership by Him pales in significance and you become protective of your inner home life with Him. When you have got God making home with you it naturally, irreligiously, un-legalistically affects what you do and how you live, because all of a sudden you don't want to lose the companionship and intimacy you have now gained. Believe me, it affects what you watch and what you do, whom you hang out with and so much more. Why? Because you become conscious of His intimate presence at home with you and you don't want anything or anyone to cause Him not to want to feel at home with you. Whatever you choose to lose will never compare to the richness of His intimate closeness.

Let me ask again, what do you want: vague acquaintance or intimate relationship and companionship?

Of His fullness we have received!

And of His fullness we have all received, and grace for grace. For the law was given through Moses, but grace and truth came through Jesus Christ.

John 1:16-17

What an incredible thought: of His (God's) fullness have we all received and do receive now daily. When did we first receive it? That moment we believed on, and received, Jesus as our Lord and Saviour. Never forget that when we believed in Jesus we became supernaturally born anew. At that exact moment we came to life as new creations in Him, no longer spiritually dead but eternally alive through Him and in Him; able to live a life that we could not live before, able to produce the righteous fruit He desires because of His divine nature and life flowing through the veins of our Christ-redeemed lives (2 Peter 1:4).

Now we are joined to Him we can expect what is in Him (His nature and life) to flow through us. Think about it: if you were to connect a limb to a body the life within the body would soon become the life within the limb. Through new birth we have been grafted into Him. Jesus once taught this in another way using a vine and its branches as a visual example to enable His disciples to understand the power of their union with Him.

> *I am the vine, you are the branches. He who abides in Me, and I in him, bears much fruit; for without Me you can do nothing.*
>
> John 15:5

Jesus taught what I have often called the 'divine order of existence' very simply because He wanted His disciples to understand the realities of where their life and potential originated from. Today we also need to rejoice in the realities of this truth. Two thousand years later, He is still the vine and we are still the branches. We are joined to Him through faith and our union with Him means that what flows through Him now desires to flow through us. It is this life and nature that springs from Him that produces the righteous fruit and lifestyle we now live.

How can we possibly add to this incredible truth except to say that we have not been grafted into or joined to some skinny, lifeless vine, but rather a healthy plump one that is bursting with life and potential? In Him there is no lack, only fullness, and today as you acknowledge that you are grafted into Him remember also that His fullness is your fullness too, and you can find all you need in Him.

When I was younger and not walking with the Lord I had a number of tattoos done. One of them was a joker on the calf of my right leg. When I had it done I was a slim young man and he was a slim joker, but now I am not as slim as I was then – guess what: neither is he. When people see him now I tell them that he is a lot bigger than he used to be, then I explain that 'of my fullness he has received'! My fullness has directly affected him because of his union to me.

As it teaches in Romans 11, at salvation we were broken from an old, wild tree that had death and lack in its very nature, and were grafted into a 'rich olive tree', which is Christ. Today your life is a branch in union with His very life and nature. He is full of everything good. Let that fullness flow again through you today and produce things you never thought were possible.

Prayer

Father, thank You that my life has been joined to You. I am a branch, Jesus is my vine. By faith alone have I been grafted in. Thank you that your life and nature is my life and nature, and today I can know your fullness again flowing in me and through me. Thank you for grace upon grace.

God created me—and you—to live with a single, all-embracing, all-transforming passion—namely, a passion to glorify God by enjoying and displaying his supreme excellence in all the spheres of life.

John Piper

The gospel was never meant to be a sedative that makes you rest, rather a stimulant that empowers you to live for a cause.

Andy Elmes

Bought with a price

Or do you not know that your body is the temple of the Holy Spirit who is in you, whom you have from God, and you are not your own? For you were bought at a price; therefore glorify God in your body and in your spirit, which are God's.

1 Corinthians 6:19-20

It sometimes seems like there are two varieties of Christians: those who are saved and then allow God to use their lives, serving at every opportunity He gives and giving whenever they are able; and those who are saved and then don't do, give or serve anyone or anything, but simply carry on like 'business as usual'.

As well as leading people to Christ and discipling people I have spent many years now trying to motivate Christians who are un-mobilised or 'just sitting there' to serve God and His kingdom and not just settle for mere church attendance. I have noticed time and time again, when you get down to the 'nitty gritty' of why some Christians are happy to do nothing or serve in a very minimum way, it is simply because they still think they own their life. They have never fully understood the truth that their life is no longer their own, that their lives were bought with a price!

You see, if you fundamentally think you own your life then that gives you the right to determine what your life does, or how your life serves others and the purposes of God. But when you realise the truth that you no longer own you, all of this changes and you start to desire to glorify and serve God (the one who bought you with the blood of His only Son) with the life and resource you now have.

We were not cheap

Let us also remember that when God bought us, He never got a bargain. In redeeming us He paid the greatest price that anyone would ever pay for anything – the blood of His only Son, Jesus. Look how Peter puts it:

> *Knowing that you were not redeemed with corruptible things, like silver or gold, from your aimless conduct received by tradition from your fathers, but with the precious blood of Christ, as of a lamb without blemish and without spot.*
> **1 Peter 1:18-19**

Like both Paul and Peter tell us to, we need to know and daily remember that our lives were redeemed back to God, not with silver or gold or any other natural commodity but with the blood of His only Son, that was shed in sacrifice for our freedom. This alone should be the thing that motivates us to Christian service, the knowledge of our redemption and the price that was paid for us.

Hey Christian, the only you that you owned was the old you that was crucified with Christ. The new creation that you now are belongs to God; you are His, bought with a price, so now glorify Him with your body and life. That does not mean do a prophetic dance on Sunday, but rather present your life to Him daily for Him to use. Guess what: as you do, He will, because sadly the workers are still few.

Don't waver but savour

He did not waver at the promise of God through unbelief, but was strengthened in faith, giving glory to God, and being fully convinced that what He had promised He was also able to perform.

Romans 4:20-21

Today's verse speaks about Abraham and how, in his journeying towards what God had promised him, he made a daily decision not to waver through unbelief, but rather to continually savour the promises he had been given.

Let's face it, it would have been so easy for Abraham to regularly drift from a place of faith back into sense knowledge, then take a look around and become discouraged. Think about it – everything in the natural (or according to his five natural senses) was in disagreement with the promises God had given him. Think about the promise given to him – of a child, and that he would be the father of many nations. If Abraham looked at these promises through the natural senses of his life, or from a natural viewpoint, he would have seen things like 'old age' and 'a barren wife'. If he allowed his natural eyes to focus on these things he would have certainly wavered in his faith, but the reality is he didn't. He chose to use faith – that force or reasoning that actually has a greater reality than the five natural senses we are born with, and that can produce far more than the five senses suggest could be possible.

He chose to believe the promises given because he knew the faithfulness of the One who gave them. He knew that the promises had been given by the One who placed stars in space, the One who lived outside of the realm of natural reason and ability; the One who could do anything He wanted and who never let His word return void.

As Abraham walked with a daily persuasion to trust the promises more than his natural senses and the things happening around him, he internally became more fully convinced and strengthened in his faith, which caused him to glorify God. Where was he glorifying God? In the moment when nothing had yet happened, and reason, based on the natural senses, said it never would. When you read on you see that a day comes when the promised child is in Abraham's arms, probably to the utter amazement of those watching his life – but not to him, because he had received the baby in his heart when the promise was first given.

How about you? Has God promised you something that seems impossible? Do the natural things around you scream, 'It can't happen'? Are your five senses desperately trying to get you to rethink what you believe so that you will be 'reasonable'? Then purpose, as Abraham did, to daily savour the promise. Don't waver in your faith, because He who promises is indeed able to do exceedingly, abundantly far above what you could ever imaging (Ephesians 3:20).

Sometimes Jesus will challenge what you think you know

When He had finished speaking, He said to Simon, 'Put out into deep water, and let down the nets for a catch.' Simon answered, 'Master, we've worked hard all night and haven't caught anything. But because you say so, I will let down the nets.' When they had done so, they caught such a large number of fish that their nets began to break.

Luke 5:4-6 (NIV)

Sometimes Jesus will challenge what you think you know and what you reason to be true. Why? He wants to teach you how to live by faith and experience the power of His word. He wants to un-enslave us from being limited to mere sense knowledge alone (knowledge based on the five natural senses) and release us into living a life where we can walk expectantly knowing that God can do anything or change anything anytime He wants or chooses.

In this account we meet Simon, later to be known as Peter. He is a fisherman, always been one, probably learned how to fish from his father, who had learned from his. When you read a little earlier you see him cleaning his nets. He and the other fishermen had been out all night and were cleaning up before going home – going home disappointed because, with all the skill of fishing they had ever learned, they had caught nothing. All of a sudden a preacher turns up who is being mobbed by a large crowd. He asks to use Simon's boat as a pontoon-type pulpit. Simon agrees, not knowing too much about this Jesus – maybe he had heard he was a carpenter when growing up who now preached and did miraculous things?

After Jesus has spoken, He looks to bless Simon and the other fishermen and instructs them to set out to fish again, but this time to put their nets on the other side of the boat. Think about what must have gone through the mind of Simon as he tried to process with his natural senses and experience-based knowledge what Jesus had asked him to so simply do. He must have thought about the hopeless night they had had, the lack of fish they had from being out earlier – so many reason-based thoughts must have passed through his mind.

But, knowing there was something different about this man who claimed to be the Son of God, he said, 'This goes against all reason and everything I know, but because you said to do it, and you have spoken your word too, we will.'

And they did – the rest is history. They caught a catch like never before and had to get their partner's boats to help them bring it all in.

Often, when God's Word or wisdom comes into your life or situation, it can also violate your reason (seem totally unreasonable or impossible). It can go against everything your tradition or life has taught you, and totally violates what your natural senses tell you. The question is, will you still do it? Will you act on His word? If you do you will always see the supernatural response God had in store for you. If you don't you will never know what could have been.

Remember, we are not called to be slaves anymore to our natural senses or earthly-based wisdom alone, but we are people of faith that see supernatural things occur as we put our trust in God's Word, when it makes sense and when it does not, knowing that, indeed, nothing is impossible for Him.

NO REGRETS

He who gathers during summer *and* **takes advantage of his opportunities is a son who** **acts wisely,** *but* **he who sleeps during harvest** *and* **ignores the moment of opportunity is a son who acts shamefully.**
Proverbs 10:5 (AMP)

Regret is a terrible thing. Lost opportunities can eat away at the soul. There are some opportunities that, when they are gone, they are gone for good. One of the greatest opportunities you have in this life is to tell people that you love exactly how you feel about them. I would very much like to have another opportunity to tell my mother and father how much I love them and all they mean to me but they are in heaven now, and that opportunity is no longer afforded me. Are there people in your life who you still have the opportunity to hug, laugh with, honour, visit or tell that you love?

Don't waste this weekend if you still have those opportunities. Act wisely in your time of opportunity so you will have no regrets.

Notes

_____

_____

_____

_____

_____

_____

_____

Leave the Christ in Christmas

For there is born to you this day in the city of David a Saviour, who is Christ the Lord. And this will be the sign to you: You will find a Babe wrapped in swaddling cloths, lying in a manger.

Luke 2:11-13

More than ever this year I have been conscious of the need for Christians to take a solid, defensive stand over what Christmas is really about.

It seems like society has gone to another level in its intention to remove everything about Jesus from Christmas time. In the adverts you watch there are lovely, wintery scenes with cute, furry animals and an array of cheery snowmen and Santas, but an incredible absence of a manger with a very important baby in it.

Last week I went to buy a new Nativity set for our living room from a large garden centre near us. This garden centre boasted a huge Christmas shop where you could get whatever you needed for Christmas decorating, so I thought it would be the ideal place to purchase an old-fashioned traditional Nativity set. After walking around the store for a long time hunting for a Nativity set I was about to give up when I came to a small corner at the very back of the shop that you would not normally go to. There I found a very small selection of Nativity sets. I was happy that I had found the one I wanted, but also left kind of disappointed that the shelves of this 'Christmas store' were filled with everything from Santa to pixies, every type of light and Christmas tree decoration you could imagine, but they felt that the Nativity was just something to put in a corner.

That sadly sums up the intention of so much of modern society, but as lovers of God we need to remain convicted and committed to turning the tide of what Christmas is about back to what it should be all about: Jesus, God's Son, given to man. Please don't get me wrong; I am no 'kill joy'. I love the trimmings as much as the next person. I love the time off work, presents, turkey and other things that accompany the season, yet I am ever more resolved to keep the main thing the main thing. I have made a fresh commitment to make sure that the new Nativity scene I have bought will be the centrepiece of our living room this Christmas, just as the message of Christmas will remain the centrepiece of all my family over the Christmas time.

Let us never let anyone take the Christ out of Christmas. That's like taking the burger out of a beef burger – all you will be left with is a bread roll and salad, and a sense that something vitally important is missing. Let's take a stand – not in some religious way, but in a way that says we celebrate Christmas better than any because we know the true meaning of it. So, sorry to those who want to be politically correct, I won't be calling it 'Happy Holidays'. It will remain 'Merry Christmas' and I will be taking time to gather my children around the traditional Nativity scene to teach and remind them about every character in it and why a special Child was born that first Christmas morning.

Defending Mary's honour

Now in the sixth month the angel Gabriel was sent by God to a city of Galilee named Nazareth, to a virgin betrothed to a man whose name was Joseph, of the house of David. The virgin's name was Mary. And having come in, the angel said to her, 'Rejoice, highly favoured one, the Lord is with you; blessed are you among women!' But when she saw him, she was troubled at his saying, and considered what manner of greeting this was. Then the angel said to her, 'Do not be afraid, Mary, for you have found favour with God. And behold, you will conceive in your womb and bring forth a Son, and shall call His name JESUS.'

Luke 1:26-31

When it comes to 'defending Christmas' and what it stands for I believe we have to be wiser about what is worth standing up for or getting defensive about. Personally I don't have much time for getting bent out of shape about trees and their apparently pagan origins, or Santa being an anagram for satan . Sorry if that gets you going, it does not me! #justbeinghonest

I want to spend my time defending aspects of Christmas that deserve good defence – things like the virgin birth. I won't get worked up over Santa or a tree, but I will get worked up when so-called experts try to remove the title 'virgin' from Mary. Why? Because this is a vital component to the whole story of Christmas. Jesus was born on Christmas morning to a virgin called Mary! The Nativity story for this young lady started nine months before Christmas Day, when an angel visited her and told her she had been chosen by God to carry His only beloved Son. What a shock that was for this young virgin girl! What courage it took for her to say, 'Let it be to me according to your word.' For this we should honour her – not worship, honour – for she was chosen to carry and give birth to God's only Son, Jesus, the One born to redeem (purchase) us back to God.

It was so vital that she was a virgin because if Jesus had been born of man, and not God, He could not save us. It was a sinless man (Adam) that ruined everything for humanity and infected us with a sin nature, so it could only be a sinless man that could restore us and un-infect us (Jesus). If Jesus was born of just a man He would have carried the nature of man, a nature that was sinful and contrary to God's nature. No, the One who would redeem us had to carry the nature of God and be sinless, in order to become the sinless sacrifice that would so fully pay for our redemption on the cross.

Jesus was born to a virgin, and Joseph was only His stepfather; His real Father was God. When He was born in the manger He carried not the corrupted nature of human man but the uncorrupted nature of His heavenly Father. Jesus was born to die – to die for us and as us (as our substitute and representative). A little later in the year we celebrate Easter where we see Jesus die on a cross for us. Why could He die for us when no other man could? Because He was a 'lamb without blemish', He was sinless because of the virgin birth. At the cross a divine exchange took place where He took our sin and nature upon Himself, and we received the nature He brought from heaven for us. This produces a new birth where, by faith, we receive salvation and restoration to newness of life and reconciliation with God.

If we are going to defend anything about Christmas let's defend what matters. Jesus was God's only Son, born to a virgin, sent to redeem us through selfless sacrifice.

The greatest Gift ever given

When they saw the star, they rejoiced with exceedingly great joy. And when they had come into the house, they saw the young Child with Mary His mother, and fell down and worshipped Him. And when they had opened their treasures, they presented gifts to Him: gold, frankincense, and myrrh.

Matthew 2:10-11

*A*ll across the world, people will be celebrating Christmas Day in many different ways. For most there will be some sort of exchanging of gifts. In third world countries these gifts may be a lot simpler than those given in the more Western nations, yet often this can make them more significant. But wherever gifts are given today, they represent something about Christmas that is important for us to take a moment to focus on: Jesus was God's gift to the world, the greatest Gift ever given.

In the Christmas verse we read today we see a well-known scene from the Nativity; the moment when three important, influential men appear bearing gifts for the newborn Saviour King. They had travelled far, been guided by a God-provided star to this simple stable to celebrate the birth of the King of all kings. When you see them appear you notice they did not come empty-handed, but came carrying precious gifts of gold, frankincense and myrrh. I have heard great Christmas messages concerning the relevance and prophetic significance of each of these gifts, but what I want to focus on this Christmas morning is simply this: gifts were present at that first Christmas morning.

Though these gifts of gold, frankincense and myrrh were expensive gifts, none could compare with the One lying in a manger, the One not given by man but given by God: Jesus. Let us remind our families and ourselves that the main reason we give gifts at Christmas time is to remind us that God gave us Jesus as a gift. Maybe you have already opened your presents, or maybe you open yours after dinner – as I said, it's amazing how the procedures of Christmas Day can differ from household to household – but the truth of the day remains the same.

As you give and receive gifts today, take a moment to consider the greatest Gift ever given. One thing I have noticed when I have received gifts over the years is that some gifts are meant to just look good, like a statue or picture frame, while other gifts are given to do something, like a drill or a slow cooker. When someone gives you a 'functional' gift there is often the accompanying expectation that you will use it to do that needed DIY or cook that special meal. Jesus was also a gift that was given to do something. He was not sent to be a statue of religion on a mantelpiece or a church altar; rather, He was sent to die for the sin of the human race and redeem them back to God. The good news is the gift was not broken – what He came to do, He did.

Christmas always leads to Easter, Easter leads us to forgiveness and salvation and, like with any gift, all God wants you to do is receive it. How? By believing that the baby born in a manger died on a cross for you, to restore you to friendship with God. Consider today, as you open your gifts, the greatest gift ever given, still working two thousand years later.

Jesus, the Gift that keeps on giving

The thief does not come except to steal, and to kill, and to destroy. I have come that they may have life, and that they may have it more abundantly.

John 10:10

___

*I*n England we call the day after Christmas Day 'Boxing Day'. Sadly, for many people, today is a 'deflated' day because in their world or understanding it's all over – the presents are opened, Christmas dinner is done, there are no more carols being sung, no more pre-Christmas parties. So they sit and watch TV or visit family, but inside feel somewhat deflated without knowing why. All they know is, after such a big build up to Christmas Day, all of a sudden it's done, gone again for another year.

That should not be the case for Christians. Yes, for us certain things we love about Christmas are also pretty much done, but not the essence of it. Though we (well, most of us!) love the sideshows and tinsel, Christmas holds a 52-week celebration because what it truly represents is not about one day in the year but rather every day of our life. As we said yesterday, the greatest gift ever given at Christmas was that very first gift: God's only Son, Jesus. He is a Gift that works for us and in us 365 days a year. He is a Gift that just keeps on giving. Giving what? Hope, life, redemption, miracles – the list just goes on and on. As all the other gifts you received at Christmas run out of batteries, He never will because He is a gift that contains His own eternal life source. He came with His own divine 'battery pack', and never needs recharging. Life finds its origin in Him!

John 10:10 says that He came to give life. That's not 'one-day-a-year-in-December', but everyday of your life – including the day after Christmas when other people feel deflated and even depressed. You see, that is what the Gift sent from heaven contained: life. As the well-known carol 'Hark, the herald-angels sing' says so well, He was 'born to raise the sons of earth, born to give us second birth'. Our problem was not so much that we had sin but that, because of Adam's disobedience, we had become through him and in him spiritually dead. We needed to be 'raised to life', and that is what God sent Jesus to do. He was sent to die on a cross in exchange for us, to take upon Himself our spiritual death and raise us up to newness of life with His spiritual life.

And that is exactly what happens when a person believes in Jesus. An old life or existence stops and a new one begins. We become born again as new creations. But not only are we 'made alive again', but that life – His life – continues to flow through us and work in us each and every day, like sap running through a branch. Every day He gives us life, and life more abundantly. That is why I call Him 'God's Gift that keeps on giving'. Enjoy that life today by acknowledging that you have been raised to newness of life with Him, and are now joined to Him – as it says in John 15, He is the vine, you are the branch. His life today is your life. It's not just 'Merry Christmas', but 'Merry the Rest of Your Life'!

If you don't know Jesus, or have never received Him as heaven's Gift to your life, you can today. He is only a prayer away. You, too, can know His resurrection life in your daily life. Simply pray:

Jesus, thank you that You are the reason for Christmas. I receive You as God's Gift to my life, sent to save me and make me alive. I believe in You, Jesus, and give my life to You today. Thank you.

Be a wise man

Now after Jesus was born in Bethlehem of Judea in the days of Herod the king, behold, wise men from the East came to Jerusalem, saying, 'Where is He who has been born King of the Jews? For we have seen His star in the East and have come to worship Him.'

Matthew 2:1-3

So here we are, after Christmas, heading towards the next landmark: New Year's Eve. It's that time when we all make great resolutions and new plans for the all-new person we are going to be next year. Let me just end these Christmas-themed devotionals by encouraging you to be a wise man or woman in what's left of this year and also the new one that is coming around the corner.

In the verse above we see the wise men – these men played a big role in the Christmas Nativity scene, being guided by a star all the way to the manger to find the King whose birth had been foretold. Their pursuit or reason for finding Him was simply to worship Him. I've heard it said, 'Wise men once sought Jesus, and wise men still seek Him today.' I want to encourage you to be a wise person. How? Be a person that seeks Jesus each and every day of your life. As others around you dedicate their life to seek other things like fame, security or momentary happiness, be a wiser person that sets your intention on seeking Jesus. You see, the truth is, when you seek Jesus first all those other things that the others seek He will freely add to your life, but without the stress they knew.

Purpose to be like these three wise men that had a simple agenda to seek Him and to worship Him. These guys were not fools; they knew that when Jesus was born something changed in life. They knew that the King of all kings had been born. When they found Him they chose not pride or arrogance, but rather humility and surrender: they bowed down and worshipped. Why? They knew that they were wise men, but they also knew they were now in the presence of the One who gives wisdom. When they turned up they walked into a worship service, joining angels and shepherds singing songs of worship to the baby in the manger. They did a very wise thing: they joined in.

Be like these wise men; don't be so impressed with who you think you are that you cannot bow and worship King Jesus. Rather, bring all He has given you and made you to be and make it an offering before Him. Live humbly before your God, and He will lift you where others only ever dream to be.

Prayer

Thank You for wisdom today, Lord, I claim what is promised in James 1:5, 'your wisdom in abundance without reproach.' Let me know this wisdom in every area of my life. Help me to be a wise person who lays aside the wisdom of this world to know the wisdom that comes from You.
Amen.

DEVOTION

I can do all things through Christ which strengtheneth me.
Philippians 4:13 (KJV)

You have read our devotionals for nearly a year now so you basically know the format. This weekend, start writing one of your own. Begin with a title and a scripture that pertains to your subject matter. Now write your thoughts down regarding whatever your subject matter is. You can begin by studying about your subject. Check out what the Bible says about the subject. Let that fire up your ideas. Personalise your devotional with examples from your own experiences. Ask the Holy Spirit to help you to organise your thoughts and write something that will get others to think about God's Word and how it can impact lives. It should be about 350 words.

This exercise is primarily to get you thinking deeply about God's Word but please feel free to send it to us here at *Breakfast of Champions*. Include your name. We won't be able to print them all but we may use some of the ones that really stand out. Send them to **info@greatbiglife.co.uk**.

Enjoy the weekend, Champion! We look forward to reading your devotionals.

Breakfast of
Champions

Sign up to receive a FREE daily devotional at
breakfastofchampions.co.uk.

The corridor of faith
PART 1

For we walk by faith, not by sight.

2 Corinthians 5:7

Oh, how we love instant arrivals and instantaneous miracles. Why? Partially because we live in such a fast-moving world, we love things to happen 'like yesterday'. The problem is, most often God is not like that. He is not in the hurry we are so often in, and does not struggle with patience issues. In fact, I believe that God is more excited about the journey we take in faith towards what He has promised us than He is about our moment of arrival.

Recently I have been considering again something that I have named the 'corridor of faith', that time between when you get a promise or a dream from God and the moment you arrive or see the manifestation of it in your life. This gap between 'leave' and 'arrive' is a corridor that God provides not with any intention to crush or destroy us but rather to refine and make us. How we perceive and behave while being in a corridor of faith can actually determine how long we spend there, because it is not a place that is a mistake but rather one of design. You see, God works in us more in the corridor of faith than we realise. Often we don't fully see what He has done until the moment we leave it. Think about all your favourite stories in the Bible – all of them have a 'leaving', a 'journeying towards' and an 'arriving' to them. This week I want to concentrate on that bit in the middle – the journey or corridor of faith you pass through en route to arriving. Hopefully this will encourage you and help you understand how to behave on that journey as God would have you.

Abraham left Haran with a promise but no map, and journeyed many years, not a few days, to his 'promised spacious place'. Did he arrive? Yes, he did – but consider all that God did in him during that journey.

Joseph had a dream as a boy of being a person of godly prominence that would lead his brothers, and indeed a nation. Did that happen the next week? No, there was a corridor of faith to walk through first. That must have been very confusing at times. Did he arrive at the moment God gave him in his dreams? Yes he did, but again, look at what God did in him and what God made him during the journey.

These, and so many other accounts, reveal to us that when God gives us a promise or a dream there is normally always a journey or 'corridor of faith' that has to be walked through. This is a God design because what He does in us as we walk by faith through the moment in between actually makes us the person He needs us to be for the promise or dream He has given us. Joseph entered his corridor of faith a dreaming boy but came out as a wise prime minister. David entered his corridor a boy with a prophecy of kingship, and came out a king able to lead a nation. What is God doing in your present corridor of faith? Are you so anxious to 'land the plane' that you are missing out on what God is doing in you and through you 'during the flight'? If God gave you the dream or promise and you refuse to quit or walk away then you will arrive exactly where He said you would – but don't forget the corridor of faith, that time between 'leave' and 'arrive', will make you everything God needs you to be for your moment of arrival.

The corridor of faith
PART 2

Now Joseph had a dream, and he told it to his brothers; and they hated him even more. So he said to them, 'Please hear this dream which I have dreamed: There we were, binding sheaves in the field. Then behold, my sheaf arose and also stood upright; and indeed your sheaves stood all around and bowed down to my sheaf.' And his brothers said to him, 'Shall you indeed reign over us? Or shall you indeed have dominion over us?' So they hated him even more for his dreams and for his words.

Genesis 37:5-8

In our text today we see the moment when the 'God dream or destination' is given. What we know about Joseph at this point is that he is just a young man, and a young man despised by his brothers. The dream related to them but was a much bigger promise, I believe, of the influential person God had appointed him to be. In the final verse you see the brothers' response to Joseph's God-dream – a response of hatred and disdain that launched him into his corridor of faith. If you read on in his storyline you don't see any form of instant arrival, rather a series of events that must have been totally confusing and given him daily the opportunity to quit on the dream. His brothers throw him in a pit and come up with a plan of faking his death; they sold him to a bunch of travellers; later in the story, when things are starting to go better, he is falsely accused of adultery, and he loses a job that looked like it was heading in the dream's direction. He does a fairly long stretch in prison when innocent, also interpreting other people's dreams while in there. But one day he opens his eyes, and he is prime minister of a nation, his brothers bowed before him, with the power and wisdom to save a nation from famine.

Let me underline this thought again: a boy with a crazy dream entered the corridor of faith, and a man able to lead a nation stepped out. Where did the change take place? In the corridor. It was what happened as he continued to journey by faith through things that did not make sense that made him the person God had seen when He gave him the promise.

God also promises us according to what He knows we really are, but sometimes He needs to journey us through a corridor of faith so that we can 'find ourselves' and discover the potential we actually possess. I am not talking about sickness or infirmity, I am talking about 'stuff' – things that happen that don't make sense at the time, but later, when you look back, you smile because you see that God was working in that moment for your good – not to harm you or allow harm on you but to make you the person He knows you can be. Faith is trusting God in the moments that don't make sense, trusting Him that indeed in 'all things He works for your good'. Trusting that God is not obsessed by our present moment, like we can so often be, but rather He is focusing on the larger picture of our lives. He is doing things now that will produce great things later. In these moments you need to believe that though weeping may endure for a night, rejoicing will come in the morning. It's often not until we are leaving a corridor of faith, or a confusing moment, that we look back and fully understand the godly 'why' to what just happened.

Trust Him – when you think you have worked it out and when you have not got a clue what His next move is, He who began a good work in you (started your journey) will complete it (bring you to a place of great arrival)!

Choose the 'Something to Declare' gate

You will make your prayer to Him, He will hear you, and you will pay your vows. You will also declare a thing, and it will be established for you; so light will shine on your ways.

Job 22:27-29

As a frequent traveller I am often in one of London's airports. After I have cleared customs and collected my luggage I have one more choice to make before I am free to leave the airport: I have to make a declaration-based choice. As I approach the exit I am visually offered two choices by our border security: 'Something to Declare' or 'Nothing to Declare'. Most of us remember being presented with this option when returning to the country, right? It's your choice which gate you choose. I have never actually chosen the 'Something to Declare' gate, and am glad to announce I have never had that decision challenged.

Yet, when we leave an old year and step into a new one, it is like we stand at a spiritual version of these Customs gates. We all have a choice – will you step into a new year declaring something you believe or will you put your head down and try not to be noticed by life? The reality is, regarding the entering of a new year, you should never go through the 'Nothing to Declare' gate, but rather choose the 'Something to Declare' one. Another reality is that we all actually declare something when we enter into a new day, even if it's with our silence – so the question really is, 'What are you declaring this year?'

What is it you are believing and confessing over this new day God has given you? Are you speaking words that are based on the promises God has given you for it, or have you settled for declaring things that are based on your fears and the negative expectancies you've developed by what you have experienced lately? I believe that our declaration should be one of faith, not fear – one that comes from dreaming God-dreams that have been fuelled by the hope that has risen in us as we have allowed His words and promises to cause us to dream bigger dreams.

Your declarations give God something to work with, especially when they are words that flow from what you honestly believe in your heart. Think again about the wonderful truths in our text today; think for a moment about what it says will happen when we dare to declare God-promised things over our lives:

• Pray, and He will hear you; pay your vows.

• Declare a thing, and it will be established!

• Then light (His light) will shine on your ways.

Make sure that what is coming out of your mouth is not going to disqualify you or cause another 'Groundhog Day' for you. Rather, let the words you declare by faith aim your life in the direction of the things God has in store for you. Declare His Word, nothing less!

Be a faith-filled watchman on the walls of your life

For thus has the Lord said to me: 'Go, set a watchman, let him declare what he sees.'

Isaiah 21:6

*L*et's continue to talk about 'declaration' and the need for you to be entering this new year declaring God's promises over your life.

Today's text says 'set a watchman and let him declare what he sees'. You need to be that watchman in your life. In days of old the watchman would be positioned on the walls, or in a tower of the city, to look and see what was coming in the distance. That's what God wants you to do in your life and the lives of others – He wants you to be looking and listening at what is coming. Not with your natural eyes and ears, but your spiritual ones, the ones that came alive again at new birth. You see, the truth is you won't ever fully see what God has for you with your eyes open – you will only see these things with your eyes closed. It is when you are reading His word and spending time with Him in prayer that you see the things He has planned for you.

As believers we need to be declaring God's goodness and intent over three specific time scales of our life:

- Where we have come from – declare it is Him that brought you safe thus far.

- Where you currently are – declare it is by His grace you are where you are today.

- Where your life is heading next – declare His promises over the next leg of your life journey.

Let me say again – you are the watchman of your life. It's not your pastor's job – it's yours! If you're not seeing much that excites you, the trouble has probably been that you have been looking at the horizon, or what seems to be happening next with your life, with mere natural eyes. With your eyes open all you see is this present reality and very real circumstance. But, with your eyes closed, God enables you to see what you have not yet experienced or not yet seen; He reveals to you the plans He has for you.

I have discovered in my life that when it comes to what I am going to declare for my life and future, I first shut my eyes to see what God is showing and I open my spiritual ears to hear what God is promising. Then I declare what He has revealed, not what I feel.

Take your position on the wall of your life. Be the prophetic watchman that God has called you to be. By that I mean, don't go by what you see when your natural eyes are open; rather see what God reveals when they are shut, and your heart is focused on Him. Then what you see, declare – knowing that, if He is the author of the image then He will be the finisher that makes it a reality in your life.

Jesus 'The Breaker'

The Breaker [the Messiah] will go up before them. They will break through, pass in through the gate and go out through it, and their King will pass on before them, the Lord at their head.

Micah 2:13 (AMP Classic Edition)

To be honest, I thought I knew pretty much every name that refers to Jesus in the Bible. I have been walking with Him a while now and had discovered so many of His incredible names, like The Great Shepherd, The Door to New Life, Bread of Life, and The Vine to whom I am connected. But recently I stumbled across another one that I had never seen before and, when I found it, it blew me away. Re-read the verse above from Micah.

Did you see it? Jesus is called 'The Breaker', the One who goes before us breaking open the way for us. Not excited yet? Then take a look at how it is written in some other translations:

The one who breaks open will come up before them.

(NKJV)

Then I, GOD, will burst all confinements and lead them out into the open.

(MSG)

If we are honest most of us have spent far too long going after breakthrough, when we should have been going after The Breaker. We have all spent so much time seeking a random event or moment rather than the One who causes it. The good news is, it's not too late; today we can correct that and set our faces on the One who causes the breakthrough in our lives: Jesus 'The Breaker'.

The disciples didn't spend their time pursuing breakthrough, did they? They simply walked in the steps and sailed in the wake of the One who caused the breakthrough, and actually that is what God wants us to do also. Every day, as the disciples simply followed Jesus, things would begin to breakthrough in them and all around them. Every town and village they went to breakthrough would break out. As they kept just walking close to Him they could guarantee continued breakthrough. Why? Because they were with The Breaker, the One who breaks open the way.

Another thing I love is that the verse above also says He goes before us. Again, how many times do we just think He is just following behind us? No, goodness and mercy follow us. He (The Breaker) goes before us and invites us, as He did His first disciples, to walk in the footsteps of His victory.

So today why not move Jesus in your life from just being behind you to also being in front of you. Stop your search for that nebulous thing called 'breakthrough' somewhere in your future and spend your energy going after and walking daily with the One who causes the breakthrough – you know who I am talking about, Jesus 'The Breaker'. As you do, breakthrough will become a daily thing in your life as it was in the lives of those who first followed Him.

So today, let your declaration be, 'Jesus is The Breaker, and He has gone before me. Today I walk in His footsteps and follow Him and, as I do, breakthrough breaks out everywhere I go.'

CELEBRATE THE NEW YOU

Therefore, if anyone is in Christ, the new creation has come: The old has gone, the new is here!
2 Corinthians 5:17 (NIV)

When you came to Christ you became a brand new creation. God didn't repair the old you. That person is gone and you are completely new!

This weekend write down some things that are changed in your life since you have become a new creation in Christ Jesus. List some of those things. When you have done that, spend some time with God thanking Him for all He has done in you.

Enjoy your weekend you lovely, new creation!

Good to get your facts right before you crucify someone

Pilate answered and said to them again, 'What then do you want me to do with Him whom you call the King of the Jews?' So they cried out again, 'Crucify Him!' Then Pilate said to them, 'Why, what evil has He done?' But they cried out all the more, 'Crucify Him!'

Mark 15:12-14

---

ust days before Jesus had heard this same crowd shout 'Hosanna' as He entered Jerusalem, now so many in unison shouted 'Crucify Him'. Sadly, this is a true testament to how fickle 'the crowd' can often be. But in reality it was no surprise to Jesus, because He knew He was born to die on a cross, and their ignorant uninformed shouts were only driving things in the direction His Father had appointed them to go.

The reality here is that, while Pilate desperately looked for facts, the crowd had made up its mind. The trouble was, their collective mind was already made up – without the facts. Their opinion was based on 'some things they heard' from people. Maybe it was because they liked the people or because the people were very earnest and convincing that they felt the information making this man guilty did not need to be proved? But the real problem was, they were wrong. As they joined in with the chant of 'Crucify Him' they were actually guilty of believing a bunch of well-presented lies, and of hanging an innocent man on a cross to die.

So the trial continued and the innocent man is condemned. He is whipped, mocked and hung on a cross to die like a common criminal, as they watched on still cheering. The problem for them is that, directly after His death, it is indisputably proven that the man on the cross was actually innocent, and the people who put Him there were actually guilty – guilty of not seeking out the truth, guilty of listening to only one side of the story, guilty of not giving the person accused an opportunity to relay His side of the facts or defend Himself.

Our lesson today is simple. After you have crucified someone is too late to realise you have made a mistake and that you did not have all the facts!

It has often been said that there are always two sides to any argument. It's just immature and unjust to not find out the other side of what has happened or to check that you are indeed in possession of all the facts before joining in with a judgement. Wisdom will always wait until it has all the needed information before passing judgement. How often can one person seem so right, until the other party is heard – like the Bible puts it so well:

The first one to plead his cause seems right, until his neighbour comes and examines him.
Proverbs 18:17

Whether it is a person, or even a church leadership, that appears to be guilty, take a moment before you join in with the crowd that shouts 'Crucify' to make sure you have all the facts, because *after* you have killed a person's reputation or integrity is the wrong side to realise that maybe you were wrong. Remember, there are always two sides to every story!

Don't forget, you don't own 'you' anymore

You were bought with a price [purchased with a preciousness and paid for, made His own]. So then, honour God and bring glory to Him in your body.

1 Corinthians 6:20 (AMP Classic Edition)

Our text today makes a very strong statement: 'you were bought with a price'. The problem with many Christians today is that they either don't know that or they have forgotten it. It's when you realise your life was bought with a price that you also have a revelation that your life is no longer your own. And when you realise your life is not your own you stop trying to be the boss of it and you allow the One who now owns you to be the Lord of it. This is actually where our lives were always meant to be, willingly under His lordship.

We were bought with an incredible price. The Bible also teaches us that nothing could pay for our redemption back to God's family but the precious blood of Jesus. Think about that again today: the Father purchased you back to Himself with the blood of His only Son. Never doubt the love He has for you and the incredible value and worth He places on you.

It's when we realise we were bought by God that we finally understand that our lives are His to use as He desires. Remember, Jesus did not pay for half of you, He paid for all of you, so He has every right to expect you to live for Him with everything you are not just with some of who you are.

Again, it's when we realise that our lives are not our own that we lay down other foolish things like our personal preferences and so-called rights. Let's face it, the only right we really ever had was to go to hell – and God delivered us from that one.

One of the greatest problems with modern Christianity is that too many people still think they have so many rights. If they still belonged to themselves then this would maybe be valid. But remember, the Bible says we don't belong to ourselves any longer, we now belong to Him and we need to allow Him to be Lord over everything.

Let me challenge you as I challenge myself: today, allow Him to be Lord of everything, because when He died on a cross for you, that is what He paid for.

Where there is no communication you will always find presumption, assumption and judgement. Communicate.

Andy Elmes

Thank You, Lord!

Enter His gates with thanksgiving and come into His presence with praise. Lift your hands to Him and bless His Name.

Psalm 100:4 (NIV)

Give thanks to the LORD, for He is good; His mercy and love last eternally.

Psalm 118:1 (NIV)

In America, the 4th Thursday of November is a national holiday called Thanksgiving. It is a day that an entire nation sets aside to be grateful to people who have been significant in their lives, and also to God, if they choose to do so, for His great bounty and blessings in their lives. Obviously some people don't acknowledge God, but a vast amount do and this excites me. Imagine a whole day set aside by an entire country to give thanks and gratitude to the heavenly Father for all the blessings we enjoy daily.

As a believer, I choose to live a life that daily flows with thankfulness towards my God. Hebrews 13:5 speaks of a continual offering of praise to God for all He's done. I take time each day to come before Him and speak out my words of thankfulness. Giving one day to God would never be enough for me to express my heart towards Him. How could I just reserve a 'one off' per year to say thanks for the breath in my body, my healthy children, my great husband, my salvation, friendships, a church family that inspires and encourages me, the beauty of His creation, and the list goes on and on and on.

Also, the fact that God Himself loves when I come into His presence daily! Imagine that, God is waiting and wanting an audience with me! Who am I that God wants me to enter His gates? The answer to that is that I am His child and He longs to be with me.

I, like David in Psalm 100:4, will come daily into God's presence with thankfulness and praise because no matter what else I need to come into His presence to discuss with Him today, God is worthy of praise and thanks for all He has already done before I even opened up my eyes this day.

Celebrate Thanksgiving with me today – don't wait for the 4th Thursday of November – and thank God for all He's already done and for all you know He is faithful to do for His beloved, you and me.

Prayer

Heavenly Father, today I enter Your gates with thanksgiving in my heart, and I enter the gates of this new day You have given thankfully. Thank You, Lord, for all You have done and given to me; thank You for all You're doing and the plans You have for me. I trust You for all that lies ahead, and know that my life is safe in Your hands; but before another moment passes in this day I just want to say thank You, thank You, thank You!

Amen

We have to pray just to make it today

Be sure that you are devoted in prayer, that you have a disciplined prayer life so that you are alert spiritually, living in dependence on the Lord and thankful to Him in all things.

Colossians 4:2 (The Truth)

J heard some song lyrics that talked about life being like a paper bag caught in the wind and I'm at the mercy of wherever the wind chooses to take me. Life can be this way, which is why Paul in the Bible is instructing the Colossian church to make sure that they are people who are regularly devoting time to spend with God. There are so many benefits to having a disciplined prayer life but Colossians 4:2 clearly lists three very important benefits:

So that you are alert spiritually
Because life can be really challenging I rely on the fact that God is going to help me and lead me through those difficult times. I need to be spiritually aware of His presence with me always. I need to be able to feel His promptings in my heart to do as He wants me to do and say what I need to say, and encourage me when I need a lift. When I spend time in prayer, my spiritual senses are heightened and I feel so much more in tune with God.

Living in dependence on the Lord
If a person thinks there is any security in this life apart from being a child of God then they are greatly deceived. Earthquakes and natural disasters have been known to wipe out everything a person puts dependence on in a moment. The systems of this world fail people all the time. A person can lose their health or great job at the drop of a hat. When our time with God is strong and steady, our trust and faith in Him grows and stays strong. This is what the Bible calls 'building your house on the Rock', the sure foundation. Whatever securities we lose, we personally know the One who actually holds the fabric of our lives together.

Thankful to Him in all things
Spending time with God and feeling His presence for yourself in your personal time with Him is so satisfying. Sometimes I come to Him with a list of things I intend to ask for, important stuff! But, when I begin to lift my hands to Him and feel His sweet peace, I begin to worship Him and thank Him. I leave my prayer time forgetting about my needs list and yet I know He has it all covered. This produces a heart that flows with thanksgiving.

Decide to devote yourself to prayer. Each day set aside some time, even if only a little, and after a while you will wonder how you got by without it!

No matter what, give thanks

Give thanks to God, regardless of your circumstances. All this is God's will for you in Christ Jesus.

1 Thessalonians 5:18 (NIV)

When I read this verse I think of specific people in my life, believers, who I have seen suffer sudden and great loss. The loss they suffered was so great I actually wondered at the time how they would then perceive God and if they would ever be able to come to Him again because of their great suffering. Would they blame God?

I prayed fervently for these dear sisters and brothers and I watched. I saw something that overwhelmed me and also encouraged me beyond words. These people, in all their grief and pain never ceased to worship and praise their God through it all. I saw broken people giving God the worship He so deserves. They knew God was not the one who caused their pain and although questions may have been in their minds of why they were going through such difficult times, they knew God was still God. He was still their Father and loved them. He was still the one who brought them peace and wholeness. I saw these folks exemplifying everything it is to be a believer.

In all of our circumstances, in life, good and bad, God wants us to continue to thank Him for who He is – NOT FOR THE CIRCUMSTANCES, but for who He is to us in those circumstances. Why?

Because when we are in:

- Grief, He is our joy (Psalm 16:11)

- Poverty, He is our abundance (1 Corinthians 1:5, Philippians 4:19)

- Sickness, He is our healing (Exodus 15:26)

- Depression, He is our joy (Isaiah 61:3)

- Trouble, He is our rescue (Psalm 50:15)

Thanking and praising God will release His power into the situation. He is the answer to whatever ails us. Bad circumstances are part of life but allowing God into that circumstance and thanking Him for being what we need Him to be in that situation is our choice.

Let God into your circumstance today and thank Him for being all you need Him to be in that area.

PRAY WITH SOMEBODY

For where two or three gather in my name, there am I with them.
Matthew 18:20 (NIV)

There are so many people who have great need in life. This weekend find a person who needs prayer and arrange to get together with them so that you can pray together for their situation.

Join your faith together in believing for God to move in this person's situation.

Notes

_____

_____

_____

_____

_____

_____

_____

_____

Where are the other nine?

One of them, when he saw he was healed, came back, praising God in a loud voice. He threw himself at Jesus' feet and thanked Him—and he was a Samaritan.

Luke 17:15-16 (NIV)

In Luke 17:11-19 the account of Jesus healing ten lepers is recorded. Jesus was met by ten leprous men. Leprosy under Jewish law was something that would cause these men to be unable to be with their families or friends ever again. On top of the fact that it causes a person's extremities to rot and fall off, it carried a social stigma and meant you had to give up whatever life you knew to become a beggar because you couldn't hold down a job. You would have been considered unclean in the Jewish religion and basically you were an outcast in every way.

From a distance the men called out to Jesus asking Him for healing. He told them to show themselves to the priests and while they were on their way they were perfectly healed. Imagine the elation they must have experienced! Not only would they get to keep all their limbs and extremities (hooray!), they also would get to hug their wives and children and sleep in their own homes. They could again be part of society and have friends and enjoy celebrations with everyone they loved! Life given back and hopelessness abolished.

Well, one leper, when he saw he was healed, came back to find Jesus and he was praising God in a loud voice. Then he threw himself at Jesus' feet and thanked Him. Jesus then asked, 'Where are the other nine?' He was pretty sure He'd healed ten in all yet only one of these guys who had been given his whole life back came to thank his healer. Jesus was interested in where those other nine men were. Why had they not come to thank Jesus too?

I never want to be found not thanking God for answering my prayers, for blessing me, and for all He does for me daily. I never want Him to say, 'I'm sure I provided that thing Gina was asking for and I never heard from her about it.' I count even the fact that I woke up today as one of God's blessings, which is why I come to Him daily with my thanks and praise. According to Google, 89,000 people die in their sleep for no apparent reason each day. I woke up today!

Thank you, Jesus! Thank God daily because He is constantly pouring out blessings on us.

Prayer

Dear Lord, let me be like the one leper who returned, not the nine that did not. For everything You do in my life, whether it be big or small, let me always return to You to say thank You. I consider the things You have done for me this month, and want to take a moment to sit at Your feet and thank You for each of them. My heart is filled with appreciation and gratefulness for all You do, Lord.

Amen

Eternity – a big space to fill!

He has also set eternity in the human heart.

Ecclesiastes 3:11 (NIV)

This scripture makes so much sense to me regarding the condition of this world. Everyone is looking for satisfaction. For many believers the search for satisfaction is what led them to find Christ. It's why young people are searching to find fulfilment in partying, drinking and sexual encounters. It's why people are willing to go broke with loans for higher education or to buy bigger, better houses or cars. It's why married couples engage in extra-marital affairs, and why people get to middle age and re-asses their lives and their goals, sometimes with great dissatisfaction. It could also be why people get to mid life and buy silly sports cars or decide they need to get plastic surgery to enhance their figure or face. People don't realise that this longing for satisfaction is the eternity in their heart crying out.

Sadly, even some Christians today are still trying to fill a void in their lives. I hear statistics for Christian marriages are the same as all other marriages, and we have all heard of Christian leaders who have drink or alcohol problems or moral failures. All the same problems as people who don't have Christ! I made the decision to follow Jesus at a young age, and yet there were times in my life that I felt I didn't have enough materially or was just on a search for something that would bring 'more' to my life because just having Jesus in my heart wasn't enough. How can that be? Jesus is the answer, right? Yes, He certainly is.

Jesus makes these claims of Himself:

- John 6:35 – I am the bread of life.

- John 8:12, John 9:5 – I am the light of the world.

- John 14:6 – I am the way, the truth and the life.

- John 15:1-5 – I am the true vine.

If anyone who has accepted Jesus as Lord of their life is still feeling dissatisfaction and incompleteness, the problem doesn't lie with the Lord: it is with the person. This person has tasted and seen the Lord is good, but a taste doesn't satisfy. A full-on meal is the only thing that can fill a hunger in a person. It would be weird if, when I went to a restaurant and ordered a delicious roast dinner with all the trimmings and sauces and I am truly hungry, all I do is nibble a corner of the roast beef and maybe dip my finger in the gravy to taste the richness of it. Well, that is exactly what many people do with Jesus. He is the bread that will fulfil and water that will remove your thirst, but you have to partake.

If you want the 'eternity in your heart' to be satisfied then fill it with what it longs for – Jesus. Begin to press in to Jesus. Are you spending time with Him? How about reading your Bible? You can know God's very thoughts from reading the Bible! In John 15 it talks about 'abiding' in the vine, not visiting the vine! To abide is 'to make a home with'. If you don't, you will wither and bear no fruit in your lives. No wonder some Christians are still feeling empty and dry with all the same troubles as the ungodly.

Decide to fill that eternal part of you with eternal food and drink and you will get back to feeling strong, vital and fulfilled. Abiding in Jesus is more than enough to fill the eternity in you.

Do we actually know what we say we know?

And if anyone thinks that he knows anything, he knows nothing yet as he ought to know.

1 Corinthians 8:2

This is a very wise saying – it's a little bit like a tongue twister but if you are able to get your head around it you will find a very powerful truth within it.

We have all become very good at telling people what we know, haven't we? We walk around claiming to know this and know that, especially when it comes to the things of God, yet Paul beautifully interrupts this practice by asking does the man who says he knows actually know as he ought or should?

The reality is, if we know something, then that thing that we know should influence how we live and the fruit of it should be seen in our life. For example, if you know you could fall off the edge of a cliff and die, surely you would not go walking on the edges of cliffs, unless you actually did not know as you should?

We all have the ability to know things in a natural sense, but this is very different to knowing truth by revelation. A good example of this is in Matthew 16:13-17 where we see Jesus ask, 'Who do men say that I am?' People give various answers and responses, then suddenly Peter steps forward with a unique answer to which Jesus responds, 'Flesh and blood has not revealed this to you, but My Father who is in heaven.' Peter had just experienced true 'knowing' – knowing something by revelation in the heart of who he was, and not just gaining knowledge in the mind of who he was.

It's when we know things in our heart and not just our mind that the things we know become convictions rather than mere opinions; and they begin to affect and guide the way that we live, the things we choose to do and indeed the things we don't do. I believe we could all do with more of this kind of knowing, right?

So let's stop a moment and listen to ourselves claiming to know things; let's have the courage to ask ourselves honestly if we really do know those things we claim to as we should or is there room to know them in a better, more life-transforming way?

That's given you something to think about – let's carry on with this thought tomorrow.

Know what you look like and live in accordance and harmony with your divine reflection and not some cheap man-made one.

Andy Elmes

Do we actually know what we say we know?
CONTINUED

If anyone supposes that he knows anything, he has not yet known as he ought to know.

1 Corinthians 8:2 (NASB)

*Y*esterday we took some time to chew over this little wise saying found in 1 Corinthians and ask the question, 'Do we actually know as we should the things we claim we know?' We took a moment to look at the difference between head-knowing and knowing something by revelation (the revealing of God).

Let me carry on today with this challenge: the modern church seems to be obsessed with the pursuit of all things new; it seems that, like the Greeks of old, we have a hunger to continually know new things. But let's stop a moment and ask, do we actually need to know anything new or do we really need to go back and know better or more effectively some things we claim to know already?

Remember what we said yesterday: what we know should influence how we live and should be manifested in our lives.

If we were to put a hold on our pursuit of new things for a moment and spend some time letting the Holy Spirit teach us some things again that we don't know as we should, would we actually be worse off or better off?

I am speaking of really basic, fundamental things like:

• What actually happened when we became born again?

• What did Jesus actually achieve for us in His death, burial and resurrection?

• What does it mean to be a new creation and no longer who you used to be?

• What did your water baptism really mean? Was it any different than the recent 'ice-bucket challenge' – did you just get wet, or do you know what happened?

These are good thoughts, aren't they – thoughts that are certainly worthy of fresh meditation. Again let me ask you what I have been asking myself: do we really know as we should the powerful realities of such things as these?

My conclusion is maybe we should stop our pursuit of all things new because actually, like Solomon said, at the end of the day there is nothing new under the sun. Instead, let's open our Bible with a heart to be taught the things we say we know so that after we are left knowing as God wants us to.

Do you know you are the temple of the Holy Spirit?

Or do you not know that your body is the temple of the Holy Spirit who is in you, whom you have from God, and you are not your own? For you were bought at a price; therefore glorify God in your body and in your spirit, which are God's.

1 Corinthians 6:19-20

Here is something else that is vitally important for us to know with a knowing that goes beyond mere head knowledge. Oh, the breakthrough we would experience in our lives if each of us knew in a greater way (more than we presently do) that our life is now the physical temple (dwelling place) of the Holy Spirit.

This needs to be so much more than a casual knowing about, or something we refer to in the songs we sing on Sunday. No, it is vitally important for the believer to have a God-given revelation that the Third Person of the Godhead now calls them home.

This was a fundamental problem with the Corinthian church: they were a Christian church, Spirit-filled, but they were living terrible lives and doing ungodly things that even the unsaved were not doing. Then, in 1 Corinthians 3:3, you see the apostle Paul's letter turn up and you can hear in his tone that he is not happy with how these people are living. He accuses them of acting like 'mere men' – for Paul to say this to them must have meant that there was an alternative available to them, otherwise he would have been wrongly judgemental towards them. A little later he gives them the alternative as he says to them, 'Do you not know that you are now His temples?' This was a Spirit-filled church that spoke in tongues, yet their lives were not walking in transformation power because the understanding or knowing that God now lived in them had not dropped from carnal knowing in the mind to knowing by revelation in the heart.

Sometimes it can be the same for us, can't it? We do things, put up with things, go places that if we really believed that the Spirit of the Living God lived in us every minute of the day we probably wouldn't. My friends, like the Corinthians Paul spoke to, it is vital that we know as we should that the Holy Spirit lives in us. He never leaves or forsakes us. We don't meet Him in meetings – we carry Him, we are His postcode (zip code). Oh, the things that would fall from us, the authority we would walk in, the things we would change, if only we could know this as we should.

The good news is, you can – God wants you to! Why not ask the Lord today to help you to know as you should that your life is His temple? Ask Him to give you a revelation concerning the One who now calls you home.

Prayer

Thank You today, Lord, that my life is the temple of the Your Holy Spirit; thank You that I am no longer a 'mere man', limited to doing only 'mere men' things, rather I now have Your unlimited ability in me by which I can do everything You call me to do. Welcome, Holy Spirit, have Your way in me again today.

Amen

PERSONAL WORSHIP

Yet a time is coming and has now come when the true worshipers will worship the Father in the Spirit and in truth, for they are the kind of worshipers the Father seeks.
John 4:23 (NIV)

This weekend, spend some time alone in worship to God.

To worship is to show honour, respect, adoration, and great love. The Father is worthy of all these things. Worship from your heart with no other agenda than to tell Him how much you love Him. It is a very intimate time with God when you come to Him with your sincere worship. Be the kind of worshipper that the Father seeks. It's not about ceremony. There is no one way or formula for worshipping the Lord. Be yourself. Sing to Him, lift your hands, be loud, be quiet, but above all, let it be heartfelt.

Enjoy your time with the Lord and enjoy your weekend!

Notes

_____

_____

_____

_____

_____

_____

_____

Consider your contents, know you're His dwelling place

But we have this treasure in earthen vessels, that the excellence of the power may be of God and not of us. We are hard-pressed on every side, yet not crushed; we are perplexed, but not in despair; persecuted, but not forsaken; struck down, but not destroyed – always carrying about in the body the dying of the Lord Jesus, that the life of Jesus also may be manifested in our body.

2 Corinthians 4:7-10

*L*et's carry on where we left off last week. We need to know as we should that our lives are not the same as they were before we invited Christ Jesus into them. When we asked Him to come into our lives He did, and that day our life became the temple of His Spirit. The Bible clearly teaches that this was always the intention of the Father – He never wanted to live in buildings made by men, but in the hearts and lives of men.

Father, help us to know as we should that our lives are Your temple, that Your life now lives in each of us by Your Spirit.

When we consider these things we must remember that our lives now contain a Person, not an experience. Jesus said when He comes, not it – He will be with you and will be in you.

All of us would stop putting up with certain things if we could grasp this as the Father wants us to. Consider your contents today, not your outward situation. A friend of mine was once standing in a New York sports stadium. He was looking around at the vast space and the many seats in this building, built to hold many people. All of a sudden he felt the Spirit say to Him, 'This place is not big enough to hold me.' Wow, what a thing to hear! But what he heard next was even better. 'But I am gladly contained in you.' Think about that for a moment: the Spirit of the Living God is gladly contained in us because that was always the plan of the Father. It's when we know this as we should that, like Paul, we can say, 'Greater is He that is in me than he that is in the world' (1 John 4:4, KJV), and, 'I can now do all things through Christ who strengthens me' (Philippians 4:13).

We often get so inspired when we read about the life of Paul and the other disciples yet we forget that they did not have a different Spirit living in them than we now have living in us. The same Spirit of God that filled the lives of the men and women of the primitive church fills the lives of those who are a part of the 21st-century church. The only difference is, they knew it, and knew it as they ought.

The same Spirit that raised Christ from the dead and empowered the life of the first disciples lives in you. He cannot be contained in a large arena, yet He gladly calls you home. Come on, that is something worth getting excited about.

Acknowledging His presence in you

That the sharing of your faith may become effective by the acknowledgment of every good thing which is in you in Christ Jesus.

Philemon 6

It is when we start acknowledging the presence of the Holy Spirit in our life that we begin to experience His leading and empowerment. Like it says in our text today, the successful sharing or living out of our faith will be directly related to our acknowledgement of Him now living in us.

As I said yesterday, the apostle Paul did not have a different Holy Spirit living in him, and that is why we are able to overcome like he did and see the things happen that he saw happening. Reading about Paul, he had a hard life as he took a stand for Jesus. You read of him being imprisoned, flogged, stoned, left for dead – to name a few things. What a résumé! Some of us moan if the water is not hot in the morning!

What gave him the power to keep getting up and carrying on? The Spirit of God that lived in Him. What stopped him being crushed by the external pressure of the things happening constantly around him? Simply this: he knew the Spirit of God in him was greater, that there was treasure in the earthen vessel of who he was.

Think about it this way. The engineers and designers of the first submarine noticed they had a problem: when the submarine went deep in the water the pressure of the water would crush it. The deeper it went, the greater the pressure. The pressure was actually able to crush the submarine like a soda can, even though it was made of iron. How did they overcome this problem? Simple: they created greater pressure within than the pressure that was pushing in from the outside. This enabled the submarine to go to great depths without being crushed.

My friend, that is exactly what God did for us. He has placed a greater power in us pushing out than the one that is outside of us pushing in. When we realise this we can experience the power of this reality and, like Paul, say, 'No weapon fashioned against me shall prosper and when I am weak then I am strong.'

Today, God in you is greater than anything that can come against you. As you acknowledge this you will experience it. The power of He who is in you is released when you acknowledge Him. Enjoy!

His ability now present in you

Therefore I take pleasure in infirmities, in reproaches, in needs, in persecutions, in distresses, for Christ's sake. For when I am weak, then I am strong.

2 Corinthians 12:10

I still feel God wanting us to consider the power of His Spirit now living in us, so let's carry on where we left off yesterday. Allow me to underline again, we can know the same power and strength that Paul and the other disciples knew because the same Spirit that was in them is now living in us.

Notice what Paul said in today's text, 'When I am weak then I am strong.' He does not say 'then He is strong', rather he refers to another strength and ability now present within himself. Was he being arrogant? No, he was speaking out of what he knew. He knew God's Spirit was alive in him and the outworking of that was that when He was weak there was a strength present within him that could enable him to do whatever he needed to and put up with whatever he had to.

When you realise the Spirit of God is in you it's then you actually begin to celebrate your inability. In the world inability is a negative thing, and not being able is a weakness; but when you understand that you are now the dwelling place of the Holy Spirit this is no longer the case. Think about it, when you know He is in you, your inability then is simply just the place where you end and He begins. Where you come to the end of your ability He starts with His. It was from this revelation that Paul was able to say, 'I can now do all things.' He was not boasting of any potential within himself, but rather stating that he could do all things through the Spirit of God in him that now enabled and empowered him.

When we know as we should that His Spirit is in us too, we also will become unstoppable. We also will live beyond the limits we once knew. We also will attempt things we never thought we could do, and declare while we are doing them, 'When I am weak then I am strong.' Put another way, when I have come to the end of my ability I find another ability within me that has no end or limits.

Father, help us today to be conscious of your Spirit now living in us. Help us to not stop when we feel unable or sense a natural inability, but rather like Paul help us to flick the switch within from what we can do to what You can do through us.

If you are too busy to pray, you are busier than God wants you to be.

Wanda E. Brunstetter

Walk worthy of who is in you

For this reason we also, since the day we heard it, do not cease to pray for you, and to ask that you may be filled with the knowledge of His will in all wisdom and spiritual understanding; that you may walk worthy of the Lord, fully pleasing Him, being fruitful in every good work and increasing in the knowledge of God.

Colossians 1:9-10

Our text today encourages us to have a walk worthy of what God has done for us and indeed placed now in us. This thought very naturally follows on from what we have been considering together recently concerning us being conscious that we are now temples of God's most Holy Spirit.

As we know this as we should, it affects what we put up with, attempt, where we choose to go and indeed the daily walk of our life. If we were to get a greater understanding that He was in us – I mean, if we were to really know this every minute of our lives – how would it affect where we went, what we watched and even our conversations? I believe as we become even more conscious of His ever-dwelling presence in our lives it does affect the walk of our lives.

One of my favourite writers is a man named Watchman Nee. He once explained this in a very understandable way. He said that if a man walked down the road with a dollar in his pocket his life would be in alignment with this knowledge. He could go anywhere, and do whatever he wanted to do. But what would happen if you were to suddenly put a million dollars in the pocket of that same man? Surely it would affect where he went, what he did, how he watched out for himself? All that changed was what he was in possession of, right?

When we realise we now carry in our lives the precious Spirit of God, in the same way as the man with a million dollars suddenly in his possession, it will certainly affect where we go, and what we do, and this is how it is meant to be. Let me pick on the men to give you another example: if a man struggles with pornography all he really needs to be free is to become more conscious of the presence of God's Spirit in him; that would solve the problem. Think about it – if that man was to stop and realise that everything he looked at he made the Holy Spirit look at through his eyes, surely that would radically change what he looked at? This is just one example, picking on one issue, but the reality is if we all had a greater knowledge of His internal dwelling it would affect us all in one way or another.

The truth is, when we all become more conscious of His presence within our lives it affects the walk of our life. It is when we know Who we now carry that we naturally begin to walk in a way that is worthy. May we all become even more God-inside-conscious.

Be openhearted towards need

By this we know love, because He laid down His life for us. And we also ought to lay down our lives for the brethren. But whoever has this world's goods, and sees his brother in need, and shuts up his heart from him, how does the love of God abide in him?

1 John 3:16-17

I can remember the first time I went on mission to the Philippines – this verse impacted me in such a profound way, and indeed I am always reminded of it each and every time that I go on mission.

While travelling throughout the more rural areas of the Philippines you constantly come across need. People needing things and needing help – you then have a choice: do you shut your heart so that you do not feel their need (and you do not have to take responsibility for it) or do you keep your heart open and allow the pain and suffering of others to affect you, to affect you in a way that you end up doing something, even if it seems incredibly small, to help them?

I believe God wants His people to have healthy, open hearts concerning the needs of others. Notice how many times Jesus Himself was 'moved by compassion' throughout the Gospels? In this verse it specifically speaks of the needs of our brothers. I believe that it is referring to those who are people of God and a part of the same global family as us. What an awesome thought – when you said 'Yes' to Jesus you became a part of a worldwide family. Even if we don't see it like that God does, and I believe He wants us to care for each member of that family as we would for each member of our natural one. Wow, what a challenge this is, especially when there is seemingly no end to the people in need of help!

It's again an issue of love – the verse says that he who shuts his heart to the needs of his brother is void of God's love in his life. That's a very hard statement but a good one, good enough to awaken us all to be more openhearted. Obviously you can't do everything: I always leave the mission field wishing I could have done more, but I always do what I can. And hey, if we all do that we will together get a lot done.

Finally, it's not just about the mission field far away, is it? Around us all daily there is no shortage of people in very real need. Let us make sure our hearts are open to them. If you can do something to bless others in need, do it – as you do you manifest the love of God that is in you.

Prayer

Heavenly Father, help me today to be open-hearted concerning the needs of others that I encounter today. Let my heart be tender, like Yours, and full of compassion for people who are in need. Let me use what You have blessed me with to make other people's lives a little brighter. Father, today, help me to see others through Your eyes, I pray.

Amen

STOP AND START

And whatever you do, in word or deed, do everything in the name of the Lord Jesus, giving thanks to God the Father through him.
Colossians 3:17 (ESV)

This weekend make a plan to **stop** something that you do in your life that is somehow hindering you from getting closer to God than you could be, and **start** a new healthier habit. For example, maybe you could **stop** going straight for your mobile phone the minute you wake up, and discipline yourself to **start** spending those first moments of the day thanking God for waking you up.

Maybe you could **stop** watching so much television and **start** reading some interesting Christian books or downloading and listening to a sermon by an inspiring preacher.

It's the small, easily 'do-able' steps we take in life that actually take us the farthest. You know your own habits better than anyone and there's always room to improve our lives and draw closer to the Father.

Notes

_____

_____

_____

_____

_____

_____

We are the transformed
PART 1

Therefore, if anyone is in Christ, the new creation has come: the old has gone, the new is here!

2 Corinthians 5:17 (NIV)

If we are going to live in the fullness of what Jesus purchased for us and see others radically changed as God intended then we must make sure that we are believing a correct gospel and preaching a correct one too. The gospel of Jesus Christ, when communicated correctly, is the most powerful of things – as it says in Romans 1:16 (KJV), it is the 'power of God unto Salvation'. The sad thing is, not everyone is preaching a gospel of power – some are settling for gospels that tickle the ears of the hearer rather than radically transform them.

It is imperative for us that we understand the gospel of Jesus is the good news of a supernatural, God-made transformation, not just one of man-made behaviour modification. It reveals and contains the power of God to change a person beyond all recognition.

So many preachers today seem to be obsessed with messages about self-development and 'being the best you' when the Bible actually reveals that the best 'you' is a dead 'you'; a 'you' that found finality for the old man in the death, burial and resurrection of the Saviour, Jesus. It's when you realise the old 'you' or self is dead in Him that you can experience the new 'you', born again to newness of life. We must start from a point of death if we want to experience the fullness of life that He has provided for us.

You see, God never had a patch-you-up plan but rather a plan that would transform you into all He intended for you to be. His plan was not to momentarily deal with the harvest of bad fruit produced from our life, but deal with the nature that was producing it, because God is always interested in the spirit or motive of the thing not just what is being produced. Through providing us a death He made a way for us to lose our past so that it is no longer there for us to return to.

The gospel is not an invitation to 'be ye modified' but to be transformed by His word and His Spirit into His very likeness. Why would a person settle for mere modification when divine transformation remains the invitation from God?

Let's carry this on tomorrow.

The crowd follows Jesus for what they can get but disciples follow Him for what they can become.

Andy Elmes

We are the transformed
PART 2

After six days Jesus took with Him Peter, James and John the brother of James, and led them up a high mountain by themselves. There He was transfigured before them. His face shone like the sun, and His clothes became as white as the light.

Matthew 17:1-2 (NIV)

We are not the modified but the transformed. There is a big difference, you know. The dictionary says that to be modified is to 'be adapted or adjusted' but it says to be transformed is to 'experience a beyond normal change of nature'. Sadly, so much of modern preaching is nothing more than an offer to be slightly adapted. The problem with this is if you have been modified or adapted it is easy to be unmodified and return to what you were; but when you're transformed through death and new birth the nature of you changes, which provides a freedom from having to, or being able to, return or revert to what once was.

The word transformation is the word *metamorphoo*, from which we get the word *metamorphosis*. Some learned the meaning of this word in science class; I learned it watching an old series called *The Incredible Hulk*. The lead character, David Banner, was exposed to an overdose of gamma radiation and every time he got angry, the opening of the show said, 'a strange metamorphosis occurred'. If you ever saw the show you know what happens: he turned into a muscle-bound, green monster with crazy eyebrows.

What was happening to him was an internal nature thing, not an external modification thing. It's amazing that it is that word *metamorphoo* that God uses when the Bible speaks of the change that occurs in us when we are saved and Spirit-filled. Not that we turn into a green monster – I hope you understand that! Rather, we too experience internal change that causes us to know new life and power.

The word transformation is used around three times in the Bible: once regarding Jesus, and twice regarding us. In Matthew 17 it speaks of Jesus being up a mountain with His disciples when suddenly He is transformed before them and glowed whiter than any linen. What happened? The disciples experienced the life that was in Him; the life of God in Him shone through the earthly container of Him. You must realise that you to have an earthly container, but you now also have His Spirit and nature working and residing within you. It's this life that changes us, empowers us, and transforms from glory to glory.

Take a moment to thank God that you are not religiously modified but divinely transformed. How, you ask? I will tell you tomorrow.

Transformed by His Word

Therefore, I urge you, brothers and sisters, in view of God's mercy, to offer your bodies as a living sacrifice, holy and pleasing to God – this is your true and proper worship. Do not conform to the pattern of this world, but be transformed by the renewing of your mind. Then you will be able to test and approve what God's will is – His good, pleasing and perfect will.

Romans 12:1-2 (NIV)

Good morning! We have been taking time to establish that we are not the modified but the transformed; we have been looking at what transformation is and how it changes us. As I mentioned yesterday the word 'transformed' appears three times in the New Testament: once regarding Jesus and twice in relationship to us and our journey into all He has for us and destined for us to be.

God uses two things to cause divine (supernatural) change in us, two things that have been around from the beginning of time: His word and His Spirit. Let's look at the first of them this morning. Romans 12 says that we are to be transformed by the renewing of our mind. What do we use to renew our minds? His word. It is vital we realise that we are now spiritually alive people, and the Bible is a spiritually alive book. When you read it with a desire to be transformed it will renew your thinking and bring you into the state of transformation.

You may say, 'that's brainwashing, isn't it?' In some way, yes it is – but when we look back at how our old thinking got us into so much trouble you will probably agree we need our brains scrubbed. The real truth is, everyone is brainwashed – at least we know and trust the One who is doing the scrubbing.

When we don't treat His word like 'pick and mix' but read, believe and apply all of it to our lives it is then we experience powerful things beginning to happen in us and through us. Like I said, it's not a normal book – it is God's thoughts and ways and contains His power to transform us.

Make sure you are daily washing your thinking in the sink of His word, allowing its truths to renew your mind, allowing it to shine like a torch within you and bring His incredible life to every section of who you are. Do you want to be transformed? Then honour His word in your life, see it for what it is, read and apply it daily and watch what begins to happen. Yes, it will sometimes offend you, but when you remind yourself that God is right and you are wrong and allow it to replace the wrong believing and wrong philosophies you have been living by, it will set you free and keep you free like you never imagined.

Prayer

Father, thank You for Your word. Thank You that it renews our thinking and breaks the power of other things that have limited and controlled us. Today, I approach Your word as a living book and read it as one who is now spiritually alive. Transform me as I read it, I pray.

Transformed by His Spirit

But we all, with unveiled face, beholding as in a mirror the glory of the Lord, are being transformed into the same image from glory to glory, just as by the Spirit of the Lord.

2 Corinthians 3:18

We established yesterday that one of the two things God uses to transform our lives is His word. Today let's look at the other thing – or should I say person: His Spirit.

His Spirit now alive in us is busy at work transforming us. Like I said before, religion does not transform you because it works from the outside in, merely modifying and suppressing behaviour in your life, and often producing hypocrisy rather than long-term change. The plan of God was to entrust His very own Spirit and nature to have residency within us, knowing that it would create transformation by working from the inside out.

Like the development of a chicken in an egg, so it can often be for us: new life develops within, then breaks through the outer shell of who we are.

The person of the Holy Spirit was not given to sit quietly within us, providing fuzzy moments in certain meetings you attend. Rather He was sent to help us be transformed from glory to glory, into the very likeness of Jesus Christ. Jesus revealed a few of the Holy Spirit's many facets in the book of John: He's the helper, comforter and guide to those who realise they are now with unveiled face and contain the glory of all He is.

Let me say once more: He is not present to slightly adapt or modify your life and existence but to radically transform you. So, today, why not go ahead and let Him. He is the very nature of the new vine we have been joined to (John 15). It is His nature that we are now partakers and sharers of (2 Peter 1:4). So begin to partake by acknowledging His presence within your life, and as you do you will feel Him deep within changing you far beyond how you could ever change yourself.

What we do and say gives license to others to do and say the same. Be careful what you do and say because people are always watching.

Andy Elmes

The Spirit and the Word dance together

So then, after the Lord had spoken to them, He was received up into heaven, and sat down at the right hand of God. And they went out and preached everywhere, the Lord working with them and confirming the word through the accompanying signs. Amen.

Mark 16:19-20

Over the last few days we have spoken of how the Word of God and the Spirit of God are the tools God uses to bring about transformational change within our lives. How awesome that God would not just call us to change but provide His manual and His Spirit to assist us.

The Word and the Spirit have always existed together and been busy synergistically producing the intentions of God. They are like two dancers who have danced together from the foundation of time. I am not picturing modern dancers but ballroom dancers, regally and gracefully twirling together. In Genesis you clearly see that in the beginning the Word and the Spirit danced together producing planets and universes. Every time the Father had an intention for something to come into being the Spirit and the Word danced, and as they did new horizons were born.

Today they still desire to dance together, but now they seek not just to dance outside of you but within you, to dance to the tune of God's transforming plans for you. All you need to do is allow them to dance – clear the dance floor and let them do what they came to do.

We have spoken of what the Word and Spirit do within us but what is our part, you may ask? What must we do to support this work of personal transformation within? Only one thing: submit! Bow the knee to what God wants to do, humble yourself under His mighty hand, resist foolish things like pride and arrogance, and allow Him to have His way. As you do the Spirit and the Word will dance the dance of transformation within you, leaving you changed for eternity.

Prayer

Heavenly Father, thank You for Your Word and Your Spirit at work within me. I humble myself before You and say, 'Have Your way.' Let my life be a dance floor for them; as they spin together let my life be changed for Your glory.

SOWING AND REAPING

Do not be deceived: God cannot be mocked. A man reaps what he sows.
Galatians 6:7 (NIV)

Everything you do and say is like seeds. If you plant seeds you will eventually get a harvest. For example, plant seeds of peace in your home and you will reap an atmosphere of peace. It works negatively as well: plant seeds of contention and anger and you will have a terrible atmosphere developing. Remember, it takes time for seeds to produce a harvest so you cannot expect anything to happen overnight; but don't be fooled, you will have a harvest. Be intentional about some things you want to see cropping up in your life. Think of an area of your life that needs some healthy seeds sown and begin sowing them today.

1. Write down that area of your life you'd like to change.

2. What would you like to see growing there? List some healthy 'crops' you hope to see from the seeds you will plant.

3. This weekend, be intentional about the seed you are going to sow and sow something to produce your harvest, including the words you speak.

4. Ask the Holy Spirit to remind you to speak life-giving words into your situation and to help you NOT sow the things that will cause an unhealthy crop. As you see healthy fruit growing in that area of your life be encouraged to begin doing this in other areas of your life too!

Area of change:

_____

Healthy 'crops':

_____

_____

_____

Don't try and box an unusual God

Now to Him who is able to do exceedingly abundantly above all that we ask or think, according to the power that works in us.

Ephesians 3:20

If you want to experience all the things God has for you then you need to make the decision to let Him out of the well-constructed boxes you have tried to package Him in. The fact is, God normally always does things in unusual ways. Think about it: when you are believing for a miracle or a breakthrough, very rarely does it come the way you anticipated or expected, right? Most often it comes in a way you never imagined or could have planned. In fact it normally always comes when you did not expect, in a way you never thought of, and involving people you never thought would be involved – that's God!

You see, God is not limited by, or to, our ways of doing things – but sometimes we can limit Him by trying to govern or work out how He will do what He promised He would do. The fact is when it comes to God and His promises the best thing we can do is lay aside all of our preconceived ideas and self-imagined routes and just turn our heads to heaven and say, 'I don't know how, when or who You're going to use to do what You have promised, but I just know You will do what You have promised', and then leave the rest to Him.

Living this way looses an unlimited God to do what He wants to do without us constantly getting in the way and messing things up at every turn. Remember, you are not God – He is. He will always do what He has promised you in a way that is exceedingly abundantly, far above what you could imagine in your wildest dreams.

Religion has always tried its best to keep an uncontainable God in a containable experience. Let's make sure we never try and do the same, rather we live to let God be God in every situation and circumstance we may be facing. Believe me, He will never do less than you thought, only ever exceedingly abundantly more. Remember, it was always religious people who got offended with Jesus, not everyday folk. Why? Because He did not look like they thought He should look and did not act like they felt He should act, and very adamantly He refused to get into the little box they desired for Him to live in, then and now. But the everyday folk He walked amongst were completely different. They were amazed by the daily deeds of an unusual God; they could not get enough of Him and were blessed and amazed by all He did. Let me encourage you: today, don't be like the religious, don't try to work Him out, limit or box Him by your expectations or way of doing things; rather, be like those everyday folk that lived to daily be amazed by who He was and everything He did.

Whatever your need today when you pray, stop trying to tell God what to do and how to do it. Instead, begin to pray that simple prayer that says, 'I don't know how, I don't know when or who You're going to use but I know You will because You have given me Your promise.' Then leave the rest to Him.

God does unusual things

The wind blows where it wishes, and you hear the sound of it, but cannot tell where it comes from and where it goes. So is everyone who is born of the Spirit.

John 3:8

What a great comparison! Just as you can't govern or control what the natural wind does, neither can you control or govern what a supernatural God does. Like the wind, He is not contained or controlled by any other and blows where He chooses and when He chooses, whether it feels usual to us or not. As we considered yesterday it is vital that we understand that God is an unusual God who does unusual things. But then remember, they may seem unusual to us but they are not to Him – they are simply the ways He chooses to do things. They just seem unusual to us because they are not what we expected and often go against the preconceived plans we had for how things should work out. Again remember, His ways are always better and never less.

It's when we begin to accept this truth that we can begin to expect Him to do unusual things in our lives and the situations we face, and be blessed and amazed when He does. It's then we can begin to experience the unlimited God 'make a way where there seemed to be no way'.

Let's face it, isn't this a better and more enjoyable way of walking with a living God? Isn't this more exciting than waking up every morning thinking you know everything He is going to do and how He is going to do it, only to later be again disappointed when it does not happen as you planned or pre-thought that it would?

Read the Bible – God has always done things in an unusual way. But in fact it's not unusual to Him, rather just unexpected or unanticipated by us.

Come to think of it, who is actually 'unusual': Him or us? 'Usual' is normally the title given to that which is original, normally whatever is done or existed first is deemed usual and whatever follows, if different, is unusual. Genesis 1:1 teaches us 'in the beginning God', which means that before anything else or anyone else existed God did, and the way He did things was the usual way to do things. Are you still with me? Then God made Man and gave the privilege to walk with and experience Him. Here is my point: should we be trying to make the original One fit into the boxes that we determine 'usual', 'expected' or 'acceptable', or should we be getting out of our boxes to live in the fullness of what is usual and normal to Him?

What would it profit a man to stand on a hill on a windy day telling the wind how he thinks it should blow? Would there be any benefit in doing that? In the same way, who are we to stand in the face of a God that does things in unusual ways trying to get Him to do what He is doing in ways we prefer? Instead, let God be God; trust Him, you won't be disappointed. His ways are always higher, greater and so much better. In fact, learn to lift a sail of faith so that the wind of what He is doing can lift you and carry you where He wants you to be.

God's unusual track record

Thus says the LORD, who makes a way in the sea and a path through the mighty waters.

Isaiah 43:16

We have been spending time considering how God often does things in ways that seem unusual to us and it's when we begin to accept that He does things in unusual ways that we can have fresh hope in situations we find ourselves; that even when it looks impossible naturally, and every road we had placed hope in has failed us, God will still do something unusual to turn it all around for our good.

Think about it – you only have to read the Bible to see God's proven track record for doing unusual things, both in the Old Testament and the New. In the Old Testament we read of a man losing the iron axe head from his borrowed axe, and then God telling the man through the prophet to throw a stick in the water to make the axe head float! You'll read of prophets telling military generals with leprosy to dip seven times in a dirty river to receive their miracle of new skin! Telling a widow to pour a small pot of oil out into large containers to get a miracle of provision! Everything from men being told to build enormous boats to parting uncrossable oceans with sticks. Come on, read it for yourself – these are just a few examples. He constantly asked people to do unusual things to get incredible outcomes.

Then we step into the New Testament and watch the ministry of the Son. In the same way we see one unusual thing after another. He spat in the eyes of the blind, stuck his finger in the ears of the deaf, turned water into wine. He left it four days before raising a man from the dead, and sent His disciple to get tax money from the mouth of a fish! And these again are just a few of the unusual things Jesus daily did in His ministry.

Now think about it for a minute: if God did things in an unusual way in the Old Testament through the prophets, and in the New Testament through His Son, then why is He going to be any different today for us? Maybe we don't experience everything we could, or see everything we are meant to, because we are always waiting for God to do things in a usual way? Maybe if we face the fact that God does things in unusual ways and begin to get excited by this truth we would experience the things we read of in His word happening more frequently in our lives? Maybe when God asks us next to do something unusual that does not make sense to our understanding we don't brush it off – instead we are obedient to it? Maybe it was not a crazy thought; maybe it was God doing something unusual?

In fact, the more I have been thinking about it the harder it is to find any account in the Bible where God did something in such a way that a person could say, 'There you go, I knew He was going to do that.' It's like God wants to keep us on our toes, to keep us reminded that He is the God who does not live in any man's box!

How about you – are you ready for God to do what He has promised He would in a way you never imagined? Get out of the box of your preconceived ideas and pray again, 'I don't know how, when or who You are going to use, I just know You will do all that You promised.'

God uses unusual people

Brothers and sisters, think of what you were when you were called. Not many of you were wise by human standards; not many were influential; not many were of noble birth. But God chose the foolish things of the world to shame the wise; God chose the weak things of the world to shame the strong. God chose the lowly things of this world and the despised things – and the things that are not – to nullify the things that are, so that no one may boast before Him.

1 Corinthians 1:26-29 (NIV)

Another unusual thing about God is that He chooses to use unusual people. By that I mean He delights in selecting and using people to do unusual things for Him that others would not pick or even consider.

Again think about the different people God selected and used throughout the Bible. They were often overlooked people who had hang ups and had made mistakes. I don't know about you, but this makes me smile because if God did not choose people this way I don't know if I would be doing what I am for Him today. Here's a brief handful of examples:

- Abraham – who would choose an old man to birth a nation?

- Jacob – who would entrust so much to a cheating liar?

- Rahab – who would use a prostitute to help a people win a city?

- Moses – who would use a man with a speech impediment to be the spokesman for a nation?

- Gideon – who would use a hiding coward to lead an army?

- David – who would pick a shepherd boy to be a king?

The list could go on and on, and when you look in the New Testament it's the same with Jesus. The men He chose as disciples were such a random bunch of men from such different backgrounds: tax collectors, fishermen and doctors to name a few. None of them had trained at theology seminary; every other rabbi in the city had overlooked them all. They had watched the Jewish rabbis select the men around them and had given up on thinking that a rabbi would ever want them. Then they met the greatest Rabbi, Jesus, who handpicked them from the crowd.

Because, you see, like we see in the story of David being selected above his brothers, God does not select like natural men do. Man looks at the outward appearance whereas God looks at the heart and what He is able to do with the person through His grace.

Again think about this: God looks for everyday people – people who are not over-impressed with themselves, people who have failed and blown it, and who need another chance. He then lifts them up, makes them what He knows they can be and uses them to do incredible things. I am so glad that God saw in me what others could not see, nor even I myself, aren't you?

Today, present your life to an unusual God, give Him everything that you are, and then watch what He does with you and through you as all the glory goes back to Him. Don't be surprised when unusual things begin to happen!

How do you respond when God promises you something unusual?

Then the word of the LORD came to him: 'This man will not be your heir, but a son who is your own flesh and blood will be your heir.' He took him outside and said, 'Look up at the sky and count the stars – if indeed you can count them.' Then he said to him, 'So shall your offspring be.' Abram believed the LORD, and he credited it to him as righteousness.

Genesis 15:4-6 (NIV)

How unusual is this account? God comes to the old man Abram and promises him and his barren wife a child, and then lets him know his descendants will be more numerous than the stars. What an unusual promise. What should Abram have done? Simple, gone and slept with his wife then sat back and waited for the birth of the unusual promise God had given him; but, as we know, that is not what he did.

When God does something unusual in our lives it can cause a number of different reactions. Sometimes anger, because we don't understand everything that's happening; sometimes it causes our faith to grow stronger as we trust God for the unknown; or maybe interference, as we suddenly think we need to help God bring to pass the unusual thing He said He would do. This is the one that normally gets us into the greatest trouble, as it did Abram.

Instead of sitting back and trusting the promise, he decides to 'help God out'. Bear in mind, if God had needed his help He would have asked for it. Abram comes up with a nice little plan that involves sleeping with Hagar, one of Sara's servants. They go ahead with the plan and produce a boy named Ishmael. This child caused great jealousy with Sara and became a great pain in his life, giving him much heartache. The child continued to produce problems for many, many generations, even causing certain ongoing ramifications in the world we know today.

Then God calmly tells Abram that was not the child of promise and then Sara supernaturally becomes pregnant and bears him the promised son, Isaac. Why did Abram not just sit back and wait for what God promised? Because it was not usual! It was not usual for an old man and woman to have a child, it was not usual for a barren lady to suddenly conceive. But remember what we have been learning: God is an unusual God who does unusual things. We need to learn that, when He gives us a promise that does not make sense, don't try and work out the 'when', the 'how', and the 'who' – just believe and hold Him to His promises.

Why does God do unusual things?

1. To show He is God, unlimited and the One for whom nothing is impossible.

2. To grow our faith and trust in Him, so we are strengthened to believe for more.

3. Because He sees the larger picture of things connected to what is happening to us that we don't see and has a wonderful way of doing many things at once.

I hope you have been challenged this week to see that God does unusual things and have become hungry for Him to do more unusual things in and through your life for His glory.

COUNT YOUR BLESSINGS

Let all that I am praise the Lord may I never forget the good things he does for me.
Psalm 103:2 (NLT)

Imagine life without your thumbs!

Most people who have thumbs don't thank God for them because we forget how useful they actually are, but if you didn't have thumbs and you tried to open a jar or tie a shoelace you'd really see what a blessing thumbs actually are!

This weekend, spend some time making a list of the blessings in your life – the obvious one's and the not-so-obvious ones. You may be an 'artsy' sort and can really make it special, with coloured pens or calligraphy, or you can get a simple pen and write it on this page! Once you've done that spend some time giving thanks to God for the blessings on your list. Keep this list in a place where you can look at it now and again as a reminder of how good God has been to you. As we remind ourselves of God's blessings, we will gain a heart of gratefulness.

Have fun!

My blessings

_____

_____

_____

_____

_____

_____

Where's the profit?

For what will it profit a man if he gains the whole world, and loses his own soul? Or what will a man give in exchange for his soul?

Mark 8:36-37

Jesus asks two questions in this verse. This is a verse that is very relevant to the headlines in the paper that so often appear, headlines that tell of another famous or wealthy person passing away. I think of the sudden death of people like the pop genius Michael Jackson, a man who seemed to the world to have everything that others wanted but, it seems, did not really enjoy them or count them as what he needed for a successful life. The truth remains concerning the applause, the fame, and the money – that none of these things could be compared as a good exchange for someone's eternal soul.

Question One

What will it profit you if you manage to gain the whole world yet lose your soul?

Short-term success (this life alone) is really not success at all. God wants our lives to have influence and success here on earth but also, and more importantly, success that goes beyond the grave. To one day stand in eternity before God, justified and forgiven by the perfect work of Christ, is man's greatest success and nothing you can earn or achieve in this realm of life could ever be a good exchange for that. To hear the Father say to you, 'Well done, good and faithful servant,' is the accolade above all others.

Life lesson:

Live to experience the promised success of God in this life but also live in the light of eternity, knowing that all of us one day will pass from what we know to what we have not yet experienced (heaven for the believer). What may profit us here could leave us bankrupt there!

Question Two

What will a man give in exchange for his soul?

The answer is nothing! No thing is that valuable, and don't ever be deceived by momentary wealth, success, or fame because they are never enough to qualify for the exchange of your saved, redeemed, God-forgiven soul.

Live for more than the momentary success this life can offer. Live to know the eternal prosperity available only in Christ!

What good would it do to get everything you want and lose you, the real you? What could you ever trade your soul for?

Mark 8:36-37 (MSG)

Do you want to be amazed at what comes out of your mouth?

Therefore settle it in your hearts not to meditate beforehand on what you will answer; for I will give you a mouth and wisdom which all your adversaries will not be able to contradict or resist.

Luke 21:14-15

We have spoken about the power of 'saying nothing at all' but what about when you have to say something? We know that according to Ecclesiastes there is a time for everything, 'a time to be silent and a time to speak'. What about those times when silence won't serve you best and you need to say something and you know that what you say could have a serious effect?

Jesus gave the promise in today's verse to His disciples as He spoke to them on the subject of the signs of the end times. He spoke of people betraying them and setting them up with loaded or trick questions intended to incriminate or defame them and their God. He told them not to worry about it but rather, when they found themselves in one of those awkward moments, to open their mouth and listen to what comes out.

The promise He made to them is still valid for us today. Why? Because His Spirit, the Spirit of wisdom and revelation, now lives in us; and He is not dumb, but speaks. When we dare to take our minds out of gear and listen for Him it is amazing the answers and responses we suddenly have to give that appear seemingly from nowhere.

Consider the promise and its implications for you today.

Jesus promised that He would give 'the mouth (courage, eloquent ability) and the wise answer (truth for the moment)' to those who would dare not to pre-meditate responses but simply trust Him in those moments for the perfect answers.

Not only will He give you the perfect answer but an answer that will not be able to be contradicted or resisted. Now that is a great response.

So remember, sometimes it is better not to speak, 'to say nothing at all', and other times when words are needed, why not let His wisdom become the 'appearing seemingly from nowhere' words you use? As you do, you will leave your hearers unable to contradict why. That is what truth does when it is spoken with wisdom!

Make up your mind right now not to worry about it. I'll give you the words and wisdom that will reduce all your accusers to stammers and stutters.

Luke 21:15 (MSG)

Blessing and have a great day.

Get pure wisdom!

Wisdom is the principal thing; therefore get wisdom. And in all your getting, get understanding. Exalt her, and she will promote you; she will bring you honour, when you embrace her. She will place on your head an ornament of grace; a crown of glory she will deliver to you.

Proverbs 4:7-9

---

ere Proverbs encourages us to 'get wisdom'! Again the question is, where do we get it from? There is no shortage of apparent wisdom being made available in the life we daily live. Everyone and their brother seems to think they have 'pure truth and knowledge'; from evolution to humanism there is no shortage of 'stores to get some'.

The problem is that all wisdom outside of God's is not pure wisdom – a lot of the other wisdom that is available is not evil but simply not as good for you as God's.

Colossians 2 actually gives us a strong warning about shopping for wisdom to form your philosophies by, outside of God. Listen to the opening of the verse from three different translations, all of them initially warning with words like beware:

> *Beware lest anyone cheat you through philosophy and empty deceit.*
>
> Colossians 2:8

> *See to it that no one takes you captive through hollow and deceptive philosophy.*
>
> (NIV)

> *Beware lest any man spoil you through philosophy and vain deceit.*
>
> (KJV)

So a wrong philosophy (wisdom given you to love and form your belief and value systems according to) has the potential to take you captive, cheat and spoil you! Be careful where you go shopping, Champion.

Also, you need to keep your philosophy pure. A world that does not love or acknowledge our God is ever wanting you to make a cocktail concerning the wisdom you are loving. For example, they offer cocktails that take a bit of humanism, a bit of paganism, add a shot of Christianity, and then give it a flashy name to make you want it. It may be a funky-looking concoction but it won't taste good to your life – in fact it's poison to your soul.

Keep it pure, Champion. Let God now be the brickyard for the wisdom blocks you need to build that new life you have been promised. Not all the wisdom that is available in the world outside of God is evil – a lot of it is just not as good as God's – so why get it from somewhere inferior when you have the opportunity and invitation to get what is genuine from the One who makes the real thing.

I know this sounds somewhat narrow-minded but let's face it – it has to be so. There is too much 'wisdom mixing' going on within Christianity today, and it's time for us to look again to the Word of God and say, 'This alone contains the wisdom I need for each and every situation I may face.'

Get God's wisdom!

Giants can be moments of opportunity, get optimistic!

Then David spoke to the men who stood by him, saying, 'What shall be done for the man who kills this Philistine and takes away the reproach from Israel? For who is this uncircumcised Philistine, that he should defy the armies of the living God?'

1 Samuel 17:26

$\mathcal{S}$o, as we saw yesterday, David turns up and finds a giant of a man called Goliath threatening and mocking the armies of Israel and, more insultingly, their God, who was also his God. They may not have taken this personally but David did – he made it his problem but also his opportunity. I think David was a bit of an opportunist; he asks the men, 'OK, what is the prize in this fight? What does the winner get?' When we back up just one verse we see that there were indeed some great opportunities for the person who dealt with the giant problem that Israel had.

And it shall be that the man who kills him the king will enrich with great riches, will give him his daughter, and give his father's house exemption from taxes in Israel.
1 Samuel 17:25

- Great riches from the king (not just riches, great riches).

- A princess to marry: that would lift you instantly in your social circle, you would become a prince overnight!

- Tax-free living for your dad and his household (I personally like the sound of this one!).

David must have thought, 'Wow, what a great deal, all that for giving that giant 'a slap he won't forget'; it's a deal!'

Again, remember – unlike Saul, David was not afraid and was in a position to think about possible opportunities because he knew that God was with him; and if God is for you who can be against you, right? (see Romans 8:31).

Unlike the rest of the armies of Israel, who were frozen by fear, David was in a 'covenant-based calm' that enabled him to see that this was not about great opposition but great opportunity. Think for a minute, Champion: what benefits will there be for you when you deal with your next giant? Be like David, see what others who are frozen by 'covenant-forgetting fear' cannot; get up and run at that giant that is in the way of you and some real great benefits!

God has anointed you to slap the living daylights out of your giant, so what are you waiting for?

Two healthy trees, not one

But the fruit of the Spirit is love, joy, peace, longsuffering, kindness, goodness, faithfulness, gentleness, self-control. Against such there is no law.

Galatians 5:22-23

O K, let's talk about character and the need for its development today.
As we daily walk with God we should be experiencing two things developing (growing) in our lives: we should be experiencing the gifts of the Spirit developing in and through our lives, and also the fruit of the Spirit. These are two very separate things and a healthy Christian always has the right amount of both! Remember, when we talk about the gifts of the Spirit as they are revealed in 1 Corinthians 12 we are talking about things that are given as gifts by God – we did nothing to get them. But when we speak about fruit we speak of things that are developed in our lives as we daily submit to, and walk in accordance with, God's ways.

If the gifts and fruits of the spirit were conifer trees standing at the front of the house of your life, would you have two healthy ones or would one be looking not so healthy? This world does not need to see any more gifted Christians, rather more God-gifted Christians who have great character too – people living lives where the fruit of the life of His Spirit now within is seen and experienced too.

We regularly see headlines concerning celebrities and football players who have cheated on their partners and lived in ways they should not have – lifestyles not fitting well with their influential public roles. Often these are young men and women thrown into a fickle industry where, very quickly, they have fame, money and anything they wanted. Sadly, many times we see that they do not have the character to carry the gift or opportunity given and it all blows up into yet another embarrassing headline. We have seen this happen in ministry too, which does the advancement of Christianity no favours at all.

Success needs to be judged more holistically – just because someone can kick a ball, sing or speak well does not mean they are successful! If the rest of their life has no character and is a mess then they are merely people with messed-up lives who do a good job performing on the stage or kicking a ball on pitch. If you want true success, Champion, then be committed to developing both the gifts God gives you and the fruit that it is down to you to grow. Don't worry, if you have the desire to then the Holy Spirit will help you all the way!

Live to be a person with two healthy trees – gifts and fruit, talent and character. God can use that time and time again!

Prayer

Good morning, Lord. Help me today to be busy on both trees in my life. Thank You not only for the gifts that You have given me but also the fruits that You are growing in me. Holy Spirit, I submit and yield to You today, work on my life where You need to, develop my character as You desire to. Cause my life to have two healthy trees that give glory to You.

Amen

LOVE YOUR NEIGHBOUR

Live a life full of love.
Ephesians 5:2 (The Truth)

Your neighbour is anyone you meet in life, but this weekend make a plan to do something for your actual next-door neighbour or person on your street. Let it be something that is so filled with God's unselfish love. I'm sure you've heard it said that 'love is an action word.' Well, put your love into action today. Maybe this person could use some help or possibly you could turn up to his or her home armed with some biscuits and a listening ear.

The possibilities are endless! Pray about how to bless them.

Notes

_____

_____

_____

_____

_____

_____

_____

_____

_____

What are you devising?

Also the schemes of the schemer are evil; he devises wicked plans to destroy the poor with lying words, even when the needy speaks justice. But a generous man devises generous things, and by generosity he shall stand.

Isaiah 32:7-8

*L*et's look at the subject of being generous people.

The promise of God to those who choose to be generous rather than stingy is an ever-enlarging life. Today the challenge is: what are you devising in your heart and what will what you're devising cause you to do? All of us continually devise stuff, the problem is that some devise wicked or selfish stuff while others devise generous stuff that causes blessing and profits the lives of others.

A generous man devises generous things

To devise is to plan, to plot, to secretly arrange. This really is the calling of the believer to be a person that is continually plotting and planning the blessing of others. This is also a real fun way to live.

We used to have a man in our church that I nicknamed the 'ten pound angel'. I knew who he was but no one else did. Every Sunday he would get some crisp £10 notes and then pray who he should give them to; then he would spend Sunday morning hiding the £10 notes in people's Bibles and bags. He caused a real stir as, each Sunday, people would discover a tenner or sometimes more in their Bible and, you guessed it, a lot of the time it came at a moment when it was really needed; but no one knew (except God). I used to love watching this man creep around church hiding £10 notes, knowing that he had spent the morning praying and devising generous things to bless others (note: he did this as well as tithe, not instead of!).

The promise to those who choose to live a life that devises generous plans for others, and not wicked or mean ones, is that you will stand. Do current news headlines of lack and recession worry you? Then take this promise personally – it clearly says that it's the generosity of the one who devises good to others that will cause him to stand, even when there is a recession or when others may fall.

Get devising: remember, generosity is not just financial. You can be generous with many things: time, energy, encouragement, the list goes on and on!

*In my experience more people are 'hard of listening'
than 'hard of hearing'.*

Andy Elmes

Give us our daily bread

The tempter came to Him and said, 'If you are the Son of God, tell these stones to become bread.' Jesus answered, 'It is written: "Man shall not live on bread alone, but on every word that comes from the mouth of God."'

Matthew 4:3-4 (NIV)

Remember today that we do not live by natural bread (food) alone, but it is God's every word coming into our lives that causes us to grow in our true strength and potential.

Natural bread (food) profits the natural man but is unable to give the needed nutrition and fibre that your spirit craves for. Only God's Word will satisfy that inner appetite. That Bible you own contains the living words of God. Each sentence, thought, and principle is power-packed and able to produce in you, and through you, incredible things. Make sure you take time to daily eat the bread of God, not just the bread of man.

Don't try and live by natural things alone. Jesus said that a man cannot do that because he needs the words of God to be all that he was designed for and destined to be.

Ever heard the term 'GIGO'? It stands for 'garbage in, garbage out'. Listen, when you make sure you have a daily input of divine bread – which is God's Word, the Bible – you change that principle to a more positive reality, which is 'God in, God out'. You will experience life and power coming from you at every corner, and not garbage.

Jesus demonstrated the power of the Word of God when He was tempted by satan in a time of physical weakness. In times of trouble or temptation you too will have the answer because you would have digested it earlier. Champion, take time to regularly eat the bread that God has given, and when you do you are fit for life.

I pray you ever fall in love with the Word of God and may God give you today your daily bread!

The Christian shoemaker does his duty not by putting little crosses on the shoes, but by making good shoes, because God is interested in good craftsmanship.

Martin Luther

Where is your storehouse?

'Bring the whole tithe into the storehouse, that there may be food in My house. Test Me in this,' says the LORD Almighty, 'and see if I will not throw open the floodgates of heaven and pour out so much blessing that there will not be room enough to store it.'

Malachi 3:10 (NIV)

The Bible says we are to bring the whole tithe (tenth part) into the storehouse – so what does it mean by storehouse? I believe that the very next thing the verse says gives us our needed explanation: 'That there may be food [or provision] in My house.' It is obvious to me that when the Bible uses the word 'storehouse' it is referring to the church, God's house. So what church or storehouse should you take your tithe to? Simple, the one you belong to, the one that pastorally cares for you and feeds you God's Word on a weekly basis.

Maybe you are reading this and you don't have a local church. My advice is simple: get one! It is a major part of God's master plan for you becoming all He has destined for you to be. The church is still God's house and still His master plan, so make sure your life is in one. Others may say, 'I give my tithe to television ministers and various charitable organisations' – my only problem with this is, God never said to do that. He said bring the whole tithe (all of it) to His house and let the leadership of the house of God distribute it where it is seen to be needed. Sorry, God never said, 'bring a bit and do what you want with a bit,' it's just not in there.

The Bible speaks of tithes and offerings, and these are two very different things. Basically, tithes are the first ten per cent of your income and offerings are anything you choose to give or sow that are above and beyond the tithe. The reality is you don't give anything till your tithe is paid – first comes the tithe then what comes next is the offering.

Your offering can be planted like seeds anywhere you choose. When you see need that touches your heart you can step in and meet it with your offering; but the tithe is not yours to distribute as you see fit, it is to be brought to God's house, the church. Why? As it says in the text, that there may be food or provision in His house. A part of that provision is to be used to meet the needs of people outside the house, but a church can't do this effectively unless they have the resource in the store to do so.

The tithe is God's plan for the provision of His house. This plan only goes wrong when people don't do it. The church was never meant to go cap in hand to the local council or beg income at jumble sales. The local church was always meant to be sustained by the faithful giving of the people that call it their spiritual home. It's a great plan that works perfectly when everybody lives by the plan.

Sorry for speaking so bluntly about this but there seems to be so much deceptive junk being taught and believed in regard to this matter and it is time to get back to the simplicity of what the Bible teaches. Bring your tithe to the place you call your local church; do so joyfully knowing you are empowering your church to make a difference in people lives, the community and even the world through missions programmes; after you have brought your tithe to God's house, do whatever you want and bless as many as you can with whatever you have left. Hey, it is now your offering and you are free to do what you want, where you want – make sure your giving is being done according to His design.

Remember, God's not trying to rob you; He is trying to bless you.

Your drought is about to end

Then Elijah said to Ahab, 'Go up, eat and drink; for there is the sound of abundance of rain.' So Ahab went up to eat and drink. And Elijah went up to the top of Carmel; then he bowed down on the ground, and put his face between his knees, and said to his servant, 'Go up now, look toward the sea.' So he went up and looked, and said, 'There is nothing.' And seven times he said, 'Go again.' Then it came to pass the seventh time, that he said, 'There is a cloud, as small as a man's hand, rising out of the sea!' So he said, 'Go up, say to Ahab, "Prepare your chariot, and go down before the rain stops you."'

1 Kings 18:41-44

In this account we see God end a drought that had been in the land. God sends the prophet Elijah to go to the king and prophesy the end of a drought they were in. This is fitting because it had actually been Elijah that had prophesied and caused the drought to happen, when the king had offended God with idol worship (1 Kings 17:1). But the time had come for it to end, and for the rains to come and refresh the land. Elijah begins to prophesy, saying, 'I hear the sound of the abundance of rain.'

This was prophetic because there was no visible evidence that rain would come anytime soon. When the people looked across the land it looked like just another sun-scorched day. But Elijah was seeing according to what God was revealing, and by faith he was speaking of unseen things that he knew had been dispatched by God. Elijah goes away and prays, and sends his servant to stand on a hill and look for evidence. Six times the servant returns and says to the prophet, 'Still no evidence.' So Elijah sends him a seventh time, knowing what God had shown him. This time the servant returns saying, 'There is a cloud, I see a cloud! It's only small but it's a cloud, and it's coming this way.' Elijah then instructs him to go and get ready because the amount of rain that is coming has the potential to stop him on the way!

Maybe you have been in a drought-like season, where everything has been dry and dusty, and provision so very short (even hopeless!). I believe that God is saying to those people who have waited in faith so patiently: 'The drought is about to end.' It's time to get to your feet and look again over the horizon with faith, and keep looking till you see the cloud – it's coming your way! It may look like the size of a man's hand right now but that it is only because it is still a way off. Believe me, it's not actually a small cloud, and when it gets to you it will be plenty big enough to flood your life with all you need.

Maybe the time you have spent waiting for the drought to end has worn you out; maybe you settled in your heart that you have looked enough? Let me encourage you to look again and, like I said, don't despise its current size. It will get bigger and bigger as the wind of God blows it in your direction. Every Christmas we sing, 'Let it snow, let it snow, let it snow' – it's time to change the words and by faith begin to sing, 'Let it rain, let it rain, let it rain!'

Get your umbrella ready – it's coming. The drought is about to end, I hear the sound of an abundance of rain!

You'll love what's coming next

We went through fire and water, but You brought us to a place of abundance.

Psalm 66:12 (NIV)

Maybe when you look back, or even look where you presently are, you can fully relate to the first part of this verse. Maybe it feels like you've been through the fire and the water. Maybe it feels like you have had your very own 'furnace experience' and – like the three young Israelites Shadrach, Meshach and Abednego in the book of Daniel, chapter 3 – you also have walked in the flames, maybe the flames of testing or affliction.

But, did you notice that the flames, though they were not fun, did not harm you? In fact, all they actually burnt away was the ropes and things that held you captive.

Maybe it feels like you've been through the waters. Like Moses and the children of Israel, you have passed through your very own Red Sea moment where all you could see was water all around you that had the potential to drown you at any moment. But now, as you look back, you see all that was drowned were the Egyptians that were giving chase to bring you back into captivity.

Those seasons when it feels like you are in the fire or in the floods can be hard; they can be confusing times but, at the end, you see that God was actually using them for your good. Normally they have a plan of freedom attached to them. Now for the good bit! If you have been through the fire and the water, according to this verse the next place for you to experience is 'a place of abundance'. Get excited, Champion, the whole time God has been actually leading you to a place of abundance; it was just that you had to come through the other places to get there free.

If you have known the fire and the floods in your life, by faith begin to now thank God for the place of abundance He is bringing you to. You may not fully understand why you had to go through those other places now but, believe me, one day you will. Remember, you came through them, you did not die in them. Like with Shadrach, Meshach and Abednego, all that was actually burnt were the ropes that were around your wrists and, like Moses, all the water actually drowned were things you did not need following you anymore!

I like how The Message puts it:

> *Didn't He set us on the road to life? Didn't He keep us out of the ditch? He trained us first, passed us like silver through refining fires, brought us into hardscrabble country, pushed us to our very limit, road-tested us inside and out, took us to hell and back; finally He brought us to this well-watered place.*

BE A WITNESS

And you will be my witnesses.
Acts 1:8 (NIV)

As Christians we are called to be witnesses for Christ, spreading the good news of the gospel to all. Our mission is to show God's love in our actions and in how we behave, and we're called to be bold and speak up about our faith when we get the chance to. It's a wonderful thing when we can have conversations with people about what we believe and how God has made a huge difference in our lives.

Your challenge this weekend is to pray for an opportunity to arise where you can share with someone about what God has done in your life and how He can make a difference in their life as well. The Bible says we should always be ready to give an answer for the hope that we have within us (1 Peter 3:15-16).

Be bold and take any opportunity God gives to introduce someone to Christ. In preparation, write down some of the reasons you chose to follow Christ and how that has made a difference in your life.

Notes

_____

_____

_____

_____

_____

_____

Relating to your heavenly Father

It was I who taught Ephraim [Israel] to walk taking them by the arms; but they did not realise it was I who healed them. I led them with cords of human kindness, with ties of love. To them I was like one who lifts a little child to the cheek, and I bent down to feed them.

Hosea 11:3-4 (NIV)

This scripture paints God in such a normal, beautiful, fatherly way.

In my head I see a regular dad in jeans and a t-shirt in the park with his toddler who is lifting his arms toward daddy. He reaches down to hold the little child's arms and catches him just as he loses his balance. The child is a bit scared at having nearly fallen so the daddy lifts the child and holds him close to his face so that they are cheek to cheek. How comforting for the child to feel the familiar, warm, bristly skin of his dad and how tender the child's soft face feels to the father.

In Hosea 11:3 we see an affection that a father has for his child as he lifts him, cuddles him and nurtures him with food. We must not ever forget that our Father God is this Dad to us. Like any good parent, He never desires for us to struggle and have pain. He wants to comfort us and provide for our needs. Any decent earthly dad would desire to do good for his son or daughter and so God, who is better than any dad, is no different.

Or what man is there among you who, when his son asks for bread, will give him a stone? Or if he asks for a fish, he will give him a serpent? If you then, being evil, know how to give good gifts to your children, how much more will your Father who is in heaven give good things to those who ask Him!

Matthew 7:9-11

Sometimes as a parent I have to teach my kids important lessons or reprimand them, but because I love them I would never teach lessons cruelly or in a way that would destroy them, and I know God would not do this either. He is our loving Father and if we remember this in the hard times we will know that it isn't God causing us pain for our good but rather it is our Father who is holding us tightly through the tough times, protecting us from the wind and waves and lifting us when we fall.

Show people you love them with your actions, don't just tell them with your words. Love is a verb.

Andy Elmes

Experiencing God in relationship

Moses and Aaron then went into the tent of meeting. When they came out, they blessed the people; and the glory of the LORD appeared to all the people. Fire came out from the presence of the LORD and consumed the burnt offering and the fat portions on the altar. And when all the people saw it, they shouted for joy and fell face down.

Leviticus 9:23-24 (NIV)

The scripture above is an account of when God in all His glory turned up in power. It says His glory appeared to the Israelites and fire came from His presence and consumed the offering!

Imagine seeing this with your very own eyes. It also says that those who saw this shouted for joy and fell face down. I bet they did! They had an amazing God experience. After seeing and experiencing God in such a visual and tangible way you would think that this would have had a deep and lasting impression on their lives and that they would be so sold out to follow after Him. You would imagine that this occurrence would have solidified their honour and faithfulness towards Him; but as you read on in the Old Testament that did not happen. The children of Israel were serially unfaithful.

I have been in meetings and have felt such a strong presence of God and I have even experienced supernatural healing. Once I had a horrible sinus infection. It was so painful and I remember saying to a friend that I was going to the doctor straight away in the morning. That night I prayed for God to take the pain away and I went to sleep. I woke up the next day and I had no sinus infection at all! Not even a drippy nose, not anything. God showed His power. God experiences are wonderful and I love when amazing and miraculous things happen, but what is even more wonderful is relationship and faithfulness.

How different the journey of the Israelites could have been if they not only enjoyed the amazing awe-filled moments but if they also daily bowed their hearts to God and, through thick and thin, chose to honour Him rather than seek out idols and other things to bring satisfaction to their lives. If you choose relationship rather than living off experiences alone in your walk with God then you will never grow cold towards Him. Some of the most amazing people in God's Word were people who daily chose to walk after God; like Daniel, who consistently spent time in prayer, and David, who spent hours in God's presence worshipping.

I love God's presence at all times and a 'God encounter' can change and impact a person forever, but I would never seek to replace the richness of knowing God and consistently living in His presence for anything. Don't seek to follow after God experiences. Seek to follow after God and His experiences will inevitably follow after you.

He will not forget

God is not unjust; He will not forget your work and the love you have shown Him as you have helped His people and continue to help them.

Hebrews 6:10 (NIV)

Any good that we ever do for either another person or to further God's kingdom should never be done with the intention to get anything in return. Whatever we do should purely be done to help another person in need, just as you yourself would desire to be helped if you were in need, and to bring God honour, no strings attached.

Unselfishly giving love away is what God is all about but that doesn't mean you won't get a reward for all the good you do for others and for God. Our heavenly Father is fully aware of every act of kindness, every gesture of pure love and every work done on behalf of His Kingdom. He is not forgetful like we are when we get tired or have far too many things going on in our lives.

Sometimes things slip our minds. If you have ever made a promise to a child about something, even if it was made in haste or out of desperation – for example, 'If you go to sleep without giving me any problems I promise I'll buy you some sweets tomorrow' – and you completely forget about it the next day, believe me, that child will remind you many times over that they did as you asked and are fully expecting those sweets! The only thing God chooses to forget is our sins.

Isaiah 43:25 (NIV) says, 'I, even I, am He who blots out your transgressions, for My own sake, and remembers your sins no more.' He never forgets all the great, wonderful and unselfish acts we perform on His behalf and He is a God of great blessings and loves to pour them out on His children. Remember also that God's blessings and rewards in our lives may not always come in the form that we think a 'blessing or reward' might, or should, look like. I couldn't even begin to say how God will bless a person. I have had blessings come into my life in all forms, from the joy that comes to me when I see how something I've done for someone has changed their lives for the better, to the flowers sent to me by a beautiful friend who knew I was going through a hard time and wanted to lighten my heaviness a little.

God is no man's debtor and although we don't do good to get from God, like any natural father, it gives God pleasure to bless His children as they bless Him.

Prayer

Father, thank You that You watch over my life and do not forget the things I do for You or for others. Help me today to continue to give my life away to benefit others. Thank You, Father, that You are no man's debtor and whatever I have given away You restore a hundred times over. Let my life demonstrate Your love and generosity again today.

Amen

God can handle our impossible

Saul replied, 'You are not able to go out against this Philistine and fight him; you are only a young man, and he has been a warrior from his youth.' So David triumphed over the Philistine with a sling and a stone.

1 Samuel 17:33, 50 (NIV)

There was a famine in the land. Then Isaac sowed in that land and reaped in the same year a hundredfold.

Genesis 26:1, 12

Abraham fell face down; he laughed and said to himself, 'Will a son be born to a man a hundred years old? Will Sarah bear a child at the age of ninety?'

Genesis 17:17 (NIV)

Abraham gave the name Isaac to the son Sarah bore him.

Genesis 21:3 (NIV)

Sometimes things look absolutely impossible in the natural. How can someone plant crops in a time of famine and yet yield a bumper crop and be considered very blessed? How does a young shepherd boy who knows almost nothing of war fight a renowned warrior who also happens to be a giant and win? How does a man and his barren wife, who is well beyond child-bearing years, produce a child?

It has almost nothing to do with human ability and everything to do with God's ability. When we are trusting God to come through on His promises concerning us and the odds do not look like they are in our favour we can still remain strong and in faith regarding God's ability. He's not in heaven sweating and wringing His hands about how bad the situation seems. He is able and we can trust in that; but also, we know who we are trusting in. Our heavenly Father is filled with love for His children.

And so we know and rely on the love God has for us. God is love.

1 John 4:16 (NIV)

He is for us and not against us. It is His good pleasure to give us good gifts and to help us on our journey. Ephesians 3:20 (NIV) says, 'Now to Him who is able to do immeasurably more than all we ask or imagine, according to his power that is at work within us.' Trust in God. He is more than able to handle even the impossible for the ones He loves. He has done it for others and He will do it for you. Believe.

No one can make you feel inferior without your permission.

Eleanor Roosevelt

Overwhelmed

The waters closed over my head and I thought I was about to perish. I called on Your name, LORD, from the depths of the pit. You heard my plea . . . You came near when I called You, and You said, 'Do not fear.'

Lamentations 3:54-57 (NIV)

---

nnoyed by Jeremiah the prophet's gloomy but true prophetic words to the unfaithful children of Israel, they cast him into a pit of mud and water and left him to die as he sank in the mire. Jeremiah knew the end was near as the water began to rise up to his nose and as he sank further into the earth. He began to call on God for help. His prayers were probably gasps coming from someone who was sinking and in desperation, but the beautiful thing here is that God heard Jeremiah's plea. Some men had a change of heart and went back and pulled Jeremiah out of the pit.

Prior to their arrival, and while overwhelmed, I'm sure he thought, 'So this is how it ends!', but still he called out to God and deliverance came.

Life is filled with deep pits of all sorts – grief, shame, depression, impossible situations, poor health, family problems, financial hardship, etc. When people going through difficult times are asked how they are doing, a common response is, 'Just trying to keep my head above water!' As a mum of five and a wife I'm also sometimes overwhelmed by life's pitfalls, some of which have been serious health issues in both my husband and one of my children, teens that have made what I feel were poor choices, large unexpected bills, grief, anxiety, feelings of worthlessness and more. But 'calling on the name of the Lord' is the key here. God loves you and cares about you.

Psalm 34:19 says that the righteous person faces many troubles, but the Lord comes to the rescue each time. So lift your head and call on God in all your troubles, even while the water seems overwhelming. He will hear your plea and forgive you whether you inflicted this trouble on yourself or not, and He will help you to feel firm ground beneath you again.

The story of Christian reformation, revival, and renaissance underscores that the darkest hour is often just before the dawn, so we should always be people of hope and prayer, not gloom and defeatism. God the Holy Spirit can turn the situation around in five minutes.

Os Guinness

MAKE SOMEONE'S DAY
A LITTLE BRIGHTER

A glad heart makes a happy face.
Proverbs 15:13

This weekend, make someone's day a little brighter. Think of someone you can do something nice for, 'a random act of kindness'. You can even bless a complete stranger if you want to. Get creative. Here are some thoughts:

- Buy a coffee and donut for a homeless person

- Offer to babysit for a friend's children for free

- Use a skill you possess to help someone for free

- Wash someone's car and vacuum it out

- Bake a cake and bring it over to someone's house

- Rake the leaves in someone's garden

Notice that most of these things are free or cost very little. It's more about showing another person that they have value and there's someone who cares.

Notes

_____

_____

_____

_____

_____

Behind the scenes

Trust in the LORD with all your heart and lean not on your own understanding; in all your ways submit to Him, and He will make your paths straight.

Proverbs 3:5-6 (NIV)

The account of Esther in the Bible is about God working behind the scenes for the good of His people. There was one plan going on at the forefront of the story and there's a 'behind-the-scenes' story that the characters in the account are not privy to in the way that the reader is.

We see an evil-hearted man named Haman who wants to destroy the Jews. He plots and schemes and thinks he is literally getting away with murder. I imagine he felt on top of the world that his evil plot was going so smoothly. Meanwhile, Esther, a young lady of Jewish heritage, although she keeps this fact a secret, is discovered and marries the king. As the reader we get to see the plan of God unfolding as an unlikely ambassador, Queen Esther, is set in place to save her people from the plot that was to destroy them. At the end of the account we see the plot to destroy the Jewish people foiled as the triumph of God's plan is fully revealed. Esther announces her Jewish heritage to her king and she also reveals that Haman would have her and all her people destroyed. Haman is sentenced to death and the people are saved!

I love the threading of the two plots in this account, the plan of destruction and the plan of salvation. This is true of the plots and the plans in our lives as well. In some of our circumstances there may seem to be a plan that is unfolding in a horrible downward spiral. We see the evidence at every turn of our ship going down. Remember, Esther knew that there was a plot by one of the king's advisors to destroy her people and because of her gender in that time in history, her word over that of a respected male member of the government would not hold water. She didn't know how this story she found herself in would end. Being queen in her time did not mean she could go have a quick chat with the king and all was well. There was every reason this account should have ended terribly.

Proverbs 3:5-6 is a promise of God that has been such a strength to me in times when I have not been able to see past my 'sinking ship' and all the evidence pointing towards a watery grave. I am assured by God that if I place my trust in Him and refuse to lean on how things look on the surface, and as I yield my will to His, the crooked paths that are before me will be made straight. Today, whatever plot is looking grim on your behalf, take it to the Lord and lay it at His feet. Decide to trust Him with your whole heart and say, 'I choose to trust that God is working in the fabric of this situation and threading His plans behind-the-scene for my good.' Also, be trusting enough to let God do things His way even if it isn't exactly how you imagined the finished product would be. Trust Him today.

Tasty!

When Your words came, I ate them; they were my joy and my heart's delight, for I bear Your name, LORD God Almighty.

Jeremiah 15:16 (NIV)

---

remember I was on a real health kick and I was trying to eat only the healthiest of foods. I cut out sugar and bad fats and everything that tasted good it seems. One day, after about 4 weeks or so of eating cardboard-like food, I got a whiff of a cinnamon role. I looked at it for about 1 second before this tasty morsel was history. Yes, I devoured it and I remember trying to savour every moment of its warm, cinnamon, gooey goodness before I returned to cardboard land. Oh, how it satisfied!

That was a few years ago and I'm salivating at the memory of that moment as I write this! This is how I feel about God's Word. I'm sure that in your human experience, as in mine, you have ups and downs and dry desert-like times as well as mountain-top experiences and utterly devastating times too. I have found that in all my situations and in everything I go through, the Word of God has always been like a choice, delicious morsel of delight that satisfies whatever craving or need that I have. I guess I have to take it back to the platform with which I read my Bible – I am delving into God's thoughts about me, and for me and I am drinking in His wisdom when I approach His Word. I know God's thoughts and wisdom supersede my own. I also know that a promise from Almighty God, Creator of the Universe and the one who allows me to call Him Father is something I can hang onto with confidence even on the darkest of days. In the following scripture the apostle Paul writes:

When you received the word of God, which you heard from us, you accepted it not as a human word, but as it actually is, the word of God.

1 Thessalonians 2:13 (NIV)

There have been days in my life when all I had was a promise from God and it was enough for me because I knew it wasn't man-made wisdom. Sometimes the promise of God so hits the bulls-eye in a situation that it is sweeter than anything you could taste on Earth. I read some great quotes from great people and I get inspired by them, but God's words more than just inspire me, they bring life where there isn't any, they challenge me and cause me to grow, they light dark places in my soul and they satisfy the deepest parts of who I am.

The truest evidence of your love for him is your obedience to Him.

Andy Elmes

Beating discouragement
PART 1

But as for me, afflicted and in pain – may Your salvation, God, protect me.

Psalm 69:29 (NIV)

There will always be a fight for your destiny because that is just how life is. Obstacles can come in the form of issues regarding money, health, jobs and just about any situation that looms in the shadows that isn't conducive to your dream coming to pass. Sometimes our own doubts, fears, and trust issues can become obstacles in our lives, especially if we seem to be waiting for a long time for God's help. When this happens and we feel in a time of lack in one way or another while we wait on God, it is easy to become discouraged. Discouragement is the loss of confidence or enthusiasm, feeling let down and disappointed even crushed. When we allow these feelings to settle in our heart we can begin to question God's love for us. Can we really trust Him? Am I alone in this situation? There are tools to overcome these feelings while we wait patiently for God to bring us through to a great testimony. The first of these tools is:

Know that God is for you and not against you

God is a good Father and He is filled with love for you, end of story, full stop. There's nothing you can add to that truth. Not even a 'but I'm unworthy'. None of us are worthy and He still loves us! You will be spoiled for choice at the verses in the Bible that reveal how much God loves you and wants to do good by you. I can't print the whole Bible here and there's so much I couldn't put because of space but here are a few verses to meditate on and get into your spirit of how much God is for you:

> *The Lord is compassionate and gracious, slow to anger, abounding in love.*
> Psalm 103:8 (NIV)

> *So do not fear, for I am with you; do not be dismayed, for I am your God. I will strengthen you and help you; I will uphold you with my righteous right hand.*
> Isaiah 41:10 (NIV)

> *This is how we know what love is: Jesus Christ laid down His life for us.*
> 1 John 3:16 (NIV)

Right now, start beating down discouragement with the truth that God is your biggest cheerleader in this life. His desire for you is only good.

Beating discouragement
PART 2

But Zion said, 'The LORD has forsaken me, the Lord has forgotten me.' Can a mother forget the baby at her breast and have no compassion on the child she has borne? Though she may forget, I will not forget you!

Isaiah 49:14-15 (NIV)

In the fight of faith for our destiny and dreams there is sometimes that wait between when we pray and when we see the fruition of our prayers and it is in this time that we must guard our hearts from discouragement.

The second tool for overcoming discouragement is to remember that God is still with you even when it seems that He has gone very quiet.

I'm a mother and in this fast-paced world where my five kids have to be in so many directions throughout the day sometimes I leave notes in prominent places for those I need to get messages to. I will often leave my son messages on how to properly get dinner ready for himself when I've left ingredients out and, yes, I'm one of those embarrassing mothers who puts sweet notes on serviettes in his packed lunches. I do this so he can find these notes and remember how much his mother loves him. The Bible, and every promise therein, is our heavenly Father's note to us of how much He loves us. What else does God need to say that He hasn't already said in His Word? He's said everything that He wants to say to us and now we have to put it in front of our faces and remind ourselves of what He's said.

Also, my oldest child, who is an adult, isn't currently living at home. I was a little worried when she ventured out on her own, but I was also aware of her maturity and knew I didn't need to treat her like I did when she was an infant or a child. I didn't need to spoon feed her squishy cereal or give her a sippy cup and wipe her chin every few minutes because I trained her to be independent. Even though she is not directly under my care anymore, she knows her dad and I are always there for her and we are only a text or phone call away. She also knows that even when I haven't been in touch for a few days that she is always in my heart and mind. God has promised that He will never leave us or forsake us. He's there and still working on your behalf.

I'll end with this:

> *Your path led through the sea, your way through the mighty waters, though your footprints were not seen.*
>
> Psalm 77:19 (NIV)

Maturity means you don't need to see His footprints to know He's leading you to your Promised Land.

Beating discouragement
PART 3

Catch all the foxes, those little foxes, before they ruin the vineyard of love, for the grapevines are blossoming!

Song of Solomon 2:15 (NLT)

The little foxes in the vineyard of love are those questions you allow to ruminate and dwell in your mind that cause you to question God's good character and see Him in a false light: Is God really for me? Is God punishing me? Has He left me?

When we dwell on these lies we allow false pictures of our heavenly Father to mar our love for Him. You fall out of love with Him degree by degree as you dwell on these little, seemingly harmless, questions. It's like those little foxes chewing away a beautiful garden and destroying its beauty. You don't see the harm right away but, after awhile, the garden has lost its lustre. Psalm 37:4 says, 'Delight yourself also in the LORD, and He shall give you the desires of your heart.'

Everything you need and desire is meant to spring out of your love relationship with your heavenly Father and by letting your love be nibbled away you are ironically cutting yourself off from your source of blessing. In the times where we are waiting in faith for God's promises to be fulfilled it can be tempting to think negatively about God and to imagine that He is going to let you down but you have to look at things a little closer. How about all the small things He does for you on the journey that help to sustain you. How about the fact that you woke up today and you're alive.

When I was in a very dark corridor of faith with a situation in my life I wasn't yet seeing any breakthrough but I saw some other amazing things in one of my children who suddenly went from someone I had to force to go to church to someone who had a real zeal and passion for God. In a time when discouragement seemed to be eating away at my soul I fell at God's feet and thanked Him for this beautiful miracle. Notice the last line of Song of Solomon 2:15: 'for the grapevines are blossoming!' What comes after blossoms fall? Fruit! Don't allow those stinky, little foxes to steal your fruit!

Your greatest tool in keeping discouragement away is to love God passionately while you are waiting in faith for His promises.

Your life is better defined when there are healthy margins in it stop living on the edge of the page.

Andy Elmes

SPEND SOME TIME ALONE

But Jesus often withdrew to lonely places
and prayed.
Luke 5:16

If Jesus needed to get alone and pray then we probably need to do that as well. As a matter of fact, I'm sure of it.

Your challenge this weekend is to find time to get away from the hustle and bustle of your life and quiet yourself before the Lord.

It doesn't need to be hours. Even a few minutes of quiet reflection in God's presence can refresh the soul, but you may find that it turns into a longer time than you planned. Your heavenly Father desires to have your full attention. Prayer is talking to God. Talk to your Father and tell Him what's on your mind. Then just sit in His presence and listen for His still, small voice.

He's waiting to meet with you.

Notes

_____

_____

_____

_____

_____

_____

Been praying?

The Lord told him, 'Go to the house of Judas on Straight Street and ask for a man from Tarsus named Saul, for he is praying.'

Acts 9:11(NIV)

At any given moment God knows who is praying and He's listening. God knew exactly when and where Saul was when he was in prayer and He knew where to send the help that he needed. Remember that, at this point, Saul was still without sight from his encounter on the Damascus Road, where he had been blinded by a bright light. The Bible tells us he was in the house praying for God to restore his sight, among other things I'm sure, and God was right on the case.

When you pray God is right there, not somewhere off in the cosmos being indifferent towards His creation. He is aware of the intimate details of our lives and knows when His children are speaking to Him. He hears you, sees you, knows your address and the deepest desires of your heart and all of your personal needs. He is ready to meet His child at the moment the first word rolls off the tongue. Proverbs 15:29 says that He hears the prayer of the righteous.

What a great privilege to have a personal audience whenever we want with the Lord of all creation, who also invites us to be His children and call Him Father. It's overwhelming if you dwell on those thoughts. If God knows when His children are in prayer then the opposite is true as well. When people choose not to pray or can't really be bothered because of a busy life or other excuses, He knows. This is not to condemn anyone but rather to inspire.

It inspires me as a pastor and also a busy woman with many family commitments to know that there is a quiet place that God wants to meet with me, and that when He hears me say His name in prayer I'm His focus and His whole desire is to help me, heal me, sort out my problems and give me all I daily need to live life.

I'm not waiting for a move of God. I am a move of God.

William Booth

What does His blood say?

To Jesus the Mediator of the new covenant, and to the blood of sprinkling that speaks better things than that of Abel.

Hebrews 12:24

That's an interesting statement, isn't it? What it is informing us is that the precious blood of Jesus, shed for us two thousand years ago, speaks better things than that of Able's. To fully grasp the powerful truth being revealed here you have to remember back to the account of Cain and Able, the sons of Adam and Eve, found in Genesis 4. In a jealous rage, and against God's warning, Cain slays his innocent brother Able. God then asks Cain about his brother's whereabouts, to which Cain responds with that well-known statement, 'Am I my brother's keeper?' God responds by saying something very interesting in verse 10: 'What have you done? The voice of your brother's blood cries out to Me from the ground.'

Despite what Cain was saying, or indeed not saying, God was listening to another voice, the voice of Able's innocent blood crying from the ground. I wonder what it was saying? Surely it was things like, 'He killed me, he is a murderer; Cain is guilty of my murder.' There was no room for cover-up because the blood was speaking concerning what was true, leaving Cain without any defence. Now let us remember our text today and, as we do, let's remember that Jesus also died an innocent man, in that He did not deserve death as He had never done anything wrong. The death He knew belonged to another: us! He was also murdered to settle an argument between God and man, yet His blood does not speak like the blood of Able's – rather it speaks 'better things' or, as the NIV says so well, 'a better word than the blood of Able'. That better word is blessed not cursed.

Actually, the blood of Jesus shed for us speaks the complete opposite to Able's; it does not declare over us 'guilty' but 'forgiven'; it does not cry out death but new life; it declares acceptance not rejection, redemption not punishment.

That's such an amazing thought, isn't it – that today the blood of Jesus declares over you, 'Washed from every sin, forgiven every trespass, purchased and restored.'

This is something that is so important for us to remember each and every day, that the blood of our High Priest and Mediator Jesus does not shut a door for us, like Able's did for Cain, but rather opens wide a door for us to come boldly before Father God. What Jesus' blood declares over us, and what it achieved for us, is what gives us the confidence to stand as those who have been totally forgiven. That blood, that spilled down an old wooden cross and into the ground, is the same blood that was presented to the Father for our eternal redemption (Hebrews 9:12), that blood still speaks loud and clear: 'Forgiven, forgiven, forgiven', to which we surely must respond, 'Amen, Amen, Amen.'

His blood produces our boldness

Let us therefore come boldly to the throne of grace, that we may obtain mercy and find grace to help in time of need.

Hebrews 4:16

God wants us and welcomes us to come into His presence with boldness. Boldness is God-given confidence, not man-made arrogance. It's a confidence that comes from a revelation that the One who made a way for you to enter by His own blood now sits and welcomes you to come on in. In Psalms 100 we are encouraged to enter the Father's presence with thanksgiving and praise – this is indeed correct etiquette that we would be wise to remember. But a third component to entering correctly and enjoying His presence as you should is to remember that you are there by His invitation. Your High Priest, Jesus, made the way for you to be able to enter. To fully understand verse 16 you need to read the verses that precede it.

> *Seeing then that we have a great High Priest who has passed through the heavens, Jesus the Son of God, let us hold fast our confession. For we do not have a High Priest who cannot sympathise with our weaknesses, but was in all points tempted as we are, yet without sin.*
>
> Hebrews 4:14-15

As well as being the Lamb of God who took away the sin of the world by shedding His own blood, He Himself is also the One who goes before us and secures our approach before the Father. I am so blessed when I read these verses that it reveals to us that our High Priest is not unapproachable or non-understanding concerning who we are and the lives we live here on earth. Rather, He knows what it is to live life on earth, to be tempted in every way. We must also remember, though tempted in every way, He did not sin; this would have disqualified Him from taking our sins upon Himself.

After Jesus rose from the dead He entered into the heavenly temple of God and presented blood to the Father for the forgiveness of sin for all humanity, but unlike the high priests in the Old Testament He did not present the blood of animals, but rather His own blood. It was only His blood, you see, that could take away the sins of the world – rather than cover them for a moment.

When He presented His blood before the Father every debt was forgiven, and He took again His former place at the right-hand side of the Father, having opened again the gates of heaven to the lost and separated sons and daughters of Adam and Eve. Why am I saying this? Because I want you to understand that when you come into the presence of God today you need to do so with confidence; not confidence found in anything that you have done but rather in what Jesus your High Priest did for you. The One who made a way for you now bids you come, so come knowing His blood was more than enough to qualify you to. Come boldly!

His blood provides our confidence

Therefore, brethren, having boldness to enter the Holiest by the blood of Jesus, by a new and living way which He consecrated for us, through the veil, that is, His flesh, and having a High Priest over the house of God, let us draw near with a true heart in full assurance of faith, having our hearts sprinkled from an evil conscience and our bodies washed with pure water.

Hebrews 10:19-22

*G*od wants us to 'feel at home' in His presence, He does not want us to feel like trespassers but those who belong. I remember as a child climbing with my friends into neighbourhood gardens to steal their apples. One of us would be up the tree while the other would keep watch because we were not welcome, and we knew it. We were waiting for the moment we would be 'found out'. Sadly, many of God's people are no different when they are in His presence and that must break His heart. You see, if you have believed in His Son and received His gift of salvation you are no longer a trespasser, you belong. No matter what you did, you have been forgiven and you are welcome.

Again, to correctly empower this truth we must remember that Jesus is our High Priest and He has made a 'living way' into the presence of God – living because it was made with His life. We have spoken a lot about His blood this week and this is vitally important because it is knowing that we have been purchased and sprinkled with His blood that gives us confidence of a new start and, as our text today says, a full assurance that we are now accepted in His presence.

'High Priest' is an interesting title; to fully understand what Jesus did you have to refer to the High Priests in the Old Testament because they were indeed a type and shadow of who would come. The Old Testament reveals to us a temple on earth, a direct replica of what things are like in heaven. It is when we watch and see how the High Priests operated in an earthly temple as per God's instructions that we can begin to grasp how wonderfully our High Priest, Jesus, secured for us a confidence of faith regarding our right to stand blameless in His presence. To highlight a specific aspect of this I want you to see that there was an etiquette in the Old Testament regarding coming into God's presence. It was very precise, drawn out and involved one man – the High Priest – representing the people. You can study for yourself all he had to do to get to the moment when he stepped beyond the veil into the place called the Holy of Holies, which was where God's direct presence was. Remember, the people did not go in, the High Priest went in representing the people. Through the presentation of animal blood, a place of standing was secured for him on behalf of the people.

Let me make this point: Jesus, being the actual High Priest and not just a type or shadow, did so much more than the High Priests of old. After rising from the dead He walked into the heavenly Holy of Holies, He removed the veil, and He did not go in alone but brought us with Him. That day a lost humanity came home. As you study the duties of the Old Testament priest you see that the High Priest would sprinkle blood on objects and people to make them acceptable and covered for a moment. Our High Priest sprinkled us with His own blood that lasts forever, not just a moment. Its power to save and forgive never wears out, which secures for us a confidence to boldly approach the throne of God. Let me say it again: Believer, you are not trespassing in God's presence, so with reverence make yourself at home – He is glad you have come.

So what's the point of the floating axe head?

They went to the Jordan and began to cut down trees. As one of them was cutting down a tree, the iron axe-head fell into the water. 'Oh no, my lord!' he cried out. 'It was borrowed!' The man of God asked, 'Where did it fall?' When he showed him the place, Elisha cut a stick and threw it there, and made the iron float. 'Lift it out,' he said. Then the man reached out his hand and took it.

2 Kings 6:4-7 (NIV)

This is one of those unusual accounts that has the potential to leave you thinking 'What was that about?' At first glance it seems a bit of pointless miracle that can't teach us much but, recently, while out praying, I asked God to teach me something from it, which He did to my delight.

I saw that the story speaks of a man who had borrowed something and was now not able to give it back to the one who he had borrowed it from. He was obviously a man of conscience and cared that he could not return what someone had lent him – we see him cry out 'but it was borrowed'. Then we see a miracle that causes the very thing that he had borrowed to be restored back into his hands so that he could then do the right thing and return it like his heart desired to do.

Wow! Think about what happened through the lens of redemption: God is able to restore all things in our life when we place our lives in His hands. He is truly able to make all things new and turn every situation around for our good, even concerning that which leaves us in debt to another! Romans 13:8 (KJV) says, 'owe no man any thing, but to love one another'. What if today you owe someone something? What if today you walk around knowing maybe, because of bad decisions or just life, that you have borrowed something and you do not have a clue how you can return it, or settle the debt like you want to or promised? It's like you stand at a lake of apparent hopelessness, and you can't see a way to get back what you need to return?

Then today let faith rise in your heart. I believe that this account encourages us to believe God to supernaturally restore what we have borrowed so that we can return it to the lender and settle every debt in or around our life, whether that is to a bank or a friend.

Let's face it, Jesus already cancelled the greatest debt on your life – why would He not help you get free from other ones that restrict you?

I believe we need a wisdom nugget here. Make sure that you have your intentions set correctly. When God restores to your hand what you borrowed you'd better give it to your debtor and not use it to get in more debt because I don't think He keeps on blessing stupidity!

OK, what about the stick that Elisha used? This, I believe, could represent a simple act of faith – like when Moses stood at the edge of an ocean of impossibility, God had him stretch out a stick to release the great miracle of deliverance. Maybe if that which was borrowed is money, then a small monthly payment to the one you owe might be the stick that causes God to place in your hands what you borrowed so you can give it back? Pray it through, that's just one example relevant to finance borrowed. The stick may mean any number of simple things he wants you to do and when you're obedient His 'super' will connect with your 'natural', and things will turn around.

PROMISES

Know therefore that the LORD your God, He is God, the faithful God, who keeps His covenant and His loving-kindness to a thousandth generation with those who love Him and keep His commandments.
Deuteronomy 7:9 (NASB)

A number of years ago I was believing for God to touch my teenage daughter's life. I knew she was struggling with all that she had learned about God since she was young while at the same time experiencing tremendous peer pressure at school to turn her back on Him. I knew God had a great plan for her life, but she needed to realise that for herself. I started to pray according to God's promises for her life, such as this:

"For I will pour water on him who is thirsty and floods on the dry ground. I will pour My Spirit on your descendants and My blessing on your offspring. They will spring up among the grass like willows by the watercourses"
Isaiah 44:34

In prayer I spoke this over my daughter's life, and other scriptural promises as well, and I began to see God move. Now, years later, I see my plans were small next to what God wanted for her. Today my daughter is blazing for God like I'd never imagined, and filled with His purposes.

This weekend, get God's promise for a situation in your life and know that God is faithful to His promises.

In the end, it's not the years in your life that count. It's the life in your years.

Abraham Lincoln

The power of kindness

Or do you think lightly of the riches of His kindness and tolerance and patience, not knowing that the kindness of God leads you to repentance?

Romans 2:4 (NASB)

When I was still at school I had a teacher that wouldn't allow us to use 'boring' descriptive words such as nice, good, or kind in any of our writing. She encouraged us to use more interesting adjectives to colour our stories so that our narratives would have more life to them. I would normally agree with this but I think the word 'kind' or 'kindness' is definitely not one of those words.

Kindness by dictionary definition means 'the quality of being friendly, generous, and considerate'. How many of us would benefit from incorporating this 'boring' word into our everyday lives. Imagine how adding doses of kindness into your marriage and relationships with your children could change the whole tone of your home. Imagine showing kindness to our workmates and making the lives of those around us even just a little sweeter in some way. This is actually very powerful and, of course, it is on this principle that God wins the hearts of people. The scripture says that it is God's kindness that leads a person to repentance. Biblical repentance is 'to change one's mind'. God's kindness causes a person to change their mind about Him, their own actions and lifestyles and their purposes in life. Kindness is one of the fruits of the Spirit mentioned in Galatians 5:22 (NIV):

But the fruit of the Spirit is love, joy, peace, forbearance, kindness, goodness, faithfulness.

As children of God, filled with His Spirit we have the potential for great kindness within us but it means nothing until we let the fruit of it out. A fruit tree that bears no fruit is not serving its true purpose, thus one of the reasons Jesus cursed a fig tree He passed that had no figs when He was hungry (Matthew 11). There is a whole sad, dying, tormented world just outside of our doorsteps that are hungry for the fruit that God wants to bring from your life. That fruit in your life is for others to eat and benefit from, not you!

A while back I was having a difficult week. Pressures were high and I felt tired and weak. I scooped my three youngest girls into the car and said. 'Let's go get hot chocolate from that new café in town!' I got there and ordered our drinks and went to pay and the cashier said, 'I'm sorry, but you have to pay cash because our machines are broken.' I was going to pay by debit card because there were no cash machines around. I looked at the girls with disappointment and said, 'Guess we have to go then. Sorry girls.' I walked out of the café and felt one more defeat, albeit a small one, it just added to my pile of sadness. I heard someone say, 'Ma'am, come here, please.' The manager said, 'It would be my pleasure for you and the girls to have the drinks for free.' I was shocked and even a little emotional and thanked him. I drank that hot chocolate with my sunglasses on so no one could see my tears because I was overwhelmed that someone would do that for me. This stranger's random act of kindness brightened my day and I even saw the favour and kindness of God in this.

Imagine how your acts of kindness can touch someone today. Allow the fruit of kindness to feed those around you who are so very hungry for it and watch the atmosphere change and the hearts of people transform for the better.

What you leave behind

A woman carrying an alabaster jar of very expensive perfume approached Him while at the table, and poured the perfume over His head. The disciples were indignant at this. 'What a waste,' they said. 'This perfume is so valuable it could have been sold and the money given to the poor.' Jesus was aware of their concern and asked them: 'Why are you worried about what this woman has done? She has blessed Me in a beautiful way. You will always have the poor with you, but I will not always be with you. When this dear woman anointed My body with the perfume, she was preparing it for My burial. I tell you the truth, what she has done for Me today will be told throughout the world in her memory, wherever the gospel is preached.'

Matthew 26:7-13 (The Truth)

One of the most important things I will do in this life is pass down what I believe to the people in my life and the people who I have the privilege to 'do life with'. In particular, I have the great joy to share and impart all that God has done for me into my children.

I love sharing with my family on a daily basis the testimonies of what God has done for me each day. The spiritual state of my family is the most important thing to me of anything in life. As their mother I want to know that they, too, are God-lovers and ready to meet Jesus whenever He should call. When I've gone to heaven, I don't want the things I taught them and showed them about God to fade away and for them to lead godless, lukewarm lives. I want to leave behind me a legacy that I was a God-lover and that He was everything to me and that I honoured Him with my life. The account of the woman with the alabaster jar is an account of a woman in the Bible that left behind a beautiful legacy which Jesus himself validated.

This lady poured out probably the most costly thing she had without hesitation and without caring what those around her thought. She knew that to honour the Lord with this expensive perfume was the best use for it because of all Jesus had done for her and because of her revelation that this was the Son of God. The most priceless thing any of us have is our lives and the best thing you will ever, ever, ever do with this precious commodity is pour it out with utter abandon for God, even if those around you 'don't get it'. Even those who should know better might mock your decisions to honour God when they roll their eyes at how you choose to spend your time, money, and resources or how you choose to conduct your lives. Even giving a few hours on a Sunday to worship God in a local church can be viewed as a waste of a good day when you've worked all week and could be spending that time with family or in the great outdoors.

Let the mockers mock on and with singleness of mind and spirit choose to pour out your life to the one who gave it to you in the first place. The only person in the room that was impressed with the lady with the alabaster jar's offering was Jesus and that's all that really matters. Everyone leaves a legacy whether they realise it or not. What will your legacy be? Will the Lord say of your life, 'You have blessed Me in a beautiful way'?

How to be great

The greatest ones among you will be those who are happy to serve others. For whoever tries to place himself in a position of prominence will be humbled, but whoever is humble before God and others will be placed in a position of prominence before God.

Matthew 23:11-12 (The Truth)

The culture of the Kingdom of God never ceases to astound me in how contrary it is to human, earthly culture. For example, we are told to love our enemies and bless those who curse us, if you want to truly live you must die to self. It's all so 'not of this world!' That's because it's not of this world. This is wisdom from God Himself and the above scripture is directly from the mouth of Jesus. If you want to be great in the eyes of God then you have to serve those around you. Our servant-hood is so important to God that Jesus says:

I tell you the truth, whatever you did for another person who I regard as My brother, you actually did for Me.

Matthew 25:40 (The Truth)

How about when Jesus washes the feet of His disciples, a king washing the feet of His subjects? Jesus gets right on the floor next to everyone's stinky feet and washes them! Then He says this:

Now if I, your Lord and Teacher, have humbly washed your feet, you should also be ready to humble yourselves and wash each other's feet! This is an example I have given you, so that you should do for one another what I have done for you. So humbly serve one another.

John 13:14-15 (The Truth)

When we are standing before God He won't be asking for our doctorates in theology or how big our church is. He won't care how eloquent we our in our delivery of an absolutely cracking four-part sermon. Don't get me wrong, these things are brilliant but according to the Kingdom of God they are not what will put anyone in a place of prominence. This is one of those other-worldly things – the one who is willing to get down on his or her knees and wash the stinky feet of humanity is the one who will be great in the presence of God. Maybe you know someone who has great need today and would benefit from your foot-washing skills. Could there be someone who needs a helping hand nearby? Maybe an elderly neighbour needs some company or a needy family could use a bag of groceries. Could a local soup kitchen or homeless outreach use some extra help? Maybe your church needs you to get on board to help out in an area such as kids' ministry or the hosting team, etc. Get creative. There's enough need outside our doorsteps that could keep us busy for our whole lives. Every life you touch, touches God's heart as you follow Jesus' example.

The treasure

We now have this light shining in our hearts, but we ourselves are like fragile clay jars containing this great treasure. This makes it clear that our great power is from God, not from ourselves.

2 Corinthians 4:7 (NLT)

*M*odern day church is amazing in its wow factor and showmanship. I don't say this in a negative way. It is wonderful to be able to have churches and functions to bring our unsaved friends and relatives to that are eye-catching, trendy and filled with people who are of their own generation, with songs that represent the sound of the current culture, all while praising God. There is nothing wrong with that but it must never be about the 'show'.

If you boil it all down and do away with the glitter and glitz there must be Jesus at the centre of it all because, although the way we express the church should be attractive, the message of the King must never be diluted or hidden. I think about Paul and Silas in prison for casting an evil spirit out of a woman and thereby ruining someone's fortune-telling business. The crowd was not pleased and Paul and Silas were flogged, beaten and then arrested. Sitting in what was probably a dark, dirty jail cell, covered in blood and bruises with chains on their arms and legs, any person would be within their personal rights to feel down, sad and hopeless but these two men are found doing this:

About midnight Paul and Silas were praying and singing hymns to God, and the other prisoners were listening to them. Suddenly there was such a violent earthquake that the foundations of the prison were shaken. At once all the prison doors flew open, and everyone's chains came loose.

Acts 16:25-26 (NIV)

These gentlemen reached inside to the power of God placed inside them, and found courage, strength and the ability to rise above the situation at hand. There were no trendy worship leaders, cool music, stage lights, or wildly cheering crowds. Nobody even preached a great sermon but the power of God was present and miracles happened.

At any given time a child of God has this great power in them. Although the lights and music are awesome and a delight to the senses, there should be a party going on inside of you all the time because of the mighty power of the living God dwelling in you. I never want to think that I need 'warming up' to call on God's power.

Several years ago I picked my little daughter up from nursery school. They had just had a Christmas party and were sent home with presents and a bag of sweets. I buckled her into her car seat and proceeded to drive off. I hadn't realised she took a sweet from the bag and popped it in her mouth. I looked over at her and I knew she was choking. I quickly pulled over and grabbed her from the seat and started doing the Heimlich manoeuvre. It wasn't working. Finally I kept hearing in my head, 'Those who call upon the name of the Lord will be saved!' I gave her one almighty last blow to the back and screamed out the name of Jesus and the blue colour left her face and I knew she was OK. Right then and there on the side of a little village road, all alone, the power of God rescued my baby and me.

I love the lights and the music and will worship God wildly along with the crowds but I will also never let that become a substitute for the treasure within – Jesus.

To know Him

It was not by their sword that they won the land, nor did their arm bring them victory; it was Your right hand, Your arm, and the light of Your face, for You loved them.

Psalm 44:3 (NIV)

Once, many years ago, I needed healing for a problem I had with my shoulder. I was in a lot of pain all the time. I had read a few books on the healing power of God and I knew a number of scriptures on the subject and I really wanted to get healed! I recited my healing promises each day and made many declarations of faith over myself. This went on for ages it seemed. Frustration started to kick in as I performed my 'healing ritual' but saw no fruit from this. In all my striving I never felt I could muster up enough faith.

Now, let me clarify, I firmly believe God heals and God has many promises of healing for us in His Word and I love and thank Him for them. I also think it is a wise thing to declare often these promises over one's life but I was missing something. In all my 'declaring' and 'believing' I was missing out on 'loving'. This whole 'being a Christian' thing is about loving God and being loved by Him. I was missing out on delighting in His presence and basking in who He is. It had all become a ritualistic 'healing formula'. Nothing about relating to your Father should come from a method. Everything I do for my children is from a heart of passionately loving them. I had somehow come to believe that I had found a 1-2-3 method for receiving from God. I had allowed my time with the Father to become so clinical. My husband and I love each other so much. When you love someone you want to look into their eyes and whisper beautiful affirmations of love to them. You desire their undivided attention and intimate personal moments. We are in a love relationship where both of us go out of our way to do things for each other that we know will impress and bless just because we are head over heels in love. There's no method to being with someone you love.

Take delight in the LORD, and He will give you the desires of your heart.
Psalm 37:4 (NIV)

To delight in someone or something is to take pleasure in, to be captivated by. As you allow yourself to be captivated by God and get to know Him intimately you begin to hear His beautiful affirmations of love about you in your spirit. Suddenly, there is no room for clinical recitations or empty declarations because every promise and declaration goes from being a bland black-and-white page in a book to a sparkling love letter that someone who is crazy about you has written. You begin to accept God's promises so easily because you know in whom you are believing. You know intimately the one who made the promise and your faith and trust become strong. To know God is to know that you are not alone in any battle but have an ally who passionately loves you which gives you confidence for even the impossible.

But the people who know their God shall be strong, and carry out great exploits.
Daniel 11:32

REACH OUT TO THE NEEDY

Whoever oppresses a poor man insults his Maker, but he who is generous to the needy honors him.
Proverbs 14:31

There is need ALL AROUND YOU!

The Word of God calls God's children 'the salt of the earth.' We are what gives this world the flavour of God, and one way to spread the flavour is to 'be the answer' this world needs. How? By spreading the love of God placed in our hearts. When we reach out to people we are reaching out to what God loves most.

This weekend, find a really needy person and help to fill that need. Have no expectation of anything in return, just like God expects nothing of those He pours His love on.

Find a need and fill it!

Notes

_____

_____

_____

_____

_____

_____

Destruction
WHY GOD WON'T LET ME HANG ONTO PRIDE, PART 1

Before destruction the heart of man is haughty, but humility goes before honour.

Proverbs 18:12 (NASB)

---

*G*od loves me so very much and, like any good father, He doesn't want me to play with poison. Imagine if I let one of my kids have a little bottle of arsenic and sent them off to play! Even the littlest bit of poison can be harmful and even deadly. Pride is one of those 'poisons' God doesn't want His children playing with.

From Genesis to Revelation we see how pride brought sin, pain and death. Right from the start it was pride that caused Eve to take and eat the forbidden fruit. The devil tempted her by causing her to think that God was keeping this fruit from her and that if she ate it she'd be enlightened just like God about all things. Even though she knew the explicit rule that God laid down about eating the fruit from that one tree here's what happened:

> *The woman was convinced. She saw that the tree was beautiful and its fruit looked delicious, and she wanted the wisdom it would give her. So she took some of the fruit and ate it. Then she gave some to her husband, who was with her, and he ate it, too.*
> Genesis 3:6 (NLT)

I can almost hear the 'In your face, God, I'm eating it!' as she takes that fateful mouthful but with regret for the rest of her life. I seriously hope that piece of fruit tasted amazing because the entire world now lives in the fallout from the pride that caused that sin.

Notice in Genesis 3:6 that it says, 'The woman was convinced . . .' There's another way to say this and it's, 'The woman felt she knew better . . .' It looked good to the eye, she heard it could make her wise, well it doesn't really matter that God, the creator of the entire universe told her not to eat it because it would cause death, she knew better and she was having it! 'I know better' is the first sin and we are all guilty of it when we hold onto things that God says we should have no part of such as unforgiveness, gossip, hatred, lust, sexual immorality and any other thing God has said is a sin. He isn't keeping you from fun and good times, He's protecting you from what has the potential to kill you, your relationships, and any good thing you have.

Let's not be like Eve and think 'I know better . . . this little bit of gossip won't hurt anyone', or 'this little bit of unforgiveness I'm hanging onto is something I'm entitled to'. Trust that God knows what He's talking about and humble yourself to His wisdom. Pride's a sneaky little bit of poison that masquerades as 'I KNOW BETTER THAN GOD'.

Don't fall for it!

Character matters
WHY GOD WON'T LET ME HANG ONTO PRIDE, PART 2

King Nebuchadnezzar, to you it is spoken: the kingdom has departed from you!

Daniel 4:31

Next to our salvation, it is our character that matters most to God. He shapes, moulds and refines us for all of our earthly days. We take who we are to heaven with us and that is why character counts. Also, it is what those around us in this world see and it is our testimony and the evidence that a living God can change and shape anyone who yields to Him. He cares about what's inside us.

> *But the LORD said to Samuel, 'Do not look at his appearance or at his physical stature, because I have refused him. For the LORD does not see as man sees; for man looks at the outward appearance, but the LORD looks at the heart.'*
>
> 1 Samuel 16:7

There is a king discussed at length in the book of Daniel called Nebuchadnezzar. He was a prideful king who attributed the greatness of his riches and the brilliance of his mighty kingdom to his own greatness and power to lead. Daniel, a godly man who worked in the kingdom, had a dream where a great and mighty tree was cut down and destroyed. Daniel woke and spoke to the king about it all. Nebuchadnezzar spoke these words of arrogance and pride:

> *Is not this great Babylon, that I have built for a royal dwelling by my mighty power and for the honour of my majesty?*
>
> Daniel 4:30

Daniel interpreted the dream. The king was to be humbled and brought low by God because of his terrible pride. In God's mercy Nebuchadnezzar would not be utterly destroyed but made to see that God is the one who is ultimately responsible for every good thing in life. Everything was taken from him. During his reign, Nebuchadnezzar loses his sanity and lives in the wild like an animal for seven years. After this, his sanity and position are restored. When this terrible ordeal ended Nebuchadnezzar says this:

> *Now I, Nebuchadnezzar, praise and extol and honour the King of heaven, all of whose works are truth, and His ways justice. And those who walk in pride He is able to put down.*
>
> Daniel 4:37

Harsh lesson but it illustrates how much God hates pride. He sees it as something that is ugly and harmful to us and he'd rather take 'the kingdom' from us than allow the evil poison of pride to infect us for the sake of our character and eternal well-being.

> *A person's pride will bring about his downfall, but the humble in spirit will gain honour.*
>
> Proverbs 29:23 (ISV)

Ask God where pride could be seeping into your life and get it out quick. Decide that you don't want to learn lessons the hard way. Humility in the sight of God is always blessed.

Pride wants the spotlight
WHY GOD WON'T LET ME HANG ONTO PRIDE, PART 3

How you have fallen from heaven, morning star, son of the dawn! You have been cast down to the earth, you who once laid low the nations! You said in your heart, 'I will ascend to the heavens; I will raise my throne above the stars of God; I will sit enthroned on the mount of assembly, on the utmost heights of Mount Zaphon. I will ascend above the tops of the clouds; I will make myself like the Most High.' But you are brought down to the realm of the dead, to the depths of the pit.

Isaiah 14:12-15 (NIV)

This is a speech expressing the pride of satan which is what got him kicked out of heaven. He had some really grand plans and he thought very highly of himself to believe he could make himself like the Most High. It was the 'Most High' that made him to begin with and the Bible says he was a creature of splendour and beauty (Ezekiel 28:17). satan's heart is revealed for what it is, foolish, prideful and selfish, but then these three things do make a perfect little trio and are often found together. Notice how many times the devil said in his heart, 'I will . . .' He could very well have worn the t-shirt with the slogan, 'It's all about me.'

In Isaiah 14 we see how pride looks to raise itself up. It desires to be noticed and it is never fulfilled. First satan wants to be as high as the heavens and then higher than the stars and oh, that's not good enough, let's get onto Mount Zaphon, a holy mountain where I'll surely be worshipped. Not high enough! Let's get higher than the clouds! Actually, I might as well just go for it and be like God. satan forgot that he was a created being and everything he had, every beautiful and wonderful thing that God created him to be and to do was a gift to lead people in bringing glory to God, not himself.

We all have beauty within us, and giftings given to us by God, and every single one of those gifts is meant to somehow be used to bring glory back to the Creator. We live in a world of incredibly talented people and we see how most people want to bring glory to themselves and it is never enough. They will never have enough fame, money or prestige to bring themselves satisfaction. Sadly, I have known Christians who used their giftings and talents for God at one point but then allowed their pride to say, 'Look at me!' It suddenly became all about being noticed, being a superstar. God forbid!

You may have talent in one way or another whether that is in music or business or art, baking, public speaking, etc. Don't let pride cause the gifts God has entrusted to you to become a show to merely entertain a crowd and bring you a momentary spotlight. Everything about us was made to worship God including our gifting. satan got a big head about his gifts and beauty and was cast out of heaven. In studying pride this week we learned that pride will be brought low and humility is honoured. Acknowledge today that your gifts and talents are from God and use them to put the spotlight on Him.

Throw off hatred

Whoever claims to love God yet hates a brother or sister is a liar. For whoever does not love their brother and sister, whom they have seen, cannot love God, whom they have not seen.

1 John 4:20 (NIV)

In the home I grew up in there was a plaque with the above verse on it hanging in the kitchen. I remember seeing this verse every day as I ate my breakfast just before running off to catch the school bus. There were days I wanted to knock it off the wall! There was a girl in my school that I did not get along with at all. What made it even worse was that she was also a sister in Christ. It should be easy to love those who are of the household of faith, right? Well, humans being humans, this is not always the case. Often I would see her and feel a searing hatred for her, but that scripture that my mother hung in the house would ring in my head, 'If I say I love God and hate my brother or sister I'm a liar!'

The Bible is so amazing in how it can encourage and uplift but it can also correct and this is what it was doing for me at that time. It is ALWAYS, ALWAYS, ALWAYS wrong to walk in hatred and this includes ALL the offshoots of hatred such as unforgiveness, backbiting, gossip, the cold shoulder, dirty looks, etc. If I am a child of God then I have no other option than forgiveness and love. If you want to block up your relationship with God then hold onto your hatred. The second part of 1 John 4:20 says if you can't love your brothers and sisters in Christ that are visible, then you certainly cannot love God whom you can't see. Hatred is a grotesque fruit in a life that shows someone actually does not love God. So, I used God's antidote from Ephesians to try to make things right:

Get rid of all bitterness, rage, anger, harsh words, and slander, as well as all types of evil behaviour. Instead, be kind to each other, tenderhearted, forgiving one another, just as God through Christ has forgiven you.

Ephesians 4:31-32 (NLT)

My efforts of kindness were often thrown back in my face, which was hurtful; but I persevered and relied heavily on God's help! We never became best of friends but things vastly improved and I became free of all my hate. I know this is a challenging thought for some of you but it's also a big key to getting your walk with God on the right track. Romans 5 tells us that God loved us so much that Jesus gave His life for us when we were still His enemies. We didn't deserve it just as those who have offended and hurt you may not deserve it but it's what God expects from one of His children. I couldn't tell you where that plaque from my mother's kitchen is these days but it doesn't matter because the truth of it is etched in my heart.

Hate has no place in a redeemed life.

Stay in step with the Spirit

Since we live by the Spirit, let us keep in step with the Spirit.

Galatians 5:25 (NIV)

$\int$ uch a great little bit of advice to start our day!

This verse follows directly after the ones that describe for us the 'fruits of the Spirit' that should be seen in our lives as followers of Christ. The verse reminds us of something then directs us to do something. Firstly it reminds us that we are now alive because of the Spirit. Every one of us came to God spiritually dead, with the spiritual death of Adam and Eve – remember in the Garden after disobeying God they died as He said they would if they ate of the fruit, not in their body or soul rather in the spiritual life they had from God from their formation when He breathed His life into them. Then, after they became dead of Spirit they gave birth to a humanity who were also dead of Spirit, because as I heard it once said so well, two dead parents can't produce a living child. No, Scripture clearly reveals we remained dead with the death they birthed us into until God the heavenly Father made a way through His Son for us to be 'born again', made alive again to Him with the very Life that Adam and Eve knew before their fall.

For as in Adam all die, so in Christ all will be made alive.
1 Corinthians 15:22 (NIV)

When you were dead in your sins and in the uncircumcision of your flesh, God made you alive with Christ. He forgave us all our sins.
Colossians 2:13 (NIV)

So through faith we enter into the grace of New Birth and we are made alive again to Him in our Spirit. His Spirit comes to live in us and we become temples of His Spirit (1 Corinthians 3:16) and are delivered from our dead-like mere existence. When we realise we are now spiritually alive to God and that His Spirit now dwells in us it is easy to understand the directive He gives in the second part of the text when He writes that we are to now 'keep in step with the Spirit'. That is really all you need to do to be a Spirit-led Christian: firstly, realise you are now alive and Spirit-filled, then purpose to listen and watch for His leading in what you do and stay in step with Him. If He goes left you go left, if He walks away from something you walk away with Him. If He wants to bless someone you allow Him to bless that life through you. This is 'abiding in Him', letting the life that is in the Vine (Jesus) be what daily flows through the branch (you).

Being Spirit-led is not hard, it's really simple if you will listen for His leading and lay down your desires to walk in an opposite or contrary way. So today, Champion, remember you are no longer a mere man or mere woman, but you have been made alive by His Spirit, so purpose not to walk 'out of step' but to stay 'in step' with the Spirit. As you do that, the fruit of who He is naturally grows in you and flows through you to bless others.

Have a Spirit-led day as you 'stay in step with Him'.

HEARTILY AS FOR THE LORD

**Whatever you do, do your work heartily,
as for the Lord.**
Colossians 3:23-24 (NASB)

Whatever we do, God wants us to do it 'heartily'. Profoundly, immensely, and completely are words that are similar to heartily.

In the Bible Joseph found himself in some places where he surely had the right to do things half-heartedly. When his brothers sold him into slavery and He was working as a servant for Potiphar he had every right to think, 'I don't deserve to be here, I will do the bare minimum so they don't kill me, and that's it!' Instead, his excellence of service and character caused him to rise to the top. He knew he was more than a slave. He was a servant of the Most High God before he was anything else, and although Potiphar thought he was getting excellent service, Joseph's ultimate motivation was to bring honour to God and this brought blessing to his life.

No doubt you will have a busy weekend ahead of you. This could involve caring for your family or lending a hand to a friend on a task, or maybe you have many chores to accomplish right in your own home. Over the next two days, whatever you find yourself having to do, do it with this thought at the forefront of your mind: 'I am doing this as if I'm doing it for God Himself.' If you're cooking a meal, imagine what care you would put into it if you were cooking it for Jesus. Are you cleaning out the car? Imagine that the Lord is going to be riding in that car.

Whatever you do, do it as you would for the Lord.

*The life that is in Christ is now
the very life that is in you.*

Andy Elmes

Decide to row deeper in

But if serving the LORD seems undesirable to you, then choose for yourselves this day whom you will serve, whether the gods your ancestors served beyond the Euphrates, or the gods of the Amorites, in whose land you are living. But as for me and my household, we will serve the LORD.

Joshua 24:15 (NIV)

Never forget that God created you and me with free will and we are not robots being forced to do or think anything that we don't want to. What kind of love would there be between a husband and a wife if when she wanted to be told she's loved she had to hold a gun to his head to hear, 'Yes, dear, I love you.' His 'I love you' wouldn't mean a whole lot under such circumstances. It's the same with God. He wants our love to be the product of our own heart decisions to love Him, unforced.

That's what it comes down to – DECISIONS.

In the early days of my Christianity I didn't fully understand this. I had a fear that one day I might not love God so much or that life's journey before me might hold some things that would cause me to grow cold towards Him. I thought of myself as a piece of driftwood in the sea taking me wherever the tide wanted to take me. This is not the case at all. I should rather have thought of myself as a person in a rowboat who, with calculated decisions, decides the direction that I will take myself in. Yes, life will have its calm, serene moments and also its dark, brooding storms and choppy seas, but I have the oars of my boat and I can choose to row deeper into God or further away.

Right now you and I are as close to God as our free will wants to be. It's not some kind of magic or fate that has gotten you where you are or are not in your spiritual walk, it's your decisions. I believe there are places in God you have yet to experience that will change you forever. Decide today that if you want more of God you are going to actively row deeper in.

Being a Christian is more than just an instantaneous conversion it is a daily process whereby you grow to be more and more like Christ.

Billy Graham

Decide your soil

However, the good soil consists of those with good sound hearts. They not only hear the Word but maintain their trust in it and, because they persevere in their faith, they produce a good harvest.

Luke 8:15 (The Truth)

*Y*esterday we talked about our decisions. We don't have to be a like a piece of driftwood being forced by the tides and waves in which direction we go in God rather we have a free will and can decide that we want to pursue more of Him and actively go in that direction. In Luke chapter 8:4-15 Jesus is teaching the parable of the sower. Jesus points out that the Word of God is like the seeds that fall on the ground. We represent the ground. Here are the scenarios Jesus shows us:

1. The devil, like little birds picking away little by little at seeds, steals the Word from their hearts to prevent them from believing and so being saved (and by saved this means salvation of the soul but also allowing the Word to handle all the things we are believing for as well).

2. Some seed falls on rocky soil. The person at first receives the Word with joy but there is not depth to their faith. They believe until their faith is tested, and then they fall away.

3. Some seed fell among thorns. This represents those who hear the Word, but the life within them is choked because they worry and focus on their material possessions and the pleasures the world offers. So they never mature in their faith.

4. Lastly, the Word fell on good soil and grew and produced a good crop, a hundred times as much as was sown! These were people who not only hear God's Word, but put it into practice.

When I read about the different kinds of soil and situations in this parable, I immediately know which one I WANT to be. I believe Jesus isn't dooming anyone here and saying, 'You fall into one of these categories and it's a real shame if you fall into one of the first three. I feel sorry for you. Hope you make it even though it doesn't look too good for you.'

Rather, I think Jesus is giving us a 'heads up' and showing us that we can allow the scenario to dictate what happens to us spiritually or like the person with the good soil, who hears the Word and then DECIDES TO PUT IT INTO PRACTICE we can have a great crop. God has given us the power to choose what happens to the seeds of God's Word as they fall into the soil of our lives. You can actively decide you want to protect it, cultivate it and cause it to grow by manipulating the scene. Don't be content to let the birds, thorns and shallow ground determine your destiny. If you have weak faith, begin to grow it! Read God's Word and meditate on it. This doesn't take hours a day. Even a few minutes of reading God's Word has great power. Things can grow from there until you are so captivated by the Word and your harvest is a bumper crop. You aren't doomed to a field of rubble. Decide that your soil will be great!

Decide to get planted

The righteous will flourish like a palm tree, they will grow like a cedar of Lebanon; planted in the house of the LORD, they will flourish in the courts of our God. They will still bear fruit in old age, they will stay fresh and green, proclaiming, 'The LORD is upright; He is my Rock, and there is no wickedness in Him.'

Psalm 92:12-15 (NIV)

Our decisions are very powerful and can make the difference in life between floating like driftwood in the tide to actively rowing the boat of our life to a place in our spiritual walk where we are close to the Father and thriving.

A while back I wanted to start my back garden looking like an actual garden. It was a plain, large square of earth and needed some life so I went to buy an apple tree. Knowing nothing about growing things I thought you just went to the local tree shop, bought a fruit tree of your choice, planted it and enjoyed the succulent fruit for the rest of your days. Nope! I was wrong. Apparently, according to the shop assistant and my computer search engine, a fruit tree needs other fruit trees in order to be a healthy, thriving fruit tree. Who knew?! It has to do with pollination. Pollination is an important topic when growing fruit trees because many varieties require pollination from a compatible donor tree before they can set fruit. However, it is a natural process and happens with ease if the right trees are in the vicinity.

When you decide to be planted in the house of God, the local church, you are putting yourself in a place with other 'fruit trees' where you are fed by God's Word and encouraged by others who are on the same journey to know God more. The Word of God often symbolically portrays our lives as trees. In Psalm 92 we see what God's wisdom is for growing the tree of your life so that it is healthy and vital even in its latter years, a season where naturally a tree would bear little to no fruit. We are encouraged to get planted in God's house alongside other believers and to 'get stuck in'. By this I mean get involved in the life of the church. Be involved in how that church worships, reaches the lost, runs its meetings, teaches its youngest members. Attend often and sow your time and finances into the projects that the church is running. Find a church that you feel you can grow in and get planted. An unplanted tree will not remain healthy for long. Dedication to a great Christian preacher on television in place of finding and growing in a church is also not being planted. We are admonished in Hebrews to meet with actual people to worship together:

Not giving up meeting together, as some are in the habit of doing, but encouraging one another – and all the more as you see the Day approaching.

Hebrews 10:25 (NIV)

A tree that is uprooted often will never grow properly. Church-hopping is not being planted. There is never time for the roots to soak up the nutrients in the ground if the tree is uprooted often. Decide to be obedient to God's plan for healthy, long-term growth. Decide what kind of tree you want to be. Flourishing, fresh, green and fruit-filled works for me!

Better is one day in your courts than a thousand elsewhere; I would rather be a doorkeeper in the house of my God than dwell in the tents of the wicked.

Psalm 84:10 (NIV)

Decide to trust in times of both joy and sorrow

For everything there is a season, and a time for every matter under heaven: a time to be born, and a time to die; a time to plant, and a time to pluck up what is planted; a time to kill, and a time to heal; a time to break down, and a time to build up; a time to weep, and a time to laugh; a time to mourn, and a time to dance; a time to cast away stones, and a time to gather stones together; a time to embrace, and a time to refrain from embracing.

Ecclesiastes 3:1-5 (ESV)

When I first gave my heart to the Lord I was a very young girl, aged 9. I am so thankful for the teaching and preaching that I heard growing up which inspired me and helped me to grow up spiritually. But, somewhere along the way, and I don't know where, I somehow came to believe that the Christian life was to be a trouble-free one as if I were in some kind of bubble that protected me from any bad infiltrating my life. Sadly, through the years I found this to be false as I lost loved ones to illness, as I've made mistakes in life and still had to pay the price for them, and as I've come into situations in life that I had to actually go through rather than round the easy way or by sailing gracefully over the top. God is our deliverer and helper no doubt but sometimes He leads us through the Valley of the Shadow of Death where He teaches us to fear no evil and where we get to experience His rod and staff comforting us (Psalm 23:4).

I also think about all the people of the Bible such as Stephen and all the apostles who were martyred for God, and even our brothers and sisters in Christ around the world today who are experiencing similar fates that don't make for happy endings. Life is not a fairytale and we will experience all the seasons of life both the good and the bad. I would always opt for no troubles but that is not reality. What is reality is that we have a Father who will never leave us and never forsake us (Hebrews 13:5). We also have the promise of peace, which we cannot even comprehend, to guard our hearts and minds in the middle of troubling circumstances as we stay focused on Christ (Philippians 4:7). John 16:33 (NIV) is Jesus' words to us actually telling us flat out that we will have troubles in this world:

> *'I have told you these things, so that in me you may have peace. In this world you will have trouble. But take heart! I have overcome the world.'*

If you want to remain a strong, lover of God all your days, not waning in your passion and zeal for Him and His Kingdom, then you have to know that bad things will happen sometimes and things we don't understand but, through it all, we have a loving God keeping us, holding us and healing our hearts. In these times we have the choice to either throw ourselves into God and His love for us or to become bitter and angry towards Him. Decide to trust God and love Him in both joy and sorrow. We aren't promised a trouble-free life but we are promised peace and comfort. The apostle Paul, who probably had more bad days than any of us, called the troubles of this life 'light and momentary troubles' because he had a revelation that this life wasn't what it was all about. In the end, we have to remember that God sees things on an eternal scale and in that light our troubles will seem small. Decide to trust God in both sorrow and in joy because He loves you more than you will ever know.

> *For our light and momentary troubles are achieving for us an eternal glory that far outweighs them all.*

2 Corinthians 4:17 (NIV)

Decide to find your life

Jesus then told them all: 'If any of you wants to be My follower, he will have to deny doing with his life what he wants. He will have to take up his cross of sacrifice every day in order to follow Me. For whoever wants to live his life for himself will lose everything: but whoever is prepared to sacrifice his life for Me will find true salvation.

Luke 9:23-24 (The Truth)

Decisions are so powerful. They can lead us into greatness or take us to dark, horrible places in life. The power of decision has been left to us with our free will and even God will not make our choices for us. Even so, He will not let us make uninformed decisions. The Word of God is so clear about the consequences of our choices.

Now listen! Today I am giving you a choice between life and death, between prosperity and disaster.

Deuteronomy 30:15 (NLT)

The way of the godly leads to life; that path does not lead to death.

Proverbs 12:28 (NLT)

Godly people find life; evil people find death.

Proverbs 11:19 (NLT)

God wants us to know exactly what our choices will bring us. There are no hidden messages. In Luke 9 Christ Himself says that there are two choices set out for people who desire to follow Him:

1. Live your life for yourself and lose everything, or

2. Be prepared to sacrifice your life for Him and find true salvation. (Some translations say 'you will find your life'.)

These are some hard choices to make. What does He mean by sacrifice? Sacrifice is an act of giving up something you value for the sake of something more important. Simply put, if you want to follow Jesus, you have to put His agenda before your own at all times. This can make life inconvenient, messy and a little awkward sometimes. It's not easy to choose to love people who are unlovable, or get out of a warm, cosy bed on a Sunday morning to go to church, or stand up for your faith in a group of mocking people. It's not easy to give our hard-earned finances in church offerings, it's not easy to let our lives be an example of Christ in a world that thinks sexual promiscuity and filthy talk is normal.

God's Word tells us that in order to find our lives we have to lose them in sacrifice to Him. He puts it this way: 'taking up our cross of sacrifice every day'.

But remember this, and this makes 'sacrifice' an easier thing, we sacrifice for those we love. I sacrifice so much for my children out of sheer love. I have given up sleep, money and time for my precious family and I wouldn't change that for anything. Because I love Jesus I make sacrifices and because He loves me He has given me the opportunity of making those sacrifices in order to 'find my life'. He's not mean, He doesn't want me to 'lose everything' as stated in Luke 9, so He's given me an option to choose well. It's my decision and I decide that I want to choose the road of sacrifice over selfishness.

> *If you cling to your life, you will lose it; but if you give up your life for me, you will find it.*
>
> *Matthew 10:39 (NLT)*

Prayer

Good morning, Father. May my life be a living sacrifice for You. Help me today to lay it down where and when I need to; help me to be the servant that You have called me to be, serving others when I see them in need. I choose to put down the life I want and pick up the one that You have called me to. Help me to do this, Holy Spirit; lead and guide me again today in the decisions I make, especially the ones that affect others.

Amen

Faith is trusting God even when you don't understand His plan unknown God does not want something from us. He simply wants us.

C.S. Lewis

SET YOUR SIGHTS HIGH

Now all glory to God, who is able, through his mighty power at work within us, to accomplish infinitely more than we might ask or think.
Ephesians 3:20 (NLT)

Is there an area of your life that you haven't had much hope for? Maybe you have given up on yourself or even on God in areas of your life that you hoped would be 'better' than they currently are. Have you accepted 'that will do' in regards to certain things. God is able. He cares and wants the best for His children. Here's your weekend challenge:

1. Write down an area of your life you had higher aims for. Maybe it's your marriage or your work situation, for example.

2. Think about Ephesians 3:20 for a while. This is meditation, to concentrate on something. Read it, say it out loud, write it down.

3. Go to Father God and tell Him about these areas of your life that you feel could be better and believe that He can help to improve those areas. Tell Him that you believe He is who He says He is and that He can do what He says He can do.

4. Lastly, based on God's Word, don't give up on Him and His ability to come through for you.

Notes

_____

_____

_____

_____

_____

Decide to remain standing

So accept everything God has made available to you, to enable you to stand steadfast when evil attacks. Yes, no matter what happens you are able to stand firm and to remain standing.

Ephesians 6:13 (The Truth)

B ecause of our free will we can make decisions and choices that can make our lives better or worse. If we choose the paths that God says lead to goodness, blessing and life, we should have no fear for the future.

Because God is a loving Father, He has given us tools to manoeuvre our way through life and protect ourselves on this journey. The following is a list from Ephesians 6 (adapted from *The Truth* version of the Bible) of the armour God has given to us for our protection and wellbeing:

1. Stand firm with His truth like a belt you keep around your waist for support.

2. His righteousness is like a breastplate that protects you. Know that you are fully forgiven and part of God's family.

3. You wear the shoes of the gospel so that you are always ready for any eventuality and can walk in peace.

4. Your faith is like a shield that you have to take hold of and enables you to overcome anything the devil throws at you.

5. The assurance of your salvation is like a protective helmet, enabling you to counter all of the devil's lies and efforts to deceive your thinking.

6. Use also your defensive weapon, the sword of the Spirit which is God's Word. Get it into your head and heart so you can know God's promises for you.

We are not defenceless, sitting ducks in life but if we choose to use the tools God has given us then we will be strong, powerful and ready for life's challenges. Often I meet with Christians who are going through tough times in life and when we dig a little deeper into why they are experiencing hard times, fear and anxiety, it's because they are neglecting the tools God has put within their reach. A shield is of no use to me if when an arrow is sailing towards me I leave it on the other side of the field. What good is the supportive belt of truth if I don't make any effort to find out what those truths are? A victorious Christian walk that will leave you standing strong is about using with consistency the tools God has given you. Why be a sitting duck when you can be a warrior standing tall in victory. The decision is up to you. Choose well.

But he who endures to the end shall be saved.

Matthew 24:13

Who is in your accountability circle?

Blessed is the man who walks not in the counsel of the ungodly, nor stands in the path of sinners, nor sits in the seat of the scornful; but his delight is in the law of the LORD, and in His law he meditates day and night. He shall be like a tree planted by the rivers of water, that brings forth its fruit in its season, whose leaf also shall not wither; and whatever he does shall prosper.

Psalm 1:1-3

I love the wisdom in these opening verses of book of Psalms. It deals with something in the church and people's lives today that is a really important issue: I am speaking about the subject of Accountability.

It seems that in this modern age we live, more and more I see people want to be a law unto themselves and ignore the wisdom of scripture that tells us that it is a good and a wise thing to be a person who is accountable to others; to be a person who recognises the need for wise council and is not too proud to allow others to speak godly council into their lives.

In this, the very first Psalm, we are warned about whose counsel and input we should avoid in our life, namely that of the ungodly, the sinner and the scornful; but what it is not saying is don't ever take counsel.

No, the sober truth is that every one of us needs a circle of wise counsellors in our life – people who love God and have experienced things we have not. Life is so varied, and a person's life has so many subsections to it, that is why you need a well-balanced circle or collection of counsellors, people who are successful in different areas of life, different challenges and choices.

To give you an example, I have people in my life that help me regarding being a good husband and raising my family, others help me understand finance and stewardship, and others give me wisdom in ministry. They did not select me, but I selected these people as I watched them walk in wisdom and success in different areas of their lives. I approached them and gave them the right to speak into my life. Their door is ever-open for me to knock on when I am seeking wisdom or advice. This circle of counsel helps me to avoid failure and stupid mistakes, keep myself from being deceived, and experience the victories God has for me in my life.

I like the way Proverbs puts it:

Plans fail for lack of counsel, but with many advisors they succeed.

Proverbs 15:22 (NIV)

How about you, do you have a circle of counsel in your life or are you a law unto yourself? Who is speaking into your life and are they bringing godly wisdom into your world that will cause you to flourish? If the answer to these questions is 'no' then what are you going to do about it? Like I said, we all need accountability and we need to be careful and selective about who we are accountable to. Find wise and godly people and give them the right to speak.

Waging a good war with wise counsel

For by wise counsel you will wage your own war, and in a multitude of counsellors there is safety.

Proverbs 24:6

We started talking yesterday about the subject of Accountability – being a person that is not a law unto themselves but rather someone who places around their life a circle of wise counsel. Today's text tells us that if we want to wage a good war and remain safe we need to have wise counsel in place in our lives – a collection of people who are wise and love God, who have an invitation to speak into your life when you want advice and when you don't.

I have pastored for quite a while now, and have learned some things. One thing I have learned is that you're everyone's pastor until you tell them something they don't want to hear – then you find out whose pastor you really are. If you are going to experience the full power of godly counsel in your life you have to remove any lids or 'no go areas'. So many times I have seen people seek wise counsel for some areas of their lives but protectively and selectively keep it out of others. You can guess what happens – they remain safe and win in some areas of their life but continually struggle and lose in the areas they have 'locked down'. This is such foolishness when you establish wise counsel in your life – give them permission to speak into every area and don't throw your toys out of the pram when they do and you don't like what they say. Grow up and have the courage to ask them 'why'. Sure, weeping or annoyance may endure for a night, but if it's godly counsel then rejoicing will come after.

The more important the area the more open you should be to the voice of those you have asked to speak into your life. If you truly value your children, why would you shut out the counsel of those who have raised great young people when they want to teach you something? Maybe it's your marriage, your finances or even your walk with God – don't shut out wise counsel, let it in, give it the right to speak, and when it does have the humility to listen, Why? Simple. If you have picked the right people then they are trying to set you up for safety and position you to win the battles you may face.

As I said yesterday, make sure you have a circle of wise counsel in your life. If you don't, pray and seek out not the ones you want but the ones you need. Give them the right to speak and, when they do from hearts that love you, listen. Let there be no lids or no-go areas; give these people AAA (access all areas). Believe me, you will be thankful you did when you experience your life winning wars instead of losing them.

Prayer

Good morning, Lord. Thank You for what Your Word says about being accountable. Help me, Holy Spirit, to lay down whatever I need to lay down to have a correct accountability circle in my life. Please show me the people that I need to ask for help and the people I should not; remove from me any rebellion or pride that would cause me to stay away from those I need. Help me to understand what being accountable looks like in my life.

Amen

What do you want from your pastor?

Plans fail for lack of counsel, but with many advisors they succeed.

Proverbs 15:22 (NIV)

What a person wants from their pastor, and what they need, can be two very different things.

It seems that so many people today want their pastor to be their best friend, when God has positioned them in their lives for so much more than that. Yes, it is right for a pastor to be friendly, but their calling is not to be your friend but to be wise counsel and godly leadership in your life. Standing alongside other godly advisors you have positioned around your life, their job is not to tell you what you want to hear about a situation you may be facing, but rather to tell you what God's Word and wisdom is for that situation. Ephesians 4:11-12 teaches us that God gave church leaders as gifts to your life, to train and equip you. He gave pastors to guide and lead you, not to agree with everything you may want to believe to be true. This can sometimes be tough for a pastor but they will be more concerned with what God has called them to be in a person's life than what that person would like them to be. Listen to how the book of Acts describes the responsibility of a pastor, and you will see why they take the lives of people in their God-given care so seriously:

> *Keep watch over yourselves and all the flock of which the Holy Spirit has made you overseers. Be shepherds of the church of God, which He bought with His own blood.*
> **Acts 20:28 (NIV)**

A pastor is an overseer in the lives of God's people. That is a very serious calling indeed – they will have to give an account for how they functioned as under-shepherds of God's flock.

So, in a world where people seek the wisdom and counsel they want to hear from a thousand and one different locations, where will you get yours? I am sure, like me, you are amazed at how some people use social media tools like Facebook – without any thought they post up their deepest situations and life challenges for all to see and then wait for the whole world to give them advice on what they should do. This is very sad – and very dumb – especially when they think it is wise to seek the counsel of random and disparate people they hardly know on something like Facebook, yet never seek advice from the pastor that God has given to their life, or the wise and godly men and women that God has positioned around them!

Once again, let me say that it is so wise to have a circle of counsel positioned around your life. Make sure you don't have any no-go areas. Seek wisdom and advice from men and women who love God and demonstrate wisdom in their own lives, especially for the areas of your life that you feel are most important to you. In the midst of your circle of counsel have a pastor that you trust, but don't expect them to be your best friend. Rather, release them to be what God gave them to be: a voice of truth and godly counsel that will help you to navigate your life correctly through this very deceived and confused world.

Thank God for Nathan

The LORD sent Nathan to David. And he came to him, and said to him: 'There were two men in one city, one rich and the other poor. The rich man had exceedingly many flocks and herds. But the poor man had nothing, except one little ewe lamb which he had bought and nourished; and it grew up together with him and with his children. It ate of his own food and drank from his own cup and lay in his bosom; and it was like a daughter to him. And a traveller came to the rich man, who refused to take from his own flock and from his own herd to prepare one for the wayfaring man who had come to him; but he took the poor man's lamb and prepared it for the man who had come to him.' So David's anger was greatly aroused against the man, and he said to Nathan, 'As the LORD lives, the man who has done this shall surely die!'

2 Samuel 12:1-5

This is a very interesting account of a man who is deceived (David) and a God who loved him enough to send a messenger (Nathan) to break the deception that was blinding him.

The storyline that surrounds these verses is really worth a read when you can. It shows David doing something very wrong – committing adultery with the wife of one of his faithful men, then arranging the man's death when he discovers the wife is pregnant. He must have initially known he had done wrong but I am sure you have learned, as have I, that a person's ability to totally justify their wrong actions is a dangerously powerful thing. Before long David had totally deceived himself into believing that he had done nothing wrong, or that he was not entitled to do.

One major problem David had was that God was watching, and He loved him too much to let him stay deceived. God sends the prophet Nathan and, like a master storyteller, Nathan shares with David a tale of injustice – the same injustice that David himself had committed, but David was so deceived at this point that he did not notice the similarity. David is enraged by the unjust actions of the man in the tale and starts to vent his outrage and what he would do to such a man. Then the finger of God hits him right in his eyes, and every deception he had built around himself so well was shattered, as the prophet said bluntly, 'It is you':

Then Nathan said to David, 'You are the man!'

2 Samuel 12:7

Thankfully, David repented in a fitting way and his chosen response to this prophetic confrontation caused him to rise out of the moment and what he had done and carry on with God's plans for his life, though he experienced painful loss.

Listen to me, every one of us has the ability to justify things in our life that are wrong and deceive ourselves. That is why we need honest, godly accountability relationships in our life – people who will tell us the truth – to stop us building self-deceiving walls around things we may be doing. I believe that, as with David, God loves us too much to leave us in a deceived state. He will always send a 'Nathan' – the question is, how will you respond to the voice of Nathan when God sends him to you? Like David, it will be your response to God's direct approach that causes the rest of your life to go one way or another.

Always thank God for Nathans!

WHAT MISTAKES?

**For the righteous falls seven times and rises again,
but the wicked stumble in times of calamity.**
Proverbs 24:16

I heard a very wise individual once say he has never made a mistake, but rather he chose
to view mistakes as learning opportunities. Obviously, we do make mistakes in life and if
so, we should own up to them. But I liked that this man wasn't going to let mistakes
bring him down and destroy him. He would learn from them.

Maybe you've had some 'learning opportunities' in your life but they still feel like
mistakes, and you may even have regrets. Here is your weekend challenge: write down
the mistake or mistakes you've made:

1. List those things. Have a good think.

2. How has making that mistake changed the way you do things now?

3. What did you learn from those mistakes?

4. Were these valuable lessons?

Notes

_____

_____

_____

_____

_____

_____

Know what spirit you are of

He . . . sent messengers before His face. And as they went, they entered a village of the Samaritans, to prepare for Him. But they did not receive Him, because His face was set for the journey to Jerusalem. And when His disciples James and John saw this, they said, 'Lord, do You want us to command fire to come down from heaven and consume them, just as Elijah did?' But He turned and rebuked them, and said, 'You do not know what manner of spirit you are of. For the Son of Man did not come to destroy men's lives but to save them.'

Luke 9:51-56

So Jesus sent some of His team ahead of Him to prepare things for when He got there. They are not received in a way they anticipated, and their response is, 'Shall we call down fire and destroy them?' I don't know about you but I think they really over-reacted to what had happened. It was not like they were beaten up, or had their donkeys stolen, or were even publicly humiliated or heard God defamed. So killing people with fire from heaven – did anything that the disciples experienced really warrant that? Listen carefully to how Jesus responds to their question, because in His response is a huge key for us today as we consider how we respond to people. He says, 'You do not know what manner of spirit you are of.'

Jesus was not concerned with what had happened to the disciples, He was concerned with how they were responding to it. The reality even for us today is that you cannot always control what others do to you but you can control how you respond! This thought leads us to an obvious question: how? Simple, by remembering what spirit you are now of.

Many of the responses or actions we would like to use are actually responses that come from the spirit of who you used to be, not of the Spirit of He who now lives in us. The best thing we can do when we feel we are being treated badly is STOP, and take a moment to remember what spirit we are now of, then act or respond out of the knowledge that His Spirit now lives in us. This is not often the preferred or easiest thing to do but it is the right thing to do in the sight of God.

We are no longer who we used to be, we have been born anew by His Spirit and His Spirit now lives in us. He desires to flow through us not just when we stand in church services singing but also as we operate in our everyday lives. Becoming more 'God-now-inside'-minded will affect the responses that come from us. We see in our text today that this was something that the first disciples had to learn. Guess what: this is still something that His disciples today – us – have to learn. We have no right any longer to respond as unsaved people do, because we are no longer unsaved. We can no longer justify responding to people and challenges in the same way that people who do not know God respond, because we are now different to them: God's Spirit now calls us His home.

So, whatever happens to you today, whatever people do to you, remember what we said at the beginning: you cannot always control what people do to you but you *can* control how you respond. Your best response will always come from you knowing what spirit you are now of: His Spirit!

Know that God's Spirit now calls you 'home'

Do you not know that you are the temple of God and that the Spirit of God dwells in you?

1 Corinthians 3:16

*Y*esterday we spoke of 'knowing what spirit you are now of'. This is of vital importance if you want to be led by the Spirit in your everyday life and respond to people and situations as God would have you respond. It's when we do not know, or we forget, that God's Spirit now lives in us that we all seem to drift back to responding or operating from the spirit we used to be led by, an old unrenewed spirit.

Paul faced this issue when he visited the church in Corinth. This church was not old, in fact it was relatively newly formed, and it was a 'Spirit-filled' church. The problem was, for many in the church 'Spirit-filled' was just a well-taught theory or title they used, and not a daily life flow like God desired. So Paul turns up and finds people living like nothing had changed, with the same attitudes they always had. They were still responding like they always did: envying, backbiting and being jealous. I love that Paul did not start beating on them for the fruit of what they were doing, rather he went to the reason or the root cause of the problem. Look at what He says to them:

> *I fed you with milk and not with solid food; for until now you were not able to receive it, and even now you are still not able; for you are still carnal. For where there are envy, strife, and divisions among you, are you not carnal and behaving like mere men?*

1 Corinthians 3:2-3

He accuses them of acting like 'mere men'. It would have been totally unrighteous of him to accuse them of that if there was no present alternative. The fact is, there was. Paul knew it, but they had not realised it. In the same conversation with them, a few moments later, he says the words we opened with this morning: 'Don't you know you're now temples of His Spirit?' The fact is, they didn't – they had not realised nor had a revelation that everything internally changed when they accepted Christ, that their lives were now the residence of the Holy Spirit.

This can be exactly the same for us. It's when we are ignorant of His indwelling presence, or we forget this momentarily, that we begin to resort to acting like we did before we received Christ. It's then that things like envy, jealousy and strife begin to flow when they really should not. But equally, when we remember that He is now in us and purpose to let Him live through us daily, all of our responses are different – in fact, they become Christ-like. Why? Because it is, in fact, the Spirit of Christ now living in us.

Today, purpose to live 'God-inside' conscious – don't respond as a 'mere man' or 'mere woman', but as a God-filled temple.

Responding from a different spirit

You have heard that it was said, 'An eye for an eye and a tooth for a tooth.' But I tell you not to resist an evil person. But whoever slaps you on your right cheek, turn the other to him also. If anyone wants to sue you and take away your tunic, let him have your cloak also. And whoever compels you to go one mile, go with him two. Give to him who asks you, and from him who wants to borrow from you do not turn away. You have heard that it was said, 'You shall love your neighbour and hate your enemy.' But I say to you, love your enemies, bless those who curse you, do good to those who hate you, and pray for those who spitefully use you and persecute you, that you may be sons of your Father in heaven.

Matthew 5:38-45

S o we have established that, as Christians, we are people of a 'different spirit' and that when we realise this we can make the decision to respond to people and situations we face differently to those around us who don't know Jesus. It's this I believe that causes us to stick out in life, not the big Bibles we carry or the stickers on our car bumpers! It's when people see us responding differently, or from a different spirit, that we catch their attention and cause them to want to know what it is that makes us different. This is a good thing that can point them towards the Jesus we love and serve.

Our text this morning is a sobering one, and is embedded in a section called The Beatitudes, which are the teachings of Jesus concerning the attitudes we should have as followers of Him. Notice that they specifically call us to be different in our responses, that when we face things that seem to strike us, take from us or put unreasonable demands on us, that we are to respond in a way that is completely different to how the world we live in trained us to respond. This, I believe, is where the rubber hits the road with our Christianity. If we just respond to situations mentioned in today's verses in the same way as everyone else then we really are no different to anyone else. Yet the truth remains: we really are different, His Spirit now lives in us to enable us and empower us to do and respond like we could not do before. When, by faith, we tap into His Spirit within us we will be amazed at what we are capable of, in the way we handle things and respond.

Our standard must be Jesus. Let's face it, none of us will ever face what Jesus did: the beating, rejection and humiliation He faced over the period He was judged and crucified was horrific and beyond anything we could fully comprehend. Yet, moments before He gave up His Spirit, listen to what He said concerning a humanity that did not deserve Him or what He was doing for them:

Then Jesus said, 'Father, forgive them, for they do not know what they do.'

Luke 23:34

Even when it's tough, even when it seems unfair, let us keep Jesus as our standard and example of how we are to respond. Let us dig deep and draw on His Spirit now within us to do what we never thought we could. As we do we will most certainly stick out and catch people's attention in a world where people are desperately seeking something that is authentically different.

Start your day thankful

Rejoice always, pray without ceasing, in everything give thanks; for this is the will of God in Christ Jesus for you.

1 Thessalonians 5:16-18

Here, in today's verses, are three very good nuggets of advice if you want to take personal responsibility for the daily atmosphere of your life. It is so easy to get involved in the 'blame game' where you put the health of the atmosphere of your life down to what others have done, or not done, to you or for you. Christians should choose a better way, and that is to put these three things into the very DNA of your everyday life. Nice and simple:

- Rejoice always,

- Pray without ceasing, and

- Purpose to be thankful in everything.

This is how we are to live, independent of what season we may be in – when things are going well and when things are not so good.

But today I want to specifically underline the third nugget in this devotional: 'In everything give thanks.' Notice firstly that it says *in* everything, not *for* everything. It would be silly to give thanks *for* everything because not everything is nice, fair or of God; but we can make the decision to be of a thankful heart *in* all things.

Growing up in church there used to be a song sung often and its very simple words were 'Count your blessings, name them one by one, then you will discover what the Lord has done.' This is great advice. Whether it be your day or your prayer time, if you start it with thankfulness you will launch yourself from an attitude of gratitude – and believe me when I say that this will certainly determine your altitude, or the height you fly at in life or prayer.

Come on, we all have things we would like to see changed, or feel we need. The good news is that God tells us He knows these things. I believe it is good etiquette to approach our heavenly Father every day not with a shopping list of need but a heart filled with thankfulness. Before you utter, 'Please will You . . .' be declaring, 'Thank You for . . .'

It's truly amazing that when you take a moment to remember what He has done and what He has already given you – not just in regard to stuff but relationships and health, etc. – it's not long before thankfulness starts to flow. Thankfulness really is a perspective changer that leaves you feeling blessed and grateful!

Let me leave you with how *The Message* translation puts this verse:

'Be cheerful no matter what; pray all the time; thank God no matter what happens. This is the way God wants you who belong to Christ Jesus to live.'

Sometimes you just gotta take His word for it!

When He had stopped speaking, He said to Simon, 'Launch out into the deep and let down your nets for a catch.' But Simon answered and said to Him, 'Master, we have toiled all night and caught nothing; nevertheless at Your word I will let down the net.' And when they had done this, they caught a great number of fish, and their net was breaking.

Luke 5:4-6

After borrowing Simon's boat to use as a floating pulpit, Jesus looks to reward Simon – but also, I believe, to catch his attention. You have to remember that the Lord is no man's debtor and will not be left owing anyone. Simon had lent Him his boat, now Jesus was going to pay him back beyond what he could have imagined.

Jesus gives Simon some simple instructions. Remember, though, that Simon was the fisherman and the instructions Jesus gave him would not have made sense to Simon's mind or experience. Simon had been fishing all night with his colleagues and caught nothing, and now Jesus – who was known as a carpenter – was telling him to fish again at daytime, to get back out there after experiencing failure and do it again! This went against everything Simon thought he knew and the tiredness he was feeling from being out all night.

Yet Simon responds to Jesus, 'At your word I will do it.' He knew there was something different about Jesus and chose to trust what He was saying over what he thought he knew. The result, as scripture records, is a catch beyond what he could have imagined!

OK, let's now apply this to our life: what do we do when what Jesus is asking us to do goes against what we think we know? Do we have the courage to live by faith in His word, as Simon did? Have you ever laboured in your own effort and produced absolutely nothing, then have God tell you to do it His way and seen a supernatural breakthrough? Tithing is a classic example – it does not at first make any sense to the person who reads or hears about it, yet as they choose to put faith in the Word of God that teaches it is what He would have them do suddenly they see a 'catch' or result beyond what could have happened doing it our own way.

Our lesson today is simple: do things because Jesus told you to. Sometimes you just gotta take His word for it and trust Him – at the end of the day you will always be glad you did.

I know I am a new creation because I was there at my own funeral.

Andy Elmes

ENCOURAGE SOMEONE

Therefore encourage one another and build each other up, just as in fact you are doing.
1 Thessalonians 5:11 (NIV)

To encourage is the action of 'giving someone support, confidence, or hope'.

Your weekend challenge is this: Find at least one person to encourage. You can write them a note, text, or letter. Call them up if you like. Tell this person how well you think they are doing at something or how they inspire you. Life can be so harsh and often we get told all the things we are doing wrong, so even a little encouragement can mean so very much to someone.

Notes

_____

_____

_____

_____

_____

_____

_____

_____

_____

Are you an iceberg or an ice cube?
PART 1

Take heed that you do not do your charitable deeds before men, to be seen by them. Otherwise you have no reward from your Father in heaven. Therefore, when you do a charitable deed, do not sound a trumpet before you as the hypocrites do in the synagogues and in the streets, that they may have glory from men. Assuredly, I say to you, they have their reward.

Matthew 6:1-2

So what do I mean by 'Are you an iceberg or an ice cube?' Both are made of the same basic material – frozen water – but they are two very different experiences. An ice cube floats on the water and if you hit it with something it moves; an iceberg has a tip that sticks out of the water with the majority of it under the waves, unseen. The difference comes when something hits an iceberg – it does not move; in fact, as *HMS Titanic* found out, what hits it will sink.

So much of modern Christianity seems to be about what happens in the sight of others (especially worship leading and preaching). It seems that a lot of people want to just do Christianity that is with others and seen by others; everything about their Christian experience is 'above the waves'. Yet I believe the Bible encourages us to build something stronger and deeper than this. Like the man who built his house upon the rock, we are to build a walk with God and an outworking of our Christianity that has great depth. By this I mean a whole lot happening under the waterline of our life, where man does not see but God does.

It's when we take time to develop what we have with God 'under the waves' of what others can see or hear that we build a faith walk that is strong and unmovable, so when an enemy ship or random life attack comes against us we do not sink or float off, rather *we* cause that which came against us to sink while we remain strong and unshaken.

Today's text touches this concept when it talks about how we are to give: it instructs us to have an 'under the water, unseen by man' reality to how we give. When we know in our hearts that man may not ever know what we have done and we may never get their applause, but God does see and know, we can know we will get His reward; and don't tell me for a minute that His reward won't be far superior to that which man gives.

We are going to carry this thought on over the next few days. As we do I want to challenge you, when it comes to what you have going on with God and the outworking of your faith, are you more like an iceberg or an ice cube?

Prayer

Good morning, Lord. Thank You for this new day and for all You are doing in my life. Help me today to build the unseen part of my life strong and to develop what is under the waterline in my life. Guide and teach me today, Holy Spirit, concerning how I can build my life to be like an iceberg and not an ice cube for You. Thank You for what You are doing beneath the waves and the wisdom You generously give; have Your way in me again today, I pray.

Amen

Are you an iceberg or an ice cube?
PART 2

And when you pray, you shall not be like the hypocrites. For they love to pray standing in the synagogues and on the corners of the streets, that they may be seen by men. Assuredly, I say to you, they have their reward. But you, when you pray, go into your room, and when you have shut your door, pray to your Father who is in the secret place; and your Father who sees in secret will reward you openly.

Matthew 6:5-6

---

*L*et's carry on looking at what we started on yesterday, where I asked, in regard to your walk with God and the outworking of your faith, are you more like an iceberg or an ice cube. With an ice cube pretty much everything you see is everything it is, but with an iceberg there is more unseen, under the waves, than can be seen as it stands above the waterline.

God is interested in building the parts of you that are not seen by others, things like your character and integrity, because He knows as you daily grow in who you are, in the unseen, who you are 'above the waves' will naturally grow and strengthen too.

In the next part of Jesus' teaching He looks at prayer, and the whole thought of 'iceberg or ice cube' continues to be very relevant. When it comes to prayer, is there a part of your prayer life that is never heard or witnessed by others, reserved just for the audience of One? With so much of today's performance-driven Christianity we have become great at praying eloquent prayers when others are around, but God is interested in what happens when it is just you and Him.

Our text today instructs us concerning our personal prayer walk with God – that we are to all have a prayer place that we go to where no other person can hear what we are saying or see what we are doing. Like the 'below the waters' part of an iceberg, this place of personal prayer should be the largest part of what we have going on in the area of our prayer and communication with God. If it isn't we can easily become 'professional prayers' who pray to be heard and given applause and appreciation by man. The problem is that those who pray to be heard by others have received all of the reward they are going to get. Those, however, who pray not to be heard by man are told that God Himself gives the reward for what they have done that no one else saw.

I hope this encourages you today to grow a prayer life 'beneath the waves' of what man observes, to have a secret place where it comes to communicating with God, to build a depth in prayer knowing that where there is depth 'deep can call out to deep' (Psalm 42:7), and Father God wants to talk to you deeply.

Are you an iceberg or an ice cube?
PART 3

Moreover, when you fast, do not be like the hypocrites, with a sad countenance. For they disfigure their faces that they may appear to men to be fasting. Assuredly, I say to you, they have their reward. But you, when you fast, anoint your head and wash your face, so that you do not appear to men to be fasting, but to your Father who is in the secret place; and your Father who sees in secret will reward you openly.

Matthew 6:16-18

Here we continue to see the principle that Jesus is teaching regarding having a part of who you are with God that is unseen outworked in certain seen things, in this example fasting. As we have established over the last couple of days, we need to be icebergs not ice cubes – people who have the greatest part of who we are in God unseen, 'under the waves', people of depth and strength. Here Jesus uses the same principle but this time picks on the subject of fasting. He says when we fast we are to do it in such a way as to *not* let others know. Don't do it in an 'above the waves' fashion, rather do it in such a way that none watching you would even know.

I am sure like me you have met people who are fasting and they just can't help themselves, they just have to let you know. They whisper quietly, 'I am fasting, don't tell anyone', or they actually don't need to say anything, the facial expressions say it all! The reality is, the minute they let you know they should probably give up because the power of fasting, according to today's text, is in others not knowing. Don't get me wrong, when others find out that's fine; its when you do it for others to know you are doing it that you have problems, and all you are doing is just starving yourself.

Jesus teaches us to wash our face, put the make-up on, put gel in our hair, and walk around in such a way that only God, who sees what happens under the waterline of your life, can see what you are doing and why you are doing it. When fasting is done to be seen by the audience of only One – like giving and prayer – He then takes the responsibility to reward you openly. The person who fasts to been seen by others better enjoy the applause they get, because that's all they're getting.

Let me challenge you to continue to grow the part of you that is 'beneath the waterline of your life', knowing that this is the part He rewards and this is the part that makes you strong and unsinkable. Let me say again, when shallow Christians who have no depth have a collision with life's various problems and situations they simply float away. But people with depth don't float away, they remain standing strong, weathering every storm that comes along. Grow and invest in the person you are beneath the waves!

There was more to Jesus than met the eye

Then those men, when they had seen the sign that Jesus did, said, 'This is truly the Prophet who is to come into the world.' Therefore when Jesus perceived that they were about to come and take Him by force to make Him king, He departed again to the mountain by Himself alone.

John 6:14-15

We have been speaking this week about having more to who we are with God than what the people around us see or witness. Like great icebergs, the bigger part of who we are and our Christianity should be 'beneath the waterline' of public view.

When you watch the life of Jesus in the Gospels you see this reality lived out by Him constantly and consistently. There was a very public part to who He was that everyone got to witness. He lived the kingdom life for all to see, as an example for us, powerfully touching the lives of those around Him. Yet there was more to Him than met the eye of those who were daily with Him. There was a 'beneath the waves' part of Him that only His heavenly Father knew about. It was this part that was His source of strength. It was who He was in His private world, with His heavenly Father, that empowered Him to be everything He was when He walked on the earth as a man.

In today's text we get a glimpse of something that happened often: Jesus slipping away alone to a private place. He had just been busy giving Himself away, blessing and touching others, then all of a sudden He 'departed by Himself to the mountain'. Why? He needed to refill and re-strengthen, He needed to get wisdom and direction for what was going to happen next. These things were not found in the public arena of life but in the private presence of His Father. Many times the disciples looked for Him and could not find Him, and then He would appear like He does later in this chapter, walking on the water.

It was the private times with God, in the place unseen by man, that gave Him everything He needed to be revived, developed, pre-armed and prepared for what lay ahead, and He knew it. His greatest delight was the time He spent with His Father; it was in this place He received all He needed. After these times you see Him appear again in strength, in control and good to go again for any demand that would be put on Him.

People only got to witness the public side of who He was, but there was more to Him than met the eye of man, a part that was reserved exclusively for the audience of His Father. How about you? What have you got going on with God in the place others can't see? Is there more to you than meets the eye?

Don't let your struggle become your identity.

TobyMac

What's the address of your secret garden?

Then Jesus went with his disciples to a place called Gethsemane, and He said to them, 'Sit here while I go over there and pray.' He took Peter and the two sons of Zebedee along with Him, and He began to be sorrowful and troubled. Then He said to them, 'My soul is overwhelmed with sorrow to the point of death. Stay here and keep watch with Me.'

Matthew 26:36-38 (NIV)

*Y*esterday we spoke of how Jesus had a 'private place' with His Father that others never knew about, a place where He gained all the strength He needed for whatever He was called to do next. At no other time do we see this reality more than in the moments before He is taken to be brutally beaten, crucified and sacrificed for the sins of the world.

In these moments what did Jesus choose to do? Did He choose the public arena of ministry, one last healing crusade? No, He actually chose a private place where He could have intimacy with His Father. With a handful of disciples He left the crowd and went to Gethsemane, to a secret garden to be with God. As He approaches this garden He strips back further the friends He takes on with Him, and then even leaves those behind, those who walked closest to Him in the last three years, until He enters a place where it was just Him and His Father.

You have to remember that He knew, was fully aware of, all that was about to happen to Him. He knew that when the button was finally pushed, all hell would break loose against Him, like unrelenting stormy waves against a coastal sea defence. In these moments His soul was troubled. We see Him enter and leave this private place with His Father a couple of times (to speak to His sleeping disciples), then one last time He kneels before the Father and says, 'Your will be done', starting the engines of all that would now take place to redeem humanity.

No one saw what happened in the secret place, no one heard what was said, yet when we see Him leave that final time He is no longer weak but strong; He is no longer looking for an alternative plan but ready for God's plan to now begin. Everything He needed for what lay ahead He found in that private place with His heavenly Father.

My point? If He was able to find all He needed in the private presence of God, who do we think we are to try to live without it? If Jesus found all He needed in a private place of prayer with Father God then so will we. We will never face what Jesus faced, but for the challenges and things we face in our own lives we can find all we need in His presence. It must be a place we go to alone; just as He left even those closest to Him to be in the audience of One, so must we – and when we do we will never regret it.

DO SOMETHING TO REACH YOUR DREAMS TODAY

Commit your work to the Lord, and your plans will be established.
Proverbs 16:3 (ESV)

Here is your weekend challenge:

1. Write down your dream(s) and be specific.

2. Take some time to dedicate and commit all your dreams to God. Ask Him for the steps to take to see your dreams become reality.

3. List some of those steps and ideas.

4. Make a plan to take those steps even if they seem small. Even a small step in the right direction gets you closer to your goal than just standing still.

Notes

_____

_____

_____

_____

_____

_____

You got the power

But you will receive power when the Holy Spirit comes on you; and you will be my witnesses in Jerusalem, and in all Judea and Samaria, and to the ends of the earth.

Acts 1:8 (NIV)

S adly, a lot of Christians are often guilty of waiting for something they already have. Worse than that, some are still begging God for what He has already given. When He said, 'You will receive power,' He was not lying. The reason why so many people never see a manifestation of the power of God in their life is not because God did not do anything, but because *they* won't. You see, God's power – the Holy Spirit ability in and through us – is like electricity: you have to put a demand on it to experience the flow of it.

Think about the natural electricity that powers the electrical appliances in your home. You may be in possession of all the energy required to boil your kettle, dry your hair or power your hammer drill but nothing happens until you put a demand on that energy, by plugging the appliance into a power socket and flicking the 'on' switch. It's when you use the appliance that you experience the flow of current through it, empowering it to do what it was designed for.

You and I are the same – we have been connected to Him when we received Him and He is waiting for us to do something so that He can empower us to be successful. Whether it is laying hands on the sick, telling someone your testimony, public speaking or starting a company to fund the work of His kingdom, until you step up or step out you won't know His flow of power through you. You'll know it when you do, though, because He is not a God that He would lie, and He gives what He has promised to all who ask.

So today, think about that thing that God has been challenging you to do – not in your strength but His. Now think about when you're going to take the plunge and give it a go. That moment you have just come up with is the very same moment that His power will be present to help you and empower you to succeed. You can stand around looking at your electric kettle all day wanting a nice cup of tea, but you will not get one with hot water until you flick the power switch. It's the same with you: flick the switch by doing something in faith, trusting Him alone, and watch His power flow.

No silent witness

But you will receive power when the Holy Spirit comes on you; and you will be My witnesses in Jerusalem, and in all Judea and Samaria, and to the ends of the earth.

Acts 1:8 (NIV)

When we talk about knowing the flow of God's power in and through our daily lives we cannot forget the primary purpose for which He has empowered us: simply, to be witnesses.

Witnesses are people who speak up for what they have seen or witnessed. We need to be those who are not afraid to be speak up concerning all we have seen Him do in our lives. The trouble with a lot of our church evangelism these days is that we have too many 'silent witnesses' – people who have been marvellously saved, supernaturally restored and healed, yet do not tell others.

Why? Usually because of fear – the fear of man silences their witness. This is such a shame, because how will others know unless we speak? The saddest thing is that they don't realise that God doesn't expect them to do it in their own ability: He has given His spirit to empower them and provide the confidence and ability they need. As we established yesterday, they will never experience this divine ability until they 'flick the power switch' – more specifically, open their mouth!

If the people of God need to take anything more seriously in this hour we are living in, it's evangelism and the reaching of others, the bringing of others to Christ. For this to happen each of us needs to take personal responsibility to 'break the silence' in our life, to no longer be a silent witness! Just imagine if enough of the church took this challenge personally today? All across the country, in workplaces, college campuses and neighbourhoods, people who once were silent are now speaking under the enablement of the Spirit of all the things they have witnessed.

God does not want us to speak of things we have only heard He did for others, but the things He has done for *us*. When you are a witness to an accident you stand in court and give an account of what you witnessed, not what you heard someone else saw. In the same way, that's all God wants you to do now: tell others what *you* have witnessed Him do for you. As you do you become a tool in His hand, no longer a silent witness.

It's time to break the silence – go ahead and open your mouth today, and as you do His ability will be there: He promised it would.

Prayer

Thank You today, Lord, for fresh boldness to be the witness You have called me to be. Thank You today that Your Spirit empowers me to represent You to the people You have placed in my world. I purpose today that I will not be silent but tell as many as I can about the wonderful things You have done for me. I choose to 'break the silence' in Jesus name.

Amen

Taking your Jerusalem seriously

But you will receive power when the Holy Spirit comes on you; and you will be My witnesses in Jerusalem, and in all Judea and Samaria, and to the ends of the earth.

Acts 1:8 (NIV)

Every single one of us is called to be a missionary in the world that He has given us. So often, when we talk of missionaries, we think of men and women leaving the shores of their own lands to sail to far-off places with the agenda of sharing the gospel with those who have not yet heard. Yes, this would be a true definition, but we also need to understand that each of us is a missionary in the local world that He has given us and is unique to us.

Don't get me wrong, I believe it is good for every person to go on short-term mission trips – they are powerful and can bless others as well as changing you. And there will be those who know God's call to long-term mission. But we also need to see our everyday world as our own personal mission field too, and realise that God has empowered us with the same power and ability to reach it as He has the ends of the earth.

Remember what Jesus taught the first disciples in our text today? He said, 'Go.' This remains His commission to each and every one of us today. He says 'go' first to Jerusalem – Jerusalem to me represents the local world around you. He then mentions going further afield, even to the ends of the earth, but first comes your local world!

God wants to empower you to be a missionary and a soul winner wherever you wake up in the morning, to be a person who understands the worth of someone's soul, whether they live on the other side of the world or just around the corner. I have said before that I believe it often takes more courage to be an ongoing witness in your everyday world than it takes to be one in a place you visit and are not known. Why? Everyone knows you in your local world, there is no pretending or faking anything. But guess what: His grace and ability are as strong – if not stronger – here than when you are anywhere else.

Be His missionary today, wherever you find yourself. Make the decision to open your mouth and move from being a 'silent witness' to an empowered soul-winner. As you do, watch the whole of heaven go ahead and back you up.

A man who is intimate with God is not intimidated by man.

Leonard Ravenhill

Our Good Shepherd

The LORD is my shepherd; I shall not want.

Psalm 23:1

The Bible is filled with stories and analogies of shepherds, the most well-known of which is probably Psalm 23. The psalmist calls the Lord his shepherd, and because of this he wants for nothing.

Imagine wanting for nothing! So what actually is a shepherd's job description? According to the Mountain Plans Agricultural Service* a shepherd's responsibility is 'the safety and welfare of the flock'. The shepherd will graze the animals, herding them to areas of good forage, and keeping a watchful eye out for poisonous plants. I love how the shepherd is keeping the sheep safe even from his own bad choices. Sometimes what may seem good to the sheep may actually be harmful and the shepherd redirects the animal.

Shepherds protect sheep from predators, such as coyotes, wolves, mountain lions, bears and even domestic dogs, which are the most common of all the listed predators! According to a report by the USDA domestic dogs will chase the sheep to exhaustion and then attack the poor weary sheep who has no fight left in him. Jesus says to come to him if you are weary and need rest (Matthew 11:28). According to the job description, shepherds carry rifles to shoot predators. Shepherds check their flocks often for minor skin ailments that can turn into big problems if left uncared for. The shepherd is expected to be on round-the-clock watch for the sheep, especially watching out for those that are most vulnerable, the very young and the pregnant ewes in particular.

Experienced shepherds will shear their sheep as well, without nicking or cutting the skin. In watching a video of a shepherd performing the shearing, it looks like it could go very wrong in the hands of someone who doesn't know what they are doing, but to an experienced shepherd, he or she knows how to handle the sheep with as little upset to the animal as possible.

After reading the job description of the shepherd, it is so clear why our Lord is called the Good Shepherd and why the psalmist has no 'want': every area of need in the sheep's life is covered by the shepherd.

> *He tends His flock like a shepherd: He gathers the lambs in His arms and carries them close to His heart; He gently leads those that have young.*
>
> Isaiah 40:11(NIV)

Today each of us who are part of God's flock, and call Him our Shepherd, can trust that He cares about our well-being, protection, and sustenance. He handles us with His expert care and He is carrying us close to His heart, a place of affection, so that not only are our physical needs met but our need to be loved is covered as well. Declare over your life today that you will allow Him to be your Shepherd and that in Him you have all you need.

* http://work.chron.com/duties-shepherd-23576.html, accessed 12/04/2016

I need a forever holiday!

He makes me to lie down in green pastures; He leads me beside the still waters. He restores my soul.

Psalm 23:2-3

*L*ife can get pretty busy sometimes as we rush around getting chores done or travelling to and from work, in traffic or on crowded tubes, trains or buses. At work you may have to deal with difficult people and situations. Then we get home and there's still more chores to get on with. Maybe you're a carer or a parent of small children and the work never seems done. Rest seems a foreign thing and when it's time to sleep you collapse with exhaustion into your pillow, knowing that you have to do it all again the next day.

Sometimes even a holiday doesn't help with the exhaustion, because you spend the whole time trying to keep all the family happy that you feel worn out and ready for a holiday from your holiday! We need a Psalm 23 holiday!

That's right, you need to get before God with your over-tired mind – whose cogs have been on overdrive – take a deep breath and sit in the presence of God. You don't need the newest worship CD or a great sermon by a great preacher, you need to get alone with the One who restores your soul.

The scripture says to be still and know that He is God (Psalm 46:10). Another version says to 'cease striving' and know that He is God (NASB). He knows what you need better than you do. He knows the 'green pastures' and 'still waters' that you personally need. Allow the Father to restore you as the Word says. The word 'restore' in Psalm 23:3 is a Hebrew verb that indicates ongoing, continuous and intensive action. In other words, when God restores us it is an ongoing thing. If you are in relationship with the Father then He is restoring you with His very own life-giving self continually. Even in the middle of chaos and stress if you take a moment to acknowledge that you know the presence of God is with you then He can calm any inner storm that may be present.

Being in God's presence is one of my favourite places to be. There are times I have come to the Lord as a frantic stress ball and have felt the restorative presence of God bringing balance to my thinking, calming me, and helping me to see situations from a different, healthier perspective. Take a Psalm 23 holiday and stay on it forever!

*L*ife's most persistent and urgent question is, 'What are you doing for others?'

Martin Luther King, Jr.

REACH OUT TO THE NEEDY

**For there will never cease to be poor in the land.
Therefore I command you, 'You shall open wide your
hand to your brother, to the needy and to the poor, in
your land.**
Deuteronomy 15:11

Your weekend challenge is this: help someone who is needy.

As God's children we are called to 'open our hands wide to our brothers and sisters.' How?
Buy some extra canned food and donate it to a local food bank, or fill up a bag with groceries
for a single parent who doesn't have much. Do you know anyone who is unwell or in prison?
Visit them. Comfort someone experiencing grief. Is anyone you know stuck indoors and suffering
from loneliness? Go round their home and have a cup of tea and some conversation.

Need is all around you and it often doesn't require much for us to help meet that need.
What may seem like a drop in a bucket to us could mean the world to someone in need.
Find a need and reach out to help.

Notes

_____

_____

_____

_____

_____

_____

Allowing the Shepherd to lead

He leads me in the paths of righteousness for His name's sake.

Psalm 23:3

King David calls the Lord 'my shepherd' in Psalm 23, which indicates that he is allowing the Lord to lead him like a sheep would follow a shepherd.

All of us are created with free will. When we choose to call God our Shepherd we are choosing to allow Him to lead us. By acknowledging Him as our Shepherd we are saying, 'I will only go where you lead me and nowhere else.' The scripture says, 'He leads me in the paths of righteousness . . .' The word 'righteousness' here has often been translated 'straight'. So, He leads us on straight paths.

I don't believe any follower of Christ would say that He ever would lead us on a path of sinfulness. When we as followers of the Good Shepherd decide to sin, we are no longer allowing the Shepherd to lead us. When a believer sins, it doesn't mean they aren't a child of God anymore, but it does mean they are not following where Christ is leading. When a sheep stops following its shepherd in the natural, it becomes vulnerable to attack by predators, or it can become injured and exposed to the elements.

The same holds true spiritually. If you aren't allowing Christ to lead because you are following a strange path not set out by the Shepherd, then you aren't allowing God's wisdom into your life. You can get into terrible situations and then find that you wandered pretty far from the Shepherd of your soul (1 Peter 2:25). The pathway of righteousness is the new life He gave you when He exchanged it for your old, sick, sinful one, and He wants to lead you on this new path called righteousness. Paul reminds the Ephesian church that they should no longer live in sinfulness like the people of the world who don't follow Christ:

> *But that isn't the way Christ taught you! If you have really heard His voice and learned from Him the truths concerning Himself, then throw off your old evil nature – the old you that was a partner in your evil ways – rotten through and through, full of lust and shame. Now your attitudes and thoughts must all be constantly changing for the better. Yes, you must be a new and different person, holy and good. Clothe yourself with this new nature.*
>
> **Ephesians 4:20-24 (TLB)**

Allowing the Good Shepherd to lead you may not always be the easy road, but as the Word says, it is the narrow one and the destination is – LIFE.

> *But small is the gate and narrow the road that leads to life, and only a few find it.*
> **Matthew 7:14 (NIV)**

Through the valley

Even though I walk through the valley of the shadow of death, I fear no evil, for You are with me.

Psalm 23:4 (NASB)

Everyone at some time or another will walk through some very scary times in life. When things in life go so very wrong and the outcome could potentially be very bleak, the scripture so poetically calls this place 'the valley of the shadow of death' – a lonely, dark, seemingly hopeless place where death's shadow seems to hover over you and it feels heavy; and although you may have friends and family with you, there remains a deep loneliness which causes you to feel isolated even in the cheeriest crowd.

When you read this psalm, you can sense the forward motion of the journey. In verse 3 he 'leads' the sheep, in verse 4 he 'walks through' the valley, in verse 6 goodness and mercy 'follow' him. You should never remain in this valley. This is not the destination, only a point along the journey and a very important one. None of us wish for difficulty in our lives, but it is inevitable because of the nature of life. In these times when we feel loneliness and hopelessness we will be more aware of the all-sufficiency of our Shepherd. When no one else can do one more thing to help your situation and you fall into the arms of your Shepherd wholeheartedly, you begin to get healing for your soul.

Knowing there are no quick fixes to remove the heaviness of your heart you find it so much easier to come to God and receive from Him and He will never disappoint. Like David you will be able to say, 'For You are with me,' because you will have felt His presence personally. You will know experientially that you are not alone. And when you are through to the other side of the valley, your relationship with the Lord will be richer for having gone through it, hand in hand with your Shepherd.

For I, the LORD your God, hold your right hand; it is I who say to you, 'Fear not, I am the one who helps you.'

Isaiah 41:13 (ESV)

Never be ashamed of a scar. It means you were stronger than whatever tried to hurt you.

Anon

The crook

Your rod and Your staff, they comfort me.

Psalm 23:4

When I think of comfort I tend to think of a fluffy, warm duvet or a soft pillow, not rods or staffs. But, on a journey with a loving, caring Shepherd, a rod and staff are exactly what will bring comfort.

Imagine the shepherd walking on rough, uneven terrain and the sheep is near the edge of a cliff. One wrong move and it'll slip right over the edge! The shepherd uses his staff – or as some know it, a crook, with its curved top – to hook the sheep round the neck and guide it onto a safer path. A crook can also be used to fend off a predator. Try that with a fluffy pillow!

As a parent, I hold to something my brother, who ran a children's ministry, used to say: 'Better a fence at the top of the mountain than an ambulance at the bottom!' I would rather be tough with my children and have rules and regulations (a safe pathway) to follow and penalties for breaking those rules in order to direct them in life, than to allow them to wander aimlessly over a 'cliff's edge'. I could give them what they consider a 'fluffy pillow' in life and say, 'Go near the edge if you like, I think you'll be fine.'

In the same way I love my children, Father God loves His children, and sometimes He needs to redirect us in life or correct us. It doesn't seem comforting at the time, but the fact that we are not splattered all over the bottom of a canyon is of great comfort, especially with hindsight after we see how God kept us safe or directed us off a path that was leading us nowhere good. Hebrews 12:5-6 says that God chastens and disciplines anyone that He calls His child. In *Strong's Concordance*, the word 'comfort' in Psalm 23 means to 'console, extend compassion, sigh with one who is grieving', and it implies a deep empathy. A parent feels with great empathy what his or her child is going through or experiencing. God has feelings, too, and John 3:16 says that 'He loves'. He feels our pains and hurts and so that is why a loving Shepherd travels with a rod and staff over us, not to beat us, but to redirect us and protect.

When you're feeling the crook of the Shepherd round your neck, it will never choke or injure you; it will only keep you in step with Him and lead you to a good place.

Prayer

Good morning, Father. Thank You that You love me enough to keep me and guide me away from harm. I thank You for Your crook in my life. You are the Great Shepherd and I can trust You in how and where You lead me. Lord, today I submit again to Your leading; keep me from the cliff's edge and lead me to the still waters and green pastures You have for me.

Amen

Come to the table

You prepare a table before me in the presence of my enemies.

Psalm 23:5

I have been to restaurants with a lovely ambience, where the lighting was just right, music played gently in the background, and the tastiest, most beautifully presented food you can imagine was served with a smile. It would be very easy to enjoy a delicious meal served in such a place as this, but how about the same meal at the same table smack dab in the middle of a war-torn country, with bullets flying over your head and people who hate you encircling you, and watching you with malicious intent while you try to enjoy your feast. Like any king, David had many enemies and he was declaring in Psalm 23 that God was blessing him even though he had enemies all around him wishing for his failure, and maybe even his death. How could anyone ever enjoy a meal in such a terrible place?

Well, first of all, if God is setting blessing in front of me, with my enemies all around me, then I know that He is protecting me. Adversaries might be all around me, but if God is for me, then who can be against me (Romans 8:31).

Next, I think David had the revelation that you don't have to wait for circumstances to be perfect in your life to enjoy what God has for you. You have to focus on the beauty and good things God is giving and doing. In the middle of some of the most troublesome times in my life I was still experiencing God's blessing, and I had to choose to be thankful for the blessings rather than complaining about the problems in my life.

Lastly, one way to really annoy your enemies is to not respond to them in the way they want you to. How irritated would your adversaries be if they were practically breathing down your neck and you were sitting there, fearless and unintimidated, tucking into a delicious meal and taking no thought about them at all?

There's nothing wrong with enjoying the blessings God brings into your life, it would be wrong not to. He very openly sets before you a table of blessing and has invited you to sit, feast and enjoy – even if there are those around you who don't like you and don't think you deserve it, particularly the enemy of your soul, the devil. Annoy the devil, and enjoy God's blessings, because God is for you!

Prayer will make a man cease from sin, or sin will entice a man to cease from prayer.

John Bunyan

Expect God's goodness

You anoint my head with oil; my cup runs over. Surely goodness and mercy shall follow me all the days of the days of my life.

Psalm 23:5-6

Expectation is 'a strong belief in a particular outcome in a situation'. It is almost like a prediction or forecast. It's very easy to face things in life with negativity and fear because we hear terrible stories about all the things that go wrong every day! We hear about planes that crash and terrorist attacks, diseases that we have no cure for seem to be striking humanity at an alarming rate, and natural disasters hit when we least expect. As God's children we need to be facing each day and each situation with King David's attitude in Psalm 23:6, where he writes, 'You anoint my head with oil.'

According to my *Spirit-filled Life Bible*, which has a note about this verse, states that of the two kinds of oil mentioned in the Scriptures – the priestly anointing oil and the oriental perfumed oil – this is the latter and shows favour and hospitality. God pours out His favour and hospitality on us to the point of overflowing.

Then David declares, 'Surely goodness and mercy shall follow me all the days of my life.' Here David sings out (remember, this is a song) how goodness and blessing will follow him for the rest of his days! The word 'surely' is used to emphasise the singer's firm belief that what they are saying is true and shows surprise that there is any doubt of this.

Each day we have a choice to fear the bad things that can happen to us or declare that we serve a God who is daily showing us favour in abundance, and because He is with us we can expect His goodness and mercy in all of our situations. Don't forecast clouds and darkness over your future; look to God who is desirous of bringing you good. Whatever you face today, accept that God wants good for you and surely you can expect this.

Don't pray when you feel like it. Have an appointment with the Lord and keep it. A man is powerful on his knees.

Corrie Ten Boom

PRAY FOR HOUSEHOLD SALVATION

Believe on the Lord Jesus Christ, and you will be saved, you and your household.
Acts 16:31

This weekend find time to specifically pray for people from your family who need to come to the Lord. They don't have to be relatives that live in your home, any relatives will do! Be praying for their hearts to be ready to find salvation.

God can touch the hardest of hearts, so don't avoid praying for those you think are a lost cause. No one is beyond God's reach and He speaks into everyone's heart differently. He speaks the language that each individual heart will understand. He desires all to be saved so be assured that you and God are in agreement for this.

Notes

_____

_____

_____

_____

_____

_____

_____

Home

Jesus replied, 'Anyone who loves Me will obey My teaching. My Father will love them, and We will come to them and make Our home with them.

John 14:23 (NIV)

I'm back home in the house of GOD for the rest of my life.

Psalm 23:6 (MSG)

I only ever remember living in one house from the time I was a very little girl till I got married and left that home.

I loved being home. I felt comfortable and safe. After being away from home, even for a few days, I remember that 'nearly home' feeling as the car would turn onto the top of my road and I'd see the green sign with the name of my road on it. There was even a familiar sweet smell to my neighbourhood because of the gigantic jasmine tree that grew in the front garden. I would run up the stairs to the front porch, and walk in through the large, wooden front door and I was home.

Since then I have moved house often. I have had many street signs and front doors to call 'home', but I never felt that same sense of belonging as I did to the house I grew up in. I've tried to recreate the feeling, and I've gotten pretty close, but it's never quite the same and I don't expect it ever will be. And that's OK because I have learned that 'home' for me will never really be four walls and a roof, although I am truly grateful to live within the safety and comfort of a house, but rather home is the place where God has made an abode with me.

As I have grown to love and appreciate God in my life, and have come to value my time spent with Him, I have longed to spend more and more time in His presence and Word. I have felt His heart and even heard His still, small voice correcting, directing, and encouraging me. In times of grief and sadness I've wept in His arms, and in happy times I have felt joy unspeakable in His presence. I have even felt completely at peace saying and doing nothing except knowing He's there with me as I sit before Him. His presence has become a familiar place for me even when my surroundings have changed again and again, and although I have become accustomed to often spending time with God, it never becomes monotonous.

According to Google there are over 900 names and titles for God in the Scriptures. These names and titles reveal different aspects of who God is, so in spending time with Him you begin to experience all His brilliant facets. He's like a mansion with an endless amount of rooms filled with treasure of all sorts, that we have the privilege to explore and discover.

King David ends Psalm 23:6 with the following words: 'And I will dwell in the house of the LORD forever.' Yes, all God's children will spend eternity in heaven, but eternity starts right inside your heart as God makes His home there, and as He furnishes your very being with the beauty of who He is. In 1 Peter God's children are called 'strangers in a strange land' but we can always have a sense of 'home' wherever our journey in this life takes us.

Pray for your enemies

You're familiar with the old written law, 'Love your friend,' and its unwritten companion, 'Hate your enemy.' I'm challenging that. I'm telling you to love your enemies. Let them bring out the best in you, not the worst. When someone gives you a hard time, respond with the energies of prayer, for then you are working out of your true selves, your God-created selves.

Matthew 5:43-47 (MSG)

People may hurt you in life and it is never pleasant, but it hurts much more the closer you have allowed that person to your heart.

I found it really difficult to free my heart from the hurt that a friend once caused me. What was worse was that they seemed to then set themselves up as an 'enemy' against me, refusing to even discuss the situation with me. I didn't want bitterness to root itself inside my heart, and I could feel it setting in, so I went to the Lord and asked for help.

I barely closed my eyes and lifted my voice to the Father when the scripture from Matthew 5 came into my mind: 'Pray for your enemies . . .' I knew it must be God because I wasn't in a frame of mind where I would have thought to pray for them. I was hurt and angry, and that combination of offence produces bad things; but I humbled myself to take God's prescription for my aching, hurt heart. I prayed. I prayed my best prayers for health and truth to come to this person. I asked God to work in this individual's life and cause them to know God more. I didn't pray for their harm but only that God would show us both where things went wrong. I gave it my best and, when I was done, I felt a lightness in my whole self. I felt like a huge, gaping wound in my heart had been closed. I went into prayer with pain and came out feeling free.

When I was praying I even felt sorry for this individual. I felt sad for them and the turmoil they had in their life, and the burden of offence they were carrying and how that might block up blessing in their life. I saw things from a different perspective.

That was not a one off. I felt so energised from praying for this person that I have done it often since that time. I don't know how God does what He does – all I know is, when He asks you to do something, DO IT! They may be your 'enemy', but you don't have to be theirs. Praying for these folks goes so against the spirit of hatred and offence and that is the heart of God. This is the heart that you now carry inside you.

The harder this task of praying for an enemy seems to you is an indication of just how much you need to do this. This truth set me free and I hope it does for you too.

Prayer

Father, today I choose to pray for my enemies. Lord, I commit them to You and pray Your blessing upon them. You see all things, and know all things, Lord, so I can trust all things to You. Today I take responsibility for my heart and mouth and purpose to use them to bless not curse, despite what people may be doing to me. Father, help me to understand them and see their lives through Your eyes. Forgive me for carrying any unforgiveness against them, I release them to You.

Amen

Living in awe of the Lord

Oh, that they had such a heart that they would live in awe of Me and always obey all My commandments. Then all will go well with them and with their children forever.

Deuteronomy 5:29 (The Truth)

In Deuteronomy 5, the people are in awe of God and they fear hearing God's voice, saying to their leader Moses, 'Who has heard the voice of the living God speaking from the midst of the fire, as we have, and lived?' They suggest to Moses that he goes to the Lord on their behalf and hear what God has to say to the people, and then he should convey the message to them. The people say, 'Tell us all that the Lord our God says to you and we will hear and do it.'

The children of Israel often grew cold towards God on their journey but in this passage they have just had an experience where they are remembering that God is awesome and deserves their respect. The Lord is pleased that they have come to this conclusion and, in Deuteronomy 5:29, declares that it would go so well for them and their children if they would always remember to keep this attitude:

'Oh, that they had such a heart that they would live in awe of Me.'

Awe is a feeling of reverential respect mixed with fear or wonder. God desires to be so personal with us. He invites us to call Him friend and Father, but we should still live in awe of who He is and revere Him for how truly stunning He is. It really isn't difficult to have awe for God. I only have to look at all God has created and I feel blown away by His vastness and wisdom.

Recently I was at the Museum of Natural History in London, and I felt overwhelmed by how astonishing our natural world is, and could see the fingerprints of God all over creation – from the intricacy of the human nervous system to the numerous plants of the rainforests that provide medicines for us. When I saw the number of different kinds of birds and their gorgeous colours and varieties, I could only see the artistry of my Father. The geological section of the museum was equally mind-blowing as I viewed the large, glowing, simulated 'earth's core' on show.

The vast wonders of this world for me point to the genius of the Creator/Scientist/Artist that is my God. This is the God that I talk to every day and rely on. This God loves me and He has become my Father. The 'awe' for God comes as I dwell on these thoughts. I have only to look at the star-encrusted night sky or a fiery sunset to know that God is broadcasting His presence in this world and His infinite love for me. The wild, crashing waves of the ocean shout out the power and strength of the Creator. As well as being friend and Father, God is King and Creator and I am comforted that there is no force of nature or majestic mountain that can surpass His greatness – and yet He loves me.

Allow your heart to become awestruck with the greatness of your God. It will help you put every care and worry you have into perspective.

But it is God whose power made the earth, whose wisdom gave shape to the world, who crafted the cosmos. He thunders, and rain pours down. He sends the clouds soaring. He embellishes the storm with lightnings, launches wind from His warehouse.

Jeremiah 10:12-15 (MSG)

God's Wisdom

For the foolishness of God is wiser than human wisdom, and the weakness of God is stronger than human strength.

1 Corinthians 1:25 (NIV)

---

*C*an God ever be weak? Seems disrespectful to even think such a thought but sometimes the things that God asks of us can seem weak, especially to the eyes of ungodly people and even to ourselves sometimes. For example, the Word of God says in Luke 6:29 (NIV):

> *If someone slaps you on one cheek, turn to them the other also. If someone takes your coat, do not withhold your shirt from them.*

(Please note the Bible is not advocating someone being violent against you, rather this refers to someone dishonouring your pride.)

Naturally speaking, if someone in some way disrespects me, I want to return the sentiment, but God is asking us here to do something so opposite. It seems a little weak to let someone get away with that. How about Matthew 5:43, where it says to love your enemies? The natural mind apart from God would say to destroy all your enemies. It seems the more solid, strong thing to go with the latter.

How about when Jesus was hanging on the cross, naked, bleeding, physically ripped apart, dying? There seems no weaker picture than this. To the natural eye, His enemies had won. That 'Jesus problem' had been taken care of, according to those that despised Him, and yet this had been a plan of God that was in place even before the foundations of the world were set out. What looked so foolish and weak was actually the greatest, most powerful thing that could ever happen, but not to the natural eye. Jesus, dying for us and then rising from the dead made a way for us to return to relationship with God. Not weak at all!

So I suppose what I am saying is this: sometimes our natural mind will not like the things that God asks of us and we may perceive them as weak. When my pride is hurt, I want to lash out, not love. When I get offended, I may want to harbour hatred. Naturally speaking, to do what God would want seems weak, ineffective and more effort than it's worth, but when we go with God's plan and not what we think looks right, we don't always see the good that God is doing behind the scenes, but things are happening. It looked like Jesus had died a pathetic death at the hands of His enemies, but what the eye could not see was that during those three days that Jesus was dead He was declaring to satan and his hosts that He had won the victory (Ephesians 4:7-10). While people were weeping over Jesus' corpse and laying Him in a tomb, He was proclaiming His triumph to the enemy.

God's so-called foolishness will always produce good, and it is far wiser than the greatest wisdom we can ever muster up. Go with God's plan. He has insight we don't possess and His plans have purpose. He sees what we cannot on the journey ahead.

God is good

The LORD is upright; He is my Rock, and there is no wickedness in Him.

Psalm 92:15 (NIV)

No matter what happens in life, if you hold fast to this truth, that God is good, then you will never grow angry, callous or offended with the Lord. The Scriptures give account after account of the graciousness and goodness of God. The Psalms are filled with King David's praise to God for His goodness.

For He satisfies those who long for Him and fills the hungry with His goodness.
Psalm 107:9 (The Truth)

Give thanks to the Lord, for He is good; His mercy and love last eternally.
Psalm 118:1 (The Truth)

In Galatians 5 goodness, not evil or wickedness, is one of the fruits of the Spirit, and that Spirit is the Spirit of God. Jesus calls Himself the 'Good Shepherd' in John 10. In the book of Acts 10:38 it says that Jesus went from place to place doing 'good things' and healing people.

Those that attribute evil things as being the works of God have clearly never read or understood their Bible, because if they did they would see a God who is wonderfully in love with humanity and did everything possible – not even sparing His own Son – to enable us to have a relationship with Him. The person who called natural disasters 'acts of God' clearly never read the Word, which reveals that God is love (1 John 4:8). He doesn't just love us, but He actually is love.

Some people are so angry at God and feel He has so much to answer for in regards to tragedies and bad things that have happened, but wickedness is not in His character. Those individuals are blaming the wrong one for the evil they have seen or experienced. 2 Corinthians 4:4 (NLT) calls satan the god of this world and his agenda is to kill, steal, and destroy (John 10:10). When bad things happen we have a wonderful Saviour who is there to help, heal and set free and bring peace. We are God's children and we, too, are filled with His goodness and love and we are called to bring His goodness to this world.

When we see evil, that is not the fingerprint of our loving, heavenly Father, and when we act evil we are not bearing the hallmarks of Him either.

My dear friend, never imitate what is evil, only what is good. He who does good is of God; he who does evil has not seen God.
3 John 11 (The Truth)

SECRET ANGEL

So then, as we have opportunity, let us do good to everyone, and especially to those who are of the household of faith.
Galatians 6:10 (ESV)

A while back I was in a group that decided to have a little fun by playing a game called *Secret Angel*. Everyone in the group chose a name of one of the other group members out of a hat, and nobody knew who had whose name. For a whole month we had to pray for that person and do nice things for them.

My 'Secret Angel' did the loveliest things for me. I would find packets of my favourite sweets sitting on my seat at church. I had encouraging notes put in my Bible, and my 'angel' was artsy so she made me beautiful crafts.

I'm not asking you to play this game but this weekend, make a plan to be a 'Secret Angel' in the lives of others. Do kind and lovely things anonymously for some people. Pray for these people too, and let them know God placed them on your heart.

Have a great weekend!

Notes

_____

_____

_____

_____

_____

_____

Guarding your heart

Above all else, guard your heart, for everything you do flows from it.

Proverbs 4:23 (NIV)

Here the writer of Proverbs gives us some very good advice. Notice the importance and emphasis he places on the advice he is giving when he says 'above all else.' He deliberately places this piece of advice at the top of the list of things he deems important for the reader to know. The Amplified translation says, 'Watch over your heart with all diligence.' Again, you can hear the great importance being placed on the act of watching over the condition of our heart. But is this verse speaking of our natural heart, our blood pump? No, though it is wise to take good care of your natural heart. It is actually referring to another heart within you: your soul, that place deep within you where, among other things, your emotions gather, decisions are made, pains and joys are felt and expressed, people are loved, and things can be harboured.

The writer speaks concerning this 'central control box' of who we are that we daily live our lives from or, as he puts it, where our life flows from. Because we live in a real world with real people it is this place, our inner heart, that can take the greatest beatings, as well as experience the greatest blessings. We need to guard our heart to maintain its wellbeing so we can live life like God intended for us to, free from negative baggage and junk. Some of the not-so-good things that can rise up or be stored in our hearts originate from ourselves. Things like pride, cynicism, and arrogance can rise in the hearts of each of us if we do not monitor their activity. One of the best ways of doing this is to have a healthy prayer life. But other external things can affect the wellbeing of our heart, namely things that are done to us by others.

The greatest of these for damaging our life and future has to be offence. Let's face it, unless we isolate ourselves – which according to Proverbs 18:1 is not wise – we will all have opportunity to 'get offended' by others, and the level of interaction you have with people will determine how many opportunities you have. The bottom line is you may have the opportunity to take offence, but that does not mean that you should. When you understand the damage that offence can do to your life, if you choose to carry it in your heart, you'll keep from letting it find a place of germination in your life.

Someone once said that offence is 'the bait of satan' – that is definitely true! Offence is like bait that is set out to entrap you. When you take the bait your life is suddenly open to all manner of other things that are bad for your life, things that will damage your heart, things like bitterness, unforgiveness and hatred to name a few.

Don't play with offence. Keep your heart free from it by daily committing your heart to God and quickly forgiving anyone you feel has wronged you. Just as a healthy natural heart will cause you to live an full, active life, so it is when the central heart of who you are is in health – your life will flourish, blossom and bloom. So guard and maintain the health of your heart today.

Absalom and the dangers of offence

As time went on, Absalom took to riding in a horse-drawn chariot, with fifty men running in front of him. Early each morning he would take up his post beside the road at the city gate. When anyone showed up with a case to bring to the king for a decision, Absalom would call him over and say, "Where do you hail from?"

2 Samuel 15:1-2 (MSG)

The account of Absalom is a very sad story, a story of how an offence that started so small turned into a monster that drove a man to his ruin. That's the problem with offences, they start so small like seeds and are often hardly noticed arriving. But once they germinate and take root in a person's heart they begin to turn and drive things in a strong way from deep within them. As we study the life of Absalom this week may it be a warning to us all to correctly deal with offence when it comes knocking on the door of our life. Remember, you are in charge of your life responses – offence may knock but you do not have to let it in.

Here is the basic storyline: Absalom had killed his brother for his inappropriate behaviour with their sister. David was not sure what to do with Absalom so he sent him away. Please note, David never stopped loving him or seeing him as his son the whole time he was gone, but things were not the same for Absalom. Sometime during his time away offence entered into his heart concerning David, and it grew into a deep bitterness and a despising of David and his leadership. With offence now fully grown within him he began to plan how he would overthrow his father's kingdom and rule.

David was completely unaware, but that is what offence is like, isn't it? A person takes offence and, instead of dealing with it correctly by talking to the person they feel wronged by, they sit and brew over what is in their hearts. Before long the brewing produces resentment, then resentment turns into action. Let's learn from this sad account and purpose to not let this happen to us.

So how should you deal with offence? Simple, go talk to person involved, forgive them quickly and don't let plans to see them suffer or get what you think they are due take any kind of root in your life. God can't and won't bless this response. It takes courage and humility to deal with offence in a godly way, but as we take time to read through this story this week, and look at how things ended for Absalom, you will hopefully be encouraged to do what is right in God's sight.

As we said yesterday, we will all have the opportunity to be offended by others, but that does not mean we have the right to be offended. What is right is to guard your heart and what you allow in to grow, and always have the courage to talk to others – especially when it involves the Davids, the leaders that God has positioned in your life. Always take the brave road of communication, not the coward's route of isolation, or worse dissension and divisiveness, because that leads to nowhere pleasant.

Be careful of Absaloms, they are out there

He would get up early and stand by the side of the road leading to the city gate. Whenever anyone came with a complaint to be placed before the king for a decision, Absalom would call out to him, "What town are you from?" He would answer, "Your servant is from one of the tribes of Israel." Then Absalom would say to him, "Look, your claims are valid and proper, but there is no representative of the king to hear you."

2 Samuel 15:2-3 (NIV)

This week we are looking at the subject of offence, specifically considering the account of Absalom, David's son. We looked yesterday at how offence was born in his heart concerning his father and spiritual leader and what not dealing with that offence did in his life, causing him to set sail for somewhere he never should have gone.

Once the seed of offence had germinated and become a driving force in his life, Absalom began to plot to get from David what he felt he deserved, and then took the next step and acted on his deceptive intentions. His plan was to take away the kingdom and the people from David, but in his deception he forgot one very important thing: that God had given David the kingdom and had not changed His mind.

Notice in today's text the sneaky way Absalom outworked his plan. Instead of confronting the one who had so offended him he worked behind his back to ruin him. I have sadly witnessed people that, in their offence, yielded to an 'Absalom spirit' and in a scary way followed his script to the letter, often not knowing they were doing it. Notice the things Absalom did and let them be a warning to you in your walk with God and submission to godly leadership. Not only do we need to deal with offence in our own hearts, we also need to be careful when we have dealings with others who have offence in theirs, especially when it comes to their leaders. When people have offence in their heart they normally always try to put that offence on others. Don't let others load their bullets of offence in the gun of your life.

Absalom is deliberately cunning and sneaky. He positions himself at the gate between David, who was God's established leader, and the people – and like a wolf in sheep's clothing starts to steal the hearts of the people passing by him with deceptive words dressed in a false sincerity of caring. David was unaware of what he was doing, and this was neither a godly, righteous or even 'helpful to the people' thing to do.

The big lesson here: be careful of sweet speaking people who position themselves between you and the leader God has given you. Always stop and ask yourself, 'Why are they offering me their ear and advice instead of encouraging me to talk to my leader?' Maybe it's because, like Absalom, they have an offence and instead of dealing with it in a godly way they want to find innocent people to join their 'coup'. Be careful of such people because though their words may be kind to attract your allegiance, know that their inner agenda is not and you really do not want to go where they want to lead you. Protect your heart from the influence of such people – in fact, do them a huge favour when you encounter them and encourage them to go talk to their David. They will normally be too cowardly to do this, but in suggesting they do so you could actually save them!

Lesson today: always guard your life from your own offences and also the offences of others.

Recognising the Absalom behaviour

Then Absalom would say to him, "Look, your claims are valid and proper, but there is no representative of the king to hear you." And Absalom would add, "If only I were appointed judge in the land! Then everyone who has a complaint or case could come to me and I would see that they receive justice." Also, whenever anyone approached him to bow down before him, Absalom would reach out his hand, take hold of him and kiss him. Absalom behaved in this way toward all the Israelites who came to the king asking for justice, and so he stole the hearts of the people of Israel.

2 Samuel 15:3-6 (NIV)

*L*et us continue to look at the subject of offence and protecting ourselves from the damaging influence of an Absalom spirit in our lives and the lives of others we may encounter on the road of life. To enable us to be able to recognise an Absalom spirit active in the life of a person let us read Absalom's story again to learn his traits.

Firstly, he subtly positions himself between the leadership and the people. This means he will be near the leadership but not with leadership. When in position he then beckons vulnerable people to himself, telling them things like, 'The leadership does not want to listen to your problems and don't really care about you, but I do, I have time for you.' In doing this he very subtly devalues and dis-empowers leadership in the sight of those he approaches.

Once he has successfully made them feel they will not be listened to or helped by leadership, he then steps in as their saviour, with offers of care and personal assistance. Again this is so wrong because there was zero evidence that David or his leadership would not have listened to or cared for the people's problems. This is nothing more than an offended man spreading his offence by mixing its poison in a sugary sweet, apparently very caring, offer. But in its true light it is nothing less than divisive and crafty, and will only cause confusion and harm. How caring he must have seemed as he took their hand, bowed down to them and kissed them with his comfort. How sad that they could not see through the performance to the reality that all he intended to do was to infect them with the same virus of offence that had infected him and separate them from the leadership God had appointed in their lives.

Can you see how subtle the Absalom spirit can be? May this be a warning to you, especially when you encounter people trying to 'win your heart' away from a leader. Don't be conned by the caring arm, the sweet smile and the offer of a listening and understanding ear. Rather, have the discernment to carry on walking until you get to your leader and talk to them about the situations or issues you may have.

Please hear my warning today – protect your heart and life from people who carry the spirit of Absalom, which is still sadly very active in the world today. Their favourite position is still 'just outside of the gate' of the church, where the pastor can't see them but where they can be heard. Be wise when you encounter this spirit operating in a person, even if they seem really sweet. Don't lend them your ear, rather walk on by less their infection of offence be sown in you and suddenly you wake up sneezing with an offence that is not yours.

Undealt-with offence will leave you hanging

Then Absalom met the servants of David. Absalom rode on a mule. The mule went under the thick boughs of a great terebinth tree, and his head caught in the terebinth; so he was left hanging between heaven and earth. And the mule which was under him went on.

2 Samuel 18:9

This week we have spoken of the negative potential of offence in a person's life, looking specifically at the life of Absalom. Absalom sadly allowed offence to grow in his heart and it caused him to do terrible things against his father and leader, David. Remember the golden rule: 'what a man sows that he will reap'. What Absalom had sown in his divisive actions was never going to produce anything good for him long term. So, let's look at what happened to Absalom, and gain a sobering warning concerning the final destination that his offence actually led him to.

Here we see him on a mule. In many ways his offence was another mule he was riding at the same time. Offence was taking him places he really did not want to go but now, deceived by his offence, Absalom is totally unaware of his journey. All of a sudden he gets his head caught in a tree and is left hanging – it literally says, 'hanging between heaven and earth!'

What an unusual thing to happen, to be caught and hung in the branches of a tree! I was so intrigued with how the Bible says, 'He was left hanging between heaven and earth.' The writer didn't say 'sky and land' but 'heaven and earth.' One way of interpreting this could simply be that his divisive actions, caused by his deep offence, brought about a behaviour that did not position him well on earth, but was also considered unacceptable in heaven. You see, when someone is deliberately divisive and causes dissension among people it is not long before people catch on and begin to avoid the person because of their behaviour. But also we need to understand that divisive behaviour really is not accepted in heaven – it is actually something God says He hates and sees as an abomination.

These six things the Lord hates, yes, seven are an abomination to Him: a proud look, a lying tongue, hands that shed innocent blood, a heart that devises wicked plans, feet that are swift in running to evil, a false witness who speaks lies, and one who sows discord among brethren.

Proverbs 6:16-19

When you read through this list of things that God hates you actually see that they are exactly the things that Absalom did. These things were not acceptable in the sight of God and also separated him from a relationship with his father and king, and others. So, in many ways, the actions that came from his offence were the things that caused him, at the end of his life, to be left hanging.

I don't know about you but I don't want to be left hanging around like he was. How can we prevent that? Simple, we must guard our heart from offence. Never allow the mule of offence to carry you away from relationships you need or toward any head-catching trees you don't.

And, in this all remember, David was unaffected. His life and leadership carried on according to God's plans for him, because the problem was not his and no weapon of offence fashioned against him was going to prosper.

Guard your heart, forgive and always love.

SHOW THANKFULNESS

I thank my God in all my remembrance of you.
Philippians 1:3 (ESV)

The attitude of thankfulness in people is a beautiful thing.

Recently my daughter, who is currently studying away from home, sent me an unexpected note with flowers. I saved this beautiful note and I will probably cherish it as long as I live, because I loved the way I was caught completely by surprise by her gratitude and love for all that I had done for her. This was such a special moment for me.

This weekend think of at least one person in your life who has done something you are thankful for and let them know. You can write a note, letter, text, whatever way you do it, just do it. Don't let life slip by without giving honor to the people who have helped you on this journey of life.

Notes

_____

_____

_____

_____

_____

_____

_____

A mixed bag

So Jesus answered and said, "Assuredly, I say to you, there is no one who has left house or brothers or sisters or father or mother or wife or children or lands, for My sake and the gospel's, who shall not receive a hundredfold now in this time—houses and brothers and sisters and mothers and children and lands, with persecutions—and in the age to come, eternal life.

Mark 10:29-31

I don't know about you but I love these verses promising a hundredfold reward and blessing for those who have lost or left things behind for Jesus and His Kingdom. This has always been a very special promise to both Gina and I as, over our time of being married, we have often left things to do what God has called us to do, including homes, lands and relationships. Truth be told we would have done it for Jesus if there was no reward, because of all He has done for us, but it is nice to know that He promises what He does.

But please notice a couple of things: firstly, God promises rewards and blessings in this life and the one to come! You see, God is no one's debtor, He will not be in debt to anyone. Whenever you lose or lay aside something for Him He will always, in His time, restore or replace – and it's never same for same but a hundredfold. It's always exceedingly, abundantly better (Ephesians 3:20). Secondly, He promises to reward and bless in the here and now *and also* in the life that is to come – how great is that?

We also need to notice that what these verses promise really is a mixed bag. They teach us that we will see His reward here *and* later, but also that it will come 'with persecutions'. Please understand, the persecutions don't come from God but from others, and they are actually healthy signs that a person is living for God. Don't confuse these with the persecutions that come from a person being unwisely or stupidly. No, these are ones that come from a life standing up for Christ and His kingdom. You see, when you leave things for Him your life starts to become radically defined, sticking out from the crowd. That will bring different responses from those around you. Maybe because your love for God, lived out in demonstration and not just theory, irritates or challenges them and their relationship – or lack of relationship – with Him?

So when you see God restoring things in your life, things that you had left behind for Him, don't be surprised or upset if at the same time you experience persecution. It's all good, and goes to prove that you are indeed in a time when God is 'paying you back' for what you left behind for Him.

And always remember He told you it was going to happen.

All three are present if you look

I am the true vine, and My Father is the vinedresser. Every branch in Me that does not bear fruit
He takes away; and every branch that bears fruit He prunes, that it may bear more fruit.

John 15:1-2

---

*L*et's take a moment to return to some of my favourite verses in John 15. If you know me, and have ever been around me, then you know it's never that long before I get back to preaching on the incredible truths found in John 15.

Today I want to point out something that I recently saw in a fresh way. In the opening verses of Jesus teaching on abiding in the vine He takes a moment to introduce all of those involved. The Heavenly Father is present as the Vinedresser or Gardener, Jesus is present as the Vine, and we also are present, as new creations, as the branches joined to the Him. But recently I had a question: 'Where is the Holy Spirit?'

Whenever I was taught about God I was always taught about the Trinity and how He is God in three persons: Father, Son and Holy Spirit. So I momentarily thought, 'Why was the Holy Spirit left out of this story or analogy?' Then I realised, He hadn't been left out at all. Though not introduced or mentioned by name, the Holy Spirit is so very present if you think about it. You see, the Holy Spirit is the life of the vine. He is present as the heavenly sap, flowing through the vine, and also flowing through us, the branches, as we abide in Him.

How exciting is that? All three are present in the story but also all three are present in our experience of the union we now have with Jesus. Today, if you have believed in Jesus, your life has been joined to Him, the vine, and you can now say with confidence, as He did concerning you, 'He is the vine and I am a branch.' Being a branch that is now fully joined or connected by His doing, you can have confidence to say that His life (sap) is now your life (sap), and the life or nature that flows through Jesus the vine now also flows through you.

Peter teaches this in a wonderful way:

> *By which have been given to us exceedingly great and precious promises, that*
> *through these you may be partakers of the divine nature.*
>
> 2 Peter 1:4

The key is simply to abide or remain in Him. As you do you are of the same sap as the One you are now connected to. His life is now your life, so your life is destined to produce fruit that glorifies Him. And don't forget the Gardener – He is the one ever working on us, pruning and trimming, never to harm our lives but to cause them to produce more fruit than we ever imagined.

Broken off and grafted in

Abide in Me, and I in you. As the branch cannot bear fruit of itself, unless it abides in the vine, neither can you, unless you abide in Me. "I am the vine, you are the branches. He who abides in Me, and I in him, bears much fruit; for without Me you can do nothing.

John 15:4-5

In our church, Family Church, people always smile when I remind them that we were not always known as Family Church. When Gina and I first opened the church around two decades ago it was called 'Abide in the Vine Family Church'. I thought that this was a great name because of the revelation that I had concerning the truths found in John 15 when Jesus spoke about abiding in the vine.

We had badges, banners and T-shirts with our name on. One morning I was putting the rubbish out and I had my 'Abide in the vine' T-shirt on. I bumped into my neighbour and, on seeing my shirt, he told me he was a member of a wine tasting club too! Realising that people who don't usually go to church did not get our name, I soon changed it to 'Family Church'. Our name changed but the teaching of abiding in the vine has always remained central to what we believe and what we preach. Its simplicity is so beautiful yet so profound. At that time our mission statement was really simple too, based on John 15: *break them off, graft them in and teach them how to suck sap.*

In this simple statement is the essence of our calling and the results of what happens and what is available to us when we give our life to Christ. Romans 11:17-24 teaches us that when we come to faith we are grafted into the true vine. But before we are grafted in we must understand we are first broken off – broken off from an old vine with an old nature. Romans calls this vine a 'wild olive tree'. It was wild because of its nature, different or contrary to God's.

In the Garden of Eden, in their disobedience, Adam and Eve were disconnected from God's life and nature, and joined to another. The nature of that other was a sin nature and that sin nature became the nature that flowed through us. That is why, before you were a Christian, it took no effort to sin. But now everything has changed, we have been broken off and Jesus has grafted us into Himself with the seal of faith.

Think about it, you are no longer joined to that old tree that is evil by nature. There's a big hole on that tree where you once used to be. Now you have been grafted perfectly to Him, which means His sap, His divine nature, is now daily flowing to you. What do you need to do now you've been broken off and grafted in? Simple: SUCK SAP!

Let His life and nature flow through every part of who you are. As you do you won't be able to stop the fruit of His Spirit growing in and through you.

Let it flow!

Live in me. Make your home in me just as I do in you. In the same way that a branch can't bear grapes by itself but only by being joined to the vine, you can't bear fruit unless you are joined with me. I am the Vine, you are the branches. When you're joined with me and I with you, the relation intimate and organic, the harvest is sure to be abundant. Separated, you can't produce a thing.

John 15:4-8 (MSG)

So, we have established that by His doing we have now been broken off from an old vine that was wicked by nature. Now we have been joined – grafted in – to the tree of life, to Jesus Himself. Romans 11:20 reminds us that we are joined to Him by faith and nothing else.

As we remain in Him, staying joined, abiding, He remains in us and as this natural ongoing relationship daily continues the life of the vine or root flows through the life of the branch, producing fruit that now gives glory to the owner of the orchard, God. It is only when we do not yield to the flowing life of the vine – maybe because of things like ignorance, stubbornness or pride – that the natural life-producing flow of the vine is hindered.

Producing godly fruit that pleases God really is a very natural thing. Sadly some Christians, when you listen to them, make bearing fruit for God such an effort, and when you watch their life they sometimes resemble 'constipated apple trees'! Come on, think about it: have you ever seen a constipated apple tree? Have you ever heard an apple tree in a garden or orchard panting like it is in childbirth when producing its fruit? No, of course you haven't. Why? Because bearing fruit happens naturally. So it is with us when it comes to producing the fruit of His Spirit. God does not want us straining, He simply wants us yielding; and as we do there is a natural flow of His life through the branches of our life, producing the fruit He desires.

It's only because of the change of nature that suddenly where there was once the fruit of selfishness there is now the fruit of selflessness; where there was once hatred there is now love; and where there was once meanness, kindness now grows. The fruit of the life of Jesus becomes the same fruit that is seen in us. Why? It's the same life!

Go ahead and yield to His Spirit today – as you do fruit will grow, good fruit that will remain.

Stop being afraid of what could go wrong and start being excited about what could go right.

Unknown

Just remain in Him

If you do not remain in me, you are like a branch that is thrown away and withers; such branches are picked up, thrown into the fire and burned. If you remain in me and my words remain in you, ask whatever you wish, and it will be done for you. This is to my Father's glory, that you bear much fruit, showing yourselves to be my disciples.

John 15:6-8 (NIV)

All we need to do is remain in Him, to stay connected. As we do His vibrant life and nature infuses our life and keeps us alive and vibrant. It's only when we don't remain that we start to wither and, as the text teaches us today, if we fully remove ourselves we become like dead wood that is only good for burning. Neither of these two things need to happen or be our experience if we just purpose to stay connected in a healthy, natural way.

Once again, let's think about this in a natural way. If you snapped a branch from a tree in your garden and threw it aside it may look alive for a short time but not for long, right? And you really would not be that surprised if, when you looked at it a few weeks later, it was dead and lifeless, would you? Of course not, you'd simply say, 'It's because it's not connected to the tree anymore.' It's really that simple for us as well. If we desire to stay alive, vibrant and continually producing good fruit, we just need to abide, and stay connected.

When Jesus was teaching this to His first disciples, He was simply teaching them what I have termed the 'Order of Existence'. By that I mean that He supports our life, we do not support His. If we separate ourselves from Him He lives on, it's us that won't because, as you know, the branch finds its life in the vine, not the other way around. The branch simply expresses the life of the vine or root it is connected to.

Jesus simply taught, 'Without Me, or disconnected from Me, you can do nothing.' That's good news for those who don't disconnect from Him, because connected to Him we can do anything. The Apostle Paul knew this, that is why he said with such confidence, 'I can now do all things through Christ who strengthens me' (Philippians 4:13). These were not words of arrogance based in a confidence of his own ability, rather they were words flowing from his persuasion that He was now connected or joined to Jesus Christ. It's the same for us!

So today, stay connected. As you remain in Him, He remains in you, and your life produces new fruit, beyond what you can imagine.

Prayer

Dear Father, thank You for pouring Your God-life into me as I remain in You. Lord, I am so grateful that I can make my dwelling place in You, and in this place I have Your strength, Your ability and everything that You are coursing through me. As I remain in the vine I find the real me, the best possible me and I am home.

Amen

PRAY FOR YOUR NATION AND LEADERS

First of all, then, I urge that supplications, prayers,
intercessions, and thanksgivings be made for all
people, for kings and all who are in high positions,
that we may lead a peaceful and quiet life, godly and
dignified in every way. This is good, and it is pleasing
in the sight of God our Savior.
1 Timothy 2:13 (ESV)

Whether you like the leader of your nation or not, he or she is in a great position of power
and needs your prayers.

This weekend take some time to pray for your national leaders, and your local leaders.
They may not be leading like you hoped they would but they still need wisdom from God
in making decisions. Maybe if you pray for them they will make wiser choices in how they
lead? No leader has an easy job and I'm sure that when they took the job on they had no
intentions of making their country worse off, even if some of the policies and laws they
made didn't pan out so well. You may think your leader is super but they are still only
human, and leading a nation cannot possibly be easy.

I'm sure your leaders would appreciate it if you would PRAY FOR THEM!

Notes

_____

_____

_____

_____

_____

It's time to open the Blacksmiths

Now there was no blacksmith to be found throughout all the land of Israel, for the Philistines said, "Lest the Hebrews make swords or spears." So it came about, on the day of battle, that there was neither sword nor spear found in the hand of any of the people who were with Saul and Jonathan. But they were found with Saul and Jonathan his son.

1 Samuel 13:19, 22

The Philistine army had come up with a great plan to keep Israel from becoming any threat to them: they just shut down their blacksmiths. What did this do? It stopped the children of Israel being able to make weapons, and without weapons they could not fight or even train to fight, making them a totally controllable non-threat to the Philistines. Oh, they could sing, but singing would not be any kind of physical threat. Basically, Israel had become a 'singing people' who were unable to fight.

When I read these verses it reminds me a little bit of the church today. You see, the modern Church has become so good at singing – we fill large arenas with singing saints and our performances are truly breathtaking. My question is, when the singing is done how many of the Christians leaving the arena know how to fight? How many have weapons of warfare and know how to use them to fight and overcome the enemy of their life?

Don't get me wrong, our praise and worship is awesome, and in itself is a powerful weapon of warfare. But we also need to make sure we are training the people of God to fight, lest we become like the children of Israel in today's account, a singing people unequipped and unprepared for battle. Recently I felt the Lord challenge me in a dream to 'open up the blacksmith's house again'. What I believe He meant by that was to make the Church a place where people can be trained and equipped for battle again; to make Church more than a great singing event alone; to let it be a place where warriors are made and weapons are forged. Isn't this the very purpose of the church as we see it in Ephesians 4?

And He Himself gave some to be apostles, some prophets, some evangelists, and some pastors and teachers, for the equipping of the saints for the work of ministry, for the edifying of the body of Christ.

Ephesians 4:11-12

Let me encourage you today to not just see your church as a place that you're loved and accepted, a place where you get to worship and sing nice songs, but also a place where you are equipped, trained and made ready for battle. Let it not just be a place of spiritual entertainment but also the workshop of the blacksmith in your life, a place where steel is fashioned and weapons and warriors are made.

Pay a visit to the Blacksmith's house too

The word which came to Jeremiah from the Lord, saying: "Arise and go down to the potter's house, and there I will cause you to hear My words." Then I went down to the potter's house, and there he was, making something at the wheel. And the vessel that he made of clay was marred in the hand of the potter; so he made it again into another vessel, as it seemed good to the potter to make.

Jeremiah 18:1-4

We spoke yesterday of how the Philistines removed the blacksmiths from Israel to make sure they had no weapons or ability to fight them, and how the Church – as well as being a place of worship – needs to again be a place where Christians are equipped and prepared for battle. The Church needs to be 'the house of the blacksmith' again – and never forget, the Greatest Blacksmith of them all is Father God.

The problem is, not all Christians want to know or experience anything else but the 'loving hands of the Father', where they feel cherished and loved. These are indeed great hands to know, especially when you first come to Him, but the truth is God also wants you to know the other potential that is in His hands as well. Jeremiah discovered His potter's hands when He responded to God's invitation to be as clay in His fingers, and we all need to experience Him as the Potter, moulding and shaping us too. But I believe that God's hands are also the blacksmith's hands – that if you will allow Him to, He will carefully fashion your life for battle and victory. The good news is that you do not have to leave the loving hands of the Father to experience the forming hands of the Potter or the fashioning hands of the Blacksmith, because they are the same hands belonging to the same God!

As well as being shepherds in your life, pastors should be blacksmiths, serving under the greatest Blacksmith of them all, the Lord. It's when you allow Him and His church to be the Blacksmith in your life that He will make you strong, unbreakable and ready for every battle you may face.

I love that moment when Jeremiah hears God say to Him to 'go to the potter's house.' God wanted to teach him something's about His creative ability that a verbal lesson would not have adequately done. Jeremiah goes and, as he watches the potter, he observes and understands how God's hands can form and shape the nation of Israel, and his own life. He has a revelation of the power of the potter's wheel.

In the same way we need to consider the blacksmith, and gain an excitement of what God can create in us if we will place our lives upon His anvil, with the assurance that He will never harm or hurt us but will fashion and shape us. Join me tomorrow as we go to the blacksmith's house to learn about God's intentions and plans for us.

God the Father, the Potter and the Blacksmith

Still, God, you are our Father. We're the clay and you're our potter: All of us are what you made us.
Isaiah 64:8 (MSG)

So, we have established that through new birth our lives are now safely in the hands of a loving Father. We also know that God desires that we know the fuller potential of His hands as the Potter and the Blacksmith in our life. As Jeremiah went down to the potter's house to learn the potential of God's hands, so let's take a moment visit the blacksmith's house to see exactly what he does and see its comparable application in our lives.

When the Lord asked me to 'open again the Blacksmith', straight away I began to study what blacksmiths did, and I immediately noticed a couple of very relevant things. Through a process using fire and water, they change the molecular structure of steel to super-steel. What does that mean? By using extremes of heat and cold, and repeated beating over an anvil with a hammer, they transform the strength of the steel from basic, brittle metal, which would easily snap under pressure, to a sword that won't be broken in the intensity of battle. This is what God wants to do for us and in us. Using the two things He has always used – the fire of His Spirit and the water of His Word – He wants to fashion us into unbreakable weapons that He can use in battle. One blacksmith I read about said, 'The hotter the fire, and the colder the water, the tougher and more unbreakable the steel produced.'

As we allow Father God to be the Blacksmith in our life, and His church the blacksmith's workshop, He fashions us using His Word and His Spirit – and, yes, even the knocks of life can be used to help. But, when He is done, we are changed; not modified but transformed. Just as the molecular structure of steel is changed in the blacksmith's hands, so the nature and character of our lives are changed in His. You might say, "What would make anyone want to stay on the anvil?" Simple: trust in the hands that are working on you and believe in what He is fashioning.

I hope this has encouraged you to know not just the loving hands of Father God but also desire the hands of the Potter to mould and shape, and the hands of the Blacksmith to fashion and strengthen. When you find yourself in battle you'll know that, though others to the right and the left of you may break, you won't because you have been through the fire and the water and have come to a place of great strength! (Psalm 66:12)

Prayer

Good morning, Father. I commit my life into Your hands again today, the hands of the Father, Gardener, Potter and Blacksmith. I trust Your hands, Lord; mold me and fashion me into all You know that I can be. Thank You that You know my full potential and I trust You to do what You need to do to let that full potential come into full expression.

Amen

So faithful

Great is his faithfulness; his loving-kindness begins afresh each day.

Lamentations 3:23 (TLB)

---

*G*alatians chapter 5 lists the fruits of God's Holy Spirit, and one of these is faithfulness. According to the dictionary, to be faithful is to be 'steadfast in affection or allegiance, to remain loyal'.

Faithfulness should be part of the character of every believer because His Spirit resides in us. This world looks at faithfulness as something pretty special. For example, when a man and a woman have been married for a very long time people are amazed at the loyalty and commitment that was involved. When a person loses an extraordinary amount of weight we applaud their faithful attitude toward their goal. Some would even attribute faithfulness to a pet that, with loyalty and affection, stays close by their owner's side.

The Bible reveals to us that it is God's nature to be faithful. There have been times in my life when, because of difficulties and problems I was facing, I wondered if God was still with me. When the going got tough I was tempted to think of God as a 'fair weather friend' who was there when the sun was shining but absent in my dark times.

Sometimes we will feel God's presence at every turn, when we see a beautiful sunset or when people show us great kindness, but the truth is He never leaves us or forsakes us – never ever, ever, ever, rain or shine. He is faithful in every sense of the word. He faithfully abides with us and faithfully keeps His promises without fail at all times, even when we don't deserve it. I have only to look at Ruth in the Bible, who showed fervent devotion and compassion toward her aged, widowed mother-in-law, who sadly was childless when her two sons died. Ruth too was a widow and she could have gone back to a life with a promise of comfort and a future, but out of love she chose to journey with Naomi.

Also, I think of Hosea who showed incredible faithfulness and love toward his bride who was completely and repeatedly unfaithful toward him, even to the point of rescuing her after she foolishly went off with another man who ends up selling her into slavery. Both Ruth and Hosea are symbolic portraits of God's faithfulness toward us. He chooses to journey through life with us, in our ups and downs, and regardless of our faithfulness toward Him. He remains unwavering in His love and grace toward us.

Just as I expect the sun to rise each day, so I expect God's faithfulness. Expect God's faithfulness and devotion toward you in every area of your life.

If we are without faith He will still remain faithful, for He cannot deny Himself.
2 Timothy 2:13 (The Truth)

Be brave

One of them said he knew a young fellow in Bethlehem, the son of a man named Jesse, who was not only a talented harp player, but was handsome, brave, and strong, and had good, solid judgment. "What's more," he added, "the Lord is with him."

! Samuel 16:18 (TLB)

It's easy to see why David was chosen by God to become the next king over Israel. Talent, good looks, strength, and intelligence are all things that we as human beings hold in great importance, but the one that I want to focus on is BRAVE.

I think that bravery is one of the most important attributes that any person can have to live a successful life. In 1 Samuel, David is attributed with bravery in being a warrior. Many of us are not warriors in the traditional sense of the word, but if you have been alive for any length of time then you've probably realised that sometimes we have to fight in this life. If we didn't have to face some scary things at times then we wouldn't need to be brave. Bravery is an enemy of fear. Everyone faces fear at some time. When times of fear assail us, we can muster up as much courage as is within us and even that sometimes isn't enough. It is not easy being brave in the face of fear. Maybe you've dealt with a phobia or hypochondria or have tried to help someone else dealing with fear.

Fear can be crippling. When we fear something that fear can seem like a mountain that cannot be scaled by mere little us. Notice the end of 1 Samuel 16:18: 'What's more, the Lord is with Him.' When I step out of my comfort zone into things that I fear, or when fear is gripping my heart, I always remind myself that in my feeble attempts to overcome my fears, I have the strength and backing of God Almighty. In 1 Chronicles King Hezekiah is trying to encourage his fearful army as they are surrounded by a horde of their enemies and he says this:

"Be strong and courageous. Do not be afraid or discouraged because of the king of Assyria and the vast army with him, for there is a greater power with us than with him. With him is only the arm of flesh, but with us is the LORD our God to help us and to fight our battles." And the people gained confidence from what Hezekiah the king of Judah said.
2 Chronicles 32:7-8 (NIV)

Well, the Lord gave them victory and the Scripture says the enemy king returned 'shamefaced' to his own land. Wouldn't you love to send all your fears 'shamefaced' back to wherever they came from? Next time you are surrounded by an army of fear remind yourself that the Lord is with you and, however powerful the fear seems, like Hezekiah put so perfectly, 'there is greater power with us.' You may not feel brave in your own ability, but with Almighty God on your side confidence will grow and the fear that has been roaring like a lion will eventually squeak away like a little mouse. You may have to remind yourself of this many times but the bravery is in not giving up. Keep bravely coming against fear with the knowledge that God's power is with you. Even if you didn't possess the power to overcome your fear, God in you is enough power to overcome a whole army of fear and send its king shamefaced back to wherever it came from.

If God is for us, who can be against us?
Romans 8:31

BLESS YOUR PASTORS

Let the elders that rule well be counted worthy of double honour, especially they who labour in the word and doctrine.
1 Timothy 5:17 (KJV)

Your pastors have a wonderful but difficult job in leading and equipping the people of God. Although many people are a joy to lead, there are always people and situations that are not so easy to deal with. Pastoring is not the kind of job that starts at nine in the morning and finishes at five in the evening, but it is a job that you carry in your heart and mind always. Pastors are often with people on the happiest days of their lives, and they also walk people through some of the darkest valleys too, and it can take a real toll on him or her.

This weekend do something to bless your pastors. Check out a book entitled *The Glass of Water* which discusses how people can be a blessing to their spiritual leader, causing refreshing in his or her life, and thus getting the best out of their leader. Be creative and find a way to bless your pastors this weekend.

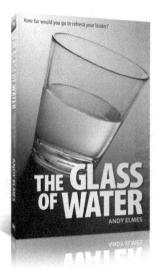

The Glass of Water
by Andy Elmes

Available from **greatbiglife.co.uk** and **greatbiglifepublishing.com** for £8.99

ISBN 978-1-4823513-1-6, Great Big Life Publishing

Some stones were left to guide us

Do not move an ancient boundary stone set up by your forefathers.

Proverbs 22:28 (NIV)

Here the writer of Proverbs gives us a warning. When it comes to our 21st century Christianity we are not to move every 'boundary stone' as some of them were left for our benefit, positioned for guidance and well being.

It seems today that so many church leaders want to change so many things to do with church, in an effort to make it more attractional or accessible to more people. This in itself is not a bad thing, especially when we are effectively removing things that are merely 'stones' that represent a previous or former style of doing things. But in our zealous landscaping endeavours we need to be really careful that we do not move, displace or try to replace certain 'stones' that were positioned by the people of God that went before us and were actually positioned to be 'boundary stones' for us as we purpose to follow the same God they did in our generation.

In the Old Testament and former times stones were used for a number of significant things. Like our modern fences they established boundaries, determining what belonged to whom. They were used as places of worship and sacrifice, in locations where God had done significant things. They were also used for direction, to let a person know which way to go, help them avoid potholes and give clear direction to people travelling a common route.

Some stones in Christianity need to be moved because they are merely preference- or style-based stones, representing a generational or cultural expression of how people once outworked their love for God. Others are more apostolic in their purpose, stones that enable us to know how to live and function in a way that pleases God. These are the stones we would do well not to move, but rather take time to understand how they can guide us in our modern-day walk with God.

These stones represent the foundational truths or godly principles that cause a believer to know and function in the ways of God. We should never desire to remove these stones or replace them with modern philosophy. Rather we should teach people to understand and interpret them correctly, because these boundary or ancient stones that were actually set in place by God through the prophets and apostles that went before us to enable us to succeed with Him as they did. Let's not dare to lay aside significant boundary stone teaching, like sowing and reaping, righteousness by faith and obedience over sacrifice, for modern-day, ear-tickling quick fixes that really do not cause any long term success in the people that choose to embrace them. You see, within scripture you will find 'ancient stones' of truth laid and established by the forefathers of our faith that went before us. They discovered things about God and His ways that caused righteousness, peace and great success.

> *The boundary lines (stones) have fallen for me in pleasant places; surely I have a delightful inheritance.*
>
> Psalms 16:6 (NIV)

It's still true, you reap what you sow

Do not be deceived, God is not mocked; for whatever a man sows, that he will also reap.

Galatians 6:7

We've spoken this week about foundational truths and principles that remain the same through every generation. Here is one of them, sowing and reaping – 'what you sow, you will reap' or, as The Message translation puts it, 'what a person plants, he will harvest.'

This principle will never expire, it was established in the days of Noah when God Himself put it into motion and chose to give it no expiration date. Certain laws and other things ended, or were fulfilled, at the cross but others did not and have been set in place to carry on until Christ returns. The law or principle of sowing and reaping is one of them – listen to how God initiates it with Noah:

> *While the earth remains, seedtime and harvest, cold and heat, winter and summer, and day and night shall not cease.*
>
> Genesis 8:22

See how God sets the principle of seedtime and harvest next to three other everyday things that a person would have no hesitation in accepting. He even chooses to place the principle of seedtime and harvest – or sowing and reaping – first. It is vital that you understand that God did not establish this principle solely for the benefit of farmers or people that worked in agriculture. It is a life principle that affects us all. By that I mean it was set in motion by God to have an effect in every single section or facet of a person's life. Sowing and reaping is not just about corn, carrots and cabbages, it is about your relationships, your wealth and provision, your health and every other part or subsection of your life.

If you want to understand seedtime and harvest you only have to watch a farmer – very simply, what you sow determines what you harvest!

Another thing to note is the principle or law of sowing and reaping can have both positive and negative ramifications in a person's life, depending on what a person is using as seed. Let me give you an example: if you sow encouragement into the lives of others you seed the field to harvest encouragement in return at a later date. Equally, if you gossip and backbite, don't be surprised when you feel nibbling on your own back – you for sowed it, enjoy your harvest!

This is just a very simple example but lays out the simple dynamics of sowing and reaping really well for us. So I suppose the question for us all is, 'What harvests do I desire to see in my life?' The next question is simply, 'What seed am I, or should I, be sowing to see that harvest?' Remember, unmanaged land left to itself normally only produces weeds, so don't let that happen in your life. Always be sowing good seeds to produce good harvests. The earth still remains, so we can still enjoy the benefits of this amazing promise.

Three parts to seedtime and harvest

While the earth remains, seedtime and harvest, cold and heat, winter and summer, and day and night shall not cease.

Genesis 8:22

*L*ike it or not, believe it or not, sowing and reaping is a very big part of the daily lives we now live. God has chosen to give us the ability to control or be involved in what we harvest in our life. When we have a revelation of this and take it seriously we can affect the harvests we experience. That is such a powerful thing when you take the time to think about it.

When you initially read the words 'seedtime and harvest' it looks like there are two parts or components that are involved in the overall process. But take another look and you'll see there are actually three. Granted, you will have to put a gap in the word 'seedtime' to see it as you should, but when you do it makes a lot more sense of the process and enables you to understand the power of that key moment between the seed being sown and the harvest being enjoyed. The bit in the middle is Time!

Again, you only have to talk to a farmer (if you even need to) to understand this simple reality: no farmer puts seed in the ground and then straight away enjoys the harvest from it, there is always 'time' involved. So it is with us, we must understand that when we sow seed we then have to wait, but after waiting there always comes harvest. And when it comes to the amount of time, God is the one who determines when the harvest comes, and His timing is always perfect.

Let us consider these three parts of the process again:

- Seed (the moment you sow something into ground)

- Time (the moments between you sowing the seed and experiencing the harvest)

- Harvest (the moment when you get to enjoy what the seed you sowed produced)

The 'time' part is such an important part. It's when we use our faith, when we trust in what God has said and not in what we see. It's when we learn to rest in the promise. A farmer rests after sowing his seed because he knows if the soil is good it's only a matter of time before the seed turns into a harvest. We too can have this confidence when we sow seed – it's only ever a matter of time before we see harvest. In my experience it's often what God does in us during the 'time' bit that is the greatest harvest in our life.

So, if you have sown good seed, relax – the harvest is coming. If you have sown bad seed you have not got away with it – repent quickly before the harvest comes, because it will. God said that what a man sows, that He will reap.

How big a harvest do you want?

But this I say: He who sows sparingly will also reap sparingly, and he who sows bountifully will also reap bountifully. So let each one give as he purposes in his heart, not grudgingly or of necessity; for God loves a cheerful giver.

2 Corinthians 9:6-7

We've been looking at the subject of sowing and reaping, a principle or ancient boundary stone that people of faith have lived by from the time of Noah. Please understand, sowing and reaping is not a new teaching invented by some televangelist to get you to give loads of money; rather, it is a principle established by God to enable you to be blessed in every area of your life.

I want to challenge you with this thought regarding sowing and reaping. What size harvest do you want to see? Once again, let's use a farmer as our example. If we would take some time to watch we would soon learn that the size and quality of the harvest produced is determined by the amount and quality of seed sown. In the same way, God gives us the ability to not only be involved in the type of harvests we experience in our life but also in the size or quality of them. Consider again our text as it lays this thought or principle in a nice, simple way. It says that we are to purpose in our hearts the crop we want and joyfully sow the right amount of seed to get it. Look at this verse in another more blunt translation:

> *Remember: a stingy planter gets a stingy crop; a lavish planter gets a lavish crop. I want each of you to take plenty of time to think it over, and make up your own mind what you will give.*
>
> 2 Corinthians 9:6-7 (MSG)

Another important part of this is to understand that 'size of seed' is not always about 'amount of seed' but 'quality of seed', otherwise the principle would not be fair. For example, it would enable a person with loads of money to sow more than a person with limited finances and that is not the case – remember the widow in the temple (Mark 12:41-44). If it had been about the amount the widow placed into the offering – a pittance in comparison to those around her that gave large amount – then why did Jesus say she gave more than any of them? It is because, when it comes to our giving or sowing, God always looks at the heart connected to it. He gives us all the chance to sow and He gives us all the opportunity to choose to sow generously or sparingly. 'Generously' refers more to what it means to the sower, the value to the sower of the seed sown.

As you purpose to take more control over the harvests of your life, determine to always sow your best seed. Why, every seed bears fruit after its own kind, so good seed in, good harvest out.

If you sow carrot seeds you get carrots!

Then God said, "Let the earth bring forth grass, the herb that yields seed, and the fruit tree that yields fruit according to its kind, whose seed is in itself, on the earth"; and it was so. And the earth brought forth grass, the herb that yields seed according to its kind, and the tree that yields fruit, whose seed is in itself according to its kind.

Genesis 1:11-12

*A*nother important truth to understand, when we consider the lifestyle of sowing and reaping, is that God designed it that every seed would bear fruit after its own kind. When we understand this reality it helps us to determine the crops we experience in life by being selective with the seeds we sow. When it comes to natural agriculture everyone of us knows that if we take a carrot seed, plant it, and wait, we will definitely get a carrot as our harvest. We would not stand in the garden shocked at what had happened, would we? Yet I have experienced many Christians shocked by their harvest – they did not expect what they had grown. Maybe they forgot the simple truth that every – not just some, but every – seed bears fruit of its own kind.

Okay, let's bring it from the garden into our daily life and run through a few simple examples. If every seed bears fruit according to its own kind then if you sow love what will you harvest? If you sow bitterness what will you harvest? If you sow finances? If you sow forgiveness? How about vehicles, homes, buildings and clothes? God didn't placed any 'no go' areas on seedtime and harvest, just a simple one-rule-fits-all: what a person sows, that they will reap!

When we grasp this truth it empowers us to be able to manage what we experience more of in life. If you are constantly experiencing not nice things in life it really is worth looking at what you are sowing. Equally, if you need something in life maybe it's time to apply God's principle and sow for it? Remember, He gives seed to the sower (2 Corinthians 9:10). He does not provide seed to the one who has no intention to sow because He is wise not wasteful, but he always provides seed to the sower according to His promise to do so. The seed is never what you need, but it contains the potential of what you need through its harvest. When you sow the seed in faith, according to His promises, He causes that seed to meet the need through the harvest.

I have personally seen this too many times to not believe it. Over our time in ministry Gina and I have often had a need, planted a seed and seen God come through! We have sown clothes, cars, finances, food and every other type of thing, and always seen God come through. Recently, on a mission trip, I was reminded that we needed a building for our main congregation in Portsmouth and while in a rural part of Philippines had the opportunity to sow finances to purchase land and a church for a local pastor there. Yep, it was great blessing him but when I gave that money it was also seed in the ground to get what we needed in Portsmouth. Remember, every seed bears fruit after its own kind. I sowed to him his dream church, big enough for what God had called him to. Guess what I am now waiting for?

How about you, what 'kind' of thing are you sowing for?

RESOURCE YOUR LIFE

For life is more than food, and the body more than clothing.
Luke 12:23

This weekend, resource your spiritual life.

Is there a subject or topic in God's Word that you would like to know more? Maybe you enjoy a good spiritual challenge? Do a little research or ask a friend to suggest a great book to read, or to recommend a good teaching to download. Maybe there's a beautiful worship CD out there that would bless your personal time with God? Our physical lives will one day end but spiritually you will live on forever. This certainly is one reason to invest into your spiritual life today!

Notes

_____

_____

_____

_____

_____

_____

_____

_____

This joy

When the Lord restored the fortunes of Zion, we were like those who dream. Then our mouth was filled with laughter, and our tongue with joyful shouting.

Psalm 126:1-2 (NASB)

---

*F*ind yourself in peaceful delight of God today, a fullness of hope that can only be described as joy.

Trust in God is the secret to joy, without it there are too many things that will come to steal your joy. This joy is entirely necessary to life on this earth. It may look like a smile or sound like laughter, but true unhindered joy is powerful and can only be found in relationship with God, in adoration of Him.

The joy of the Lord may look very 'otherworldly' in some places, such as in a dry work atmosphere or a broken home – your joy will not go unnoticed. Your joy will turn heads and hearts towards a God that is love, Just by living with joy you will stir hope and instil peace.

Find your joy in the Lord today, and let it seep into everything you do and say. Let joy be our trademark as lovers of God. Joy is not ignorant, it is very aware yet stubborn enough to remain.

Olivia Elmes

Pray this today

Father God, right now I ask that You would fill me with Your joy. Let Your joy overwhelm my sorrows and my fears. I give You my anxieties for today, God, I lay every other dominant thought down before you. Thank you for taking my heaviness in exchange for peace and joy. By laughter and lightness let it be known, today, where my joy flows from!

The best and most beautiful things in the world cannot be seen or even touched they must be felt with the heart.

Helen Keller

Free indeed

Jesus answered them, "Truly, truly I say to you, everyone who commits sin is the slave of sin. The slave does not remain in the house forever; the son does remain forever. So if the Son makes you free, you will be free indeed."

John 8:36 (NASB)

Good news this morning: the Son has set you free! You're no longer a slave to sin, you are free to leave the house of your captivity! No longer do you have to be hesitant or fearful, because you are free.

You are free to dance today, you are free to do the things that scare you, you are free to be exactly who God created you to be, and nothing can stop you! Let your freedom release freedom in the people around you.

I pray that you would find the freedom that I have found in Christ, it is so good that my only desire is to worship Him for it! Focus on the One who freed you today. He freed you for freedom's sake, so praise Him! He is all-powerful, all-wonderful and all good! Turn your eyes to the God of freedom – He is so good and His intention is that you would be free today; free from shame, free from guilt and free from fear.

Use your freedom to worship the one who freed you.

Olivia Elmes

Prayer

God, I thank You that You have freed me. I am no longer captive to sin, I am free because of You. I thank You and I praise You because You are a good Father! Release freedom everywhere I go today, Father.

Let your faith roar so loud that you can't hear what doubt is saying.

Unknown

Holy burning
NAZIRITE, PART 1

He was a burning and shining light.

John 5:35 (KJV)

What does it mean to be burning for God? To be 'set ablaze' or 'on fire' are such common terms, easily and cheaply thrown around in the Church today. To burn for God is to desire God, and to desire God is to desire holiness.

To break that apart, what I mean is that burning for God doesn't truthfully look like jumping higher or screaming louder. It really looks like a heart that is so passionately gripped for God that it would forsake all else in pursuit of Him. As you begin to desire God more, you desire other things less.

I cannot desire to know God and seek Him 'wholeheartedly' if I desire to watch Netflix for three days straight. That may seem petty, and you are probably asking, "What does Netflix have to do with my desire for God?" but my point is that a heart that really desires God will not be semi-passionate, it will be utterly consumed. It will willingly forsake all other desires, for a burning and fervent pursuit of the living God.

If you are not consumed and burning with desire for God, then you need to check if it is really God that you desire?

Olivia Elmes

Prayer

God, consume me totally. I abandon myself and my desires to You, consume my heart with Your love. It is You that I truly desire. Come and speak to me, show what I need to lay down to know You, God!

Sometimes the grass is greener on the other side because it's fake.

David Avocado Wolfe

Others can but I cannot
NAZIRITE, PART 2

Therefore be careful and drink no wine or strong drink, and eat nothing unclean, for behold you shall conceive and bear a son. No razor shall come upon his head, for the child shall be a Nazirite to God from the womb, and he shall begin to save Israel from the hand of the Philistines.

Judges 13:4-5 (ESV)

Nazirites were raised up in the Bible as people who lived with a burning desire for God. The intensity and commitment that these people had would turn nations back towards God.

The heart of a Nazirite was to pursue God above all else, and because God is holy they pursued holiness. To become closer to God Nazirites would do things not required of them for acceptable living, but necessary to be closer to God. They chose to abstain from legitimate and acceptable pleasures of the world, because they desired the ultimate pleasure of knowing God. They would stay away from anything that was dead, and they would not cut their hair, as an outward sign of an inward commitment.

For us today, it is time for people to rise up that so desire God, and the things of God, that they will make these unnecessary and seemingly ridiculous changes in their lives, because they desire holiness. This call for Nazirites is not a call for self-seeking, works-based Christians; it is a cry for a generation to lay down themselves and seek after God in a radical way, that will turn nations back towards God.

Olivia Elmes

Prayer

God, I lay myself down. Root out anything that is unholy. I want to know You, I want to hear from You and be close to You, so I am chasing You and chasing holiness. God, I commit every part of me and every desire to You.

Helping one person might not change the whole world, but it could change the world for one person.

Unknown

The Artist

"To give them a beautiful headdress instead of ashes, the oil of gladness instead of mourning, the garment of praise instead of a faint spirit; that they may be called oaks of righteousness, the planting of the Lord that He may be glorified."

Isaiah 61:3 (ESV)

When we realise that on our own we are weak and insufficient, we realise how much we need God to be our sufficiency. Our gaps and cracks become obvious as we are stretched. We can pridefully allow these flaws to consume us, or we can allow God to fill them. For everything that we lack in – patience, kindness, goodness – God is more than able to complete in us, if we would only invite Him to.

Live in surrender today, take your eyes off of yourself and off of others and focus completely on God. There is no fear in His eyes. When you stare deeply and willingly into the face of God, the broken and empty pieces become whole. Alone we are fragmented and confused, we were not designed to be without God. He begins and completes us.

He longs to take our broken pieces of bitterness and envy, jealousy and strife, and rework His masterpiece to be what He originally intended to create. What He longs to create in you is a pure and unique work of art. Just give Him your broken pieces today, in prayer and surrender. The Artist of creation is not afraid of your brokenness – He sees the beauty that only His hands can create with it.

Olivia Elmes

Prayer

God, I need to You to complete me, I need You to make my brokenness beautiful. My fear and anxiety, my hatred and envy are all Yours, God. Take these broken pieces and create in me what You have wanted to create since the beginning. I trust you, God, to create in me a masterpiece.

Your greatest test is when you are able to bless someone else while you are going through your own storm.

Unknown

FAST AND PRAY

When you fast, do not look somber as the hypocrites do, for they disfigure their faces to show others they are fasting. Truly I tell you, they have received their reward in full. But when you fast, put oil on your head and wash your face, so that it will not be obvious to others that you are fasting, but only to your Father, who is unseen, and your Father, who sees what is done in secret, will reward you.

Matthew 6:16-18 (NIV)

Fasting and praying is part of the Christian life. There are a number of reasons why we should fast and pray. When you are praying for something, and you really need to see a breakthrough, fasting can be very beneficial. Fasting is for our good, not God's. Our fasting doesn't make God move any faster or hear us any louder. It helps us to focus on spiritual things with more clarity as we deny our physical selves comfort for a set time. Most often fasting pertains to abstaining from food, but it can be giving up any of the luxuries we enjoy for a set time and to use that time to pray and focus on God in regards to our situation. This weekend set aside a time to fast and pray for something you need a breakthrough for. Maybe you can skip one meal or give up TV or video games for the day. You don't have to do a full 24-hour fast, but you can if you want to. My prayer is that you get the breakthroughs that you need.

Have a great weekend!

Notes

_____

_____

_____

_____

What an introduction

James, a bondservant of God and of the Lord Jesus Christ.

James 1:1

---

*A*s you open the book of James, with a heart to both read and learn, one of the greatest lessons is actually taught in the opening statement. Some would call it James merely introducing himself, but I would call it James sharing a deep revelation that he had concerning who he was first and foremost. It's amazing that actually, when you read the opening statements of most of those who wrote letters in the New Testament, they all use this same common introduction. Why? Because they all, like James, had a revelation of who and what they were before anyone added any other title; before 'Apostle', 'Pastor', 'Evangelist', 'Teacher' or 'Prophet' they were simply 'Bondservant'!

I love this. We live in an age where much of the church seems to be obsessed with titles: Bishop this or Apostle that. It is vital that we remember that all of us, before we are anything else or call ourselves anything else, are firstly servants with the high calling to serve. Other titles are not bad, when they are used for functional purposes or to help people know who does what, but it becomes a dangerous thing when people start to find or place their identity in those titles. If we are going to find our identity in any title let it be the same one that James and the other disciples used to introduce themselves to the world: Bondservants.

You see, it was learned behaviour – they were just copying and imitating the One they followed, Jesus. Never did they hear Him introduce Himself, when entering a room, as Pastor Jesus, or correct someone when they addressed Him wrongly by saying, 'Excuse me, that's Apostle Jesus to you.' No, He was secure in what He had been sent to do which, according to Matthew, was to serve:

> *And whoever desires to be first among you, let him be your slave—just as the Son of Man did not come to be served, but to serve, and to give His life a ransom for many.*
> **Matthew 20:27-29**

As I said, other titles in themselves are not wrong and certainly have their place in the church; and yes, according to Ephesians 4, God has given offices of ministry with certain titles, etc. But those titles, or the desire for them, should never drive us or what we do; rather a simple desire to be what James and the other disciples were more than content to be: first and above all else they were servants of Jesus ,the great Servant King, sent by the Father to serve.

Bondservants, not servants

Paul, a bondservant of Jesus Christ, called to be an apostle, separated to the gospel of God.

Romans 1:1

*Y*esterday we saw how James introduced himself in his letters. Today we see Paul doing the exact same thing. If you know anything about Paul then you know he certainly was an apostle, an incredible teacher and a man set apart to carry the gospel beyond Jerusalem. But note again, the first thing he calls himself is 'bondservant of Jesus Christ'.

And also note that he doesn't say 'servant' but 'bondservant'. You see, bondservants were very different to your everyday domestic servant. In the Old Testament you read about them as people who were once servants or slaves but had been granted their freedom and been given the option to go and be a freeman yet, most often because of the love they had for their master and his house, took the freedom and gave it back, binding themselves to their master permanently. You can read all about this in Deuteronomy 15:12-17. If the servant decided they did not want to leave then their ear would be pierced by being nailed to the door, and from that day they were known as a free slave or bondslave in that house.

> *And if it happens that he says to you, 'I will not go away from you,' because he loves you and your house, since he prospers with you, then you shall take an awl and thrust it through his ear to the door, and he shall be your servant forever.*
>
> Deuteronomy 15:16-17

The disciples had a great understanding of this and knew how it applied in their lives. Among other things they knew that each of them had once been slaves, and they had found their freedom at the hand of Jesus. They had also purposed that, though thankful for their freedom, they did not want it – they did not want to be free from Jesus being their master. So in their hearts their 'ears' had been nailed to the door of His kingdom and their lives were now His, and His by choice.

May each of us, as Paul and James, see our lives not only as slaves now set free (Galatians 5:1) but also purpose, as they did, to not run off and enjoy our freedom but rather to lay it at the door of the One who saved us and set us free. May we purpose to be His bondservants in our generation, as they did in theirs.

I remember growing up in church hearing a song that I never fully understood back then. Today I do and sing it with meaning, revelation and desire:

> *Pierce my ear, O Lord my God // Take me to Your door this day. // I will serve no other gods, // Lord, I'm here to stay.*

> *For You have paid the price for me // With your blood You ransomed me // I will serve You eternally. // A Free man I'll never be.*

"Pierce my ear", Steve Croft ©1980 Dayspring Music, LLC (admin. By Small Stone Media)

The solution for pollution

Religion that God our Father accepts as pure and faultless is this: to look after orphans and widows in their distress and to keep oneself from being polluted by the world.

James 1:27 (NIV)

Here James reminds us of a couple of important things; that if we want to live out our Christianity in a way that God deems faultless we are to firstly purpose to not overlook orphans and widows in their distress. Orphans and widows still exist in our time so we are still called to care for them, as indeed we are any person we find in need.

The second thing, that is quite unrelated to the first, is "we are to keep ourselves from being polluted by this world". This is most certainly something that we all have to purpose to do because we live in a very polluted, sin-stained, fallen world; but always remember the Bible teaches us that we are in the world but no longer of it. You see, when you were born again your life was supernaturally translated out of darkness (pollution) and positioned into the kingdom of the Son of His love (Colossians 1:13). So the truth is we are now citizens of another kingdom that is pure to the core, but we reside in a polluted kingdom. Not only is this world polluted, the pollution seems to be getting worse!

Have you ever noticed how easy the natural pollution of a city can get on you? Have you ever visited a major city like London or New York, then got home and showered, or blown your nose, and been totally amazed at the dark grime you managed to attract and absorb in your pores, nose and every other place? It's the same with spiritual pollution – you can live to avoid it but even then it can so easily get on you. The good news is if we wash correctly each day (be people of the word and prayer) we can keep the pollution from remaining a part of us.

It really is such a strange time that we live in, where things that have the potential to pollute our lives are everywhere we turn: television, cinema, computers, smart phones – they all have the potential to pollute as well as entertain or help. This, mixed with the ever-changing platform of things that people deem acceptable in school, college and the workplace, make keeping yourself unpolluted a daily thing not a casual hobby. Seems that everywhere we turn there is the potential for pollution. The key or solution to pollution is having a heart that desires to live beyond it. How? Firstly by guarding certain important gateways to your heart and mind, gateways like your eyes and your ears. These are vitally important to protect if you want to live unpolluted.

The truth is it may be on TV or the movies but we don't have to watch it. They may be having that wrong conversation but we don't have to listen or join in. Let's face it, unless we ignore the Great Commission and hide ourselves away, we can't always fully protect ourselves from the pollution around us. But as I said, if we wash regularly we can avoid it sticking.

There are ways we can avoid spiritual pollution and live in a way that protects our life from it. May we all purpose to do this, because as we do we shine for Jesus in this polluted world and our lives stick out, leading others out of the pollution into His glorious light.

How to get away with eating while you fast!

Is this not the fast that I have chosen: to loose the bonds of wickedness, to undo the heavy burdens, to let the oppressed go free, and that you break every yoke? Is it not to share your bread with the hungry, and that you bring to your house the poor who are cast out; When you see the naked, that you cover him, And not hide yourself from your own flesh?

Isaiah 58:6-7 (NIV)

Here is an interesting take on fasting that pleases God!

Please don't hear what I am not saying – I fully believe in fasting that involves laying aside eating and doing things we like to seek Him and His will more. But here we read of a type of fasting that God says 'He chooses' that doesn't involve us not eating. What it does involve is us rolling up our sleeves and helping others.

I don't know about you but I want to fast in a way that pleases Him and, according to Him, this type of fast involves being actively involved in helping people get free from the grip of wickedness, oppression and slavery in their life. Instead of not eating we actually share our food with the hungry and our clothes with those who need them. It's interesting that, in the Gospels, we see Jesus talk about these same things as being an evidence of those living in a way that serves Him.

> *Then the righteous will answer Him, saying, 'Lord, when did we see You hungry and feed You, or thirsty and give You drink? When did we see You a stranger and take You in, or naked and clothe You? Or when did we see You sick, or in prison, and come to You?' And the King will answer and say to them, 'Assuredly, I say to you, inasmuch as you did it to one of the least of these My brethren, you did it to Me.'*
> **Matthew 25:37-40**

Isn't it amazing how this teaching of Jesus runs so parallel with the desires of God expressed through the prophet Isaiah! There is certainly a point here for us today. Maybe fasting is a bigger subject than what we first thought? Yes, there is a fasting that involves the abstinence of food for a period of time, but another bigger, more important fast involves us *sharing* our food with others. It is a fast that is very practical and makes a difference in the lives of others. This is apparently a fast that truly pleases God. Don't get me wrong, if you want to you can help others while not eating yourself, but you should never not eat yourself while ignoring the needs of others.

Hey, let's face it, we are surrounded daily by people with need. In this nation and abroad we have the opportunity daily to get involved with things that break the grip of wickedness and oppression off of the lives of others. So jump on in with both feet and remember, whatever you do to the least of them you also do to Him.

Forgive and Forget?

God's love in us is not rude, nor self-seeking. We are not roused to anger quickly, and we certainly do not keep a mental record of the wrongs others have committed.

1 Corinthians 13:5 (The Truth)

The Word of God is so wonderfully challenging. When I'm reading the parts of the Bible that my soul finds uncomfortable, I can almost feel the sandpaper of God rubbing away rough edges in my life. God's Word offers up life-changing words but sometimes they feel like bitter pills to swallow. As if forgiveness on its own is not enough, I'm now asked to forget what that person has done or said!

In its context, the above scripture from 1 Corinthians refers to Christians who are legally suing one another in the Corinthian Church. Paul feels that God's love is not present in this situation and that they should be working out the wrong between themselves like mature followers of Christ. He points out the things that love is NOT and says that we need to purposely not recall the wrongs that were committed.

We are not able to wipe the mind like we would a computer. It's just not naturally possible, but like so many other principles in God's Word, we have to decide that we are going to do something. We have to make a conscious choice.

I so vividly remember my parents arguing when I was a little girl. The argument would start out about one thing and as the anger and words became more bitter, so the list of all the wrongs would come out, accusations of past hurts and pain would come out, until the argument was no longer about one small thing any more but about a lifetime of unforgiveness.

Imagine if God kept a scroll with all our sins and wrongs on it, even after we asked for His forgiveness. Even if that scroll were hidden away somewhere, you would always know that at any time God could take that list out and recite it to you, and you would be as if you were never forgiven. You would feel the guilt of every evil thing you did and said and it would be there for others to see as well. It is the same when we create a mental scroll of the wrongs people have committed against us. God keeps no record of our wrongs.

As far as the east is from the west, so far has he removed our transgressions from us.
Psalm 103:12 (NIV)

Ephesians 5:1 tells us we are called to be imitators of God because He is our Father. Can you feel that sandpaper smoothing you out yet? This is challenging stuff but it will set us free and cause us to be more like our Father, which is the goal! Maybe you feel that someone's wrong toward you is still on your mental scroll and you just can't rid yourself of it. Talk to God about it. Remember, He's on your side and if He wants you to do something He will help you to do it. In the meantime you can make some choices on your journey and you can choose to never bring up those wrongs again, just as you would never want God to bring up the wrong that you have committed. Let God's Word do its work of perfecting you and making you more and more like your Father in heaven.

NO COMPLAINTS

Do everything without complaining and arguing.
Philippians 2:14 (NLT)

Complaining is something that does NOT impress God. This was one of the reasons it took the children of Israel forty years to get to the Promised Land!

Believe me when I say, 'I'm preaching to myself here!' How easy it is to find fault in things or people and to speak it out. Really, is this doing anyone any good? No, it isn't.

CHOOSE NOT TO COMPLAIN this weekend.

Things may still annoy you but choose not to speak them out and pollute the atmosphere with negativity. Instead, choose to speak about the good stuff! Challenge yourself this weekend to avoid complaining of any form. You may find yourself biting your tongue but that's good! The Holy Spirit is your helper and will help you with this challenge.

Choose words of life! Happy weekend.

Crowd or Disciple?

And it happened, as He was alone praying, that His disciples joined Him, and He asked them, saying, "Who do the crowds say that I am?"

Luke 9:18

When you read through the gospels you constantly read about 'crowds'. Crowds followed Him, watched Him, asked Him for things, and daily He ministered to these crowds, selflessly giving Himself away. But there was also another group of people that followed Him daily – these men followed Him not for what He could do but rather for who He was. These were called Disciples.

In some ways Jesus had two ministries going at once – He had His 'crowd ministry' and He had His 'discipleship program'. The crowd got to know Him from afar and experience Him in one way, but the disciples got to walk with Him and experienced Him in a far more intimate way. It was the disciples that got to sit with Him every morning, sleep around the campfire every night with Him, and walk from place to place asking any and all question that popped into their mind, each time getting a personal answer. To me the disciple's experience was the far superior one of the two.

In today's text we hear Jesus ask the disciples, 'Who do the crowd say I am?' When you read their response you hear a very group-minded response: 'You are this' and 'You are that.' It's like they typed "who is Jesus?" into Google and then repeated what Google told them: 'John the Baptist', some say 'Elijah' and others say that 'one of the old prophets has risen again.' But then Jesus gets personal and asks the disciples who they think He is. Suddenly you hear Peter's answer based on his personal daily experience of Him: 'You are the Messiah, the Son of the living God.'

Still today people have the choice of a crowd- or disciple-type relationship with Jesus. How about you? Are you in the crowd or more of a disciple? When you speak of Jesus, do you speak of Him with 'part of the crowd terminology' or from a place of personal relationship? As I said, there was and still are two groups of people following Jesus: the Crowd and the Disciples. One has intimacy and daily interaction, the other just watches and hears about what He does from others. May I encourage you this week to be ever leaving the 'crowd' experience to follow Jesus in a more personal, life-changing way.

God's design for your life is not that you attend Church, but become it.

Andy Elmes

Disciple was His intention and desire

Then Jesus came to them and said, "All authority in heaven and on earth has been given to me. Therefore go and make disciples of all nations, baptizing them in the name of the Father and of the Son and of the Holy Spirit.

Matthew 28:18-19 (NIV)

It's good to be reminded that the central call of the Great Commission is one of discipleship; it's to make disciples, not just reach people and see them respond to the message of salvation. This shows us the heart of Jesus very well – yes, He wants people to come to Him, or encounter Him in a crowd-like experience, but then He also wants to be ever drawing people from that crowd-type experience into a more personal walk of discipleship, where they become followers of Him in their life.

When you realise this you suddenly, when you read the gospels, notice Him calling people out of the crowd to follow Him or become disciples everywhere He went. Whether they were fishermen, tax collectors or doctors, you regularly hear Him say, 'Come and follow me and I will make you . . .' Still today He says the same to us – He does not violate our will or choice, but simply offers more of Him to those who desire it.

The reality is, we all start in a crowd-like way. We find Jesus in a moment of encounter, often at a meeting or with others around, and that's good. But we are not meant to stay as crowd, every one of us are meant to be ever stepping toward knowing Him in a much more personal way. To be honest, saying you must be 'crowd' or 'disciple' is not that accurate, is it? That's like placing two poles in the ground and saying 'Which one are you?', whereas in reality it's more of a natural progression than that. Each of us are somewhere in between those two poles of absolute, aren't we? Hopefully none of you are still where you were when you met Him! Each of us have taken steps away from the crowd toward being more of a disciple or having a personal walk with Him.

My encouragement today is to keep moving in that direction, even if it's inches or centimetres. Be ever moving forward into a growing relationship of personal discipleship with Him. Why? Because that was always His will for you, and what He established His Church to help you do. He has not done all He has done so you would be vaguely saved and have a limited experience of Him on a weekend basis in a meeting somewhere. (Though meeting together regularly is a part of His plan for you). Rather, that you would daily walk with Him, know His voice and leading, and be falling ever deeper in love with Him and His kingdom.

Take another step away from crowd and towards being disciple. How? Maybe pull away from the crowd and go spend some time with Him, just you and Him. As you pray and open His word listen for what He is saying to you personally. As you do you will hear more than what He is saying to the crowd. What a privilege, that we can know Him personally and follow Him, just as those first disciples did.

Two very different experiences

As evening approached, the disciples came to him and said, "This is a remote place, and it's already getting late. Send the crowds away, so they can go to the villages and buy themselves some food." Jesus replied, "They do not need to go away. You give them something to eat." "We have here only five loaves of bread and two fish," they answered. "Bring them here to me," he said. And he directed the people to sit down on the grass. Taking the five loaves and the two fish and looking up to heaven, he gave thanks and broke the loaves. Then he gave them to the disciples, and the disciples gave them to the people.

Matthew 14:15-18 (NIV)

We've been looking at the subject of being 'crowd' or being 'disciple', and specifically asking, 'Do you have a crowd-like relationship with Jesus or do you desire to be a disciple?' When you read through the gospels, as with today's text, you really do see these two groups of people present wherever He went. He never had a problem with drawing a crowd and always blessed them, but He was also constantly calling people out of the crowd to follow Him in a more intimate way. The two groups of people were very different in what they wanted and what they were with Him for.

The crowd really was only there for what they could get and He tirelessly met their every need. But the disciples were different; though they had started by being with Him for what they could get, something had changed – they were now with Him for what they could become. Their excitement was found now in what 'He was making them' and the life change He was causing in them as they daily followed Him.

In today's modern church not much has changed – there are still crowds and there are still disciples. There are still people that want Him when He can do something for them – then, sadly, they leave until the next time they have a need. There are also those who want to stick around Him because they see their lives changing for the better when they do. Out of the two experiences the second is far superior. Let me encourage you, in your journey, to choose to be a disciple, daily journeying to know Him more and walk with Him closer.

Not only did the disciples give more, they also got more. Think about it: the crowd only ever got to watch the miracles, but the disciples got to handle them. A great example is with the feeding of the five thousand – the multitude needed feeding and Jesus gave the bread and fish *to the disciples* to do the miracle (Matthew 14:13-21). Do you just want to witness miracles or handle them? When it came to teaching, the crowd got to hear His 'crowd messages'. Don't get me wrong, these were amazing; but the disciples got to both hear these and His daily individual input and wisdom into their lives. There are many examples I could use but what I am basically saying is this: yes, being a disciple will cost you more but your experience of Him will be so far beyond that of a person who stays in the crowd.

Today, take another step away from a crowd experience of Him into following Him as a disciple. Believe me when I say, you will not ask for your money back!

Two different pathways

To the Jews who had believed him, Jesus said, "If you hold to my teaching, you are really my disciples.

John 8:31 (NIV)

By this everyone will know that you are my disciples, if you love one another."

John 13:35 (NIV)

---

*A*s well as being two very different experiences, being 'crowd' or being 'disciple' also puts a whole different demand upon your life. Remember what we have said all along, everyone starts in a crowd-like way by encountering Him as Lord and Saviour. But then people really do have a choice: do they want to believe in Him and receive assurance of their salvation, attend His church, and enjoy relationship with His people, or do they want to walk as disciples by doing what He says? That's where the rubber hits the road – when deciding what we are more like, isn't it? Do we want to sing songs about Him and attend groups discussing Him, or do we want to do what He asks us to do and be what He asks us to be? In today's text there are two very sobering descriptions of what a disciple is, made by Jesus Himself.

1. **They hold to His teaching.** This means they choose to live by and live out His teaching on a daily basis. They apply it to their daily life, not just recite it when there is opportunity to do so. For example, if they need to forgive, they forgive!

2. **They love each other.** Not just the people they like or get along with, but *everyone*! It is this love that they have for each other that actually demonstrates to a watching world that they are followers of Him.

We spoke earlier this week about the two comparable poles we can place in the ground called 'crowd' and 'disciple' that can help us to locate where our life currently is in the common journey we all face between the two. Two really good and honest ways to help us locate where our life truly is, is to ask yourself, 'Am I living by His teaching and am I truly loving others, especially those of His household? Or am I still doing what I want to do when I know His word teaches for me to live differently? Am I loving some and hating others as I deem fair or reasonable, maybe according to how I feel they have treated me?'

Let's not kid ourselves, being a disciple is different and it places your feet on a narrower path. But the real difference is that though the crowd may one day experience heaven when they die, disciples get to know it and live it out here on earth. Be a disciple, walk according to His teachings and love one another.

God's Word: your Lamp, your Bread and your Sword

*G*od's Word, the Bible, is a very powerful thing and was given to be a number of powerful things in the believer's life. It was given by God for your benefit and wellbeing – among other things it was given to be:

Your 'daily' bread

Jesus answered, "It is written: 'Man shall not live on bread alone, but on every word that comes from the mouth of God.

Matthew 4:4 (NIV)

Just as your natural man needs bread (good food) each day to remain strong and be productive, so your spirit man, that part of you made alive at new birth, needs to be fed and nourished each and every day. You can't feed your spiritual man with the food your natural man consumes; rather it thrives on the nutrition of God's Word, which contains a perfectly-balanced diet for you that, when digested and applied, will create a strong and healthy Christian life.

A lamp for your feet and light for your path

Your word is a lamp for my feet, a light on my path.

Psalms 119:105 (NIV)

God has given you His Word to be the flashlight to your feet. Like any torch its purpose is to show you the way forward and reveal to you what is ahead and how you should walk. As you turn the lamp on every day it will stop you tripping over things you shouldn't, and falling down holes you were not meant to.

A sword in your hand

Take the helmet of salvation and the sword of the Spirit, which is the word of God.
Ephesians 6:13-17 (NIV)

God's Word is also His Sword, the sword of His Spirit, in your hands. As with any sword it is for both defence and attack. Daily you can use it to protect yourself, and those you love, from the lies and attacks of the enemy. But you can also use it to tear down things the enemy may have established, and take back the ground he may have stolen from you. God has not left you unarmed. Pick up His Word and use it as a sword in your life, and as you do you'll see victories breaking out all around you.

So consider these three powerful reasons to use your Bible. Pick it up and let it feed you, lead you and protect you.

CREATE SPECIAL TIME FOR FRIENDS

A friend loves at all times.
Proverbs 17:17 (NIV)

Life is very busy but it should never be so busy that we don't take some time to keep in touch with friends.

This weekend get in touch with a friend you haven't contacted in a while. Friends are a gift from God and just maybe a friend out there needs to know they are being thought of.

Notes

_____

_____

_____

_____

_____

_____

_____

_____

_____

_____

Timing is everything

I foretold the former things long ago, my mouth announced them and I made them known; then suddenly I acted, and they came to pass.

Isaiah 48:31 (NIV)

Have you ever prayed and prayed and prayed and believed for something that you so desired, and it seemed like taking forever, and then suddenly it happens and you are actually physically living in the promise you were trusting God for? Oh, how wonderful that day is! It's all about timing: God's timing, not ours.

Always remember, with God our character – who we are – is so much more important than what we have. Along our journey He is building our character, our inner person, and making us more and more into His image with each step of the way.

When I have had to wait for what I believed God had promised me, I saw God working in my situation and for my benefit at every turn. My faith was made stronger as I saw each problem resolved and as He helped me climb the mountains of impossibility. I saw God's provision and felt His comfort and strengthening when I felt weak and faithless. I was on a journey trusting God for something for a number of years, something I did not expect. I certainly didn't think my prayers would be instantaneously answered, but I thought maybe a couple of months – but it was five years. Five years! Sometimes I joke and say, 'In dog years that's 35 years!' I started out my journey as one person, but God did so much good in me in those five years that I hardly know the person who started that walk of faith. Somewhere along the journey I realised that God had a beautiful agenda that was so much more about 'making me' than it was about making my dreams come true. God knew what I needed more than I did.

I am the Lord your God who teaches you what is best for you, who directs you in the way you should go.

Isaiah 48:17(NIV)

Take heart though, He does care about what you desire and have believed Him for. He is a good Father and loves to give us the desire of our hearts. Isaiah 49:8 (NIV) says this:

In the time of my favour I will answer you.

God will bring about your desire when He's ready! Just like you wouldn't want to eat a meal that has been under-cooked, God has a perfect, favourable time for when He will bring His answer to you – and then SUDDENLY you will be living in the promise, but you will get so much more than what you asked for. He wants to enrich you not only with your desires, but He also wants to do a beautiful work inside you, where you'll be made more like Him along the way.

Walking in the dark

Let the one who walks in the dark, who has no light, trust in the name of the Lord and rely on their God.

Isaiah 51:10 (NIV)

If you have any area in your life where you are at a loss for answers then you need to start trusting the Lord. Maybe you don't know what next steps you need to take in regards to a business or career, or a relationship. Maybe you need God's intervention in how you relate to your children or to other family members because what you've been doing and saying so far isn't getting through to them or doesn't seem to be making a difference. Whether you have big or small life decisions to make, you need to be relying on God and His wisdom if you want to have success in what you do. He knows the pathway to the answers we need, even if we don't.

Get some time away with God and bring to Him in prayer all your dilemmas, dead ends and impossibly tangled situations. When I bring my 'messed up' situations to the Father I see them as a big, tangled-up ball of wool where the end and the beginning and everything in between is knotted, matted and messy, and I have every expectation that He will work it out for me. I know better now than to implement my own wisdom to my problems. Have you ever tried to untangle a wildly chaotic ball of yarn? It's very frustrating. God wants to help you.

Isaiah shows us that when we by-pass God's wisdom in our lives then we are asking for trouble:

> *But now, all you who light fires and provide yourselves with flaming torches, go, walk in the light of your fires and of the torches you have set ablaze. This is what you shall receive from my hand: you will lie down in torment.*
>
> Isaiah 50:11

Rather than making a sticky situation even stickier, or a tangled ball of wool more tangled, go to God and ask Him to bring you His enlightenment. He will bring you the wisdom that you need and the answers you require.

> *If any of you lacks wisdom, you should ask God, who gives generously to all without finding fault, and it will be given to you.*
>
> James 1:5 (NIV)

Patience is not the ability to wait but the ability to keep a good attitude while waiting.

Unknown

Beautiful seasons

To everything there is a season.

Ecclesiastes 3:3 (KJV)

Every season brings a beauty all of its own.

In particular I'm thinking of a large tree that was in the garden of the last place I lived. I lived there for five years and for those five years I sat in just about the same seat almost every day in my quiet time with the Lord and stared out into the garden at the same tree. I've seen the tree in its full Summer bloom, with luscious green leaves and the birds coming to rest in the cool of the shadowy branches. In Autumn I've watched its golden and red crowning glory flutter to the ground. You'd think all of the beauty had gone but then the leafless boughs show off their elegant form against the grey backdrop of a Winter sky. Then, with the coming of Spring, each day the tree takes on a little more colour until it is bursting with flowers and leaves again.

In my walk with God I am not unlike that tree, and I have gone through many seasons in my spiritual walk. There have been times when I have felt God's presence with me in an almost tangible way and, like the green lushness of Summertime, I felt so alive spiritually. During this season I hardly voice a prayer and it seems answered in the next breath. I have walked through the Autumn when my branches have begun to shed the old leaves and lose the things I no longer need, as I am pruned at the hands of the Master Gardener; a time of preparation where God trims back parts of me that would hinder future growth. I have also been through seasons of Winter, that felt barren and distant from God. In these times I have known God was with me but I couldn't feel the closeness I had felt in other seasons, and during this time I held onto faith, knowing that there was still life in the tree even though the branches looked empty. I chose to believe the Father was still doing His perfect work. It is during these times that God shows me that it is not about how I 'feel' but about what He promised, which was that He would never leave me (Hebrews 13:5). In these times I have a sense of what it means to be what the Scripture refers to as a 'prisoner of hope' (Zechariah 9:12), always knowing inside that the Father is taking care of me and will bring me through the Winter.

Those who sow with tears will reap with songs of joy.

Psalm 126:5 (NIV)

When the Spring comes, I sense new life bursting in me again as blossoms and buds declare that 'He is making all things new' (Revelations 21:5). Seasons of my walk with God change and vary but God never changes (Malachi 3:6). He is the 'constant' in my 'ever-changing'. What I am learning is to take every season and enjoy what is beautiful about that season. There were things I learned in 'Winter' that I could never have learned in 'Summer', and no season lasts forever.

Don't despise the season you're in. Go to the Master Gardener and ask Him what He has to say to you at this time and He will show you things that make whatever season you're in so very precious and beautiful.

Focus on what is unseen

So we fix our eyes not on what is seen, but on what is unseen, since what is seen is temporary, but what is unseen is eternal.

1 Corinthians 4:18 (NIV)

Whatever a person sets his or her focus on is what they will follow after, and what they will become like. I'm sure you've heard the saying, 'You are what you eat.' I could never understand this when I was younger, it was nonsense to me! But as I learned more about good nutrition, I suddenly 'got it'. If I eat at fast food restaurants all the time then I will become overweight, and unhealthy. My arteries will begin to harden up from exposing my body to poor nutrition. Likewise, if I choose fresh, healthy foods then my body will reap the benefits of the healthy properties of the food; thus I become what I choose to eat. I have to focus on the healthy input if I want the healthy output. This principle is the same with what a person chooses to fix his or her eyes on in every area of life. The problem with this world is this:

> *The god of this age has blinded the minds of unbelievers, so that they cannot see the light of the gospel that displays the glory of Christ, who is the image of God.*
>
> 2 Corinthians 4:4 (NIV)

The world is spiritually blinded to Christ and the good news of the Gospel. They only see what this world has to offer and so they follow the only thing they can focus on: the flesh. By focusing on 'flesh' unbelievers only sow to the flesh (Galatians 6:8) and that's where self-gratification comes in: if it feels good then do it (no matter who or what gets destroyed). They cannot help themselves.

As believers in Christ the Word says that we are to, 'Fix our eyes on what is unseen', the eternal. Notice, though, the Scripture doesn't say that as believers we will automatically see as if through some kind of 'spiritual filter.' We must choose to fix our eyes on what is unseen, the eternal. If you choose to see and act only on what is visible to this world then you cannot expect anything from the eternal but if you choose to see with your spiritually-opened eyes then you can expect all that heaven has to offer. What is impossible to man can now become possible because you are reaching into the eternal. No longer are you limited by what can only be seen with your natural eyes but you can believe God to handle the things that seem like impossibilities in your life. Choose today to fix your gaze on the King and His kingdom, and the Scripture says that you will reap life and peace.

> *The mind governed by the flesh is death, but the mind governed by the Spirit is life and peace.*
>
> Romans 8:6 (NIV)

Prayer

Thank you God that there is more to our lives as believers than just what our natural eyes see. Thank you Father for the eternal.

His name is Jealous

Do not worship any other god, for the Lord, whose name is Jealous, is a jealous God.

Exodus 34:14 (NIV)

---

*A*fter having walked with the Lord for a while now I thought I knew all the names He uses for Himself in the Bible. But recently I discovered there was another one I hadn't noticed before, and it took me a bit by surprise, because the name was 'Jealous'. To tell you the truth, I did not expect that God would call Himself by the name 'Jealous'. I know He says that He is jealous *for* us, but to *call* yourself by the name Jealous, that's huge.

Then I started to ask myself, 'But isn't jealousy wrong, should He be jealous?' I studied it out and found that the Hebrew word used for 'jealous' is *Qanna* and it can mean two things: 'envious of' or 'zealous for'. Now we know that God is not envious of us because we have nothing that He did not give us in the first place, so that means He is 'zealous for' us – He is jealous *for*, not *of*.

I thought that jealousy and envy were very similar, but they are actually very different. Look at what I found in an article I read in *Psychology Today*: 'Envy occurs when we lack a desired attribute enjoyed by another, jealousy occurs when something we already possess (usually a special relationship) is threatened by a third person.'

This again helped me to understand what God means when He says His name is Jealous. He is jealous for us in a zealous way, just as any husband would be over their wife, or a wife would be for her husband. That's not wrong when you're married because you belong to the other person, and if a third party arrives on the scene singing love songs you'd better believe your back goes up – that's normal! In the same way, He is jealous for us because we are His bride, and He does not want to share us as we would not want to share our spouse.

He is jealous over us as a parent is jealous over their children. I am jealous over my kids in that I don't want this world to have them, I want them to know God's plans for their lives. Again, don't forget that we are His children and He has plans for us.

Finally He is jealous over us like a craftsman is over their workmanship. We are His workmanship, created for His good works (Ephesians 2:10).

So when God says His name is Jealous, it's a good thing. For us it means we are loved and He does not want to share us or have other things lay claim to us or damage us. We are His. In the same way, may we be as jealous over Him.

Prayer

Father, thank You that Your name is Jealous, that You love me so very much, and that You are jealous over me. Help me to live conscious of your jealous love, and to love You with the same commitment and passion. Forgive me for when I have made You share me with other things; You deserve so much more than that. Let my heart be set apart for You, I am Yours. Lead me deeper into Your love today.

Amen

FAMILY TIME

And you shall rejoice in all the good that the LORD your God has given to you and to your house.
Deuteronomy 26:11 (ESV)

Spending time with family is one of the things I love most about this life.

This weekend spend some quality time with your family. Maybe you have a sibling or a cousin you haven't seen or talked to in a while. Husbands, take your wife on a date! Mums and Dads, get out those board games and play with the kids. One of our favourite family adventures is going for long walks in the forest. Give the people you are blessed to call 'family' some extra undivided attention today.

Have a wonderful weekend of family fun!

Notes

_____

_____

_____

_____

_____

_____

_____

How can we amaze Jesus?

For I myself am a man under authority, with soldiers under me. I tell this one, 'Go,' and he goes; and that one, 'Come,' and he comes. I say to my servant, 'Do this,' and he does it." When Jesus heard this, he was amazed and said to those following him, "Truly I tell you, I have not found anyone in Israel with such great faith.

Matthew 8:9-10 (NIV)

The answer to today's titular question is found in today's scripture, and is very simple: 'understand authority'. I love this simple account of a centurion approaching Jesus and asking Him for a miracle for one of his servants. Notice what he says to Jesus: 'For I myself am a man under authority.' What was it about this statement that amazed Jesus in such a way that He would then boast about this man? Let's have a look.

It was not the first part, where he states his gender: 'I myself am a man.' This would not have impressed Jesus as He dealt daily with many men. Yes, as a centurion, he was probably a strong man, maybe even a real 'man's man'! But it was not this that turned the head of the Lord.

It was when he said the next bit: 'a man *under authority*.' What was he saying in this statement? Simply that he was a man who acknowledged, respected and understood what authority looked like and how it worked.

Maybe it was good parenting, or the fact that he was in the military, that had taught him these things? Whatever it was that had been his classroom, he had certainly learned well. He then begins to relate his understanding on how authority worked in a simple yet profound way. 'I have people under me, I ask them to go and they go, to do and they do.' Then he says, 'Just say the word, Jesus.' It was this that impressed Jesus the most – that the man knew that the word of Jesus, and the authority it contained, was enough that he did not even need the person with authority to be present at the place of need to get what he desired!

This man's understanding of authority notably impressed Jesus. He commended him even to the point of saying, 'I have not found anyone in Israel with such great faith.' What a huge commendation for this man! They had never met before, and Jesus was not a person that He would exaggerate or say things just for the sake of it. He always meant what He said, even when He compared this man to a whole nation. Wow!

Again, let me underline – Jesus was not impressed by the fact he was a man or that he was a centurion; He was impressed by the man's understanding of what true authority looks like in a person's life and how it works.

May this simple account get us thinking about authority. What is our understanding concerning it? Would how we see authority be enough to amaze Jesus? All authority comes from God and is set into position by God, and how we respond to authority dramatically determines the boundary lines of our life and what we will experience.

Let's carry on with this thought tomorrow.

God sets authority in the home

Wives, submit yourselves to your own husbands as you do to the Lord. For the husband is the head of the wife as Christ is the head of the church, his body, of which he is the Savior. Now as the church submits to Christ, so also wives should submit to their husbands in everything. Husbands, love your wives, just as Christ loved the church and gave himself up for her to make her holy, cleansing her by the washing with water through the word.

Ephesians 5:22-26 (NIV)

*Y*esterday we started talking about authority and how, like the centurion, our understanding of it has the potential to turn the head of Jesus. According to Jesus, to understand authority – specifically the authority contained in the word of a person – is 'great faith'. So if we want to fully understand faith and the working dynamics of His kingdom, we must be able to understand, and be able to submit to, authority.

We may not always like it but it is vital that we understand that it is God who sets authority into position in our lives. It is He who watches how we respond to it, whether we will choose the healthy road of submission or the destructive roads of rebellion and pride. It is God who sets correct authority in the home, and society seems to be ever trying to remove it. I don't know about you but I have made up my mind, as for me and my house we are going to do marriage and family God's way!

As we see in today's text, He sets a clear authority within marriage. This is not so a man can rule over his wife in some authoritarian way, but rather that he can lead, guide and protect her as the *co-heir* of the gift of life that she is. Call me old school, I really don't mind, but I still believe that, in a marriage, the man is set in position by God to be the priest of the household. Let me say again, not to dictate, dominate or abuse but rather to lift his spiritual arms and natural arms to protect, nourish and bless. Every godly husband needs to realise that God has called them to be the priest of the household. In the same way, I believe that it's God who positions parents in the household to have authority over the children – again, not to be abusive and mean but rather to raise, nurture, protect and lead in a God-fearing way.

I fully understand that as I speak about marriage, home life and parenting, other people's personal experiences or preferences may be different to mine, and that's okay. I just want to encourage you, wherever you may be at, to be ever making God's Word the guiding light in your home concerning who has authority. Today, take time to think about what godly authority looks like in your home, whether you are a husband, wife, parent, single parent or child. God has a perfect way for how your household should function. Let's not lay this aside for the cheaper, non-effective ways of a fickle society that is totally out of control. God's ways, when lived out properly, still work; they still produce strong, lasting marriages and families.

And finally husbands, don't go forgetting your bit:

'Husbands, love your wives, just as Christ loved the church and gave himself up for her.'

Something for everyone

Wives, submit yourselves to your husbands, as is fitting in the Lord. Husbands, love your wives and do not be harsh with them. Children, obey your parents in everything, for this pleases the Lord. Fathers, do not embitter your children, or they will become discouraged. Slaves, obey your earthly masters in everything; and do it, not only when their eye is on you and to curry their favor, but with sincerity of heart and reverence for the Lord. Whatever you do, work at it with all your heart, as working for the Lord, not for human masters.

Colossians 3:18-23 (NIV)

*A*s we continue to consider the subject of 'understanding authority and submission', today's verse is really a 'one-stop shop' for everyone. It includes husbands, wives, parents and children, and it also brings in the workplace and our bosses. We spoke yesterday about godly authority in the home, but what about understanding authority correctly concerning your government or the boss you work for?

Here Paul speaks predominantly to slaves – in the time he was living there were many people who were slaves, servants or bondservants to masters. I believe that it is fair to compare this, in some ways, to the modern workplace or boss we may know today. Paul teaches regarding submitting to authority, that we should respect the authority of those who are positioned over us, whether that be government, law enforcement, or our boss at work. Romans 13 makes for a great read on this subject, especially verses 1-7. Listen to how Paul starts his teaching:

Let everyone be subject to the governing authorities, for there is no authority except that which God has established.

Unless they ask you to do something immoral or illegal we should always endeavour to walk in submission concerning their authority in or over our life. Notice in our text that, regarding our boss or employer, teacher or leader, we should obey and work for them as if we were working for Christ Himself. This is great if you have a lovely boss, who is super-caring and excels in leading you. But what if they are not like that and are hard to work for or seem unreasonable? The Bible does not teach that we are to act any differently to them, but that we should walk honourably towards the authority they have over us. No, we are not slaves, and we have trade unions and committees to make sure our work environment is reasonable and fair, but the Bible talks more about our attitude towards them. We are, according to Paul, to acknowledge and submit in all godliness to those who have authority over us; as we do we walk in a way that pleases God.

Depending on your workplace experience this may bring different levels of challenge for each of us, yet the same instruction belongs to us all. In a world that does not honour or submit to authority, God wants us to honour authority so that we will shine as an example to those who are watching. Watch what happens when you do – there is every chance that, like Daniel, you will begin to experience favour and see promotion within your workplace, or God may see what you do and move you on to better things Himself.

What about authority in the Church?

Have confidence in your leaders and submit to their authority, because they keep watch over you as those who must give an account. Do this so that their work will be a joy, not a burden, for that would be of no benefit to you.

Hebrews 13:17

We have spoken a lot about understanding authority, and looked at how God has set in place different types of authority, in the home, the government and the workplace. Let's now consider the Church.

To understand this correctly we need to firstly remember that the Church, among other things, is God's household (Ephesians 2:19), so if He has established a clear line of authority in our households do you not think He would do that firstly in His own? Sadly, for some people, it's when you start to talk about authority in Church, or submitting to this kind of authority, they can suddenly have a problem. Sometimes this is because they have a problem with *any* type of authority in their life, other times it's because they have seen people abuse or misuse their position of spiritual authority.

Whatever the case, we need to always remember that it is God who established the authority in His house and you need to always be ready to submit to it, knowing that God has made church leaders the overseers of your soul – and they will have to give an account for it.

Church should actually be a visual demonstration to an ever-watching world of what true authority, and submission to authority, actually looks like. But until we see spiritual authority as God wants us to we will not do this, though the world desperately needs us to.

My personal opinion is that you should be able to willingly submit to the spiritual authority He has positioned in your life, and if you can't you need to ask 'why not?' As I have said before in my devotionals, you have to see your church leaders as more than just men or women, or you will only ever hear the words and guidance of 'a human' when they speak. And this would be such a shame because God wants to use you church leader to help you spiritually grow and develop, and help lead you through the various mazes of life.

Ephesians 4 teaches that God sets people in position in His church and He anoints and enables them to function in the role He has given them. If you do not believe your church leaders have been 'set in position by God' or can hear God on your behalf, then the question is 'why not?' Maybe it's a personal issue or the style of their leadership, but it is vital that you get to a place where you can trust them and submit to their authority. Why? Because God wants to lead you through them, and as you submit to them you actually are submitting to Him.

Maybe you are fine with your church leadership – then do what the verse says and make their role a joy not a burden. But maybe today's devotional has caused you to ponder on how you view authority in the church. That's also good – pray and study the Word some more to find out what God thinks.

The final authority of His Word

When Jesus had entered Capernaum, a centurion came to him, asking for help. "Lord," he said, "my servant lies at home paralyzed, suffering terribly." Jesus said to him, "Shall I come and heal him?" The centurion replied, "Lord, I do not deserve to have you come under my roof. But just say the word, and my servant will be healed. For I myself am a man under authority, with soldiers under me. I tell this one, 'Go,' and he goes; and that one, 'Come,' and he comes. I say to my servant, 'Do this,' and he does it."

Matthew 8:5-9 (NIV)

The story of the centurion teaches us one more important thing concerning authority, and that is that authority is always found in the *word* of a person. When Jesus offered to physically come and help the centurion's servant he calmly responded, 'No need, Jesus, just speak the word and they will be healed.' It was the centurion's faith in the power of Jesus' word, and in the authority it had over sickness, that I believe amazed Jesus the most.

The good news for us is that God's authority is still found in His word today, and as we give His Word centre place in our lives, like the centurion, we release our faith in it. As we hear it or read it regarding our lives we should treat it as if the words are coming straight from the mouth of Jesus. We should not only do this when we like what we hear but also when we don't. We need to always be ready to act on it, even when it instructs us to do things that we would prefer not to.

It was when the centurion acted on the authority of His word that he received everything that Jesus intended to do for him. In the exact same way, when we honour God's Word above all else and act on it or purpose to live by it, we do not need Him to be 'physically' present in the place of our need to see His supernatural power or provision break out. When the centurion got home his servant was completely healed. I don't think he was at all surprised when he walked through the door and saw this, because he knew that Jesus had said it would happen and the authority for what was needed to make it happen was contained in His word.

Let us always make His word the final authority in our life, higher than any other authority. Let us allow it to be what determines how we manage our relationships, our finances, our home life and workplace, and how we navigate the daily choices we all have to make. Let His Word determine what is true and what is not, what is truly possible and what is good for us. His word is still powerful and, as we submit to its authority in our life, things are always healed and established correctly, and we get to see some mountains moved.

The best view comes after the hardest climb.

TobyMac

AN INVITATION

Love one another with brotherly affection. Outdo one another in showing honor.
Romans 12:10 (ESV)

This weekend, invite a person or family from church round to your house for dinner. Look for people that you don't know too well but would like to know better. If they are new to the church this is a perfect opportunity to help them feel at home and comfortable.

The point here is that you should know the people that go to the same church as you. Don't worry about making a complicated meal, something simple will be fine. It is not about the food, it's about cultivating friendship and building a sense of community. If you aren't able to invite folks round to where you live then meet up with them for coffee somewhere for a chat. Getting to know people is fun!

Enjoy.

Notes

_____

_____

_____

_____

_____

_____

_____

He is your redeeming God

For you know that it was not with perishable things such as silver or gold that you were redeemed from the empty way of life handed down to you from your ancestors, but with the precious blood of Christ, a lamb without blemish or defect.

1 Peter 1:18-19 (NIV)

Never forget that your God is a redeeming God, and that He has redeemed you back to Himself with the blood of His only son, Jesus.

This will not mean much unless you understand what redemption is. Redemption can be one of those Christian words you hear used around church, but it needs to be so much more than just another Christian word in your understanding. The dictionary gives many definitions for the word *redemption*, the most common one being 'The action of regaining or gaining possession of something in exchange for payment, or the clearing a debt' (Oxford Dictionary). This sums up perfectly what Father God did for us in redeeming us back to Himself. He bought us back to Himself at great cost. Why? Because of His unstoppable love for us. Though the Bible has many different themes and individual storylines, there is actually one main theme that runs throughout it all, from beginning to end; that is the storyline of our Redemption.

Allow me to briefly summarize this storyline for you. We were originally made by God to walk in intimacy with Him. We were lost to God through the disobedience of Adam and Eve, but we have now been restored back to God by the redemptive work of Jesus in dying on a cross, *for* us and *as* us.

Through Jesus, and Him alone, we have now been redeemed and reconciled back to God. We could never pay the debt held over us, but the One who originally made us sent His only Son as payment for that debt, freeing us from it to be His again. That actually means we are twice His! He both made you and bought you back to Himself. How loved are you? The good news is that when Jesus rose from the dead His resurrection sealed the deal for us to have confidence that our redemption is an eternal one. After paying for us Jesus rose from the dead, never to die again, and in Him neither will we. Praise the Lord!

Not with the blood of goats and calves, but with His own blood He entered the Most Holy Place once for all, having obtained eternal redemption.

Hebrews 9:12

For further study on Redemption get a copy of my book *iamedemption* (Great Big Life Publishing, ISBN 978-0-9928027-4-5)

Being easily offended is a symptom of immature love.

Unknown

The redemptive heart of God

Now these are Your servants and Your people, whom You have redeemed by Your great power, and by Your strong hand.

Nehemiah 1:10

*B*ecause of Jesus, and what He did for us, we too can now say, 'We are your people, redeemed by Your great power and strong hand.' As we speak about redemption it is vital we understand that it is not just 'what God does', it is 'who He is'. Redemption is not just the work of His hand but the very heartbeat within Him. Father God is a redemptive God who did everything that was needed to provide for us a secure, eternal redemption so that we do not need to fear what lays the other side of the grave. But you also need to know that He has a redemptive heart for you concerning your life on earth in the here and now!

God is not just thinking of your salvation and entitlement to be with Him in heaven one day, though this is indeed the greatest redemptive priority in our life. He also cares about restoring and making new the things in our life here. His heartbeat is to mend things that are broken, heal things that are sick and restore things that are in need of restoration in our lives – whether that be a marriage, an opportunity, or your health.

God is for you and has a redemptive heart concerning you! He loves to take things that look like they are dead and finished and cause them to live again – including our hopes and dreams. He is the one that, as it says in Revelations 21:5, 'makes all things new.' What seems broken in your life today? What seems like it is too late to see it turn around? Put it in the hands of your heavenly Father who has a redemptive heart towards you.

When you read through the Bible, time after time you see Him take people's seemingly impossible situations and storylines and turn them around in such marvellous ways. Page after page reveals relationships being restored, dead people being raised to life, sick people getting healed, justice becoming established where injustice previously reigned. Through accounts like that of Hosea and his redeeming love for his unfaithful wife, Mephibosheth being restored to David's court and table, and Ruth's life being rebuilt by Boaz her 'kinsmen redeemer', we see God demonstrating and declaring His redemptive intent and capability towards mankind, and we must be left with the conclusion that He is indeed a redeeming God.

The good news is His heart is full of redemptive intention for you and what you may be going through right now, so no matter what may be going on, bring it before Him and ask Him to step in and turn it all around! Redemption is all about how God can 'change the story of people's lives', so let Him get involved with your manuscript, let Him rewrite some things. Believe me, His ending will always be better than any you may have had.

For further study on Redemption get a copy of my book *iamedemption* (Great Big Life Publishing, ISBN 978-0-9928027-4-5)

Let the redeemed of the Lord say so

Let the redeemed of the Lord say so, Whom He has redeemed from the hand of the enemy.

Psalm 107:2

When I was growing up in Church we used to sing these simple words in a chorus. Most Sundays I remember singing, 'Let the redeemed of the Lord say so' but to be honest, though we sang it to a jolly tune, I never really understood what I was singing. It was not until I understood what redemption was – what it meant to be redeemed and what it cost for us to be redeemed – that I started singing it with conviction. And it was only a couple of years ago, when I happened to read today's verse in another translation, that I fully got it.

Let the redeemed of the Lord tell their story.

Psalm 107:2 (NIV)

Suddenly it made a whole lot more sense: let those who know how God bought them back to Himself be busy telling others and not keeping it a secret. Then I realised that it's not just about telling others how He saved us but also about all the other redemptive things He has done for us since.

Take a moment to look back and think about the things He has redeemed in your life: relationships, situations and things that seemed so impossible until He stepped in and made a way forward where there seemed be no way. I don't know about you, maybe it's because I have lived a 'colourful' life, but I see many, many times when He stepped in and changed the storyline of my life by redeeming something else. When we start to consider how He has saved us, and all that He has done for us, it's overwhelming. The next thing we need to do is purpose not to file these memories away in some 'inner library of thankfulness', like we have done so many times before, but rather start telling other people.

Become one of the 'redeemed of the Lord' in telling your stories. As we do this our lives become naturally evangelistic, they become visible billboards that advertise His grace, mercy and ability to those all around us that desperately need Him. How can we stay quiet when we consider all He has done? What motivates us to tell our stories of redemption to others should not be any sense of obligation, rather an overwhelming inner thankfulness for all He has done, and is still doing, and will continue to do.

So often we can make the Great Commission so seemingly unachievable, but it really is so simple. Remember, He commissioned us in Acts 1:8 to 'be a witness' in our local worlds, as well as further afield. It is so easy to be a witness, you just tell others what you have seen or experienced. And because you are telling of things that happened to you there is great authenticity that empowers your words, and that will get people's attention.

For further study on Redemption get a copy of my book *iamedemption* (Great Big Life Publishing, ISBN 978-0-9928027-4-5)

Carrying the redemptive heart of God

The Lord is not slack concerning His promise, as some count slackness, but is longsuffering toward us, not willing that any should perish but that all should come to repentance.

2 Peter 3:9

*L*et's carry on speaking about God being a redemptive God. We have spoken of how He has a redemptive heart for us, but we need to remember that it is not just for us but for everyone. His desire is that none should perish but all should experience redemption. I believe that He does not want any to perish eternally and this is indeed man's greatest need, but also He does not want people to perish in their lives here. When God looks down and sees people's suffering He does not delight in what they are going through but rather has a heart filled with redemptive love and intention for them.

This is where we come in. God wants us to be His representatives that carry His redemptive heart for people and also practically outwork it in the lives of others. So many times we can look at people in need and ask, 'Why don't you come and help them, God?' The answer is closer than we think – He has sent us! It's not that He can't help, it's that He has chosen to send *us* to help. We are the body of Christ and, just as we have thoughts in our hearts that we then practically outwork using our bodies, so it is with God. Yes, He can do miracles and supernaturally turn things around for people, but most of the time He wants to use our hands, our feet and our wallets to make a difference in the lives of those who are suffering or struggling around us. But do we hear His promptings?

This is a 'rubber-hits-the-road' thought. Will you let the redemptive intentions that are in the heart of God for others flow through your life to bring practical change to others where they may need it? It is no less God doing it Himself, because we are His body! What an awesome thought: God *wants* to use you today to be a redemptive interruption in the life of another and what they are going through. They may be heading towards the edge of a cliff and not know it, but then God drops you in their life and uses you to re-route them to a better tomorrow, not just using your mouth but often your hands, feet, time and wallet also. Today, be a person who knows the Father's redemptive heart and carries His redemptive heart, and lets Him use your life to outwork His redemptive intentions for others wherever you go. Be His Good Samaritan to people in need, not a religious person who crosses the road.

Homework

Read the account of the Good Samaritan and then prayerfully consider how you would spend your life for others when you find them in need.

For further study on Redemption get a copy of my book *iamedemption* (Great Big Life Publishing, ISBN 978-0-9928027-4-5)

Reconciliation trumps gift

Therefore, if you are offering your gift at the altar and there remember that your brother or sister has something against you, leave your gift there in front of the altar. First go and be reconciled to them; then come and offer your gift.

Matthew 5:23-24 (NIV)

In today's text we can see clearly what God values the most when it comes to the things we offer Him and the relationships we have with others. Always remember, the Bible teaches us to live with 'two-way success' when it comes to our relationships. God wants us to have health in the 'vertical-type relationship' we have with Him, and He also desires for us to have health in the 'horizontal-type relationships' we have with others.

Jesus left us with two simple commandments in the new covenant that summed up all of the others in the old: 'love the Lord thy God with everything you have and are, and love thy neighbour as yourself' (Matthew 22:37). God still takes this two-part commandment seriously, and we would do well if we did too. If we are honest, most of the problems we face – like offence and hurt in our hearts – involve the people we live with, not the God we serve and worship. Yet God says that we are to have harmony both vertically and horizontally if we want our gifts and offerings, our worship, to please Him.

So, what could that look like? You come to church to worship and all of a sudden the Holy Spirit reminds you of someone who has something against you; note that today's verse doesn't say 'you have something against them' because these things should have been dealt with long before. No, you are suddenly prompted concerning someone you know who has something against you. God's Word says you are to get up and seek reconciliation before you do *anything* else. Practically this may mean you leaving the room to go and see them, or make a call, but also it could be you purposing in your heart to extend the hand of reconciliation as soon as you can after the service, especially if they are not local to where you are.

But what if they don't take your hand? That's okay, that's down to them. But you know before God that you have done everything you can to make reconciliation with them possible. You then commit them to the Lord, ever leaving your heart open for future reconciliation, and your hand extended to initiate it.

I believe it is when our hearts are empty of our own offences against others, and our consciences are clear that we tried to bring reconciliation to others that may have problems with us, that we can offer worship to God in a way that truly pleases Him. Just as obedience trumps sacrifice (1 Samuel 15:22) so seeking reconciliation with people who hold things against you trumps giving God your offerings and gifts. This is an opportunity to be a peacemaker.

REFRESHING

The generous will prosper; those who refresh others will themselves be refreshed.
Proverbs 11:25 (NLT)

To refresh is to give new energy to.

This weekend find someone who could use some refreshing, someone going through a hard time maybe and could use some recharging of the soul. You could text them encouraging words, call them, or maybe visit them. Maybe you know someone who is exhausted and you could refresh them by helping them out in a way that they need. For example, a tired parent of small children may need some help with childcare, or a student who has been studying for exams may need you to take him or her for an ice-cream sundae break.

Pray about who to refresh and remember, those who refresh others have the promise of being refreshed themselves!

Notes

_____

_____

_____

_____

_____

_____

_____

Who's judging who?

Who are you to judge another's servant? To his own master he stands or falls. Indeed, he will be made to stand, for God is able to make him stand.

Romans 14:4

Here Paul warns us about judging people in a wrong way, and gives us a very strong caution about doing so.

To get a correct context for this verse, as always, you have to read the verses directly before and after it. In these verses you read about being loving and sensitive regarding people who may have different levels of conscience or faith about doing certain things, such as eating certain foods or keeping specific days. Paul teaches that we are not to be a stumbling block to others with our personal persuasions, but equally we need to be careful not to set ourselves up as judge and jury against those with persuasions different to ours.

The reality is, we all have a master, don't we? It doesn't matter that for most of us He is the same master, He is the master of our lives. This makes us all His servants, personally accountable to Him. Please don't hear what I am not saying – when it comes to things like immorality in the life of a believer or the church I believe we need to have an absolute based on His word, and that absolute causes an element of judgment in itself as we purpose to live by it. But this actually makes His Word the Judge more than us.

But today I am talking about other things that are normally just the produce of different preferences, or having a lack of all the information needed to make a true judgment. It's here that we are to remember that we all belong to another Master and Judge: God.

I love what it says next: 'And He (God) is able to make them stand.' Remember, each of us are on a journey, none of us have yet fully arrived but equally none of us are where we were when we started. Let's always try to keep away from the 'seat of the judge' and instead be the person that cheers people on, guiding them forward as and when we can.

In my experience a lot of the time judgment comes when people actually do not know the entire truth or all the facts. Let us ever withhold our judgment until we are in a position to make a correct, unbiased one, knowing that God has more to say about judging people. He says that 'with the measure we use it will be measured back to us.' This is a sobering warning that should provoke us all to leave the judge's seat to the One it belongs to.

> *'Judge not, that you be not judged. For with what judgment you judge, you will be judged; and with the measure you use, it will be measured back to you.*
> **Matthew 7:1-2**

I don't know about you, but these verses inspire me to be careful when it comes to the judging of others.

How's your legacy coming along?

A good man leaves an inheritance to his children's children, but the wealth of the sinner is stored up for the righteous.

Proverbs 13:22

It's healthy to think about legacy – specifically, what mark you will leave behind when you have 'graduated' from this earthy life. This should not be a morbid thought, rather one that inspires us to live in such away that we leave something behind in the life of others when we are 'gone'.

Yes, 'gone' may mean death, but it could also mean when God moves you on to another place or another mission. The question in both instances is, did you leave anything behind with others worth leaving? Or, put another way, did your life have a positive, lasting effect on those you did life with? Today's text speaks of a good man 'leaving an inheritance' that affects the generation that follows, and also beyond. This verse certainly has a financial context, but legacy is actually a much broader subject than being just about money. We should all have hopes and desires to leave a financial inheritance to those we love but what we will all leave behind is so much more.

You see, your legacy is not just about what you accumulate or own, it's about who you are. Your life is the legacy you leave with others. Everyone is building their legacy right now but only some people realise it or live like they are. Everyone will leave some kind of legacy, so the real question is, will yours be formed by design or default?

Parenting is a great example of building and leaving legacy, and can sadly display another truth: that legacy can be positive or negative, according to the builder. I have had the privilege to meet many people who were handed a great or noble life legacy from their parents. Again, that doesn't just mean money, it also means things like a godly heritage or they were shown how godly parents raise their kids. But also I have met and ministered to many people who were not left a good life legacy or example by their parents – what was handed down to them was not usable or positive. I am not sure which of those examples you relate to most closely, but the good news is that, though you may not be able to change what was handed you, you can decide and purpose that what you are going to hand on to those in your world will be positive and life-giving.

Legacy is something we are all building right now. So much about what we leave with others is up to us. How we live, what we stand for, the things we build – these are all things that are 'real time' in our lives right now. Maybe you haven't thought about your legacy before – may I encourage you to give it real consideration, because whether you do or not you are building one right now.

Let us purpose to be as today's verse says, good 'men' (people) who leave a good inheritance, not just to our children's children but to everyone who knew us. May our lives, and what they stood for, live on long beyond us.

Your life is your legacy

And so it was, when they had crossed over, that Elijah said to Elisha, "Ask! What may I do for you, before I am taken away from you?" Elisha said, "Please let a double portion of your spirit be upon me."

2 Kings 2:9

This text is from the well-known account of the moment when Elijah the prophet graduates to heaven, and his mantle is caught by his young protégé Elisha, who then picks up the mantle and uses it for all the Lord has for him next. So often, when you hear this account taught, you build a mental picture of a magical moment where Elisha gets his 'double portion' from Elijah's life – it's like a Disney sequence how this supernatural moment takes place! I don't believe it was like that. Yes, I believe that in that moment Elisha received an anointing, something godly and supernatural from his mentor's life, and it was powerful. But you also need to remember that in one very strong way he had already received a major chunk of his 'double portion'. 'When', you may say? When he daily walked with Elijah in the years leading up to this zenith moment.

You see, if you watch Elisha, the first thing he does is part the river water just like he had seen Elijah do. Then, as you watch his life, you see so many similarities, even double the amount of things done by Elijah.

This is legacy. As they walked together in seemingly non-dramatic moments the 'values and ways' of Elijah were sown into or impressed upon the life of Elisha. So although Elijah's epic ending is an amazing account, it was in many ways just the cherry on the top (though a very supernatural cherry!).

This is the same for us with the legacies we are leaving with our children, those we lead and those we love. Daily, without realising, our 'ways and values' are being impressed on those around us, and often become many of *their* 'ways and values'. Then, when we are no longer with them, the values we impressed on them begin to be the ones they live by and for. This is a great way of looking at the legacy you are leaving.

Today you are having an impact on those around you, especially those closest to you. Be purposeful concerning the kind of legacy of 'value and ways' you leave with them because, like Elisha, they will carry on living out your values and ways long after you have gone. Think about the disciples: they followed Jesus, and His ways and values became theirs. When Jesus rose from the dead He, as with the account of Elijah, empowered the disciples with a supernatural touch. But watch their lives from that moment – they begin to exemplify Him. When you watch them it's like watching Him.

When it comes to spiritual legacy, the disciples' legacy has become ours. Let's live that legacy of faith out loud and clear, as they did.

Developing your spiritual core strength

I pray that out of his glorious riches he may strengthen you with power through his Spirit in your inner being.

Ephesians 3:16 (NIV)

Recently, while travelling with my son Ethan, we had the chance to receive a surfing lesson. Neither of us had surfed before, and it seemed like a good idea at the time. The first part of the lesson was on the beach, learning everything '101' that we needed to know once we were in the water – how to get up on the board, and how to stay standing. Then into the water we went.

After about thirty minutes I noticed Ethan standing upright on his board and riding a wave. Me, I was laying like a stranded seal on my board, catching my breath. I explained to our instructor that the reasons for this were probably that my son is 15 and I am 51, that he is thin and I am not quite so thin, and that he has shoulders and I used to have shoulders! The thing that frustrated me the most was that I knew what I had to do in my head, but my body would not/could not do it fast enough. The main problem was the state of my 'core strength'. Given a couple more days I think I could have cracked it, but in my present state I could not because my body was not fully ready for the moment.

There's a great lesson here. You are a spirit man/woman as well as a natural one. If you want to be ready to do the things that God has for you next, you need to be strong in the core of who you are, your inner man. If you're tired of constantly falling off your board when the waves of life rise under you or come against you, you have to develop good balance that comes from the strength of your spiritual core. To get a good core naturally you need to eat well and exercise; it's the same for the spiritual you. If you want to strengthen who you are in God on the inside then take in the nutrition that's in His Word daily, and be working it out with a healthy prayer life and active faith.

Make sure your life is ready for when God sends you a wave or a brain wave, a thought of something He wants you to do. Like a surfer sitting on their board, waiting for a great wave, be ready. Just as the Bible says, 'in season and out of season.' Let your inner man/woman be ever 'good to go'. Maintain your personal walk with God so you are constantly in a state of core fitness – then you can jump on up and ride that wave all the way to the shore.

Prayer

Good morning, Father. Help me again today to develop my spiritual core strength, so that I am ready for all You have for me next. Forgive me for any laziness that has held me back. I proclaim it a new day, where I will eat from Your Word and be guided by Your Spirit. Help me today to develop my inner man so that I can stand, and remain standing, when different things come like waves against my life. Thank You that You are for me, You're on my side.

Amen

Disposing of your cares responsibly

Therefore humble yourselves under the mighty hand of God, that He may exalt you in due time, casting all your care upon Him, for He cares for you.

1 Peter 5:6-7

Peter shows us in these verses how to responsibly dispose of our cares. But how often do we all not take his advice and instead carry them ourselves?

One thing we all have in common is that, at one time or another, we will have cares. Cares are simply anxieties, worries and concerns that come from living a real life in a real world with real people. But Peter is telling us that, though we may get them, we do not need to keep holding onto them. So what do with them? We give them, or cast them like a fisherman casts his line, upon Jesus. Why? Simply, because He cares about us.

Jesus does not want you carrying those cares, rather He wants to dispose of them for you. But you have to give them to Him before He can to do that. Cares can be compared to weeds and thorns – just as these are not good for a garden so the cares of this life are not good for you. In Mark 4:18 Jesus teaches that the 'cares of this life' come to choke the Word and life of God out of you. That's why you must pull them up like you would weeds and cast them on Him. Weeds and thorns can also cause you, as with a natural plant, to become unfruitful – and that is certainly not God's plans for your life. He wants you to bear much fruit, and fruit that remains.

Just like when you do the gardening you need to make the decision to pull up those cares in your life that are like weeds and thorns, and then throw them somewhere that they can't affect you anymore or grow back again. That place is at the feet of Jesus. Remember, at the cross they placed on His head a crown of thorns. He wore the thorns so we did not have to. What a great example this is – the thorns were pressed upon His head – and it's in our heads, isn't it, that cares, anxieties and worries try to do their damage. But we must remember, He wore the thorns so we do not have to.

So what are those concerns, worries and anxieties that are trying to take root in your life? Take a moment to pull them up, disposing of them responsibly by casting them on Him – He invited you to do it.

Cast your cares on the Lord and he will sustain you; he will never let the righteous be shaken.

Psalm 55:22 (NIV)

Life has no remote. Get up and change it yourself.

Unknown

PRAY THROUGHOUT THE DAY

Rejoice always, pray without ceasing, in everything give thanks for this is the will of God in Christ Jesus for you.

1 Thessalonians 5:1618

Without ceasing! That is a lot of prayer. Don't worry, you are not being asked to do something impossible here; rather the Apostle Paul is asking us to be God-minded all throughout the day and to let prayer become a way of life. Talk to the Father in the day as you carry on with your life.

When you're in the supermarket, taking a walk, working, cooking . . . be aware that God is ever present and loves you. He desires to hear you and also to speak to you. Don't limit time with God to your devotional time.

One of my favourite times to talk with God is while I drive, and also when I'm walking the dog. You don't have to make a spectacle of yourself. I often pray quietly if I'm in a crowded place and more loudly if I'm alone. Sometimes I 'think' prayers to God. He hears me no matter how I do it.

Be God-conscious this weekend and talk to Him throughout the day.

Allow this to become a way of life.

Notes

_____

_____

_____

_____

_____

About the Authors

*A*ndy and Gina are the Senior Pastors of **Family Church**, a multi-congregational church located on the South Coast of England. Andy is a visionary leader who has grown the church from twelve people on its first day to now being a significant and influential church in the UK and beyond.

Andy is also the founder of **Synergy Alliance**, a network of like-minded churches and ministries walking shoulder to shoulder, championing the development of healthy, cross-alliance relationships, and of **Great Big Life**, a ministry established to see people equipped and empowered not only to lead effectively in Church but also in every other section and sphere of life too.

Andy has a wealth of experience and wisdom to offer that comes from a very successful time in ministry. As well as planting churches, he has been involved in many forms of evangelism including travelling as an evangelist for many years across the UK and throughout the world.

A dynamic visionary, Andy helps people to see things outside of the box and, as a strategist, he helps others to set goals within their lives and ministries and move towards them quickly. His experience, combined with his life-coaching skills, makes him a valuable asset to any pastor or leader seeking personal development encouragement and to address change.

A highly sought-after conference speaker for events and conferences, Andy regularly shares on a whole range of subjects including leadership, motivation and evangelism. Andy's versatility allows him to communicate as a pastor, an evangelist, a teacher or coach reaching individuals of all ages and in a variety of settings. Andy is very natural and irreligious in his approach, using humour well and being very animated and often unconventional in his delivery. His desire is to lead people to Jesus and help them to discover all that is now available to them through what Jesus has done for them. His personal mandate is 'to know the King and to advance His kingdom.'

Originally from Portsmouth, this is where Andy and Gina, along with their five children, Olivia, Ethan, Gabrielle, Sophie and Christina, now reside and lead the different ministries from.

Useful websites

Family Church: **family-church.org.uk**
Great Big Life: **greatbiglife.co.uk**
Breakfast of Champions sign-up: **breakfastofchampions.co.uk**
Synergy Alliance: **synergy-alliance.org**
Synergy Christian Churches: **synergychristianchurches.com**
iamredemption: **iamredemption.org**

Andy & Gina's social media links

Facebook: **facebook.com/Andy-Gina-Elmes-722484461120666**
Facebook: **facebook.com/breakfastofchampionsemail**
Twitter: **@andyelmes, @GinaElmes**
Instagram: 'andyelmes', 'gina_elmes'

Prayer

I hope you enjoyed this book and that is has been both a blessing and a challenge to your life and walk with God. Maybe you just got hold of it and are looking through before starting. Long ago, I made the decision never to take for granted that everyone has prayed a prayer to receive Jesus as their Lord, so am including that as the finale to this book. If you have never asked Jesus into your life and would like to do that now, it's so easy. Just pray this simple prayer:

> *Dear Lord Jesus, thank You for dying on the cross for me. I believe that You gave Your life so that I could have life. When You died on the cross, You died as an innocent man who had done nothing wrong. You were paying for my sins and the debt I could never pay. I believe in You, Jesus, and receive the brand new life and fresh start that the Bible promises that I can have. Thank You for my sins forgiven, for the righteousness that comes to me as a gift from You, for hope and love beyond what I have known and the assurance of eternal life that is now mine. Amen.*

Good next moves are to get yourself a Bible that is easy to understand and begin to read. Maybe start in John so you can discover all about Jesus for yourself. Start to pray – prayer is simply talking to God – and, finally, find a church that's alive and get your life planted in it. These simple ingredients will cause your relationship with God to grow.

Why not email me and let me know if you did that so I can rejoice with you? Tell me about your redemption story.

Andy Elmes
response@greatbiglife.co.uk

Further Information

For further information about the authors of this book, or to order more copies, please contact:

Great Big Life Publishing
Empower Centre
83-87 Kingston Road
Portsmouth
Hampshire
PO2 7DX
United Kingdom
info@greatbiglifepublishing.com

Are you an Author?

Do you have a word from God on your heart that you're looking to get published to a wider audience?

We're looking for manuscripts that identify with our own vision of bringing life-giving and relevant messages to Body of Christ. Send yours for review towards possible publication to:

Great Big Life Publishing
Empower Centre
83-87 Kingston Road
Portsmouth
Hampshire
PO2 7DX
United Kingdom
info@greatbiglifepublishing.com

breakfast of
CHAMPIONS

260 daily devotions
by Andy Elmes

Breakfast of Champions is a mid-week devotional written with the purpose of inspiring you to live the most effective, influential, God-filled life you can. Packed with wisdom and tips taken from his own colourful walk with God, Andy will inspire and challenge you to daily "run your best race". This devotional, served up alongside your Bible each day, will give your spirit the nutrition and fibre it needs to grow strong and healthy. God's Word truly is the breakfast of Champions!

PAPERBACK: ISBN 978-0-9928027-0-7
EBOOK: ISBN 978-0-9928027-1-4

WHAT ARE THEY SAYING?

"Andy Elmes lives life to the full with contagious joy, constantly extending the kingdom of God. He communicates with one person as though he/she is the most important person on earth. A very engaging and humorous preacher, he hits the mark every time and large crowds of people remember his messages for years. Andy is a great leader who is impacting thousands of lives around the world."

Ashley Schmierer, International President, Christian Outreach Centre global movement of churches

"It's been my privilege to be a friend of Andy's for several years now and I have come to know and value his visionary and inspirational leadership. Andy has a wealth of experience to offer in so many ways and I particularly value his regular 'devotionals' which, like me, so many have found to be very relevant and helpful in their daily lives. I'm sure this book will bring prosperity and success to all who read it. Well done, Andy."

Linvoy Primus, professional footballer and co-founder of Faith & Football

It's time for the 21st century church to return to a 1st century vision

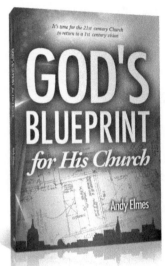

PAPERBACK: ISBN 978-0-9928027-2-1
EBOOK: ISBN 978-0-9928027-3-8

Two thousand years ago, when Jesus declared that He would build His Church, He rolled out a blueprint of what the Church was meant to be – relevant and effective through all generations. We now find ourselves in the 21st century, and we need to ask ourselves, "When we roll out the blueprint we currently have for 'building the Church', does it look the same as His? Are we building the Church Jesus wants built?"

In this compelling book, Andy Elmes, speaking from years of experience as a church leader, evangelist, and leadership coach, sends out a passionate call to the modern-day Church to return to "the blueprint" of God, building Church once again according to the pattern handed down to us by the architect, Jesus.

Andy challenges us to reconsider the importance of topics like:

- The Great Commission – is Church to be seeker-friendly, mission-minded, or both?
- Discipleship – what place should it have in modern church?
- The power of God – are we building safe churches or supernatural ones?

Together we will revisit these and other subjects to see how today's Church lines up with God's original plans and intentions for His House. Is it time for the 21st century Church to return to a 1st century vision? And how do we do that both effectively and relevantly in our generation?

Also available from

gbl Great Big Life Publishing

greatbiglifepublishing.com • @GBLPublishing

How far would you go to refresh your leader?

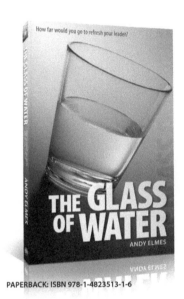

PAPERBACK: ISBN 978-1-4823513-1-6

'If truth be told, most senior pastors would love to write a book for their leadership teams called *How I Would Serve Me If I Was You*. The reality is most won't, yet what is on their heart needs to be heard. So I dared to write it for them!'

In this sometimes brutally honest book, Andy shares insights on what it is like to be a senior leader of a church, looking with great transparency at the natural and spiritual pressures facing the leader who has decided to do something for God. He also asks the question, 'Where are the mighty men?' – those men and women whom God desires to surround the leader with. He asks a number of very honest questions:

- What do mighty men look like and what do they do?
- What are the hallmarks and characteristics of a mighty man?
- What does the leader need their team to do for them?
- What have 'holding up Moses' arms' and 'being an armour bearer' got to do with us in the 21st century?

This book is written to be intentionally provocative. You will journey into the often unseen world of the leader God has given you, seeing things you never knew and that they would never tell you, and discovering how challenging the calling they received can sometimes be.

'My desire in writing this book is to stop pastors quitting by initiating vital conversations. I want to provoke the mighty men and women that are out there to have a greater awareness concerning the leader God has given them; to stand up and step up to a new level; to be what they should be so that the leader and their family can be all that God has commissioned them to be.' *Andy Elmes*

Take this thought-provoking journey to discover what a difference a simple glass of water can really make.

IAMREDEMPTION

Catching God's heart

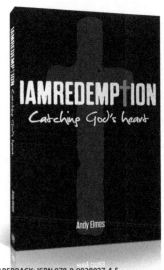

IAMREDEMPTION

Catching God's heart

Andy Elmes

PAPERBACK: ISBN 978-0-9928027-4-5
EBOOK: ISBN 978-0-9928027-5-2

Are you ready to be challenged? Are you ready to be dangerously provoked? Are you ready for Christianity to get exciting again? Then read on . . .

IAMREDEMPTION is not just a book – it's a mandate, a challenge, a clarion call for the people of God to understand afresh the power of redemption. To be mobilised to tell others of their story of redemption and to be a carrier of redemption to the lives of others. In this book, you will read about the moment when the redemptive heart of God came into Andy Elmes' world and turned it upside down. Instantly he understood God's love for humanity like never before, realising afresh that the desire of His heart is still that none would perish.

The question is, what are we prepared to do about that desire?